ULTIMATE GUIDE TO THE WORLD'S BEST

WEDDING & HONEYMOON

DESTINATIONS

InterContinental Beachcomber Resort Bora Bora- Photo Credit: Tim McKenna

A comprehensive guide designed to assist you in choosing
the perfect destination, whether it be for the most romantic
wedding ceremony, or for an unforgettable honeymoon.

Photo courtesy of: British Virgin Islands Tourist Board - www.bvitouristboard.com

DEDICATED TO BRIDES AND GROOMS EVERYWHERE!

May their wedding and honeymoon be a time of
love, celebration and new beginnings.

TABLE OF CONTENTS

POPULAR WEDDING AND HONEYMOON DESTINATIONS WORLDWIDE

Find complete descriptions of the most romantic and beautiful locations around the world.

TABLE OF CONTENTS

WORLD'S BEST WEDDING & HONEYMOON DESTINATIONS

These resorts were selected for their quality of service, ideal location,
outstanding facilities and beautiful surroundings.

TABLE OF CONTENTS

TABLE OF CONTENTS

TABLE OF CONTENTS

INTRODUCTION

Hilton Maldives Resort & Spa - The Maldives

*C*ongratulations on your engagement! You must be very excited to have found that special person with whom you will share the rest of your life. And you must be looking forward to what may be one of the happiest times of your life -- your wedding and honeymoon! Planning these special times can be fun and exciting. But hours of research are required in order to make the right decisions. That is why Wedding Solutions, the nation's most renowned wedding publishing and consulting company, has created *The Ultimate Guide to the World's Best Wedding & Honeymoon Destinations*.

The Ultimate Guide to the World's Best Wedding & Honeymoon Destinations highlights over 150 of the best wedding and honeymoon hotels and resorts in the world. These resorts were selected for their quality of service, ideal location, outstanding facilities and beautiful surroundings.

This guide includes detailed descriptions of these resorts, such as contact information, room rates, website URL, as well as romantic features, nearby attractions, on-site facilities, wedding services and more.

The Ultimate Guide to the World's Best Wedding & Honeymoon Destinations also features complete descriptions of the most popular destinations (islands or regions) for an elegant destination wedding or an unforgettable honeymoon. Some of the destinations featured in this guide are: Hawaii, the Caribbean, Fiji, Thailand, Tahiti, Bora Bora, Moorea, Italy, Greece and many more.

These areas are described in detail, including the following information:

Ice Hotel Québec-Canada © Xavier Dachez

- General overview of the area with indispensable travel tips and information about its culture and history, as well as things to see and do in the area such as nightlife, cuisine, activities, shopping and more.

- Information about traveling in the area, entry requirements, climate, language and more.

- Complete information and guidelines on weddings; how to get married and obtain a marriage license.

Manchester Grand Hyatt - San Diego, CA USA

With over 900 full color photographs, *The Ultimate Guide to the World's Best Wedding & Honeymoon Destinations* is truly an indispensable guide to making the best choice when deciding on a destination.

We are confident that one of these beautiful resorts will satisfy all your needs. Tell them WeddingSolutions.com sent you. They will surely make your stay as memorable as possible.

The entire staff at WeddingSolutions.com wishes you a romantic and unforgettable wedding and honeymoon!

Sincerely,

Elizabeth H. Lluch

Regent Beverly Wilshire, A Four Seasons Hotel - Beverly Hills, CA USA

welcome to the
CARIBBEAN

ANTIGUA - CLIMATE		
MONTH	HI	LO
JAN	81°	72°
FEB	82°	72°
MAR	82°	73°
APR	83°	74°
MAY	85°	76°
JUN	86°	78°
JUL	87°	79°
AUG	87°	79°
SEPT	87°	78°
OCT	86°	77°
NOV	84°	76°
DEC	82°	74°

Temperatures are provided in °Fahrenheit. Information is based on averages and are subject to change without notice.

A N T I G U A

In 1784 the legendary Admiral Horatio Nelson sailed to Antigua and established Great Britain's most important Caribbean base. The island had warm, steady winds, a complex coastline of safe harbors, and a protective, nearly unbroken wall of coral reef. It made a perfect place to hide a fleet. Little did he know that over 200 years later the same unique characteristics that attracted the Royal Navy would transform Antigua and Barbuda in one of the Caribbean's premier tourist destinations!

The Trade Winds that once blew British men-of-war safely into English Harbour now fuel one of the world's foremost maritime events, Sailing Week. The expansive, winding coastline that made Antigua difficult for outsiders to navigate is where today's trekkers encounter a tremendous wealth of secluded, powdery soft beaches. The coral reefs, once the bane of marauding enemy ships, now attract snorkelers and scuba divers from all over the world. And the fascinating little island of Barbuda -- once a scavenger's paradise because so many ships wrecked on its reefs -- is now home to one of the region's most significant bird sanctuaries.

Antigua, the largest of the English-speaking Leeward Islands, is about 14 miles long and 11 miles wide, encompassing 108 square miles. To the south are the islands of Montserrat and Guadaloupe, and to the north and west are Nevis, St. Kitts, St. Barts, and St. Martin. Barbuda, a flat coral island with an area of only 68 square miles, lies approximately 30 miles due north.

The nation also includes the tiny (0.6 square mile) uninhabited island of Redonda, now a nature preserve. The current population for the nation is approximately 68,000 and its capital is St. John's on Antigua.

THINGS TO SEE AND DO

Dickenson Bay and Runaway Bay, located along Antigua's developed northwest coast, are the place to go for those who want the fully-loaded

resort experience. The beaches most convenient to St. John's are Fort James, a locally-popular public beach, and Deep Bay. Galley Bay attracts surfers during the winter months and joggers during the evening. The series of four crescent beaches at Hawksbill are also highly regarded, one of which is nudist.

The beaches of the hilly southwest corner of Antigua are generally less developed than those around St. John's further north. On the road that winds along this coast are Frye's Bay, Darkwood Beach, and the beaches around Johnson's Point. Rendezvous Bay and especially Doigs Beach, both located on the central southern coast at Rendezvous Bay, are especially quiet beaches worth the rough travel necessary to reach them.

On the southeast corner of the island is Half Moon Bay, now a national park and a good choice for an outing. Long Bay, on the easternmost point of the island, is another good choice for families, as it is completely protected by its reef.

Sailing has been a central part of Antigua's culture for centuries, ever since the British under Horatio Nelson made English Harbour their Caribbean base. Today, the stately Georgian architecture of Nelson's Dockyard hosts a more pleasure-seeking fleet - the international racing boats, recreational yachts, and sailboats of Antigua's annual Sailing Week.

With such a rich marine tradition, it's no surprise that boats of all sorts can be hired in Antigua.

Antiguans are more than a little devoted

to cricket. The island has historically been a very strong contributor to West Indian and international cricket, and the Antigua Recreation Ground is one of the finest places in the Caribbean to take in a local, regional, or international match. Devotees of the game can visit the Antigua and Barbuda Museum for a look at the infamous cricket bat of Vivian Richards, native Antiguan, former captain of the West Indies Cricket Club, and one of the greatest batsmen of all time. Matches can be found almost anywhere on the island, at almost any time.

One of Antigua's most exciting and thrilling activities is Swimming with the Dolphins. This once in a lifetime adventure gives participants the opportunity to experience, up close and personal, playtime with dolphins. Not only is this a fun time, but it also gives participants a much greater understanding of these fascinating mammals and a greater appreciation for marine life and the environment in which they live. Housed in a 5.5 million gallon lagoon at Marina Bay, these precious animals are sure to make your vacation unforgettable.

Special Points of Interest: Betty's Hope Sugar Plantation was the first large sugar plantation on Antigua, and its success led to the island's rapid development of large-scale sugar production. Although the only surviving structures are two stone sugar mills and the remains of the stillhouse, the site's importance in Antiguan history has prompted the government to begin developing it as an open air museum. About a hundred stone windmill towers dot the Antiguan landscape, and the two restored examples at Betty's Hope provide a dramatic sense of the way these mills must have dominated the island during the hundreds of years that sugar production was the dominant industry.

Fig Tree Drive, Antigua's most picturesque drive, meanders from the low central plain of the island up into the ancient volcanic hills of the

Parish of Saint Mary in the island's southwest quarter. The none-too-smooth road passes through an area of lush vegetation and rainforest and rises to the steep farmlands around Fig Tree Hill (figs are what Antiguans call bananas) before descending to the coastline again. Along the way are banana, mango, and coconut groves, as well as a number of old sugar mills and pleasant little churches.

Although St. John's has long been Antigua's capital city, the island's historic heart is across the island at English Harbour. One of the finest natural harbors in the Caribbean, and located at a highly strategic position, English Harbour was used by Admirals Nelson, Rodney and Hood as a secure home for the British Navy during the Napoleonic wars. Today, Nelson's Dockyard forms part of a designated national park, complete with a museum, shops, hotels, restaurants and a yacht haven. The park embraces the whole of English Harbour and Shirley Heights.

The 'megaliths' that initially drew curious visitors to Green Castle Hill are almost certainly geologic features, but they are no less impressive and picturesque for being natural features. Green Castle Hill also provides an excellent view of the island's interior, including both the southwestern volcanic mass (of which it is a part) and the interior plain.

Nightlife: Although Antigua is no Las Vegas in terms of nightlife, it is one of the more happening spots in the region. The island boasts 3 casinos, many clubs and nightly entertainment at most hotels.

Much of the nightlife in Antigua revolves around the resorts and hotels. Often, the hotel entertainment features some of the best steel bands and calypso singers in the Caribbean. Outside of the hotels, Antigua offers plenty of hot spots featuring good drink and great entertainment. Live entertainment can be found at many of the popular bars.

Dining: Antigua has a wonderful mixture of local delicacies, West Indian, International, and exotic cuisines. There is an excellent choice of bars, restaurants, cafes and pizzerias. Visitors should sample fish and fresh seafood that are caught and served daily. If looking for a local dish, ask a native Antiguan where to get Fungi and saltfish or Ducana.

Shopping: Antigua offers a variety of shopping experiences for travelers...from saving money while shopping at a duty free store to window shopping for the perfect vacation memento.

Antiguan folk pottery dates back at least to the early 18th century, when slaves fashioned cooking vessels from local clay. Today, folk pottery is fashioned in a number of places around Antigua, but the center of this cottage industry is Sea View Farm Village. The clay is collected from pits located nearby and the wares are fired in an open fire under layers of green grass in the yards of the potters' houses. Buyers should be aware that Antiguan folk pottery breaks rather easily in cold environments.

Red Cliff Quay (St. Johns) is a former slave compound, but is now a shopping district with some of the finest stores and restaurants on the island.

Heritage Quay (St. Johns) provides duty-free shopping in a seaside mall.

Museums/Galleries: Located in Brown's Bay at Nonsuch Bay, Harmony Hall Art Gallery is the center of the Antiguan arts community. Exhibits change throughout the year, but the annual highlights are the Antigua Artist's Exhibition and the Craft Fair, both in November. The sugar mill tower, around which Harmony Hall is built, has been converted to a bar and provides its patrons with one of the island's best panoramic views, including a fine prospect of Nonsuch Bay.

The Museum of Antigua & Barbuda is a charming museum that tells the story of Antigua & Barbuda from its geological birth through the present day. A cool oasis in the middle of St. John's, the museum contains a wide variety of fascinating objects and exhibits, ranging from a life-size replica of an Arawak dwelling to the bat of Viv Richards, one of the greatest cricket players of all-time.

Visitors can watch an impressive multimedia presentation of Antigua's history, from its initial settlement to independence at Dow's Hill Interpretation Center. Observation decks provide a fine view of English Harbour.

Nature/Sightseeing: Antigua has many trails and tracks that are well suited to hiking. Most of the popular hikes lead to one or another of the island's many hilltop fortifications: Fort George sits atop Monk's Hill, and Fort Barrington (captured by the French in 1666) is on the promontory at Deep Bay. The Historical and Archaeological Society frequently arranges group hikes.

Much of the appeal of the natural environment in Antigua and Barbuda is the multitude of bird species to be found there. The Frigate Bird Sanctuary on Barbuda, though accessible only by boat, is the largest bird sanctuary in the Caribbean and contains over 170 species; Long Island and Great Bird Island also offer outstanding opportunities for birdwatchers.

WEDDINGS ON LOCATION

More and more people are getting married while on vacation, and it's now easy to do in Antigua and Barbuda. Even cruise ship visitors can now get married.

There are three simple steps:

1.) Visit the Ministry of Justice located on lower Nevis Street in downtown with your valid passports, complete the application and pay applicable fees.

2.) Confirm a date and time for the ceremony with a Marriage Officer.

3.) Get married - Congratulations!!
There is a registration fee of US$40 that must be paid at the courthouse in the new government buildings on Queen Elizabeth Highway. The application fee for the special marriage license is US$150, and the Marriage Officer's fee is US$50.

Marriage Requirements: Both bride and groom will need valid passports as proof of citizenship. If either has been previously married, then bring along the original divorce decree or, in the case of a widow or widower, the original marriage and death certificates.

Both parties must be over 15 years of age, if under 18, written authorization from parents or guardian is required. It is important that all documents presented are original or certified original by the issuing departments or offices. Ensure that all documents are in your legal name, and provide affidavits in cases where you are known by another name. Your marriage must also be solemnized or celebrated in the presence of two or more witnesses, apart from the Marriage Officer. (You can ask a guest or two to do this for you).

Your Antigua/Barbuda marriage ceremony is both legal and binding. Additionally, consent must be expressed by both parties to accept each other as husband and wife.

To be married in a church requires the permission from the church authorities where you wish to be married. Have your pastor contact the church to establish the requirements. Some churches ask that the couple attend pre-nuptial consultations. Therefore, allow some extra time if planning a church ceremony.

To get a list of churches in Antigua, contact the Antigua and Barbuda Department of Tourism for a list of churches on the island.

Often, most hotels and resorts in Antigua and Barbuda offer wedding and honeymoon packages.

LOCAL INFORMATION

Climate: Temperatures generally range from the 75° in the winter to the 85° in the summer. Annual rainfall averages only 45 inches, making it the sunniest of the Eastern Caribbean Islands, and the northeast trade winds are nearly constant, flagging only in September. Low humidity year-round.

Language: English is the primary language on Antigua.

Currency: The official currency is the Eastern Caribbean dollar (XCD) which is fixed to the US dollar. (Recent exchange rate was US$1.00 = EC$2.65). US dollars are widely accepted, as are traveler's checks and credit cards.

Time Zone: GMT (Greenwich Mean Time) – 4 hours. Daylight Savings is observed.

Entry Requirements: Proof of US citizenship is required in the form of a passport. You will also need an onward or return ticket. No Visa is required for trips under six months in duration.

Customs Regulations: You may bring back $400 of goods per person. Depending on the types of goods (cigarettes, non-Cuban cigars, or alcohol over a liter) you may be charged an additional custom.

Safety: Antigua & Barbuda are relatively crime-free, but exercise normal precautions; i.e. don't leave valuables unattended in rental cars or on the beach.

Peak Season: December 15 – April 15

For more information, contact:
Antigua and Barbuda Dept of Tourism
610 Fifth Avenue – Suite 311
New York, NY 10020

Telephone (From US): 212-541-4117
Website: www.antigua-barbuda.org

© Greg Johnston

B A H A M A S

Sun, sand, and sea are merely perimeters of the Islands Of The Bahamas. At the core of the islands you'll find a big heart, open arms, and a way of living life that is both timeless and new. It is the heritage of the Islands Of The Bahamas. It is your departure from everyday life.

The Islands Of The Bahamas is a 100,000-sq-mile archipelago that extends over 500 miles of the clearest water in the world. The 700 islands, including uninhabited cays and large rocks, total an estimated land area of 5,382 sq miles, and register a highest land elevation of 206 ft. Most notable, however, is that each island has its own diversity that continues beyond geography, carrying through to the heart of The Bahamas, the Bahamian people. You'll find it in their heritage, in their culture, and in the irony of their humble pride. These are The Islands Of The Bahamas.

Nassau/Paradise Island: Come visit the jewel of The Islands Of The Bahamas -- Nassau/Paradise Island. As the cultural, social, political and economic centre of The Bahamas, it is the most visited destination in the islands. Nassau/Paradise Island has much to offer visitors. There are more sights and activities here than you can experience in one trip. This island pair maintains a distinct blend of international glamour and tropical ease, giving travelers freedom to do everything or nothing at all.

Grand Bahama: Grand Bahama Island is an ecological wonder waiting to be discovered. Endless beaches, emerald green water, charming fishing villages and enchanting marine life are just some of the Island's attractions that make this a unique destination.

© Julian Bajzert

The Out Islands: They are called the Out Islands because they are the most remote in The Bahamas' archipelago of islands. But please don't confuse being secluded with being sleepy. Activities are numerous, islands and cays are seemingly unending, and the farther you leave everyday crowds behind, the more you are drawn in to the Bahamian culture before you. So you can be as relaxed or as active as the day allows.

THINGS TO SEE AND DO

With hundreds of activities on land and sea to choose from, visitors to The Islands Of The Bahamas will find there's not enough time in a day to do everything that the islands have to offer. Vacationers looking for an active holiday will find a myriad of choices for sports – from sailing, windsurfing, fishing and scuba diving to golf, biking and hiking on land. Those in search of edification will not be disappointed as The Islands Of The Bahamas is rich in history and culture as displayed in museums, communities, and in live performances.

The emerald and turquoise waters of The Bahamas archipelago naturally form breath-taking beaches. Countless meandering miles of sand, white or pink. Where ocean meets land here, the possible rewards are genuinely endless.

Coral reefs. Blue holes. Walls. Caves. Shipwrecks. Sharks. Dolphins. Stingrays. The variety of islands in The Bahamas present a variety of diving experiences. Beginners and experts are welcome. Lessons and guides can be found throughout the islands.

Anyone in search of the perfect beach should start in The Islands Of The Bahamas. Most beaches are secluded with soft, sugary sand and surrounded by a beautiful spectrum of light blue to dark green colors that paint the ocean, palm trees and sky. The shallow flats allow visitors to wade hundreds of yards out into the ocean and snorkel the brightly colored coral reefs that teem with virtually every variety of marine life known to man. Here you can be alone with your thoughts or a loved one and never have to worry about the rest of civilization. But if civilization is what you're looking for, you can find beaches alive with action, too! Just as beautiful as the secluded beaches, most of these tourist beaches offer fishing, windsurfing, waterskiing, diving, sailing, parasailing, picnic tables, restaurants, bars and local music to keep you entertained. If you can do it, you'll probably find it being done on one of the islands' beautiful beaches.

Exploring nature and the environment is a fun and exciting vacation activity. The Islands of the Bahamas has many national parks that protect and preserve the natural environment and offer unsurpassed viewing of rare and indigenous wildlife.

Nature lovers will enjoy discovering new species of plants and animals, both above and below the water, and even have the chance to safely interact with many of them. Everything from bird-watching to swimming with the dolphins is available on almost every island in The Bahamas.

When visiting these sites, don't forget to bring your camera. Many of the activities you will do and sights you will see are experiences that can only be had in The Islands of the Bahamas. Each island offers different activities, so check with your local ecotour operators and guides to get information on each island you visit.

© Bahamas Ministry of Tourism

Lucayan National Park is filled with pine trees, huge caves and rare flower species. It's also the only place in The Islands Of The Bahamas where you can explore all six of the islands' eco-systems, including one of the world's longest underwater cave systems.

Grand Bahama Island is privileged to host the second-highest amount of native birds on all the Bahama islands. This accounts for 18 of the 28 species of Bahamian birds. An ideal spot for birding is Rand Nature Centre. Visitors to this 100-acre sanctuary will encounter many West Indian flamingos, Antillean Peewee, Red-legged Thrush and endangered Bahama Parrots.

Accessible only by boat, Peterson Cay, a national park, offers exceptional snorkeling and diving. Visitors who adventure out into the surrounding waters will be rewarded with stunning views of coral reefs, tropical fish, sunken rocks and the occasional barracuda.

With over 65 species of birds on The Abaco Islands, they are truly a bird-watcher's paradise. As the national bird of The Islands Of The Bahamas, the flamingo remains the most identified bird on the island. That identifiable color comes from a diet of crab, shrimp, algae and other microscopic plants and animals.

Located just 8 miles north of Cherokee Sound, Great Abaco, the 2.100-acre Pelican Cays Land And Sea Park contains beautiful underwater caves and extensive coral reefs, abounding with terrestrial plant and animal life.

Located off Green Turtle Cay, the miniature park of Black Sound Cay comprises a thick stand of mangrove vegetation and is an important habitat of the Abaco population of the wildly colorful Bahama Parrot.

A great place for birding, Tilloo Cay offers twenty acres of wild and pristine natural environment which provides nesting for tropical and exotic birds. It is located between Marsh Harbour in The Abaco Islands and the Pelican Cays in The Exuma Islands.

Exuma Cays Land and Sea Park provides a 176-square-mile preserve

© Bahamas Ministry of Tourism

for land and sea life and is only accessible by boat and is of unusual interest to yachtsmen, skin divers and adventurers. No hunting, fishing or coral collecting is permitted. It is one of the few places in the world to view completely undisturbed marine life.

Nightlife: One of the real pleasures of The Islands Of The Bahamas is that each island has its own personality. No matter what kind of nightlife entertainment you want, you'll find it on one of the islands. Peaceful nighttime serenity abounds on The Out Islands. A world of glamour and gaming thrive on Grand Bahama and Nassau/Paradise Island. Whether you choose to spend your vacation nights under the stars or under the bright lights, there's an island waiting for you. If it's variety you seek, some islands offer both!

The nightlife on Grand Bahama Island is an exciting part of the island experience. Casinos, Las Vegas-style shows and night-clubs will keep you entertained well into the evening hours. And don't forget your danc-ing shoes! Live music fills the night air on Grand Bahama Island -- Goombay, disco, jazz -- everything you need to keep your feet movin' and your soul groovin' can be found at any of the lively dancing clubs. Check out

© Julian Bajzert

Port Lucaya's open-air Count Basie Square for live bands, fire-eaters and other local entertainers. Casinos and nightclubs here keep you entertained well after the sun goes down. Many local clubs offer a variety of music, dancing and a taste of live Junkanoo music -- the Bahamian music of choice.

Dining: Dining in The Islands Of The Bahamas can be an eclectic experience, dif-fering from meal to meal. Most dishes center around seafood like conch or rock lobster, but you'll find a tremendous variety of fare throughout the islands. Even dishes with the same name may have their chef's own special ingredients and signature flavor. Eating establishments range from five-star intimate restaurants to busy beach gatherings called "Fish Frys." Whether you're looking to expe-rience the local flavor or are wanting an old-fashioned American hamburger and fries, you'll find exactly what you're craving in The Islands Of The Bahamas.

To sample authentic Bahamian cuisine, find a restaurant participating in the "Real Taste of the Bahamas" program sponsored by the Ministry of Tourism. They should be marked with the "Real Taste of the Bahamas" logo in their window. These restaurants stand out among the best.

The restaurants of Nassau/Paradise Island offer virtually every type of cuisine – from simple dishes to the exotic Bahamian and International menus.

Grand Bahama Island presents visitors with the chance to enjoy a unique dining experi-ence and true Bahamian cuisine. Roast conch was developed by Grand Bahamian chef Joe Billy and can now be found throughout The Islands of the Bahamas. Crawfish is another island delicacy that visitors find delicious. It can be found at most local restaurants.

Dining on Eleuthera/Harbour Island can take you on appetizing adventures that range from upscale resort restaurants with an international flair to local "peas 'n' rice" places famed for their unique touch with freshly caught seafood specialties. And the renowned sweet Eleutheran pineapple wine is available everywhere, as is the tempting selection of tropical drinks made from it throughout the islands.

Shopping: If you love to shop, The Islands Of The Bahamas is the place for you! With shelves piled high with products from around the world and the discounted duty-free prices lurking at every corner, travelers should be armed with a strong will power or

© Bahamas Ministry of Tourism

an extra stash of money for a shopping spree. Some of the best buys include deals on Perfume, Crystal, Leather Goods, Jewelry, Fine Linen, Watches, Photographic Equipment, China, Binoculars, and Telescopes where savings can be between 25% - 50% below US prices.

When going out shopping, be sure to bring an appetite for authenticity. Today's Bahamians continue the tradition of early island natives by using local resources to create distinct items that reflect their heritage. Straw markets reveal foods, spices, ceramics, crafts, art, and music.

At the Bahama Craft Center (Nassau/Paradise Island) browse through booths of Bahamian arts and crafts made from indigenous products found all over The Bahamas. Crafts include paintings, sea treasures, blown glass, conch shell jewelry, Junkanoo art, clothing, driftwood paintings, straw work, ceramics, pine seed dolls, and more.
You can also find many treasures at numerous designer boutiques and jewelry shops throughout the Nassau/Paradise Islands.

© Julian Bajzert

Port Lucaya Marketplace (Grand Bahama Island) features numerous shopping and dining opportunities in a picturesque waterfront setting with live entertainment in the Count Basie Square. Boat lovers will want to glimpse the impressive array of luxurious yachts anchored at the marina, an official port of entry.

WEDDINGS ON LOCATION

Couples choose to get married and honeymoon in The Bahamas because of the many ways the Islands bring them even closer together: "the beauty, the beaches, the experiences, the memories."

Experience the wedding and honeymoon of your dreams in The Islands Of The Bahamas. Whatever your style, getting married in The Islands Of The Bahamas is an experience you'll treasure forever. And, planning your wedding in The Islands Of The Bahamas is easier than ever! Romance Directors are readily available to facilitate all your needs.

~Experience a Classic Wedding between the romantic columns of the 14th century French Cloisters on Paradise Island overlooking Nassau Harbour.

~Visit the Botanical Gardens, or any of the many beautiful garden settings in The Islands of the Bahamas, to find your ideal Tropical Wedding site. Say "I do" amid the colorful bougainvillaea, blooming hibiscus and the raging orange poinciana trees.

~For a truly Romantic Wedding, imagine saying your vows beneath tall palms swaying in the balmy island breeze with soft, white sand underfoot as the sun sets over an ocean horizon. The perfect way to celebrate one of life's most precious moments.

~What's a Party Boat Wedding? Imagine sailing off into the sunset on the sparkling crystal Bahamian seas as you lovingly exchange your nuptial vows. Then, dancing the night away under the twilight stars with friends and relatives.

© Greg Johnston

BAHAMAS

Let The Islands Of The Bahamas host a Unique Wedding you'll never forget. Take your vows undersea, on a romantic surrey ride, Junkanoo style - whatever your imagination desires.

The Weddings and Honeymoon Unit of the Ministry of Tourism offers services to assist you in organizing your own ceremony or, by acting as a facilitator between you and on-island wedding consultants, help you to plan any type of wedding.

Officers can be contacted at 1-888-NUP-TIAL (1-888-687-8425), by telephoning the Weddings and Honeymoon Unit directly at 242-302-2034, or faxing to 242-325-5835. You can also e-mail an officer at romance@bahamas.com.

Marriage Requirements: Both parties must reside in the Bahamas for one day prior to the wedding. The license costs $100 and both parties must apply in person. You will also need to obtain an affidavit from the US embassy in Nassau stating that both of you are American citizens who are free to marry (both are single, divorced, widowed, etc.) The cost is $55 per person. If you are divorced or widowed, you will need to provide proof at the time of application. If you have questions about current fees and requirements, you can contact the embassy at 242-302-2034.

LOCAL INFORMATION

Climate: The trade winds that blow almost continually throughout The Islands of the Bahamas give the islands a warm, agreeable climate which varies little year-round.

The most refreshing time is from September through May, when the temperature averages 70-75 degrees Fahrenheit. The rest of the year is a bit warmer with temperatures between 80-85 degrees. Rainfall is scarce from November through April each year; however, showers can occur during the months of May through October.

The temperature typically never drops below 72 degrees F with averages of 82 degrees in summer and 76 degrees in winter.

Language: The official language of The Islands of the Bahamas is English, more British than American, and generally intertwined with a special Bahamian dialect. Some Indian words like "cassava" and "guava" have been retained in the language.

Currency: The local currency is the Bahamian dollar (B$1), which is equivalent to the US dollar (at time of print). Both US and Bahamian dollars are accepted interchangeably throughout the islands.

Time Zone: GMT (Greenwich Mean Time) – 5 hours. Daylight Savings is observed.

© Terrance Strachan

Entry Requirements: US citizens must provide proof of citizenship (passport, certified birth certificate with photo id, or proof of naturalization) and a return ticket. Travelers will be given an immigration card to fill out and turn in upon departure from the islands.

Customs Regulations: Visitors from the US have a higher duty-free allowance than others, and amounts are based on length of stay. Check at your point of exit/entry for details.

Safety: Crime against tourists is relatively unheard of and the Bahamas has little panhandling. Normal precautions should be made however, like keeping valuables in hotel safes, being wary in remote areas, and always locking rental vehicles. As far as driving, British rules apply, so please remember to drive on the left and watch those roundabouts!

Visitors may use their home driver licenses for up to three months and may also apply for an international driver's license. Pedestrians should remember to look right before crossing streets.

For more information, contact:
The Bahamas Ministry of Tourism
640 Fifth Avenue
New York, NY 10019

Telephone (From US): 1-800-BAHAMAS
Website: www.bahamas.com

© Bahamas Ministry of Tourism

© Barbados.org

BARBADOS

BARBADOS - CLIMATE		
MONTH	HI	LO
JAN	82°	73°
FEB	82°	74°
MAR	83°	74°
APR	84°	76°
MAY	85°	77°
JUN	86°	79°
JUL	86°	78°
AUG	86°	78°
SEPT	86°	77°
OCT	85°	77°
NOV	84°	76°
DEC	83°	75°

Temperatures are provided in °Fahrenheit and based on averages.

Barbados is a relatively flat island with an abundant supply of large, gradually sloping beaches fringing the land. In some areas, coral and sandstone cliffs rise straight out of the sea reaching several hundred feet in height.

On the flatter coasts, you may walk for miles along unbroken white sand beaches, sometimes stopping at a cluster of coral rocks jutting out to sea. All along the shore large and small beaches are broken by coral formations, the soft coral rocks weathered by the ocean surf, forming abstract sculptures to an artist's eye.

Of course, not all of Barbados' coast is sand; there are mangrove swamps, cliffs, tide pools and areas where beds of low lying coral rock, sandstone, clay or shale reach out to the sea. Cliffs of coral and sandstone overlook calm bays and rugged coastlines and sometimes small, cozy soft sand beaches nestle between heads of coral sculptured by the sea.

© Barbados.org

From the air the island is in the shape of a pear. Graced by gently rolling hills, sugar cane fields and spectacular beaches - Barbados is one of the most densely populated islands in the Caribbean and visitors quickly experience small winding roads that strain with weight of traffic as cars drive on the left hand side past pastel colored homes, gardens, historic stone buildings, churches, statues and parks. As far as islands go it is not very big, measuring only 166 square miles. But just about everything on her 166 miles makes Barbados unique. First of all, the island actually sits just to the east of the Caribbean islands that arch down toward nearby South America.

Another unique feature is that the island is made up of limestone with no massive volcano rising from the sea to challenge the sky. This limestone formation created some of the best tasting water in the world as well as incredible beaches that seem to pop up on every nook and cranny on the coastline.

The island is also unique with her mixture of English traditions and Caribbean style. Often called "Little England" the island is home to stone buildings, homes and churches built centuries ago. If one did not see nearby swaying palm trees he might be convinced he was in some London neighborhood.

Other similarities to England can be seen in the cricket fields, polo grounds and elegant restaurants where people pause for afternoon tea. But these highly educated people with their unique British-West Indies accent are proud of their vibrant nation and gladly welcome people to their shores and quickly make them feel at home.

Today, the people of Barbados are often called by their nickname Bajuns. The island has a literacy rate of 98%. They are proud of their ties to England and enjoy cricket and afternoon tea. People still wear light jackets for dinner, observe manners and speak with more of a British accent than a pure "West-Indies" accent found on other Caribbean Islands. But while they respect their ties to England and observe many English customs, they are equally (if not more) proud of who they are and what Barbados has made of itself. For the most part the people are outgoing, friendly and very patient with visitors. In fact, one of the reasons so many people enjoy going to Barbados is the friendly people and the feeling that the resort or hotel they are staying in is part of the "neighborhood" rather than just staying in a resort "compound" with a wall dividing the people!

THINGS TO SEE AND DO

Sink your toes in the warm sand, lie back and relax under our blue skies and you'll start to savor the special way of life found only on Barbados.

Over 70 square miles of beaches await you in Barbados - welcoming you in hues ranging from delicate pink to purest white.

The west coast of Barbados is often referred to as the "Platinum Coast" and is renowned for the clear warm waters that lap gently onto golden sands. There are several magnificent beaches along this coast ... which is the best? Only you can decide! You can choose from Brandons, Batts Rock, Paynes Bay and Folkestone Park in St.James or Mullins Bay and Heywoods in St.Peter, and many more along the way! At each of these beaches you will find calm azure waters that are perfect for swimming and clean coral sands on which to relax and soak up the brilliant sunshine.

The south coast of Barbados is a curious mixture of the Caribbean Sea and the Atlantic Ocean. This coast is more lively than the West Coast but calmer than the East or North Coasts. The South coast offers something for everyone - calm swimming, snorkeling over inshore reefs and tidal pools, and at the southernmost tip of the island - windsurfing!

On the east coast of Barbados huge Atlantic waves crash along the shore and these beaches are better suited for walking and sunning. However, there are a few good places to splash along this coast. As the waves break over rocks and reefs, small pools are formed close to shore creatin natural swimming pools! The "Soup Bowl," located at Bathsheba, is the surfer's choice; while the East Coast Road is a popular picnic spot. Cattlewash offers a breathtaking landscape. With the

© Barbados.org

© Barbados.org

constant washing from the Atlantic, the East Coast is the perfect place for beachcombing.

The northern coast of Barbados is known for it's panoramic and breathtaking views! Here you will find quiet, private coves and bays ... areas of respite from the huge waves that crash onto ragged cliffs - throwing mist and foam into the air!

When the world was created, Barbados was given an abundance of potential for becoming a surfer's paradise. The island's location far out in the Atlantic Ocean allows waves to travel thousands of kilometers on the bottom of the sea to finally unload all the power it developed during its long journey over Barbados' coral reefs.

As Barbados is a Coral island, a coral reef stretches all around Barbados' coastline, providing for unlimited surfing conditions all over. No matter whether a swell approaches the island from a northerly or westerly direction or whether it's moving in from the East or the South, Barbados is guaranteed to have surf somewhere along its shores at almost any given day of the year.

Special Points of Interest: St.Lawrence Gap, a 1.3 km stretch of road in the parish of Christ Church, is famous for it's fine restaurants, diverse accommodation, lively nightlife and good shopping. 'The Gap.' as it is commonly known, is a place where various cultures meet and merge ... it is an experience that should not be missed!

A great treasure of Barbados is the Coral Caves and Underground Lakes around the island. The island itself is a fabric of soils and flora, on top of sandstone rock and coral pushed out of the sea by ancient volcanic action. The land is hilly and rocky with a vast underground system of rivers, caves and lakes that supply clear, delicious drinking water. The coral rocks that contain the underground water systems, are covered with a thin film of top soil measuring less than a foot on average and hardly more than a few feet at the deepest point. It is a delicate and critical balance that has supported the great sugar plantations of the past and continues to sustain a diversifying base of agricultural production.

Harrison's Cave is one of the island's most famous attractions. A unique phenomenon of nature, Harrison's Cave is an amazing gallery of stalactites hanging from the roof of the cave, and stalagmites that emerge from the ground, with streams of crystal-clear running water that drop from breathtaking waterfalls to form deep emerald pools. The stalactites and stalagmites were formed over thousands of years and in some places the stalactites have reached down to the stalagmites and a spectacular pillar has been formed.

Visitors are driven in electrically operated trams down through the extensive system of caves and at the lowest level point in the cave, visitors are invited to leave the tram and walk alongside a spectacular waterfall which plunges into a deep pool below.

Nightlife: As the sun sets, the action shifts from the beaches and clear waters to a wide selection of night time dining, dancing and entertainment fun! Take in an exciting murder mystery show, a romantic cruise, a historic dinner play, or jump to the beat in nightclubs throughout the St. Lawrence Gap. Check with your hotel for the latest information on all the current happenings on the island.

Dining: Watch the sun sink slowly into the turquoise Caribbean Sea while enjoying a sumptuous dinner at any of the excellent restaurants in Barbados.

© Barbados.org

There is an abundance of fine restaurants on the island that offer local cuisine, seafood and continental cuisine. Besides the fresh bounty drawn from the sea, the island keeps thousands of acres under cultivation so that restaurants can receive fresh vegetables, fruits as well as island grown pork, chicken and beef. The wide range of dining options available in Barbados ensures that there is something to suit every taste and budget.

By day informal attire is acceptable in most Barbados restaurants, but at night a more formal dress code is enforced. It is also recommended that dinner reservations be made in advance, especially during the winter.

Shopping: Barbados is an island filled with artistic talent ....from skilled local potters at work fashioning their wares as has been done for centuries, to modern fashion designers, abstract artists and poets, Barbados has it all! Pelican Village, on the outskirts of Bridgetown, is the place to get local handicrafts including straw bags, wall hangings, batik, paintings, rum cakes, and much more! Walkers Caribbean World offers Barbadian crafts and other useful items. On the sidewalk you will find several craftsmen and jewelry makers displaying their wares.

In The Gap, you will find the Chattel House Shopping Village which is comprised of several shops selling souvenirs, gift items and more! These shops are all replicas of the tra-

ditional Bajan Chattel House and are painted in beautiful pastel colors. The Chattel House was originally the design of the plantation workers' home. They were modest wooden buildings set on blocks so that they could be easily moved from one lease holding to another.

Aside from local wares, duty-free shopping is especially popular, with prices typically being 30 to 50% less than in Europe and North America! When making duty-free purchases, be sure to have your passport or airline ticket with you. Your packages can be delivered to the airport or sea port for your convenience.

The heart and soul of shopping in Barbados is Broad Street in the capital city of Bridgetown. There you will find several large department stores and duty free shops. In addition to the specialty stores, there are several shopping malls offering a wide variety of products and services. Just outside of Bridgetown is the Bayshore Complex, worth a stop for its shopping, and historic value.

Barbados has a rich history and has preserved and restored many of its historic buildings. Visit a plantation house for a trip back in time, see the towering lighthouses that once led ships to safety, Visit a local museum, or explore the historic towns that are an important part of our past and present.

The Barbados Museum contains many artifacts, collections and furnishings, as well as an interesting collection of rare historical maps.

The Sunbury Plantation House is over 300 years old, featuring mahogany antiques, old prints and a unique collection of horse-drawn carriages.

The Hutson Sugar Museum is a record of how sugar was produced in Barbados in the eighteenth and nineteenth centuries.

"Hike Barbados" takes you through cane fields, gullies, tropical forests and coastal communities to explore the unique geological and social structure of Barbados. Along the way you will meet new friends, enjoy healthy exercise and observe the delicate balance of the unique heritage and environment of Barbados.

WEDDINGS ON LOCATION

Imagine awakening to the warm caress of the Caribbean sun. Palms whisper and coves beckon. Languid sands stretch out before you. A breeze embraced by turquoise waters gently cools you. This is your wake-up call, inviting you to live out your daydreams, and begin your most important beginning, in Paradise.

Barbados is an island of infinite possibilities. It is elegant and it is casual, full of unspoiled charm amid sophistication. It is an island of song, dancing to the rhythms of the Caribbean or resting in the tranquil music of the wind and waves, serenading lovers in their hideaways. It is beaches and hills, flower forests and caves, sitting in the calm Caribbean sea and jutting out into the Atlantic ocean to break the march of rollers as they meet the eastern shore. It is a paradise for lovers, in nature's garden on the sea.

Here you can get married on a boat, in a church, in an elegant plantation home, under the cool shade of a flamboyant tree, by sea cliffs or soft sand beaches. Barbados agents cater to your every need.

Marriage Requirements: It is very easy to get married in Barbados. There is no required waiting period or minimum length of stay. Application for a marriage license must be made by both parties in person at the office of the Ministry of Home Affairs.

Both bride and groom will need valid passports or the original, or certified, copies of their birth certificates. If either party was divorced, an original Decree Absolute or a certified copy of the Final Judgment must be presented. If either party was previously married and widowed, a certified copy of the Marriage Certificate and Death Certificate in respect of the deceased spouse must be presented. Where necessary, all documents not in English must be accompanied by a certified translation. The applicable fees, if neither party is a citizen or resident of Barbados, are approximately US$75 and a US$25.00 stamp.

LOCAL INFORMATION

Climate: It is mostly sunny and fair in Barbados, featuring warm days with cool winds and cozy nights.

It rains most in summer and a good rainfall is refreshing and much needed. Rain is usually followed quickly by sunny skies and within minutes everything is dry. Tropical rainstorms sometimes occur in the hurricane season, which runs from June to October (as is said in Barbados - "June too soon, October all over!"). Tropical rains are spectacular but the island is very porous and the heaviest rains quickly drain off into the underground lakes or the sea.

Language: The official language of Barbados is English with a broad dialect.

Currency: The official currency is the Barbados Dollar - BDS. Most establishments will also accept U.S. currency.

Time Zone: GMT (Greenwich Mean Time) – 4 hours. There is no Daylight Savings Time in Barbados.

Entry Requirements: Every person entering Barbados should be in possession of a valid passport and a valid return ticket. A visitor who is a citizen of the United States of America or Canada traveling direct from

© Barbados.org

these countries may be admitted without a passport for a period not exceeding three (3) months. However, that person will be required to produce proof of nationality, by means of an original birth certificate or citizenship papers, and photo identification.

Safety: Crime isn't a major problem in Barbados, but take normal precautions. Don't leave valuables unattended on the beach or in plain sight in your room, and don't pick up hitchhikers.

Barbados is known as one of the healthiest places in the world. The very first tourists that came to Barbados were enticed here because of the clean air, sunshine, and a spirit of vitality. The East coast with its rugged landscape, strong winds and pounding seas became the retreat of choice for the wealthy European and American visitors and a number of health services and retreats grew up to cater to this clientele. Over the years, tourism has widened and diversified, but Barbados has continued to attract the health conscious because of its well known healing qualities. It remains a haven for those needing to get away and relax and those who seek a more spiritual experience.

For more information, contact:
Barbados Tourism Authority
800 Second Avenue
New York, NY 10017

Telephone: 1-800-221-9831
Website: www.barbados.org

TORTOLA	-	CLIMATE
MONTH	HI	LO
JAN	84°	70°
FEB	84°	69°
MAR	85°	70°
APR	86°	70°
MAY	87°	75°
JUN	90°	75°
JUL	91°	76°
AUG	89°	75°
SEPT	89°	74°
OCT	88°	74°
NOV	87°	72°
DEC	85°	71°

Temperatures are provided in °Fahrenheit and based on averages.

BRITISH VIRGIN ISLANDS

Located where the Caribbean meets the Atlantic, the British Virgin Islands contains sixty islands. With hundreds of secret bays and hidden coves, they have long been a seafarers' haven. Inhabited by Arawak and Carib tribes and later renamed by Columbus, the islands were once teeming with pirates and privateers who preyed on the Spanish galleons bound for Europe with Incan gold.

When you think of The British Virgin Islands, don't think big, think numerous. There is more of everything in The British Virgin Islands, but only in the ways that count. With more beauty, more isolated beaches and more unsurpassed sailing. These islands are truly one of nature's little secrets. The BVI's main islands include: Tortola, the largest island and primary home of its yachting fleet; Virgin Gorda, an isle of natural wonders and home to The Baths; Picturesque Jost Van Dyke, the Caribbean as it used to be; Isolated Anegada, a coral atoll with miles of deserted beaches.

Each has its own special character and charm. But these are only a few of the chain's dozens of islands, islets and cays, all unique and beautiful in their own right.

Yes, there are a lot of hotels, small resorts, villas and inns in The BVI. Rather than mega-resorts, we have lovely hotels and intimate guest houses, some located on swathes of white sand, others tucked into tropical hillsides. All are personal and caring. When staying in The BVI you won't be part of a crowd and you won't be just a number.

Prefer the sea to the land? The BVI offers even more. The Caribbean's largest bareboat and crewed charter yacht fleets call The British Virgin Islands home, yet the anchorages remain unspoiled and the sailing waters are unsurpassed. With dozens of anchorages to sail to - all within an hour or two cruise - no wonder The BVI is one of the world's top sailing destinations.

Low-key yet special, The British Virgin Islands offer the best of the Caribbean lifestyle. There is night life here, but no razzle-dazzle. Excellent restaurants offering international and local cuisine abound, but there are no fast food franchises. There is good island-style shopping, but no designer goods. What there is plenty of though, is unsurpassed natural beauty and limitless fun on land and water all adding up to more of nature's little secrets than you ever imagined.

THINGS TO SEE AND DO

Relaxation is the order of the day in The British Virgin Islands, as nature intended it to be. Here, the sights, sounds, and friendly service will help you let go and just relax. Visit the British Virgin Islands and escape from the mad world for a retreat to tranquility.

Here in The British Virgin Islands, you will relax and renew your soul. The possibilities are endless!

In addition to peaceful relaxation...sun, sand and warm caribbean water await you!

British Virgin Island beaches have been voted the best beaches in the Caribbean. Some BVI beaches, like Cane Garden Bay Beach on Tortola, Loblolly Bay Beach on Anegada, White Bay Beach on Jost Van Dyke, The Baths on Virgin Gorda and

Deadman's Bay Beach on Peter Island were rated world class.

The beaches of The British Virgin Islands are peppered throughout the entire archipelago of 60 islands and cays. Some we have discovered and others are just waiting to be. Not only do they possess such natural beauty and character not seen elsewhere in the world, but they also allow you to be a part of a captivating marriage of the Caribbean Sea and the northern Atlantic Ocean.

Nevertheless, a love affair with the beaches in The BVI is not really uncommon for those who have returned to them or for those who have yet to explore their shorelines. It's no wonder why BVIslanders continuously take advantage of these natural wonders as they take great pride and care in their country's tourism and appreciate your visit each and every time - all BVI beaches allow you to enjoy the ambience and close up feeling of nature, together with a relaxed and environmentally friendly lifestyle.

TORTOLA

Named in Spanish for the turtle dove, Tortola is the largest and most centrally located of the British Virgin Islands. The territory's capital, Road Town, lies in the middle of the island on the south shore and is the center for commerce and international finance, government and tourism, and is home to the largest number of charter yachts in the Caribbean. The island's south side is easily navigated by a road which winds along the Sir Francis Drake Channel and is dotted with marinas and anchorages. The north side is lined with beautiful sand beaches, Atlantic surf, lovely villages, small hotels and private villas.

Recreation: If you are passionate about water sports or just an enthu-

siastic novice, Tortola offers the perfect playground to get you wet, wild, spilled and thrilled! Whatever activities you choose, the professionals at our many water sports establishments will tailor an action plan of recreational fun and relaxation.

Catch the breezes as you sail our beautiful coastline. Learn to scuba dive from our certified professionals. Spend the day snorkeling along our many reefs deep sea fishing for Marlin, or fly fishing for Bone Fish. Discover our islands and waters in a powerboat; kayak our beaches, coves and cays; surf Tortola's North Shore beaches, including Little Apple Bay and Josiah Bay; windsurf, board sail or parasail and take in the breathtaking views, or swim with the dolphins and experience the thrill of a lifetime.

Beaches: Whether you are a sun worshipper, a windsurfer, or just want to enjoy a good book under a tree or in a hammock, the beaches of Tortola can make your island getaway dreams come true. There is a beach to suit every mood. You can socialize or be completely alone, dance until the sun sets, lazily snorkel above colorful reefs, body surf in thunderous waves, or simply float in still water as warm as a bath.

Special Points of Interest in Tortola: Tortola is endowed with Caribbean charm, beautiful beaches and dramatic mountain peaks. The largest of nature's little secrets (population 17,233), Tortola is base for The BVI's diverse charter boat fleet and is the gateway for the territory's infinite sailing destinations.

The capital city, Road Town, located on the island's south shore, is built around a deep u-shaped harbour fringed with hotels, restaurants, marinas and a number of quaint West Indian shops. Situated on a small bluff on the western end of the harbor is the residence of the islands' British Governor and the stately Old Government House Museum.

The island's north shore contains several beautiful white sand beaches, some accessible by road, others only by boat.

Cane Garden Bay, one of several popular yacht anchorages on Tortola, is the centre for great island night life as well as the location of many inns, guest houses, restaurants and water sports activities.

Nature/Sightseeing: Ridge Road runs along Tortola's spine and offers breathtaking panoramic views of the surrounding sea and many of the islands. Local homes dot the ridge, many built in traditional West Indian fashion with large verandahs, colorful hip roofs and gingerbread trim. Scattered along the island's steep hillsides are banana groves and stone terraces containing local root crops and vegetables. The ruins of plantation era buildings can also be seen throughout the island, remnants from the 18th and 19th century when sugar and rum were the basis of the islands' economy.

Sage Mountain is the oldest National Park in The BVI and has the highest point in all the Virgin Islands (1,716 feet above sea level). There are several hiking trails that lead not only to the peak, but also to a small rain forest sometimes shrouded in mist. Within its lush boundaries, visitors will find several rare and endangered plant species as well as mahoganies, hanging vines, enormous elephant ears, white cedars, and kapok trees, thick ferns and many other local flora.

The windmill in the Mount Healthy National Park is an outstanding symbol of the sugar plantation era in The BVI. It is the only one of its kind remaining in the entire British Virgin Islands. The 18th century mill overlooks the north shore of Tortola and, apart from the Callwood Distillery in Cane Garden Bay, is the only relic from a period when sugar was "King." The windmill was one of two types used in The BVI. The other mill was operated by mules, horses or oxen.

Named after the territory's leading conservationist, the J. R. O'Neal Botanic Gardens are a cool and peaceful refuge located in the center of Road Town. The Gardens feature a lush selection of exotic and indigenous plant life, including palms, orchids, cacti and local herbs. A pergola walk, lily pond, waterfall, tropical birdhouses and miniature rain forests are just a few more of the gardens' attractions.

VIRGIN GORDA

Virgin Gorda is an island of rolling hills, beautiful beaches and spectacular geological formations. This little secret capitalizes on its quiet charm, "small town" appeal and amiable people. Tourism may be Virgin Gorda's main industry, but with a population of just over 3,000, the way of life is still old-time Caribbean.

Virgin Gorda, which means the "Fat Virgin" in Spanish, reportedly received its name from Columbus who was impressed by the island's feminine curves when viewed from a distance. Two distinctive areas define Virgin Gorda. They are the Valley, with its rolling hills and sprinkling of round granite boulders and North Sound, which is a large sheltered harbor that contains the small community of Gun Creek as well as several resorts. Bridging the two areas is a narrow neck of land fringed by the lovely Savannah Bay beach and the steep mountain leading up to Gorda Peak.

Recreation: Discover the many beaches on Virgin Gorda offering a unique experience and magnificent scenery both above and below the water. From the world famous and exotic natural "indoor swimming pool" of The Baths, to the spectacular white sand beaches at Trunk Bay, you will understand why Virgin Gorda is considered the beach-blessed jewel of the Caribbean. All you need to do is visit...and leave your footprints in the sand!

Special Points of Interest: The island's most famous and most photographed attraction is the enormous granite boulders that line a series of Virgin Gorda's northwestern beaches. The Baths, where these boulders create a series of sheltered grottoes and sea pools, contain the most spectacular of these formations and is often referred to as one of the wonders of the natural world.

The Copper Mine, now a national park, was mined in the 1860s by Cornish miners. The remains of the mine's smoke stack, engine house and shafts are still there. Indigenous flora, including cactus, bromeliads and wild ferns grow on Gorda Peak. From the viewing platform of this national park there is a sweeping view of Tortola, Beef Island and the Dogs. North Sound is one of The BVI's most popular yachting anchorages. A world unto itself, Virgin Gorda is a secret worth discovering.

Nature/Sightseeing: One of the most dynamic and frequently visited parks in The British Virgin Islands is The Baths. The Baths are a maze of granite boulders, some as large as 40 feet in diameter, with exotic pools and grottos formed by giant boulders along the southwest coast of Virgin Gorda.

A popular charter stop, The Baths can be accessed both by water and by land. Hiking to The Baths takes approximately 15 minutes from the Ferry Dock. There are several restaurants, facilities and concessions near by.

The Copper Mine is one of Virgin Gorda's most impressive landmarks. It is the only one of its type in the entire English-speaking Caribbean and a very important link to the island's past.

Amerindians, who dug tunnels into the rock to find copper, were the first to mine the area. They used the copper to make tools and jewelry to trade with people of other islands. There are several mineshafts in the area around the ruins. Some go as deep as 100 feet beneath the sea. An effort has recently been undertaken to preserve the mines in hopes to have the site recognized as a World Heritage Site.

Devil's Bay, declared a National Park in 1964, is one of the most picturesque settings in The BVI. Crystal clear waters, white sandy shores and ample shade provided by Sea Grape trees, combine for a perfect beach experience.

Devil's Bay can be reached from the top of the Baths, via two trails. One trail takes you through a natural setting of boulders and dry coastal vegetation. The walk to the beach is approximately 15 minutes. For the more adventurous and physically fit, an alternative route is via the trail leading from the Baths. This trail starts on the beach at the Baths and winds around, under and over boulders, through tide pools and wet sand. Users of this trail should be prepared to climb ladders, crawl and wade through shallow water.

Gorda Peak is the highest point on Virgin Gorda and stands among 265 acres of Caribbean Dry Forest. Animal life is just as vibrant as the plant life. Tree frogs, soldier crabs, snakes and several species of birds can be observed. Another unique feature of this park is that it is home to the world's smallest reptile, the Virgin Gorda Gecko.

To the east of the Baths is Spring Bay, declared a National Park in 1964. Large granite boulders are the hallmark of Spring Bay National Park. The beach provides excellent swimming and snorkeling opportunities and, because fishing is not permitted in the park, marine life is teeming. A unique enclosure of boulders forms a natural pool called The Crawl. In the past, local fishermen used this as a hold for turtles and fishes. Today, The Crawl makes an impressive attraction not to be missed and is an excellent snorkeling area.

Nightlife: The nightlife in the BVI is quite different from the nightlife found on neighboring islands. Here, you will not find a fast-paced nightlife scene; rather, the pace of the unhurried day flows into the night. Indulge in fine food and drink at one of the many resorts or local restaurants.

Absorb the local flavor and hospitality at one of the islands' many outdoor beach bars. The experience will stay with you for a lifetime! You might find yourself sitting next to a local business owner who has just closed up shop for the night, or chatting with a financier who

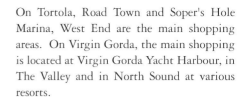

came ashore from a yacht. It doesn't matter, as long as you have fun!

Get up and dance to the music or just lean back and reflect on how lovely your life has become in the beautiful British Virgin Islands. You haven't lived until you've stood in the warm waters of The British Virgin Islands and toasted the full moon! Now that is living!

Dining: The local cuisine represents a palate of tropical tastes extracted from the multiple cultures that have made the BVI what they are today. The Caribbean, of course, is well known for its wealth of spices. Combine these with indigenous fruits, vegetables and seafood, and the results are a colorful and palatable taste extravaganza.

From West Indian to Cordon Bleu cuisine, the BVI has restaurants to satisfy every palate, mood and budget. Some restaurants are on the beach, others can be found along the islands' dramatic ridges offering breathtaking views of the sea. Some are located in historic sugar mills, surfside shacks and fragrant tropical gardens.

Try sampling some of the local dishes - it's a fantastic way to experience the BVI culture, savor some "home food" and get a chance to mingle with the locals. With hundreds of restaurants, whatever your taste, the variety is endless and the dining is delicious!

Shopping : The British Virgin Islands offer a variety of shopping experiences - ranging from local handcraft markets to farmers' markets to traditional boutiques.

On Tortola, Road Town and Soper's Hole Marina, West End are the main shopping areas. On Virgin Gorda, the main shopping is located at Virgin Gorda Yacht Harbour, in The Valley and in North Sound at various resorts.

Since there is no duty-free shopping, consumer goods tend to be expensive because of duty and shipping costs associated with bringing these items to the islands. Try to pack enough toiletries, film, sunblock, etc. for the duration of your vacation as familiar brand name items are limited and usually quite costly.

WEDDINGS ON LOCATION

You have found that perfect partner. Now here's the perfect place to have your perfect wedding. Many couples choose a British Virgin Islands wedding, possibly because it is so easy to get married here. A marriage license is simple to arrange and the marriage certificate is valid in the United States.

The Caribbean setting couldn't be more romantic. The ceremony can take place on a soft beach in the quiet of sunrise, aboard a yacht, beneath the spectacular ocean's reef for an underwater adventure, on a secluded island, in a lush tropical botanical garden, a friend's lawn, your favorite restaurant's poolside or gazebo, the traditional church, the local registrar's office or the great outdoors of a mountain top.

Some couples invite family and friends to share this blessed moment, but others choose local people to serve as witnesses. After all, in the three days it takes to qualify for a marriage license, a BVIslander can become a lifelong friend.

Marriage Requirements: You can apply immediately upon arrival in BVI for a license at the Attorney General's Office, situated on the second floor of the Central Administration Complex, Road Town, Tortola. The Attorney General's office is open Monday through Friday, 8:30AM through 4:30PM, except for holidays. The license will take 3 working days to process, so plan accordingly. Once the license is granted, it is good for three months.

At the Attorney General's office, you will be required to purchase a $110 postage stamp for a special license if you have been a resident of BVI for one day or a $50 postage stamp for an ordinary license if you have been a resident of BVI for fifteen days or more. You will have to show proof of your residency status (proof of the day on which you arrived) in the BVI, via your passports. In addition, you must show proof of marital status (including certified copies of Absolute Decree of Divorce or death certificates, if applicable), and have two witnesses to witness and sign your application form for the license. Please note that these witnesses need not be the same two witnesses who are present at your marriage ceremony. You can ask anyone to be the witnesses at the Attorney General's office and the ceremony.

Having applied for your license, you will need to go to the Registrar's Office in the heart of Roadtown, above the post office, to schedule an appointment for the date and time you want to be married. If you have made an appointment via telephone from abroad, you will need to confirm it at the Registrar's Office. The Registrar's office is open 9:00AM – 3:30PM, Monday through Friday. Weddings can be performed between 9:00AM and 6:30PM, Monday through Saturday. At the office, you will be required to fill out a form showing your names as shown on your travel documents, your age, occupation, marital status, and the names of the two witnesses, who must then be present at the ceremony.

If you wish to be married at the Registrar's Office, you will be required to pay a fee of $35.00. If you wish the Registrar to perform the ceremony outside the office, there is a fee of $100.00. If the Registrar needs to leave Tortola to perform the ceremony, you will also be required to pay for the transportation to and from that island. If you wish to be married in the church of your choice, Wedding Banns must be published on three consecutive Saturdays or Sundays in that church. You must make advance arrangements with the minister of that church.

LOCAL INFORMATION

Climate: The British Virgin Islands enjoy a balmy, sub-tropical climate. Temperatures rarely drop below 77°F in the winter or rise above 90°F in the summer. The average temperature is around 83°F with slight variations between seasons.

Peak Season: The peak tourist season is December to May, but this has more to do with the weather in North America and Europe than it does with the reliably balmy weather of the BVI. It can be beneficial to visit outside this period, when you can expect room rates to be about two-thirds of the rates charged during the busier months. And as an additional bonus, between April and August, the calmer weather tends to keep the waters clearer for diving.

Language: English

Currency: US Dollar - USD

Time Zone: GMT (Greenwich Mean Time) – 4 hours

Entry Requirements: Valid passport is the principal requirement for entry into The British Virgin Islands; however, Canadian and US citizens may also enter using an authenticated birth or citizenship certificate along with current picture identification.

Customs Regulations: All imports are subject to varying rates of duty. Imports entering The British Virgin Islands on a temporary basis will not be subject to duty.

For more information, contact:
British Virgin Islands Tourist Board
1270 Broadway, New York, NY 10001

Website: www.bvitouristboard.com
Telephone (from US): 800-835-8530

BRITISH WEST INDIES

The islands of the British West Indies are a popular destination for honeymooners. Pristine beaches, luxury resorts and world-class spas are popular draws for couples desiring a romantic holiday.

Of the islands that make up the British West Indies, Anguilla, the Caymans, and Turks & Caicos are very popular with discerning travelers.

ANGUILLA

Anguilla is often referred to as 'tranquility, wrapped in blue' - chosen by visionaries as the destination of choice for luxurious, five-star resorts; and by all visitors for the pervasive quality found in each level of accommodation.

Why Anguilla? ...body, mind and spirit.

For Your Body ...Gentle seas to swim, astoundingly beautiful beaches for relaxation, reflection, contemplation - and beach games, jogs and picnics. The pinnacle of gastronomic delights including over 70 dining experiences presented by a cadre of world renowned international and award-winning local chefs, and enlivened by, roadside barbecues and beachside bistros and grills. Resorts and independent spas offer the latest in spa and wellness facilities, services and treatments. Unhurried, uncomplicated, easy-to-explore Anguilla invites bike tours and hiking excursions as well as a myriad of activity choices. For Your Mind ...Unhurried, uncomplicated time to concentrate your thinking on nothing more than choosing which pleasurable activity you will select to round out your day of beach and sea pleasures. A visual pleasure, or intellect pleasure? Art galleries featuring original oils, pastels and watercolors; fine wood and metal sculptures; driftwood tables, and mantle pieces are scattered throughout the islands. Museums with exciting artifacts detailing this small island's history from its beginning to the present are also found on Anguilla. Choosing the evening's dining pleasure based simply on your mood - a romantic, candlelit dinner? A convivial pub? A beachside bistro? No lines. No hassles.

For Your Spirit ...Visitors to Anguilla are met by caring, friendly and welcoming Anguillians, and quickly embraced as friends. Innkeepers, whether of five-star luxury resorts or smaller hotels, apartment hotels, villa and condo beach clubs, value their guests and strive to ensure that vacationers here return to their homes and careers fully rested and restored, in body, mind and spirit. It is this very nurturing and gracious spirit that has set Anguilla apart from many other vacation destination, in the Caribbean and around the world. It is one of the common answers, in varying words, that you'll receive when asking of our past visitors - "Why Anguilla?" The people.

THINGS TO SEE AND DO

There's always a choice of activities on Anguilla... daytime or nighttime. Lazy beach days to rejuvenate your body and lift your spirit. Or art gallery and museum tours, boating to an offshore cay for a secluded picnic, or a long stroll on an uncrowded beach. Each day of your visit can bring a different watersport adventure, or the single adventure of beach chair, umbrella, book and tired toes in refreshing, pristine waters. The choice is yours to make each day.

Recreation: First and foremost, of course, are the 33 magnificent, powdery soft, white sand beaches that ring this small island. So many splendid beaches and such a small island!

Beachgoers here are assured of peace and serenity - even when visitors fill every room on the island. No crowds, no hassling; just you, your lounge chair or beach blanket, and the breathtaking beauty of Anguilla's beaches and the turquoise waters that gently meet soft white sands. Beaches for every pleasure: strolling, jogging, sunbathing, shelling, beach games, sandcastles, book reading, boat watching, birdwatching. Beaches for romance, rest, relaxation, rejuvenation and meditation. Visit us and discover why those in the know name Anguilla beaches as the best in the Caribbean - some say the world!

In addition to beach fun, you will find watersports and land activities to round out your day. Anguilla's turquoise waters boast seven marine parks: Dog Island, Prickley Pear, Seal Island Reef System, Little Bay, Sandy Island, Shoal Bay Harbour Reef System, and Stoney Bay Marine Park. Dive sites include wreck dives, shore dives, mini wall dives, night dives and heritage diving.

Snorkels and fins are available at most hotels, dive shops, charters, and at beaches where either beach operators or casual, beachfront restaurants are located.

Cruising and sailing to many of Anguilla's offshore cays or secluded beaches can be a great way to experience some of the island's most pristine spots. Picnics on board or ashore, sunset cocktail cruises,

secluded snorkeling trips and excursions to sand cay restaurants are just some of the fun itineraries available.

Dining: Unmatched in the Caribbean — more gourmet choices here per acre than in New York City. From award winning chefs and elegant restaurants to beachside bistros and sand cay barbecues, Anguilla offers a dining experience for every mood, taste and budget. French, Italian, Creole, West Indian, American, and other culinary styles are masterfully influenced by the flavors of the Caribbean to create an eclectic mix of mouth-watering delights.

Nightlife: For a small island, Anguilla has a number of nightlife options and musical entertainment to offer its visitors. Classical pianists and guitarists, a quiet saxophone, reggae, steel drum and calypso bands are just a few options. What We Do in Anguilla and Anguilla Life list 'what, where and when' for night owls. These publications are available from the Anguilla Tourist Board and most properties.

Local hot spots offer an opportunity to dance barefoot to Caribbean tunes that move your body and shake your soul. Generally, Sandy Ground is the "Hotspot" on Fridays and Saturdays, while Sundays and Wednesdays the crowds move to Shoal Bay East. There is music and entertainment almost every night of the week somewhere on the island.

Shopping: Anguilla is home to a veritable colony of artists who have come from many parts of the world to join Anguilla's noted local artists in the pursuit of their creative muse. The diverse art forms include pottery, sculpture, handcrafts, paintings and woodcraft. There is also a growing collection of tribal artifacts, textiles, antiques, carvings and furniture from many exotic destinations, in the Caribbean and beyond, which can be found in art galleries and studios around the island.

CAYMAN ISLANDS

Nestled in the calm, turquoise waters of the western Caribbean lies the peaceful British Crown Colony known as the Cayman Islands. Consisting of three islands just 480 miles south of Miami, Grand Cayman, Cayman Brac, and Little Cayman remain a little piece of paradise.

The island country consists of Grand Cayman (76 square miles), the largest and most populated of the trio, and the Sister Islands of Cayman Brac (14 square miles) and Little Cayman (10 square miles), which lie approximately 89 miles east-northeast of Grand Cayman and are separated from each other by a channel about seven miles wide. Grand Cayman is approximately 22 miles long and 8 miles at its widest point, reaching a maximum elevation of 60 ft at east End.

Between the Cayman Islands and Jamaica lies the deepest part of the Caribbean, the Cayman Trough, which is over four miles deep. South of Cayman is the Bartlett Deep where depths of over 18,000 ft. have been recorded. All three islands are surrounded by healthy coral reefs which lie at the top of dramatic walls and drop-offs close to shore, creating ideal conditions for diving and sportfishing.

THINGS TO SEE AND DO

You'll never be short of things to do in The Cayman Islands. World-class scuba diving,

snorkeling and sailing are just the beginning of your Islands' adventure. Whether it's a trip under the sea to feed the stingrays, an excursion to the Turtle Farm for a hands-on experience of one of nature's most inspiring miracles, or a journey into the past to revisit the first landing by Christopher Columbus, a feast for the senses-and sensibilities-awaits. Recreation: People travel to the Caribbean for many great reasons, but hands down one of the main reasons people travel to the Caribbean for vacation is because of the great beaches. Visitors want to see destinations where sun, sand and clear water are prevalent. The Cayman Islands are just that kind of destination and are world re-owned for their beautiful beaches.

At first glance, it's just the start of another day in paradise. The sun rises brilliantly, the breeze rustles through the fronds of silver thatch palms, and a flock of Grand Cayman parrots alight on a mango tree. A green turtle slides off to sea, skimming over the reefs, after depositing her eggs in the sand. The white and purple petals of a wild banana orchid flutter from their perch on a Mastic Trail mahogany tree, and a clutch of baby blue iguana scuttle into the underbrush, ready for anything.

At second glance, such seemingly casual

occurrences are actually hard-won victories. Were it not for the efforts of an army of volunteers, bolstered by two decades of far-sighted legislation and a government committed to education and preservation, the Cayman Islands might be "just another pretty face" of beaches and hotels-minus the endowments that make them one-of-a-kind in natural history and heritage. The Caymanian love of nature, coupled with inherent sensibility and economic vision has caused the Cayman Islands to lead the way in establishing policy for eco-tourism development.

Caymanians have embraced every aspect of what is referred to as Nature Tourism, saving more than their water, land and the creatures that inhabit both. They are saving their heritage, as evidenced in social, agricultural, and architectural markers of the past. It is an undertaking of major proportion, but Caymanians know it is their lifeline to the future.

Special Points of Interest: One of the largest tourist attractions in the world, Stingray City, is in 12 feet of water and mainly, but not exclusively, visited by scuba divers.

Today you can swim under, over, and along

with the rays. Their favorite food is squid, which you can feed them by hand. At Stingray sandbar, which is only waist deep, you can use a mask and snorkel and watch the rays swarm around you, brushing their velvety bellies against your hands and feet. Don't worry: this is the rays' way of begging for food. The rays have no teeth, but use a powerful sucking motion to draw in their food. Some are big, nearly six-feet in diameter. Their only means of defense is a barbed, venomous tail. As long as you don't lift the rays out of the water and treat them with the respect they deserve, you'll have a wonderful experience.

The only one of its kind in the world, Cayman Turtle Farm is home to over 16,000 sea turtles, ranging in size from six ounces to six-hundred pounds each! The farm is a modern-day reminder of the turtle's role in the history of the Cayman Islands. When Christopher Columbus first discovered the islands in 1503, he named them "Las Tortugas," meaning The Turtles. According to legend, there were so many turtles that the islands looked like they were covered with rocks.

The turtles are a protected species, and you can witness the majesty of these unique creatures hands-on. Nowhere else can you see an endangered species so successfully raised for conservation. In fact, since 1980, the Farm has released 29,000 turtles back into the sea to help replenish the wild population.

Museums/Galleries: The Cayman Islands National Museum exists in the restored Old Courts Building in George Town. The attractive building overlooks Hog Sty Bay, and is one of Cayman's few remaining 19th century structures, a survivor of hurricanes and countless Nor'westers. During its 150 years, it has served as a jail and courthouse - and meeting place of worship. The meticulous restoration project won the 1990 American Express Preservation Award for the Caribbean.

Nightlife: The Cayman Islands offers an enjoyable variety of nightlife and entertainment.

The Matrix nightclub and Bobo's Iguana attract a younger crowd of locals and tourists alike along Seven Mile Beach. Each night, DJ`s at both of these clubs spin to the sounds of Hip Hop, Disco, Calypso, Reggae, Salsa and Meringue. Occasionally there are live performances by bands.

If it is dancing you are after, DJ's spin to the latest hits at many of the hot spots each night. Other popular clubs and bars include Illusions, Legends, XTC, Jungle, Club Inferno, Bed Lounge, West Bay Polo Club, Lone Star and Next Level. The Link's at SafeHaven Club House, Benjamin's Roof, The Westin, the Marriott, the Hyatt Regency, and Decker's 269, all regularly feature live music.
For a great laugh, visit the Coconuts Comedy Club at Captain Morgan's in the West Shore shopping center and Chuckles at West Bay Polo Club.

Shopping: An amazing variety of local items await you! These include shell jewelry, thatch work, wood carvings, Caymanian-style birdhouses, crocheted items, pepper sauces, tropical fruit jams, honey, Caymanite (Cayman's semi-precious stone) jewelry and sculpture, and a unique selection of antique and treasure coin jewelry. On Grand Cayman, The Farmer's Market Cooperative on Thomas Russell Way, and Frankie's Fresh Fruits & Juices on Red Bay Road sell delicious unusual local jams, hot sauces, fruits, fresh juices and baked goods.

A growing interest in developing local art and crafts has led to the opening of art and craft galleries featuring local and Caribbean art. Underwater photography services and an excellent selection of underwater photos and prints framed as art pieces are available as well.

TURKS AND CAICOS

The Turks and Caicos Islands are famous for the 1,000 square miles of reef that surrounds them. The islands have been ranked in Rodales' Scuba Diving Magazine as "Best Fish Life," "Best Overall Destination," "Top Fifteen Most Popular Dive Destinations Worldwide," " Best Wall Diving" and " Best Beginner Diving."

The Turks and Caicos consist of 40 different islands, only 8 of which are inhabited. The islands of the Turks and Caicos are almost as diverse as its people. From the main tourist center of Providenciales to the quiet and tranquil islands of North and Middle Caicos to the historic Capital Island of Grand Turk; each offers a different experience and a unique character, but all offer great climate, beaches and underwater activities year round!

Most of the islands are only about 10 to 25 minutes by air from Provo, and most can be reached by boat too. There are also regular ferries from North to Middle Caicos. Providenciales is the most well known of the Turks and Caicos Islands and is the center of the tourism industry with a wide range of hotels, restaurants, attractions and facilities.

Grand Turk and Salt Cay offer history with great Bermudian architecture and a rustic

charm as well as some of the best diving and probably the most "relaxing" time you will ever have.

Middle Caicos and North Caicos represent the best of the environment, with lush green woodlands, the biggest cave network in the Caribbean on Middle Caicos, cottage pond and flamingo pond in North Caicos and a vast range of plantlife and birdlife.

South Caicos is the center for fishing, with lobster and conch exported from the islands, the historic cockburn harbour and the natural phenomenon of the boiling hole. This small yet friendly island offers many secluded beaches with awe inspiring views of the turquoise waters and surrounding islands.

Parrot Cay and Pine Cay are privately owned islands and are home to the exclusive resorts Parrot Cay Resort and Spa and the Meridian Club.

THINGS TO SEE AND DO

Recreation: The islands are arrayed around the edges of two large limestone plateaus, the Turks Bank, with deep offshore waters that serve as major transit points for Humpback Whales, spotted Eagle rays, Manta Rays and Turtles. Anglers who are fishing for Tuna, Wahoo and Blue Marlin use these same rich waters. Bordering the

edges of the islands are lines of coral reef and some of the most impressive walls of coral in the Caribbean.

In the last decade on Turks and Caicos, divers have begun to discover some of the finest coral reefs and walls in the world. From the legendary walls of Grand Turk, West Caicos and Provo's Northwest Point to the historic wrecks south of Salt Cay, a dozen world-class walls have become a Mecca for the serious diver.

From late December through April, the entire Atlantic herd of 2,500 Humpback Whales pass through the shores on their annual migration to the Mouchoir Bank, just 20 - 30 miles southeast. During this period divers can listen to an underwater concert of the whales' songs. During the summer, divers encounter Manta Rays cruising the face of the walls. Encounters with Dolphin are not uncommon either.

The salt ponds and inland marshes serve as excellent feeding grounds for resident and migratory birds. Search for Great Blue Herons, Flamingos, osprey and Pelicans alongside Egrets, Terns, Frigates, Boobies and other water birds. As part of the National Parks system, more than twelve small cays have been set aside and protected for breeding grounds.

On some of the less disturbed and smaller islands, such as Little Water Cay or Great Sand Cay, it is the Turks island Iguana that dominates the land. The Iguana is endangered and delicate but thrives on these

deserted islands, away from the influence of man. These islands are also protected by the National Parks system.

The National Parks were designed to protect the scenic environment and habitats, to preserve and conserve them for future generations, and to make them available for public recreation.

In 1992 the government set aside 33 specific protected areas, a list that includes nature reserves, sanctuaries and historical sites totaling more than 325 square miles. 210 square miles of this total amount are sensitive and ecologically essential wetlands ratified under the international Ramsar Bureau. Other protected areas include marine replenishment areas as well as breeding grounds for turtles, seabirds and other creatures. A marine mooring buoy system is just one of the many projects currently underway.

Nightlife: There are about 70 restaurants throughout the Turks and Caicos Islands offering local cuisine, seafood, conch, lobster and other specialties and Caribbean dishes as well as a selection of restaurants offering more Mediterranean, Italian, British and American dishes.

Shopping: In Providenciales there are three main shopping centers: Ports of Call; Market Place, and Central Square. All of these centers include a place to buy souvenirs as well

as clothing, beach and sportswear. Resorts also offer boutiques for those in need of a little 'retail therapy' during their stay.

For arts and crafts, there are a number of places to visit in Providenciales and in the family islands. You should notice smaller art and craft outlets as you travel around the Islands. Innovative work can be found by artists who use the natural environment to create designer mirrors, lamps and other household as well as fashion items - try the Shell Shack in Grand Turk or Greensleeves in Central Square in Provo. Craft work, specifically the beautiful handmade straw hats, bags and baskets, can be purchased in Middle Caicos at the Middle Caicos

Cooperative, in Bottle Creek in North Caicos or at Daphne's Native Gift Shop in South Caicos, as well as at outlets in Grand Turk and Providenciales. These items are highly regarded in the region and are of extremely high quality.

Nature/Sightseeing: Hike the Crossing Place Trails. A great way to explore the island is hiking with a local guide along the old coastal paths known as the Crossing Place Trails. Once used for trade, the islanders would walk to the end of the trail near Pine Barrel Landing and wade over to North Caicos when the tide was low, hence the name. Facing north-east and towards the prevailing winds and currents, the beaches along the trail collect large amounts of interesting flotsam and jetsam, including the occasional message in a bottle.

Sail the local sloops. The Turks and Caicos sailing boats have always been made by hand and cut from the local forests. This practice is still common in Middle Caicos where they make around two boats each year. The boats vary in size, the largest being about 28 feet. Join the boat builders in Middle Caicos for a day. They will tell you how they construct these boats and then take you sailing for a few hours around the bay.

Culture and History Tours. Enjoy a sightseeing tour by taxi around the historic and picturesque sites of Middle Caicos. Visit the flamingos at Village Pond, pass through the settlements of Bambarra and Lorimers and take a short walk to the Haulover plantation ruins and Sir Lorimer's grave. Stop for lunch in Conch Bar and then relax and swim at the sensational Mudjin Harbour beach. Finish this day with a tour through the extensive Conch Bar caves.

Captivating sunsets, gentle breezes, friendly smiles and gracious hospitality, casual elegance and relaxed informality are just some of the reasons Modern Bride's readers named Anguilla one of the best honeymoon destinations in the world. Be it Anguilla, the Cayman Islands, or Turks & Caicos, the British West Indies will provide the perfect atmosphere to make your honeymoon the trip of a lifetime!

Take an afternoon beach stroll and leave only two sets of footprints on the stunningly white, exquisitely soft white sands. Bask in the sun, swim, snorkel, sail, scuba, or windsurf to your heart's content. Visit an art gallery and take home an original watercolor for a permanent memory of the most romantic time of your lives.

Savor outstanding gourmet cuisine, touched with Caribbean spices and flavors; enjoy fine wines in a host of delightful restaurants overlooking the sea. Sip a rum punch while taking in a magnificent sunset. Dance to the romantic and sensual sound of Caribbean music.

Enjoy the warmth of the sun, cooling ocean breezes, lazy beach days or invigorating daytime activities, evenings of dancing and camaraderie, or tranquil serenity, alone just the two of you.

LOCAL INFORMATION

Climate:
Anguilla is a dry island with an average annual rainfall of 35 inches and average monthly temperature of 80°F. The island is continually cooled by prevailing trade

winds, with little change of temperature in the summer. Water temperatures are in the upper 70's to lower 80's. Optimum diving conditions are in the summer months when visibility is at its highest and there are little or no ground seas.

The average temperature of the Turks and Caicos ranges between 85 and 90 degrees (29-32 degrees celsius) from June to October, sometimes reaching the mid 90's (35 degrees celsius), especially in the late summer months. From November to May the average temperature is 80 to 84 degrees (27-29 degrees celsius). Water temperature in the summer is 82 to 84 degrees (28-29 degrees celsius) and in winter about 74 to 78 degrees (23-26 degrees celsius). A constant trade wind keeps the climate at a very comfortable level.

Hurricane season can vary but usually runs from June to October.

Language: English is the official language on all three islands.

Currency:
Anguilla: Eastern Caribbean Dollar (XCD) US currency is also widely accepted.

Cayman: The Cayman Islands Dollar (KYD) is the official currency (fixed rate: US$1.00 = CI$0.80); US currency is also widely accepted.

Turks & Caicos: The United States Dollar (USD) is the official currency.

Time Zone:
Anguilla: GMT (Greenwich Mean Time) – 4 hours. Anguilla does not operate Daylight-Saving Time.

Cayman: GMT (Greenwich Mean Time) – 4 hours. Cayman Islands does not operate Daylight saving Time.

Turks & Caicos: GMT (Greenwich Mean Time) – 5 hours. Daylight Savings Time is observed from April to October.

Entry Requirements: Proof of U.S. Citizenship required. Tickets and documents for return or onward travel. No visa

required for stay up to 30 Days.

Visitors from U.S.A. and Canada may enter the British West Indies with proof of US Citizenship (a passport, if they have an original birth certificate (or, a notarized copy) and a photo id (e.g.. Driver's License).

All visitors must hold a round trip ticket. Visitors are allowed to stay for 30 days; this is renewable one time only.

Safety: There is very little crime in the British West Indies; however, travelers should take normal precautions such as locking doors and securing valuables.

For more information, contact:
Anguilla Tourist Board
c/o Turnstyle Marketing Inc.
Two Park Lane, Suite 6B
Mount Vernon, NY 10552
Telephone.: 914-668-2854
Website: www.anguilla-vacation.com

Cayman Island Department of Tourism
3 Park Ave, 39th Floor
New York, NY 10016
Telephone: 877-4-Cayman
Website: www.caymanislands.ky

Turks and Caicos Tourist Board
P.O. Box 128 Front Street,
Turks & Caicos Islands, B.W.I.
Telephone: 649-946-4970
Website: www.turksandcaicostourism.com

JAMAICA	-	CLIMATE
MONTH	HI	LO
JAN	82°	71°
FEB	83°	71°
MAR	84°	72°
APR	86°	73°
MAY	87°	74°
JUN	88°	75°
JUL	88°	76°
AUG	89°	77°
SEPT	88°	77°
OCT	87°	76°
NOV	85°	75°
DEC	83°	72°

Temperatures are provided in °Fahrenheit and based on averages.

J A M A I C A

Jamaica is one of the most special places on earth …rich culture, vibrant art, picturesque beaches, and world famous all-inclusive resorts.

The island of Jamaica is the Caribbean's largest English-speaking island and the third largest in the region (after Cuba and Hispaniola). It is a land of lofty mountains, plateaus and plains all rich with flora and fauna. The climate varies from tropical on the coast to higher temperatures inland, creating a diverse mix of tropical and sub-tropical vegetation. With endless coastlines, the beaches range from reef-protected white sand in the north to black sand beaches in the south. Jamaica's rich ancestry, with ties to Africa, Asia, Europe, the Middle East, Great Britain, India, China, Germany, Portugal, and South America, has woven a nation that is truly uniquely Jamaican …"out of many, one people." It is this rich ancestry that has created a rich unique culture setting Jamaica apart from other Caribbean destinations.

Catch a show at one of the many theaters and stage shows, revel at Carnival and Augus' Mawnin, or just dance in the street to the infectious reggae beat pouring from nearly every street corner and rum bar across the island. No matter where you are, music is likely to entertain you. The Jamaican people love to dance; in fact, it is an integral part of everyday life. You'll find it everywhere and in all occasions from social events and celebrations to formal events and times of worship. In fact, it is said that the heart of the Jamaican people has never ceased to dance since that proud moment on August 6, 1962 when Jamaica became an independent nation. The transition was celebrated with dances, parades and ceremonies all commemorating the rising of Jamaica's own flag and colors of black, green and gold.

Enjoy a meal as unique and diverse as the island and its people. Food is celebrated and enjoyed in Jamaica. With fertile grounds and a tropical climate, everything grown on the island seems to taste just a little sweeter and just a little more flavorful. Treat yourself to a flavorful cup of local coffee or a cup of cocoa sweetened with condensed milk - an island favorite. Or, share a meal of local flavor - ackee and salt-fish, the Jamaican national dish, a concoction made from imported salted cod and the fruit of the ackee tree, mixed with onions, peppers and tomatoes. Or, try red beans and rice, curried goat, boiled green bananas, crab and pepperpot soup, red snapper or lobster. Jamaica offers such a culinary variety, whatever your tastes, you're sure to find a flavorful dish you'll absolutely love!

The beautiful landscape of turquoise beaches, glistening sand, swaying palm trees, statuesque mountains, flowing rivers, spectacular waterfalls, sweeping plains; the vibrant atmosphere with a reggae beat, jazz, calypso, dancing; all-inclusive resorts; and the romance of it all make the island of Jamaica a perfect vacation getaway.

All-inclusive resorts are a very popular option with travelers looking for a trouble-free vacation. Touring Jamaica on your own is possible, but may be intimidating to some. Jamaica's dramatic inequality of wealth and social tensions influence the local people and, since Jamaicans tend not to beat around the bush, they often let their feelings know to tourists. With an all-inclusive resort, you step off the plane and are immediately swept away to your own private Jamaica where you can live the vacation of your dreams without ever leaving the resort. You will be catered to in a manner fit for royalty.

THINGS TO SEE AND DO

These people -- with their different backgrounds, traditions and beliefs -- shaped Bahamian culture into the unique, colorful patchwork of life and lifestyles that it is today.

Anyone in search of the perfect beach should start in The Islands Of The Bahamas. Most beaches are secluded with soft, sugary sand and surrounded by a beautiful spectrum of light blue to dark green colors that paint the ocean, palm trees and sky. The shallow flats allow visitors to wade hundreds of yards out into the ocean and snorkel the brightly colored coral reefs that teem with virtually every variety of marine life known to man. Here you can be alone with your thoughts or a loved one and never have to worry about the rest of civilization.

But if civilization is what you're looking for, we have beaches alive with action, too! Just as beautiful as the secluded beaches, most of these tourist beaches offer fishing, windsurfing, waterskiing, diving, sailing, parasailing, picnic tables, restaurants, bars and local music to keep you entertained. If you can do it, you'll probably find it being done on one of our beaches.

© Jamaica Tourist Board

Xanadu Beach: Grand Bahama Island boasts some of the most beautiful and exciting beaches in all of The Islands Of The Bahamas. Many guests of the Freeport hotels frequent the Xanadu beach. It's a popular beach and tends to get crowded at times, but you'll find most water sports equipment here. The premier beach on Grand Bahama Island is Gold Rock Beach. It is a secluded beach with BBQ pits, picnic tables and benches and a spectacular low tide. Just north of the beach are the Lucayan Caverns, the world's longest underground surveyed cave system.

Barbary Beach: If you are looking for a more secluded beach, travel down to the Barbary Beach. You'll find beautiful seashells and in May and June there's a spectacular display of white spider lilies. Many locals believe that Barbary is the most beautiful beach in all of Grand Bahama Island.

Harbour Island: The setting: three miles of the most beautiful pink sand you'll ever see. Harbour Island is simply encircled by what many say is the most striking beach in all of The Islands Of The Bahamas. You can pursue almost any water sport at the resorts there – or just relax and soak up the sun in your own favorite spot. Can't miss!

Governor's Harbour: This beautiful pink sand beach is usually crowded with vacationers at one end, and virtually people-free at the other. The privacy and isolation can be great, but if you want more activities, there are plenty of local activities and tours to choose from.

Tropic Of Cancer Beach: This graceful crescent of pale sand borders the phenomenally blue-green water along the coast of Little Exuma. The longest beach on the island, it is also the prettiest in the Exuma chain and you will probably have it all to yourself. The imaginary line that defines the northern extent of the tropics is said to run right along this beach.

Exuma Cays Land And Sea Park: In the early morning, beach visitors here may be interrupted by iguanas begging for a breakfast handout, but please don't feed them.

You will adore the pristine, sandy beaches of Nassau/Paradise Island. Cable Beach (west of Nassau) and Paradise Island (across the harbour) offer an endless variety of activities, especially if you stay at one of the fabulous resort hotels that line the beaches. Sailing, waterskiing, windsurfing, diving, fishing, parasailing, seaside restaurants, beach bars, local entertainment -- all this and more are waiting for Sunning, swimming, snorkeling, diving, canoeing, hiking, biking, relaxing, horseback riding, reggae music, dancing, partying, world-class resorts, river rafting, golfing, reefs, caves, historical sites…you name it, Jamaica's got it.

Recreation: Sip on a refreshing rum drink while relaxing on a sparkling white beach looking out over clear blue water. What could be better? Not much, the beaches of Jamaica are a destination in and of themselves. At the Blue Lagoon, you could spend the entire day watching the colors of the lagoon change with the movement of the sun. The Blue Lagoon is over is Port Antonio's most famous attraction.

Visit the World Famous Doctor's Cave Beach, Jamaica's most beautiful beach located in the heart of Montego Bay.

For snorkelers and divers, Jamaica's waters are just as beautiful below the surface as they are above. The North Coast, an excellent place for scuba diving, offers reefs and canyons just a few hundred yards from shore. The west side of the island offers limestone caves and caverns for the experienced adventure seeker. Hop aboard a sailing cruise and be taken to the finest snorkeling spots in the Montego Bay Marine Park. Snorkeling equipment is typically provided on sailing cruises and instructions for beginners are provided.

The "Coral See" is a new attraction providing visitors with a unique view of the Montego Bay Marine Park. Passengers of this semi-sub reef vessel go down into the hull of the vessel where panoramic viewing windows allow full visual access to the colorful marine life and fishes living below.

Swim with a family of Bottlenose dolphins in their home at Dolphin Cove, adjacent to the world-famous Dunn's River Falls in Ocho Rios.

To top it all off, visit the Margaritaville Caribbean Sports Bar & Grill. This entertainment complex offers restaurants, water-sport events and entertainment.

Either a romantic or adventurous horseback ride is a great way to explore Jamaica. Most resorts offer organized rides ranging from rides through plantations to trekking into the island's interior.

Jamaica features 10 championship golf courses, some of which are regular stops for the PGA and LPGA tours. The pre-eminent course, Tryall Golf Club, is located just 12 miles west of Montego Bay.

Special Points of Interest: A one-of-kind-attraction, Aquasol Marine Park (Montego Bay) offers several water-sports, sunbathing comforts, picnic spots, restaurants and bars, gift shops and boutiques, tennis courts and the only go-cart track in Montego Bay.

© Jamaica Tourist Board

Take a boat ride up the meandering Black River (South Coast), past sultry crocodiles and through mysterious mangroves.

Discover the legend and spirit of Bob Marley at Bob Marley Experience & Theatre (Montego Bay). This retail and entertainment center includes complimentary admission to an air-conditioned theater where visitors watch a film on the life and work of Bob Marley on the big screen.

Cuddle with Sugar, get rubbery, wet kisses from Mitch, or let Cometta and Betta take you for a spin around Dolphin Cove (Ocho Rios). These exotic and friendly mammals wait to entertain you.

Said to have been a haven for 'runaway slaves' in the 18th century. The Green Grotto Caves (Ocho Rios) are characterized by coastal limestone and are easily accessed.

Greenwood Great House (Montego Bay) is over 200 years old. Formerly owned by the family of Elizabeth Barrett-Browning, the famous English poet, Greenwood is one of the best-preserved great houses on the island.

Located east of Treasure Beach, Lover's Leap (South Coast) is a sheer 1,700-foot cliff overhanging the sea. It was here that two slave lovers leaped to their deaths rather than be separated.

Today, walking along Port Royla's (Kingston) quiet streets, where children run freely and sun-worn fishermen mend tattered nets, it is hard to imagine that this quaint town was once called the "wickedest and richest city of the west". Yet, if you hone your senses, you'll pick up clues that cast aside Port Royal's humble facade. You'll see the pirate flag waving proudly over the town, old cannons peering out at the horizon, and haunting monuments honoring men from centuries long ago. As a former buccaneer and British naval base, it has played host to notorious pirates and legendary admirals, and profited from their riches and glory. Two-thirds of the town lies at the bottom of Kingston harbor, the result of a massive earthquake in 1692. This sunken city represents one of the greatest repositories of 17th century artifacts in the Caribbean and is one of the most important archeological sites in the region.

Nightlife/Dining: Jamaica is the home of reggae, and every Jamaican town has some degree of nightlife, whether it is a cluster of small bars with a jukebox, cabaret-type entertainment, high tech dance clubs, beach parties, or karaoke ensembles. Fashionable street dances featuring well-known sound systems have become the rage for younger, dancehall audiences. Check with local newspapers for nightlife happenings when you get there.

Jamaica's "jerk meat" is the island's most distinctive style of cooking. Meat, usually chicken or pork, and sometimes fish, is seasoned in a special blend of island-grown spices, including pimento, hot peppers, cinnamon and nutmeg, and then grilled slowly for hours over a fire of pimento wood and under a cover of wooden slats or corrugated zinc sheets in a specially designed drum. Seafood is plentiful as is the selection of fresh fruit and vegetables. Foods of all types can be found while dining in the resorts. Further outside the resorts and outside of Kingstown, international eating options are limited.

Shopping: The Ocho Rios area has a wide variety of shopping possibilities. Main Street in the center of town is a shopping hub that includes the local craft market, and some of the duty-free delights include Taj Mahal, Soni's Plaza and Ocean Village Shopping Centre.

Museums/Galleries: Animal Farm (Montego Bay) is the place for the nature lover. It is Jamaica's newest animal sanctuary and nature retreat where you can explore the habits of exotic birds, learn about solar electricity, or relax by the river with a cup of tea from their herb garden.

The Bob Marley Museum (Kingston) is dedicated to the memory of the late reggae superstar, Robert "Bob" Marley. The museum is located on Marley's original studio, where he recorded many of his songs.

© Jamaica Tourist Board

Coyaba River Garden & Museum offers the serenity of a genuine water garden fed by streams that rise on the property, exquisite Jamaican Spanish architecture, and a natural aquarium.

ReggaeXplosion (Ocho Rios) is an involving exhibit that celebrates Jamaican music by using images, videos and soundtracks (both music and interviews) from the 1950's to the present day. It is housed in a two-story building with soundbooths for each genre and DVD monitors that are genre specific; in addition there is a giant screen that shows compilation DVDs and provides the ambient music.

Escape to the Royal Palm Reserve and discover the enchantment of Negril's hidden treasure. This 300-acre site boasts 114 plant species including the Royal Palm, unique to this area. There are over 300 animal species, including birds, butterflies, and reptiles. Come and experience the beauty and tranquility of this local sanctuary.

The Royal Botanical Gardens at Hope, (popularly called Hope Gardens) is a national attraction frequented by visitors from all over the world. The Gardens have many exotic species along with some endemic trees of Jamaica. At the Hope Gardens, visitors can also visit

© Jamaica Tourist Board

the Coconut Museum, the Sunken Gardens, the Orchid House, the Lily Pond, the Maze and Palm Avenue.

Take a Plantation Tour and visit picturesque estates, brimming with famous crops like sugar cane, banana, coffee and tasty tropical fruits.

The Hilton High Day Tour has been operating since 1983. Their tour includes return transportation with a tour guide from your Montego Bay Hotel or Villa, a fully hosted and guided tour, a Jamaican-style buffet country breakfast, complementary drinks and rum punches. Another tour will take you through the Jamaican countryside to visit the German Village and local primary school. You will be entertained by the plantation Calypso band and village children and enjoy a plantation luncheon with roasted pig and exotic vegetables.

Nature/Sightseeing: Bloody Bay (Negril) boasts talcum white sand and warm clear water.

Buccaneer' Beach (Montego Bay) is literally beside the airport, so while lying on the sand you can almost touch planes' bellies as they swoop in for landing. This small, narrow beach hugs the quiet roadside. There's a shallow swimming area that opens onto the Montego Bay Marine Park.

Locals will tell you that Doctor's Cave Beach is the most famous in Jamaica. True or not, it is certainly the most beautiful and best-maintained in the area. Its pristine white-sand, glistening waters and excellent facilities have charmed beach lovers from the 19th century to today.

The point at which Dunn's River Falls (Ocho Rios) enters the Caribbean Sea is marked by 600 feet of mountain spring water cascading down the rocks toward the ocean. This most photographed attraction in Jamaica can be climbed even by the non-athletic. The operators of the park recommend the assistance of an official guide, since at points the rocks may be mossy, slippery and just dangerous enough to put a small

damper on what otherwise might have been a perfect vacation. Along the route are clear pools to swim in, small whirlpools, caves to explore, and a garden to picnic in.

Located just 20 minutes from the hustle and bustle of Ocho Rios, James Bond Beach is spectacular -beautiful beaches surrounded by crystal clear water on three sides and an amazing backdrop; the lush mountains of St. Mary reach straight down into the sea.

Situated on a five-acre property, Mayfield Falls (Negril) is a great spot for camping, hiking and picnicking. Other activities include cliff jumping, cave diving, relaxing in one of the natural Jacuzzis, and enjoying a massage. At Mayfield Falls, visitors are taught local folk dances and how to prepare local dishes with spices and herbs.

Plunging into a jade-colored pool, the secluded waterfall at Reach Falls (San Antonio) is one of Jamaica's best-kept secrets. Come renew your spirit and refresh your soul in the cool mountain spring water.

Stake out a blanket-sized spot of paradise or meander along soft foot-friendly white sand at Seven Mile Beach (Negril). The beach is lined with funky eateries oozing ice cold drinks by day and sizzling hot reggae by night.

WEDDINGS ON LOCATION

Visitors can get married just 24 hours after arriving in Jamaica providing prior application has been made for a marriage license. The cost of a license is approximately US$87 (at time of printing). To apply for a marriage license, contact the Ministry Justice at 876-906-4908.

Unlike many countries, Jamaica does not expect you take a blood test before getting married. However, the following documentation is required:

• Proof of citizenship - certified copy of birth certificate, which includes father's name.

• Parent's written consent if under 18 years of age.

© Jamaica Tourist Board

• Proof of divorce if applicable (original certificate of divorce).

• Certified copy of death certificate for widow or widower.

• Italian nationals celebrating their wedding in Jamaica must notify their embassy and a certified copy of their marriage certificate forwarded to their embassy to be legalized and translated.

• French Canadians need a notarized translated copy of all documents and a photocopy of the original French documents.

There are non-denominational Marriage Officers who can officiate either at their offices, in their homes or at a place chosen by the couple, and are able to provide witnesses. Marriage Officers charge anywhere from US$50 – US$250.

LOCAL INFORMATION

Climate Jamaica has a tropical climate at sea level and a temperate climate towards the highlands of the interior. The island sees two rainy seasons: from May to June, and from September to November. Of note, also, is the hurricane season from June to September, during which time large storms may, but rarely do, pass over the island. The average temperature is between 66 and 99 degrees Fahrenheit year-round.

Peak Season: Mid-December through mid-April

Language: The official language is English, but most Jamaicans speak a local patois influenced by a combination of several different languages.

Currency: Jamaican Dollars - JMD

Time Zone: GMT (Greenwich Mean Time) – 4 hours. Jamaica does not observe Daylight Savings Time.

© Jamaica Tourist Board

Entry Requirements: A valid US passport is required for entry, along with a return ticket.

Customs Regulations: You can leave Jamaica (for trips of 48+ hours) with $600 worth of duty-free merchandise (there is a 10% charge on the next $1000 worth of merchandise). No fresh food is allowed into the US.

Safety: Use the same caution you would exercise as you would at home. Stay away from remote areas, especially at night.

For more information, contact:
Visit Jamaica
1320 S. Dixie Highway
Coral Gables, FL 33146

Telephone (From US): 212-856-9727
Website: www.visitjamaica.com

© Jamaica Tourist Board

PUERTO RICO - CLIMATE		
MONTH	HI	LO
JAN	83°	71°
FEB	83°	72°
MAR	84°	72°
APR	86°	72°
MAY	87°	74°
JUN	88°	76°
JUL	88°	77°
AUG	89°	78°
SEPT	89°	78°
OCT	88°	77°
NOV	85°	75°
DEC	84°	73°

Temperatures are provided in °Fahrenheit and based on averages.

P U E R T O   R I C O

Whether you're planning a wedding or a honeymoon, a getaway for the entire family or just yourself, are young or old, Puerto Rico offers the excitement of overseas travel with the convenience and comfort of a domestic trip.

Puerto Rico is 100 miles long by 35 miles wide—but don't let these measurements fool you. Close to 4 million people live on the "Island of Enchantment," with more than a million in the greater San Juan metropolitan area alone. It is a vibrant, modern, bilingual and multi-cultural society, one that has been molded by Spanish, African, Indian and U.S. influences. Residents of Puerto Rico have much in common with their fellow Americans in the continental United States, yet they retain a decidedly Hispanic heritage.

THINGS TO SEE AND DO

Recreation: Whether you're dreaming of spectacular surfing waves, a challenging golf course, or the perfect sunbathing beach, Puerto Rico offers the active traveler a tremendous array of opportunities. Surfing and golf compete with tennis, fishing, kayaking, scuba diving, and horseback riding, not to mention windsurfing and parasailing, for your active time. Puerto Rico's perpetual summer weather begs you to enjoy the sport of your choice!

Puerto Rico is home to some of the most beautiful beaches in the world, and its hundreds of miles of coastline harbor an almost endless selection for the beach connoisseur. Beaches come in every size, color, and form, from the pure white dunes of Isabela to the black volcanic sands near Punta Santiago. You can find a beach for any

level of seaside activity, from a stroll in the shimmering shallow waters at Luquillo to a thrilling ride in the boisterous surf of Rincón.

The beaches mentioned here are just a few suggestions. Ask a local, and you will get a dozen more!

Isla Verde Beach is actually a series of beaches stretching for miles in front of luxury resorts and posh high-rise residential apartments, restaurants and private clubs, guesthouses and private homes, parks, and even a cemetery! A tranquil place during the week, Isla Verde really comes alive on weekends and is otherwise known as "San Juan's playground." Beach lovers stream in from everywhere to get some sun, splash in the sea, party with family and friends, play beach volleyball, or walk along the sandy shores. There is no shortage of places to eat or drink. Many hotels and restaurants have bars and casual restaurants adjacent to the beach.

Of all the truly gorgeous beaches on the island of Culebra, nine miles off the main island's eastern coast, Flamenco leads the pack. This island municipality is a paradise of beaches so perfect they are almost impossible to believe. The crowning jewel is Flamenco Beach, recently named one of the Best Beaches in America and Best Escape Beach by the Travel Channel. A magnificent mile or so of pure white coral sand framed by Culebra's arid, sun-toasted hills, it is protected as a Marine Wildlife Reserve by the Department of Natural and Environmental Resources. Here you can escape from the crowds, jet skis and motorized sea vessels found on many of the major beaches on the main island of Puerto Rico.

The long stretch of Atlantic coast from Arecibo in the northwest to Rincón, the town at the westernmost tip of the island where the Atlantic meets the Caribbean, is home to an incredible variety of beaches. About halfway between these two points are the spectacular white sand dunes of Isabela. Among the favorite beaches in Isabela is Shacks. It has an international reputation as one of the premier windsurfing spots in the world and is often compared with Maui. Despite its worldwide reputation, Shacks is almost never crowded.

Caja de Muerto means "coffin" in Spanish, but the name refers only to the shape of the cay, which lies 8 miles off the coast of Ponce in the south of Puerto Rico. Other than its reputation as a pirates' den, there is nothing funereal about it. Indeed, it is a favorite destination for people who seek unspoiled natural beauty. The island has beautiful foliage and fauna. It rarely rains in Ponce and its environs, so perfect beach weather is almost guaranteed every day of the year. It is the largest of the three cays that make up the Caja de Muerto Nature Reserve. For those in search of spectacular scuba diving and snorkeling, the shallow reefs surrounding Caja de Muerto will provide an unforgettable experience. For those more interested in landmark monuments, the lighthouse, built by the Spaniards in 1887, will make for memorable sightseeing between swims.

The Mediterranean style town of Aguadilla is situated on the northwest coast of Puerto Rico, where the nearby mountains afford good vantage points for viewing the majestic shoreline below or watching the sun disappear into the sea. The waters closest to the town are usually too rough for safe swimming, but Crashboat Beach is on every dedicated beach enthusiast's must-see list. It is very popular with the younger crowd. It is certainly worth navigating the narrow, winding, tree-lined access road to be able to walk along the beach's shell-covered sands and gaze at the roaring sea. Unless you are a strong swimmer or an avid bodysurfer, you may prefer to enjoy the calmer waters a few miles away. Waves at Crashboat can be unpre-

dictably large and break quite near the shore. An abandoned cement pier is said to give the beach its name, since the heavy surf damaged many of the fishing boats that were tied to it. Plenty of palm trees and other coastal vegetation line the dramatic beach and provide shelter from the sun's rays as well as place to take in the wonder of nature at its challenging best.

Special Points of Interest: Puerto Rico offers nothing if not diversity. On one small island, 100 miles long and 35 miles wide, you can experience thousands of years of history and four distinct cultures.

Investigate ancient Indian ceremonial parks, compare two of the oldest and most architecturally interesting Spanish Colonial churches, or see a 19th century coffee plantation in action. Survey a pair of the largest and most complex castle-like fortifications built by the Spaniards in the New World, or join the modern era when you tour the Arecibo radio telescope or the Bacardi Rum distillery.

El Morro, officially known as Fuerte San Felipe del Morro, sits atop a high promontory overlooking the entrance to San Juan Bay. It is the result of the efforts of many different Spanish engineers over a period of more than 200 years and is one of the largest forts built by the Spaniards in the Caribbean. Visit dungeons and hidden passages, aim your camera on the cannons that still guard the harbor, and gaze over the 60-foot tall walls at the ocean. Stroll on the lawns where soldiers once marched and watch the children fly their kites in the afternoon sea breezes.

PUERTO RICO

Gothic churches are rare in the New World, but Puerto Rico has two: Porta Coeli, built in 1606 in San Germán, and San José, built in the 1530's in Old San Juan. The honor of being the first church on the island—and perhaps the oldest church in the western hemisphere—goes to the San Juan Cathedral down the street from San José, although the original building was blown away in a hurricane and the current cathedral structure dates from the 1800's. Be sure to visit the Dominican Convent next door. Built in 1523 on land donated by Ponce de Leon, it has served as a convent, barracks, and U.S. military headquarters. It is now the home of the Puerto Rico Institute of Culture and hosts many concerts and exhibitions.

The Bacardi Rum Distillery, the largest in the world, is only a 15-minute drive from San Juan and is one of the most popular visitors' destinations in Puerto Rico. Visitors are treated to a fascinating free guided tour of the facilities at the "Cathedral of Rum." Everything from the vast fermentation vats to the high-speed bottling machinery is at work and on display. A trolley takes you to

the Bacardi family museum, where a history of the product and landmarks in its development are seen. The tour ends at the lofty, bat-like pavilion, which you may have seen if you have gazed across San Juan Bay from the southern walls of the Old City. Here you can sample the world-famous rum and buy souvenirs or a variety of Bacardi products at the gift shop.

The little town of Maunabo is located precisely at the point where the east of Puerto Rico meets the south. One of its best-known attractions is the lighthouse at Punta Tuna, still in operation. It was built by the Spanish in the late 19th century, shortly before Puerto Rico was turned over to the United States as spoils of the Spanish-American War. Although its antique fresnel lens has been supplanted by modern technology, the Punta Tuna lighthouse still warns ships of the risks of sailing too close to Maunabo's shores. Visitors will see a spectacular view of a magnificent beach, the unbelievably blue waters of the Caribbean, and on the distant horizon, a hazy view of Vieques. This is the place for classic photographs of a brilliant white lighthouse, shimmering in a picture postcard setting. When you can finally pull yourself away from the view, drive down to

Playa Maunabo, which is almost a mile of lovely beach encircling a tiny port. Small stands sell seafood fritters and ice cold coconut juice in their shells. Here you will find Puerto Rico at its most unspoiled: a genuine seaside village where nothing much happens. Don't be surprised if you are the only visitor in town!

Treat yourself to a walking tour of San Juan. Narrow cobblestone streets, colorful colonial buildings, centuries-old fortresses overlooking the Atlantic Ocean, fascinating museums and art galleries, handcrafts on the corners - and everything bathed by a tropical breeze - these are some of the characteristics of legendary Old San Juan. Wear comfortable shoes, grab your camera, and get ready to marvel at the perfect marriage of the past and present on these very lived-in streets. A walking tour is a wonderful way to get acquainted with the Old City. If you need a break, hop aboard the no-charge trolley cars that make the rounds to and from La Puntilla and Covadonga parking lots at one of the clearly marked stops.

Nightlife: The Caribbean has a well-deserved reputation as a quiet, laid-back place, where hammocks are more common than discos. But Puerto Ricans truly know how to party, and the nightlife in the island's bigger cities and resort hotels rivals that of the world's most cosmopolitan cities!

San Juan is the Caribbean capital of nightlife and entertainment, where you can indulge in bar hopping, fine dining, Vegas-style gaming or anything in between.

Throughout the San Juan area, bars, discos and popular restaurants are found on nearly every corner of the city, but be sure not to miss the vibrant nightlife out on the island, including the special charms of resorts in Dorado, Rio Grande, Ponce and Mayagüez.

You will find fine restaurants and wild clubs in Santurce as well as the Condado-Isla Verde strip, best for less hectic bar- hopping or trying your luck at a hotel casino. In Piñones you'll remember you are in the tropics, for here nightlife meets the beach.

Many island towns have their own special flavor of fun. Boquerón, a students' haven; Luquillo and Piñones, local favorites; and family choices such as La Quancha's boardwalk or a boat ride on the bioluminescent bay at Parguera are always a treat. You can also leave the big island entirely and head to Vieques, , , where you can take in some live jazz before you head for a midnight swim in phosphorescent waters.

Dining: Dining in Puerto Rico can be a full-time adventure. From boutique restaurants serving the latest fusion cuisine to traditional Puerto Rican Mesones, from snack shacks on the beach to classic steak houses, Puerto Rico offers as many choices of dining atmosphere and cuisine as any major city on the mainland.

Be sure to eat at one of the thirty traditional eateries participating in the Mesones Gastronomicos Program sponsored by the Puerto Rico

Tourism Company. These restaurants, located throughout the island, serve up Criolla cooking at its best. Criolla cuisine is a blend of Taíno, Spanish and African influences incorporating all kinds of delicious fruits and vegetables, unforgettably savory rice dishes, meat and poultry, as well as abundant seafood from local waters. One island favorite, tostones, or fried green plantains, are enjoyed alone or as a side dish with nearly every meal. Mofongo is another star preparation of mashed plantains and meat or seafood in a delicious garlic and tomato-based sauce. Getting hungry?

Museums/Galleries: Puerto Rico has scores of museums exhibiting everything from millennia-old Indian artifacts to 20th century modern art. The most prestigious collection of fine art in the Caribbean is yours to visit at the Ponce Museum of Art, where you can see the famous "Flaming June," in addition to a fine collection of more than 850 paintings, 800 sculptures, and 500 prints culled from five centuries of Western art that is featured here. The building alone, which was designed by famed architect Edward Durrel Stone, is worth the one hour-plus trip from San Juan.

The Museo de Arte de Puerto Rico incorporates a modern five story structure designed by architects Otto Reyes and Luis Gutierrez with a neo-classic building – the West Wing – that was part of the San Juan Municipal Hospital, designed and built by architect William

Schimmelphening in 1920. The modern East Wing centers on an atrium three stories high that gives access to the 400 seat theater, a restaurant, the museum shop and gardens.

Birthplace of Antonio Paoli, the Casa Paoli Museum is now a haven of cultural and art objects. They also offer conferences, seminars, and visits to other cultural sites.

The Serralles Castle is a magnificent Spanish Revival mansion, built in 1930 for the Serralles family, owners of the Don Q rum distillery. The antique furnishings recall the era of the sugar barons. A short film tracing the history of the rum and sugar industries enhances your visit.

Nature/Sightseeing: There is no place quite like a tropical volcanic island, and no island in the Caribbean quite like Puerto Rico. The geography of the island is very unusual, as it encompasses distinctly different kinds of topography and micro-climates in a relatively small area.

A rugged mountain range runs across the center from east to west, which often prevents rain clouds from passing to the south. The north side of the island is covered by dense vegetation and rushing streams, while the south side is sun-toasted terrain, home to tropical dry forests and many species of exotic birds. Puerto Rico is only about 100 miles long and 35 miles wide, so its most distant points are only a three-hour drive apart. It also means that just about every tropical landscape in existence is a short trip from wherever you happen to be!

From leisurely drives and walks to serious hiking, rock climbing, spelunking, kayaking, and camping on deserted islands, the nature lover and adventure traveler can find it all in Puerto Rico.

Thanks to the huge diversity of Puerto Rico's natural attractions and the island's size, you can participate in a variety of outdoor adventures during a day trip from San Juan. If you have a bit more time, don't miss the exquisite beauty of the smaller islands. You can hike rugged terrain, rock climb in forested gorges, kayak in white water, and

more. Not an athlete? Don't worry – many sites require no more than an easy walk and some actually require sitting down!

How would you like to have your own little island, just for you, your family, and friends? On Gilligan's Island (or Gilligan Island, as it is also known), you can be king or queen for a day and rule over white sand beaches, mazes of mangroves, and crystalline waters. Think sun, think picnic, but especially think snorkeling. The shallow waters around the island and the fascinating series of mangrove-lined channels that crisscross it are amazingly clear and brimming with marine life.

There are only two other places in the world where you will find a cave system as massive or dramatic as the Río Camuy Cave Park – and neither of them has a tropical underground river thundering through it! Ride a trolley that descends into a sinkhole lined with dense tropical vegetation After a walk across ramps and bridges and through the dramatically illuminated, 170-foot high Cueva Clara, another tram shuttles you to a platform overlooking the 400 foot deep Tres Pueblos Sinkhole. Another attraction is the Spiral Sinkhole and Cave. You can walk the 205 steps down into the sinkhole. Cathedral cave is home to an enigmatic collection of petroglyphs etched into the walls by the ancient Taínos.

Nature lovers will not want to miss the phenomenal experience of visiting a tropical phosphorescent bay! Imagine the blackness of the sea on a moonless night. Now watch it sparkle with the darting lights of a million fireflies. The phosphorescence is actually bioluminescence generated by microscopic organisms in the water. The phenomenon occurs sporadically in warm seas around the world, but Puerto Rico is one of the only places on the planet where you can depend on it every evening at two different protected bays, La Parguera and Vieques. Truly magical!

The Caribbean National Forest, often called El Yunque Rainforest, has the highest visitation of any natural site in Puerto Rico. When you see it, you'll easily understand why: El Yunque is the only rainforest in the U.S. National Forest System! More than 100 billion gallons of precipitation fall each year, creating the jungle-like ambience of lush foliage, sparkling leaves, shining wet rocks, and shadowy paths occasionally pierced by sunlight. Spectacular waterfalls rush alongside its well-maintained (but slippery) trails. There are many favorite spots for visitors to take photos or a refreshing dip in the pristine pools. Seek out the noisy, ubiquitous tree frog, el coquí, or the endangered Puerto Rican parrot. You can park along a roadside tower to see the view, take a guided tour, or simply explore on your own.

WEDDINGS ON LOCATION

Puerto Rico is romance. A moonlight walk along the beach. A swim in a phosphorescent bay. A stroll along a rain forest trail. A slow dance as the sun sets. A drink under a lavish crystal chandelier. A horseback ride through a coffee plantation. A carriage ride through the Pearl of the South.

PUERTO RICO

From opulent hotels to delightful restaurants and sizzling clubs, from wind surfing to lazing in the sun, from gallery hopping to serious shopping, Puerto Rico has the perfect settings for weddings and honeymoons.

For the most variety, stay in cosmopolitan San Juan, where you can explore the Old City in the morning, head for the rain forest in the afternoon, catch some sun and the sunset on the beach, and spend an electrifying night on the town. If you want to share your time with only one other person, for the utmost in privacy and tranquility, spend a few days and nights on Puerto Rico's own Virgin Islands, Vieques and Culebra. Whether you tie the knot in Puerto Rico or spend the first days of your marriage here, you will cherish the experience forever. You and Puerto Rico: the perfect match.

Marriage Requirements: With Puerto Rico's exotic ambiance and spectacular sunsets, there's no better place to be swept up in the romance of a wedding! Here's what couples planning to marry in Puerto Rico need to know before they can tie the knot:

• Each person will need to bring a photo ID or passport; if either party has been divorced or widowed, a divorce decree or death certificate is also required.
• Each party will need to take a blood test from a federally certified laboratory (in the US or Puerto Rico) within 10 days of the wedding date.

• A marriage certificate can be acquired in advance from the Puerto Rico Department of Health; Call 787-767-9120 for more information.

• A doctor will need to sign and certify your marriage certificate and blood test in Puerto Rico.

• The couple will then visit the Demographic Registry to obtain the marriage license, and purchase two license stamps (total stamp cost is US$30.00).

• Couples can expect to receive their marriage license within ten days of their wedding date.

LOCAL INFORMATION

Climate: Puerto Rico is a tropical destination blessed with lots of sun and enough rain to keep the waterfalls flowing and the flowers growing. The climate is as close to perfect as it can get, averaging 83°F (22.7°C) in the winter and 85°F (29.4°C) in the summer. In other words, it's always summer! The trade winds cool the coastal towns and the temperature decreases as you go up into the higher mountains.

Peak Season: December 15 through April 15.

Language: Spanish & English are the official languages. Although Spanish is the norm, English is widely spoken in all major tourist areas throughout the island.

Currency: U.S. Dollars - USD. Major credit cards accepted in most establishments.

Standard Time Zone: GMT (Greenwich Mean Time) – 4 hours.

Entry Requirements: Passports are not required for US citizens, as Puerto Rico is an unincorporated territory of the United States.

Customs Regulations: There are no customs duties on articles bought in Puerto Rico and taken to the US mainland. The US Department of Agriculture inspects bags for fruits and plants forbidden entry to the United States. For more information, contact the US Department of Agriculture at 787-253-4505.

Safety: Puerto Rico's many attractions and resort areas are very secure, thanks to the concentrated efforts of local and state police to ensure traveler safety. In San Juan, travelers should take the same precautions as in any other major city in the world.

For more information, contact:
Puerto Rico Tourism Company
PO Box 9023960
San Juan, PR 00902-3960

Telephone (From US): 787-723-0017
Website: www.gotopuertorico.com

ST. LUCIA - CLIMATE		
MONTH	HI	LO
JAN	81°	78°
FEB	82°	79°
MAR	83°	80°
APR	84°	82°
MAY	85°	82°
JUN	85°	83°
JUL	85°	83°
AUG	86°	83°
SEPT	86°	83°
OCT	86°	82°
NOV	84°	82°
DEC	83°	80°

Temperatures are provided in °Fahrenheit and based on averages.

S T . L U C I A

St. Lucia is rich in natural beauty – and there is so much to see and do. This tropical island beckons the visitor to explore. Historical, cultural and heritage sites can be found throughout the island. Local tour companies combining several of the sites and attractions offer a large variety of tours. Attractions and tours can be sought by location as well as by type. More recently St. Lucia has developed a multiplicity of community based heritage tourism sites; these are well marked with Heritage Tourism Site signage.

THINGS TO SEE AND DO

Recreation: Holidays on St Lucia can be exciting. There are plenty of challenges for sporting visitors, whether it be on land or in the water!

Imagine the crystal clear, warm waters. Picture the fine white sand beaches, lined with gently swaying palms. Where better to go windsurfing, sailing, para-sailing or water-skiing than St Lucia?

Watersports: With the sparkling Caribbean Sea on one side and the mysterious depths of the Atlantic Ocean on the other, sailors and fishermen will fall in love with St Lucia. Not only is it possible to charter any form of sea-going vessel anywhere on the island, but St Lucia also offers opportunities for some of the best deep sea fishing in the world. Described as "an angler's dream come true", it is home to several species of big game fish, and you may even catch a trophy white marlin as your prize!

Watersports are a way of life on this island,

where a coastline of rain-forested mountains is frequently interrupted by natural harbors and bays. The island boasts some of the best underwater dive sites in the Caribbean. Many hotels offer scuba diving facilities and snorkeling equipment, as do a number of independent dive centers. Saint Lucia has also become one of the region's main centers for yacht charters, with operations at the Rodney Bay Marina and at Marigot Harbor. Deep-sea fishing charters are also available for whole and half-day excursions.

Windsurfing: Windsurfers will be challenged by the waves at Cas en Bas and Vieux Fort, the most popular spots for advanced and intermediate windsurfers, while beginners will find the calmer waters of the west coast perfect for sharpening their skills. Top-of-the-line equipment and instruction is available at most hotels and several windsurfing centers around the island.

Snorkeling: There are several companies that offer boat trips to the popular snorkeling areas such as Anse Chastanet. The watersports at most of the major hotels and the scuba diving companies rent snorkeling equipment to guests.

Water-skiing and parasailing: Available at most hotels, water-skiing in Saint Lucia can be enjoyed by beginner, intermediate and advanced skiers. For an aerial thrill, visitors are encouraged to try parasailing, which allows riders to view spectacular sights as they soar above Rodney Bay.

Diving: St Lucia is a diving paradise. The island is at the tip of an underwater volcano where both beginner and experi-

rainforest and the 29 miles of trails that run through it.

The rainforest is respected as a habitat for rare birds and plants, a world where lushness is overpowering, where elusive parrots squawk overhead, orchids scent the air, hummingbird buzz near brilliant heliconia and climbing palms encircle tall trees like lovers in a parting embrace.

It has taken centuries for St Lucia's tropical island rainforest to become its current well-developed refuge. Nonetheless, two thousand years ago, Arawak tribes associated the dark woods with evil spirits and for centuries the forest remained untouched and the spirits the Amerindians feared evolved into island folklore.

The local craft markets sell baskets that have been woven from climbing foot palms and aralie (a hanging root) and beautiful necklaces made from colorful dédéfouden seeds from the mammoth trees which form the forest's canopy.

Nightlife: Most hotels and resorts offer some form of entertainment throughout the week - including local live bands and cultural performances. There are also a number of bar and restaurants all over the island that are fun spots at night. Some popular nightclubs include: Indies, Rodney Bay; Rodney Bay; Shamrock's Pub, Rodney Bay; The Jazz Lounge, Rodney Bay; The Wharf, Choc Bay.

Dining: St. Lucians enjoy food and this is evident by the large number of restaurants, cafes, and fast food outlets on the island. The cuisine is largely a combination of international and Creole utilizing fresh local produce. There are also specialty restaurants such as French, Italian, Indian and steakhouses. And of course, as one would expect, almost every restaurant offers fish and seafood dishes.

Shopping: St. Lucia has a variety of shopping experiences to suit all types of travelers. Whether you are arriving for the day on a cruise ship, spending a romantic holiday at an all-inclusive resort, or challenging your senses on a sporting or diving holiday near the world-famous Piton Mountains, you will find the shops and markets compatible with your needs and tastes.

In and around St. Lucia's city capital of Castries, visitors can find a variety of unique shopping experiences. Pointe Seraphine, a new harbor-front shopping complex, offers duty-free designer perfumes, crystal, china, jewelry, cigars and clothing as well as wood carvings and other local arts and crafts in more than 20 modern shops.

The 100-year old Castries market is a must-see for visitors to the island, where local vendors offer thousands varieties of island memorabilia, spices and foods, and local fishermen offer the daily catch. The Castries Market is particularly vibrant on Saturdays, especially during St. Lucia Jazz and Carnival. Gablewoods shopping center, just north of Castries, offers a full array of shops and services including international books and news, postal services, restaurants and a supermarket. In Castries at Artsibits Gallery you can find St. Lucia's distinctive paintings and carvings.

enced divers alike will enjoy the stunning variety of coral, sponge and marine life. Artificial reefs have developed around a number of sunken ships which have become home to huge gorgonians, black coral trees, gigantic barrel sponges, purple vase sponges and black lace corals. Exciting Caribbean diving trips will reveal turtles, nurse sharks, seahorses, angel fish, and golden spotted eels, to name but a few, among the dazzling cross section of Caribbean marine life.

Special Points of Interest: Deep in St Lucia's mountainous, tropical island's interior, almost 1,800 feet above sea level, lies 19,000 acres of

St. Lucia is very proud of it's heritage in the arts. For a sampling, head to the Eudovic studios in Goodlands 10 minutes south of Castries to see beautiful works of art sculpted from wood. Or combine sightseeing and shopping at the 100 year-old Caribelle hilltop house, where you can watch artisans make batik and screen-prints while you shop in the exotic boutique. On the southern coast of the island you will find the Choiseul Arts & Crafts center, a wonderful source of hand-woven baskets, unique placemats, chairs and woodcarvings.

In the vacation paradise of Soufriere you will find local and resort-run shops with a variety of gifts, clothing and local art. At the north end of the breath-taking waterfront Maurice Mason Street walk, you will find the town market where all sorts of gift items are available.

Gros Islet, on the north end of the island, offers a beautiful setting for shopping whether you are arriving by yacht or staying in one of the district's world-renowned resorts. The Rodney Bay Marina offers a modern shopping arcade with a selection of stores and services including gift items,

clothing, banking and restaurants. For golfing needs, the St. Lucia Golf & Country Club offers a full selection of equipment at the Pro Shop.

Duty-free shopping is available at the following shopping centers in St. Lucia: La Place Carenage, Castries; Pointe Seraphine, Castries; J.Q. Mall, Rodney Bay.

Museums/Galleries: St. Lucia is rich in natural beauty – and there is so much to see and do. This tropical island beckons the visitor to explore. Historical, cultural and heritage sites can be found throughout the island. Local tour companies combining several of the sites and attractions offer a large variety of tours. Attractions and tours can be sought by location as well as by type. More recently St. Lucia has developed a multiplicity of community based heritage tourism sites; these are well marked with Heritage Tourism Site signage.

Culture Heritage Tours: Experience the truly St Lucian way of life with a tour that takes you to a community in Babonneau, known as Fond Assau. There you will experience traditional practices such as preparation of cassava bread, cooking on macambou

leaves, catching crayfish in the river, collecting honey from a beehive and the very authentic display of wood-sawing while a "Chak Chak" band plays traditional music in the background.

Enjoy the Castries Heritage Walk where the historic buildings of Castries come alive as well informed tour guides take you on a walk through the architectural history of an old colonial island city, whilst at the same time enjoying the spirit and life of the modern Caribbean.

Pigeon Island contains more history than any other part of St Lucia. Once the home of the Amerindians, it has been used as both a pirate hideout and military base. Visit Fort Charlotte, now a college but once the site of some of the firecast fighting between the French and the British. Or view the Choiseul Heritage site, a village rich in history, crafts and offering spectacular views.

Plantation Tours: Enjoy the tropical island's natural beauty on a tour that combines historical St Lucia with the tranquility of a nature habitat. The Find d'Or Nature Historic Park includes symbols of the Amerindian settlement and historical buildings of the sugar age. Follow a hiking trail through an estuarine tropical forest to a wide white sand beach that is frequented by nesting Leatherback Turtles, then visit and relax at the Interpretation Centre. From there, drive to the Latille Waterfall where a twenty-foot waterfall surrounded by lush vegetation and additional pools await you. To book, contact Heritage Tours.

Follow the scenic country road to a tropical Caribbean-style working plantation called Fond Doux Estate, where you will heighten your senses by smelling, touching and tasting a variety of tropical fruits and plants. Once you have explored the plantation you can relax in the plantation house while sipping local rum punch, local fruit juices and coconut water before being treated to an authentic Creole Lunch.

The Morne Coubaril Estate with its worker's village, sugar mill, manioc and cocoa houses is a meticulously preserved museum, restaurant and botanical garden. The Marquis Estate is another nearby plantation where you can tour and see the production of St Lucia's main export crops, bananas and copra.

Botanical Gardens: Visitors can choose from three exquisite tropical botanical gardens, each brimming with rare and exotic flora. These tropical gardens present a riot of color, perfume and lush tropical vegetation. Mamiku Gardens is situated on an historic site with a fascinating history. Nature trails meander through the gardens with scenic vistas and peaceful resting points.

The Diamond Botanical Gardens in Soufriere features mineral baths and a picturesque waterfall. On the Vieux Fort Highway, Mamiku Gardens encircle the ruins of an 18th Century Micoud Estate. In the North of the island is the lovely Tropica Gardens.

Nature/Sightseeing: Not interested in lazing on the beach all day long, day after day? St. Lucia is the right choice for your vacation. Organizations like the St. Lucia National Trust and the Department of Forestry offer a number of nature trails, some more strenuous than others. In the mountainous rainforests of St. Lucia there are approximately 30 species of birds. You may be lucky to spot the rare and beautiful parrot, Jacquot.

Biking has also become popular way to enjoy the island, and there are some excellent biking tours for beginners and the more experienced off road riders. There's a lot to see on 2 wheels in St. Lucia. For the adventurer, head into Soufrière for an ocean-side trail ride at Anse Chastanet. With a beautiful view of the world-famous Gros Piton and Petit Piton mountains, this is one ride you can't find anywhere but St. Lucia.

Hiking is another great way to enjoy the beauty of the island. In fact, exploring the beauty of Saint Lucia's majestic rain forest is a great way to relax, appreciate the island and reflect on the memorable time you are having on holiday. A variety of natural trails lead hikers through the rain forest, to the top of Saint Lucia's mountains, through old plantation grounds, along beaches, to Cactus Valley, to Pigeon Island and more. Hikers will have the opportunity to see spectacular rain forest waterfalls, flora and local birds like the Saint Lucia Parrot, the Saint Lucia Oriole and the Saint Lucia Black Finch. Comfortable shoes are a must.

WEDDINGS ON LOCATION

St. Lucia is the perfect destination for Caribbean weddings and honeymoons. The natural beauty of the tropical island seems to have been created for romantics. Palm fringed beaches, elegant old plantation houses, the soft tropical air, hypnotic steel band music, the tantalizing aroma of the cuisine combined all make weddings, honeymoons and anniversaries popular on St. Lucia.

Wonderful climate, astounding beauty and friendly islanders makes St. Lucia simply perfect for your special wedding day. St. Lucia offers you the freedom of doing your wedding the way you want.

Marriage Requirements: It's easy to get married in St Lucia. You just need to stay on the island for 3 days before the wedding. After you've stayed for two days, a local Solicitor can apply for a license on your behalf. You need to have received this two working days before the wedding date. Most tour operators can make all the arrangements. All you need to bring is the following documentation:

- Passport

- Birth Certificate

- Decree Absolute (if one of the parties is divorced) or a Death Certificate (In the case of a widow/widower of first spouse)

- If a name has been changed, a Deed Poll is required

- If one of the parties is under the age of 18, evidence of a consent of parents is required in the form of a sworn affidavit stamped by a Notary Public

- If any required documents are not in English, an authenticated translation must be available.

Notorial Fees & Marriage License are approximately US$150.00. Registrar Fees are approximately US$37.00. Marriage Certificate US$3.00

Typically, all of these details can be taken care of by your hotel. In fact, most hotels offer a variety of Wedding packages. The hotels can also usually arrange any other requirements, such as floral arrangements, photos, video, steelband music, wedding cake etc. Prices vary.

LOCAL INFORMATION

Climate: St. Lucia has tropical year-round temperatures of 70°F to 90°F with refreshing trade winds coming from the northeast. The rainy season is from June to November and the drier period is between December and May.

Peak Season: Mid-November through mid-March

Language: The main language in Saint Lucia is English, although many St. Lucians also speak French and Spanish. Kwéyòl, St Lucia's second language, is widely spoken by the St. Lucian people including doctors, bankers, government ministers and the man on the street! Kwéyòl is not just a patois or broken French, but a language in its own right, with its own rules of grammar and syntax. The language is being preserved by its everyday use in day-to-day affairs and by special radio programs and news read entirely in Kwéyòl.

Currency: Eastern Caribbean Dollar - XCD

Standard Time Zone: GMT (Greenwich Mean Time) – 4 hours

Entry Requirements: US citizens do not require a visa or a passport, however it is recommended. You will need proof of citizenship and supporting photo ID and a valid return ticket dated within six months.

Customs Regulations: You may bring in 200 cigarettes, 250 grams of tobacco, or 50 cigars and one liter of liquor or wine.

Safety: There is crime in St. Lucia, just as there is everywhere. Don't leave valuables in plain sight, and take reasonable precautions while in secluded areas.

For more information, contact:
St. Lucia Tourist Board:
800 Second Ave Ste 400
New York, NY 10017

Telephone (From US): 888-4STLUCIA
Website: www.stlucia.org

© U.S. Virgin Islands Department of Tourism / Steve Simonsen

U.S. VIRGIN ISLANDS

The United States Virgin Islands (St. Thomas, St. Croix, and St. John) are among some of the most popular tourist destinations in the Caribbean.

The USVI's long standing, enviable international reputation is not solely based on pristine beaches, warm weather, and crystal-clear waters, the islands also offer the most culturally diverse, ethnically rich, and artistically vibrant society in the tropics. The islands' biggest asset is the sun-kissed people. Residents are island-spiced, friendly and quick to smile. Contemporary Virgin Islanders are literally from everywhere, and are as diverse as the peaceful Arawak and fierce Carib Indians and as culturally rich as the peoples of Africa, England, Holland, Denmark, Spain, France, India and the United States.

© U.S. Virgin Islands Department of Tourism

Nowhere else in the Caribbean offers such a vacation value as the US Virgins: secluded beaches, national parks, duty-free shopping, camp-grounds, kayaking, hiking, ecological tours, world-class diving, superb sailing. tropical forests, local craftsmen. island art, sunbathing, fine dining, nightlife. And, it's all wrapped up in the safety, security, and efficiency of the American flag. The United States Virgin Islands: St. Thomas, St. Croix, and St. John. Three lively islands - one gentle people.

Shimmering beaches framing unbelievably clear waters. Posh resorts and intimate villas. Wonderful restaurants serving foods from all over the world. Colorful underwater trails and coral reefs. Friendly people with their own unique music and West Indian cuisine. First-class sailing and challenging sport fishing. Where can you find all of this? In the United States Virgin Islands!

It's no wonder that millions of vacationers choose the islands of St. Croix, St. John and St. Thomas as their destination of choice, year after year. As an American territory, the U.S. Virgin Islands offers United States citizens significant advantages over other Caribbean vacation getaways. Even if you are an international traveler, you will find the American system of laws and customs under which the U.S. Virgin Islands operates to be convenient and trouble-free.

Vacationers frequently visit all three islands during their stay. St. John is only 20 minutes away from St. Thomas by ferry, and frequent small-plane service, sea-planes, hydrofoil, charter boats, catamaran service and commercial airlines link St. Thomas and St. Croix. The inter-island flight takes approximately 20 minutes. Helicopter service also connects the islands.

Whether you arrive by sea or air, you may choose from among a wide range of beach-front, hillside or downtown accommodations, take advantage of the best shopping in the Caribbean (many say in the world) and make friends with some of the most gracious and hospitable people you'll ever meet.

Each of the three major islands possesses a unique character all its own. The Danish influence on St. Croix is perfect for visitors who prefer a laid-back experience. The historic towns of Frederiksted and Christiansted offer quaint shops, charming pastel buildings and refreshing cultural diversity. From horseback riding near eighteenth-century sugar mills to playing golf on one of the island's three scenic golf courses, you're sure to find something to suit your tastes.

Two-thirds of St. John is a national park; its comfortable pace is perfect for enjoying the island's world-renowned beaches such as Trunk Bay, Cinnamon Bay, and Salt Pond Bay. A nature lover's favorite, St. John offers hiking, camping, specialty shopping, and breathtaking views. If you take just a few hours to visit this island, you'll find it well worth the trip.

St. Thomas boasts one of the most beautiful harbors in the world. As the most visited port in the Caribbean, downtown Charlotte Amalie offers elegant dining, exciting nightlife, world-class, duty-free shopping, and even submarine rides. While it's full of energy, especially in Charlotte Amalie, this island also possesses numerous natural splendors, such as stunning views of the Caribbean from 1,500 feet above sea level.

THINGS TO SEE AND DO

The US Virgin Islands offer an endless array of sports and activities for visitors. Scuba enthusiasts will find unspoiled coral reefs and historic shipwrecks. Golf lovers can take advantage of world-class courses, including courses designed by Robert Trent Jones and Tom Fazio. Whether you're seeking an adventure filled with snorkeling, hiking and horseback riding, or a relaxing week of tennis, golf, and fishing, you'll find what you're looking for on our islands.

ST. CROIX

The largest of the US Virgin Islands, 28 miles long and seven miles at its widest point, St. Croix lies entirely in the Caribbean Sea with

© U.S. Virgin Islands Department of Tourism / Steve Simonsen

all the beauty and warmth of a tropical destination. However, it is this island's distinct history and cultural heritage that set it apart from other Caribbean islands. St. Croix is rich in diverse history that remains alive in the architecture, national parks, historic landmarks, botanical attractions, and traditions that are an integral part of island life.

Recreation: Land Activities: Golf is extremely popular on St. Croix. The Buccaneer Resort's Bob Joyce-designed par-70 course offers magnificent panoramic vistas of Christiansted harbor to the west, St. Thomas and St. John to the north, and Buck Island National Park to the east. The award-winning Carambola Golf Club course, designed by Robert Trent Jones, is the site of the annual LPGA Golf Tournament and winner of the Golf magazine gold medal. The Reef Golf Course on Teague Bay offers a nine-hole course.

Adventure seekers can explore St. Croix's beautiful west end on horseback or by bike. Guided tours are available for all experience levels. Hikers will find several indigenous and migratory species in the forest and in the Sandy Point Wildlife Refuge.

Watersports: St. Croix offers some of the best snorkeling in the world. Buck Island, famous for its striking natural beauty and underwater snorkeling trails, is one of only two underwater National Monuments in the United States. Cane Bay Reef, Davis Bay and Salt River Bay are popular scuba diving spots known for the 13,000-foot deep sub-sea canyon and steep diving walls. Divers off the coasts of St. Croix may also experience close encounters with rare species of sea turtles that nest seasonally on the island's beaches. Kayakers can see snowy egrets, great barracudas, spotted eagle rays, and hundreds of other species in Salt River Bay National Park and Ecological Preserve.

© U.S. Virgin Islands Department of Tourism / Steve Simonsen

U.S. VIRGIN ISLANDS

Special Points of Interest: Once the capital of the U.S. Virgin Islands, Christiansted is the perfect place to begin your visit to St. Croix. Fort Christiansvaern, built by the Danish as protection from pirates and other plunderers, stands over Christiansted Harbor. Nearby, the Steeple Building houses artifacts from St. Croix's Carib and Arawak Indian settlements and colonial sugar plantations.

St. Croix's Heritage Trail crosses the entire 28-mile length of St. Croix, linking historic attractions, cultural landmarks, scenic overlooks and other points of interest. Discover the unique influences of Danish, French, Spanish, West Indian, African and other cultures on the architecture and history of the island. Using a trail map and following the Heritage Trail road signs, visitors can explore the island on a self-guided driving tour.

Visitors to the Cruzan Rum Distillery, once a working sugar mill, will discover the time-honored process of producing rum and will enjoy free samples of Cruzan's distinctive line of flavored rums. Few travelers return home without a bottle of the island spirit to share with friends and family.

© U.S. Virgin Islands Department of Tourism / Steve Simonsen

Estate Whim Plantation. Venturing into the countryside, visitors to St. Croix discover reminders of bygone days when sugar and rum shaped the island's life and land. With an imposing windmill tower, the fifty-four sugar mills each have their own factory chimney and rest in the shadows of stately eighteenth - and nineteenth - century greathouses.

Buck Island National Reef Monument, an 880-acre nature preserve, boasts an underwater snorkeling trail that has become one of the most popular attractions in the U.S. Virgin Islands. Visitors are ferried by boat to the island one mile northeast of St. Croix to view the stunning array of coral and sea life.

Shopping: Christiansted and Frederiksted's quaint boutiques offer hand-made local crafts as well as designer fashions and exquisite jewelry. King's Alley is the center of Christiansted's shopping district. In Frederiksted, visitors will find shopping between Strand Street and King Street.

Museums/Galleries: St. George Botanical Gardens is a 17-acre park built over a pre-Columbian Indian settlement and the ruins

of a 19th century sugar plantation, displaying a plethora of colorful, tropical flora. A rain forest walk and a cactus garden are among the attractions. On the property are a gift shop and nursery.

Lawaetz Museum offers visitors a look into St. Croix's rich heritage. The grounds, a former sugar and cattle plantation, have been owned and farmed by the Lawaetz family since 1896. Little La Grange is still an operating farm, growing fruits, herbs and vegetables for a local market.

St. Croix Archaeological Museum holds a rare collection of remains dating back more than 2,000 years, including axe heads, pottery, ceramics, and shell and stone tools.

Outdoors: Located off the shores of St. Croix, Buck Island National Monument is one of only two underwater national monuments in the United States – the only one occurring naturally. Water enthusiasts can expect to encounter tropical fish, beautiful coral reefs and exotic flora and fauna in a dramatic array of colors during an unparalleled snorkeling experience through the monument's 700 acres of protected national park.

© U.S.V.I Department of Tourism / Steve Simonsen

© U.S. Virgin Islands Department of Tourism / Alex Cerulli

ST. JOHN

sThe smallest of the US Virgin Islands, St. John offers an exciting mix of attractions to ensure that every visitor experiences paradise when in America's Caribbean. There is plenty of sun, sand, and lots of fun for vacationers to enjoy on this island.

St. John retains a tranquil, unspoiled beauty uncommon in the Caribbean or anywhere else in the world. Settled in the early 1700s by Danish immigrants attracted to the island's potential as a sugar cane-producing colony, St. John soon blossomed into a thriving society.

The extensive sugar cane farming, however, did little to affect the natural beauty of St. John. Its unspoiled forests and stunning beaches attracted the attention of wealthy families, such as the Rockefellers, who sought privacy and tranquility on the island. In 1956, Laurance Rockefeller was so moved by the island that he bought and donated broad expanses of land to the National Park Service to keep St. John "a thing of joy forever."

Recreation: Two-thirds of St. John is part of the Virgin Islands National Park, featuring fascinating trails, secluded coves, and dazzling white beaches. The Reef Bay Trail takes hikers through dense forests, plantation ruins, and rock outcroppings marked by well-pre-

served petroglyphs. Trunk Bay, Hawksnest Bay, Cinnamon Bay, and Maho Bay are just four of the dozens of beaches. Cruz Bay, the center of activity on St. John, contains colorful shops, lively bars, and fabulous restaurants.

Special Points of Interest: The ruins of the Annaberg Sugar Plantation provide a glimpse into the island's agricultural history. The estate, built in the early 1700s, offers tours guided by the National Park Service. The Annaberg Historic Trail takes visitors through restored ruins on the plantation grounds. The views from the plantation are magnificent.

Cinnamon Bay's beautiful beach includes a National Park campground offering equipped cottages and tents, as well as basic campsites. Kayaks, windsurfing equipment, snorkeling equipment, and mountain bikes are also available for rental. Snorkeling is especially popular. A nature trail, sugar plantation ruins, and wild donkeys are some of the other attractions along the beach.

Cruz Bay is the "Downtown" of St. John. Shopping and dining are plentiful, with local artwork, luxury items, and local and international cuisine. The Elaine Ione Sprauve Library and Museum near downtown Cruz Bay contains historic artifacts and works created by local artists. Nearby Hawksnest Bay has a pristine beach, popular with snorkelers for its nearby reef.

Visitors seeking a low-impact, environmentally sensitive vacation will find several options on St. John. The eco-resorts of the island, including Maho Bay Camps and Concordia Eco-Tents, provide tents with porches, basic kitchens, and beautiful views. Harmony on Maho Bay offers cottages built almost exclusively of recycled materials that use solar and wind power.

Trunk Bay is one of the world's most photographed beaches and the most popular on St. John, Trunk Bay also offers an exciting under-

© U.S. Virgin Islands Department of Tourism / Steve Simonsen

water snorkeling trail. Underwater signs identify the various types of coral and aquatic life that inhabit the area. Snorkeling equipment is available for rental.

The Elaine Ione Sprauve Library and Museum contains historic artifacts and works created by local artists.

Two-thirds of St. John's 19 square miles is designated as protected national park land. Laurence Rockefeller deeded approximately 14,689 acres of rolling green hills and underwater preserve to the federal government more than 40 years ago. There are 22 self-guided hiking trails within the Virgin Islands National Park, where visitors can discover ancient petroglyphs and beautiful foliage along the way.

St. John's natural wonders are what set it apart from other Caribbean destinations and destinations all around the world. Its unspoiled forests and stunning beaches have been preserved by law since 1956, when Laurence Rockefeller bought and donated broad expanses of land to the National Park Service to keep St. John "a thing of joy forever."

You can't visit St. John without experiencing Virgin Islands National Park. Over 12,500 acres of protected forest, water and submerged land, the park offers 22 trails totaling over 20 miles. Views from many points along the trails can only be described as breathtaking. The famous Reef Bay Trail takes hikers through dense forests, plantation ruins, and rock outcroppings marked by well-preserved petroglyphs.

ST. THOMAS

For the more than one million cruise ship passengers and overnight guests who visit St. Thomas in the US Virgin Islands each year, the island's prominence as one of the Caribbean's most renowned shopping meccas is one of its most alluring attractions. With duty-free shopping exemptions unrivaled by any other Caribbean destination, and fine dining and accommodations at an exceptional value, St. Thomas is indeed a treasured discovery for travelers.

© U.S.V.I. Department of Tourism / Steve Simonsen

Recreation: Both National Geographic and Conde Nast Traveler have named heart-shaped Magens Bay one of the most beautiful beaches in the world. You can judge for

yourself. Snorkeling, kayaking, and other water gear is available for rental.

A George and Tom Fazio design, the Mahogany Run Golf Course course boasts 18 of the most beautiful and challenging holes in the Caribbean. Golfers extol the virtues of the 6,022-yard, par-70 championship course for its sheer beauty and exhilarating play, especially on the 13th, 14th and 15th holes. This signature trio, aptly nicknamed the Devil's Triangle, turns an already ambitious round of play into a veritable cliffside drama, where golfers must overcome a formidable stretch of Caribbean Sea that sprawls between the tee and the green.

Special Points of Interest: Located on St. Thomas' northeast shore at Coki Point, Coral World Marine Park & Observatory contains an underwater observatory tower, a tropical nature trail, a marine gardens aquarium, and an 80,000-gallon coral reef tank. The circular, glass-enclosed tank lets visitors glimpse the beauty of the Caribbean without

© U.S. Virgin Islands Department of Tourism

© U.S. Virgin Islands Department of Tourism / Steve Simonsen

for several regattas, yacht chartering services, and fishing guides.

Treat yourself to a taste of more recent island history by stopping at MountainTop for a famous banana daiquiri. This site has offered their legendary concoction of local rum, cane sugar, and bananas since the 1960s. Estate St. Peter Greathouse and Botanical Gardens contains local art and over 200 kinds of West Indian trees and plants.

The Paradise Point Tramway takes visitors up an almost 700-foot peak over Charlotte Amalie, offering a stunning view of the town, the island, and the Caribbean. Running between Havensight and Paradise Point, the tramway can hold up to ten people in one car.

The former Danish sugar plantation of Annaberg Ruins maintains a wealth of history and cultural folklore. Visitors can revisit the remnants of plantation life on St. John and the occupation of slaves during the 18th century. Demonstrations of cultural traditions, including basket weaving, music and dance, are conducted by park rangers each week.

Museums/Galleries: St. Thomas' history and culture alone is worth a visit to the island. Fort Christian, a U.S. National Landmark, is the oldest standing structure in the Virgin Islands. Today Fort Christian in Charlotte Amalie is home to the Virgin Islands Museum, where early island memorabilia and old maps trace the islands' history.

Market Square, a bustling produce marketplace, was once one of the West Indies' busiest eighteenth-century slave markets. Nearby Emancipation Garden was named in commemoration of Governor Peter von Scholten's emancipation of the slaves on July 3, 1848. Also of interest is the Synagogue of Beracha Veshalom Vegmiluth Hasidim, the oldest synagogue in continuous use in the United States.

On nearby Government Hill looming over Charlotte Amalie stands Blackbeard's Castle. Known during colonial times as Skytsborg, this seventeenth-century fortified tower is the only one of its kind in the Caribbean. Today this attraction also serves as a popular restaurant and hotel. Also on Government Hill is the Crown House, the stately former home of a St. Thomas harbormaster and governor general of the Danish West Indies.

Seven Arches Museum on Government Hill is fully restored eighteenth-century home furnished in Danish West Indian style. Its Danish kitchen and slave quarters reflect the lives led by its former inhabitants. Located in the hills not far from the heart of Charlotte Amalie, Government House has been the center of government in St. Thomas since the mid-1860s. Visitors interested in seeing St. Thomas' political life may tour the building's first two floors. The 99 Steps, made by bricks that were once used as ballast on Danish and British ships, were built into the hillside to keep the orderly grid of the city intact.

Nature/Sightseeing: Visitors to St. Thomas should take advantage of Virgin Islands Ecotours' guided kayaking and snorkeling tour

getting wet. Other exhibits include an open-air shark pool and a children's touch pool.

Resting over Charlotte Amalie harbor since 1672, Fort Christian is the oldest standing structure in the Virgin Islands. Now a U.S. National Landmark, this brick fortress protected the town from pirates and European armadas. The fort has served as St. Thomas' first Government House, a church, and a community government center. Today it is home to the Virgin Islands Museum.

Numerous attractions can be found in and around Charlotte Amalie, the capital of the U.S. Virgin Islands. Blackbeard's Castle, Crown House, Seven Arches Museum, and Government Hill offer many days worth of exploring for visitors catching a rest from the town's world-class duty-free shopping and dining. Charlotte Amalie is also the base

through St. Thomas' Marine Sanctuary and Mangrove Lagoon. Led by experienced local naturalists, these tours let visitors see the fragility and beauty of the mangrove lagoons firsthand. Snowy egrets, great barracudas, dwarf herrings, spotted eagle rays, jellyfish, mangrove crabs, and breeding nurse sharks are only a few of the species visitors might see on the tour. Snorkeling is done in designated areas without fins to protect the delicate marine environment. Virgin Islands Ecotours also offers a new tour on Magens Bay. On the north end of the island, Humpback whales can be seen breeding from January through April. Both Jacques Cousteau and "Wild Kingdom" filmed specials on whales in the waters off of St. Thomas.

St. Thomas is a mountainous island, so visitors will find that climbs to the peaks offer dramatic views. Drake's Seat, one of the island's most famous views, overlooks Drake's Passage, the channel where Sir Francis Drake sailed among the islands in the late 1500s. Visitors will also note the abundance of the yellow cedar, one of the world's most beautiful flowers found in the U.S. Virgin Islands.

Nightlife: There are several clubs throughout the US Virgin Islands, most of which feature live music, for those interested in the local nightlife. For a taste of the Caribbean's musical style, seek out one of the many local Calypso bands. There is also a casino on St. Croix for visitors interested in testing their luck.

For a taste of the local beat, check out Mocko jumbies (dancers in colorful costumes wearing stilts), reggae and calypso, steel pan bands, and pulsating salsa which are all among the fascinating sights and sounds that add to the island's cultural mix. The Caribbean Dance Company (CDC), a year-round performing ensemble that preserves and teaches the dance heritage of the Caribbean and West Indian culture, established itself on St. Croix in 1977. The CDC and their traditional folk dances, many with African roots, are a common sight and sound around St. Croix.

© U.S. Virgin Islands Department of Tourism

St. Croix's unique culture is still celebrated in customs such as the European-inspired "quadrille" dance and "quelbe," or "scratch," music. The early settlers' tradition of dancing from estate to estate has evolved into an organized town parade, performed to sounds of drums, flutes, trumpets, and gourds that are "scratched" for percussion.

The Crucian Christmas Festival, one of St. Croix's most popular events, includes a month-long celebration that culminates in the Three Kings Day parade.

Island traditions come alive during celebrations throughout the year. The Three Kings' Day festival on St. Croix, St. John's Fourth of July celebration, and St. Thomas' annual Carnival are just three examples of the dozens of special events that take place each year. However, on any given day, visitors can catch a glimpse of the unique culture of the islands.

Dining: Often the most difficult issue facing visitors in the US Virgin Islands is how to choose from among the island's eclectic array of quality restaurants. "Fusion" cuisine, which combines the latest cooking trends from around the world, has found its place on menus at many exciting eateries. French, Mexican, Chinese, Pacific Rim, and Italian add to the mix of ethnic fare available, and American favorites

© U.S. Virgin Islands Department of Tourism

© U.S. Virgin Islands Department of Tourism / Carol Lee

cocted from ginger root, yeast, herbs, and the bark of the maubi tree. Non-alcoholic ginger beer, bush tea, soursop juice, and the creamy sea-moss cooler are also popular. Although restaurants in the U.S. Virgin Islands feature international cuisine such as French, Japanese, Italian, and Chinese, we encourage you to try island specialties such as conch fritters, fried plantains, sweet potato pudding, and curried chicken. Other Virgin Island specialties include: Kallaloo, a simmering stew of okra, meat, seafood, local greens, and spices; Souse, a lime-flavored stock of pig's head, tail, and feet; Fungi, a cornmeal and okra side dish that accompanies fried or boiled fish; and Johnnycakes, a deep-fried delicacy of unleavened bread. Lobster, wahoo, grouper, mahi-mahi, tuna, and other daily catches are staple menu items as well. If you have room for dessert, you might try a coconut or guava tart, locally made soursop ice cream, or rich rum cake and bread pudding.

Shopping: The U.S. Virgin Islands are a duty-free port, with no sales or luxury taxes on items such as watches, cameras, fine jewelry, china, and leather goods. Christiansted's King's Alley on St. Croix offers handmade goods and designer fashions. Mongoose Junction on St. John is a shopper's paradise, featuring jewelry, clothing, crafts, and artwork. Charlotte Amalie on St. Thomas has been hailed as the best shopping port in the world. In short, you're sure to find unique, inexpensive shopping no matter what island you're on.

Shops in the downtown areas are usually closed on Sundays, unless a cruise ship is in port. Shops at the larger hotels are usually open on Sundays. Look for bargains on perfume, liquor, cameras, china, porcelain, crystal, imported clothing, leather goods, watches, jewelry, and gold, as well as crafts made by local artisans. Many of these items can be bought for 40 percent less than in the United States; liquor and cigarettes are often 60 percent less.

U.S. citizens are allowed a duty-free shopping quota of $1,200--twice that of any other island in the Caribbean and three times that of European countries. A flat rate of five percent duty is charged on purchases over your $1,200 allowance, up to a maximum of $1,000

can be found on many menus as well. Caribbean lobster, wahoo, grouper, mahi-mahi, tuna and other daily catches from the sea are staple menu items. Local specialties include "Fungi", a cornmeal based side dish; "kallaloo", a soup made from okra, spinach and fish; sweetpotato pudding; fried "johnnycake" bread; plantains; peas and rice; curried chicken; "old wife" fish; and conch fritters, a batter-fried delicacy, which headlines many island menus.

The US Virgin Islands culture expresses itself in its unique cuisine, which has its origins in Africa, Puerto Rico, other West Indian islands, and Europe. Since many island recipes originate from times when imports were scarce, today's typical island fare includes locally grown and raised spices, tropical fruits, root vegetables, and meats.

One favorite local beverage is maubi, a slightly fermented drink con-

© U.S. Virgin Islands Department of Tourism / Alex Cerulli

more. Besides your personal exemption, you can mail friends and relatives at home an unlimited number of gifts (other than perfume, liquor, or tobacco) worth $100 or less per gift.

WEDDINGS ON LOCATION

If you want your wedding to be a beautiful and unforgettable experience, why not get married in the U.S. Virgin Islands? Nothing could be more romantic than beginning your life together in one of the most gorgeous places on earth. The U.S. Virgin Islands is the premier upscale wedding destination in the Caribbean, and for good reason.

On a mountaintop or underwater, on a beautiful beach or in a botanical garden, in a formal church wedding or an African "Jump the Broom" ceremony, our islands have every setting you can imagine. No matter which site you choose, the U.S. Virgin Islands have several experienced wedding consultants and planners who can help you arrange the perfect ceremony and reception.

You don't have to go far to find your perfect honeymoon spot when you get married in the U.S. Virgin Islands. Luxury resorts, intimate guesthouses and condos, island villas with private pools, and private yachts are all available. Whichever you choose, you are sure to have the time of your life.

Marriage Requirements: Because the US Virgin Islands operates under the laws of the United States government, legal marriage requirements are simple and hassle-free. Couples need only request an application for a marriage license from the US Virgin Islands Territorial Courts or go online to www.usvitourism.vi. There is a required eight-day waiting period after the notarized and completed application is received in the islands. (Additional documentation is required if either party has married previously.) Couples should specify whether a territorial court judge or a clergy member will perform the marriage ceremony, as an appointment is necessary to be married in the court. The marriage application fee is only $25, and the marriage license is $25. Weddings performed in the court by a judge

© U.S. Virgin Islands Department of Tourism

will incur another $200 fee for the ceremony.

LOCAL INFORMATION

Climate: The US Virgin Islands have year-round warm temperatures. The average temperature ranges from 77 degrees in the winter to 82 degrees in the summer.

Peak Season: Winter

Language: English, though approximately 45% of the population of St. Croix speaks Spanish.

Currency: U.S. Dollars - USD

Standard Time Zone: GMT (Greenwich Mean Time) – 4 hours

Entry Requirements: The US Virgin Islands is a United States territory, so US citizens do not need to carry a passport to enter, but you should be prepared to show evidence

of citizenship upon leaving (such as a certified copy of a birth certificate and photo id, or a passport).

Customs Regulations: With no customs duties or sales tax on tourism related items, the US Virgin Islands is a shopping lover's paradise. US citizens are allowed a duty-free shopping quota of $1,200 – twice that of any other island in the Caribbean and three times that of European countries.

For more information, contact:
United States Virgin Islands Department of Tourism
PO Box 6400
St. Thomas, USVI 00804

Website: www.usvitourism.vi
Telephone (From US): 800-372-USVI or 213-739-0138

welcome to the
CONTINENTAL
U.S. & CANADA

© Robert Holmes / CalTour

CONTINENTAL U.S.

LOS ANGELES - CLIMATE

MONTH	HI	LO
JAN	70°	47°
FEB	70°	49°
MAR	71°	51°
APR	73°	53°
MAY	76°	58°
JUN	80°	60°
JUL	85°	64°
AUG	83°	66°
SEPT	82°	65°
OCT	79°	61°
NOV	73°	52°
DEC	69°	48°

Temperatures are provided in °Fahrenheit and based on averages.

From "sea to shining sea," the United States is the ultimate travel destination. Almost certainly the most dynamic country on earth, its wide range of terrain, diverse cultures, vast cities and small friendly towns offer something for everyone.

Among romantic areas in the US, The state of California and Florida are popular honeymoon destinations. For destination weddings, no place can beat the infamous city of Las Vegas, Nevada.

THINGS TO SEE AND DO

CALIFORNIA

10 Reasons To Visit and Fall in Love with California.

• Three drive-through redwood trees along Highway 101 between Laytonville and Klamath.

• A herd of 400 buffalo on Catalina Island.

• 700 wineries (and counting), according to Wine Spectator's 2000 California wine guide.

• 90 types of mammals in Sequoia and Kings Canyon National Parks, including 10 kinds of bats.

• 160 rooms and more than 10,000 windows in San Jose's Winchester Mystery House.

© Robert Holmes / CalTour

• 45 snow resorts offering downhill and cross country skiing, snowboarding and more.

• World's tallest living tree (367.5 feet).

• 2, 425 feet of falling water at Yosemite Falls, the longest drop in the United States.

• Huntington Beach, 8.5 miles of uninterrupted strands of pristine beach.

• 20 million acres of National Forest and 50 significant wilderness areas for backpacking.

San Francisco: Whether you want to climb the hills of the San Francisco Bay Area or explore the more urban delights of the "Cities by the Bay", you will never run out of things to see and do. Within every neighborhood, from San Jose in the "South Bay", Oakland in the "East Bay", San Francisco or Mill Valley, a diversity of tastes and interests are thriving! You will see it in the cuisine, the boutiques, the theater and the arts, word-class museums and boundless recreational opportunities.

San Francisco is California's Casablanca, a bubbling bouillabaisse of exotic ingredients, from the rainbow nation of the Castro district to the vibrant counterculture in Haight-Ashbury to the young and glamorous tech survivors in their South of Market lofts. Beyond their distinctive neighborhoods, all of these people peacefully coexist in the city's many public places. Just steps away from the dot-commers, for example, is the stylish Museum of Modern Art and an urban oasis called

Yerba Buena Gardens. Other city residents seek out the meditative azalea garden in Golden Gate Park, jog along the Marina, or prowl the fresh produce stands in Chinatown.

To the south of the city are Santa Clara and San Jose, the anchors to the "Silicon Valley." Lest you think that the valley is all business, though, spend a day at Paramount's Great America, delve into the wonders of technology at the Tech Museum of Innovation, or explore the Winchester Mystery House. Along the coast is the college community of Santa Cruz, best known for its beach boardwalk, where riders scream as they ride a historic wooden roller coaster.

The East Bay also has its share of thrills. Livermore Valley is home to one of California's oldest wine regions. Established in 1849, it's one of the wine world's best-kept secrets. In Oakland, jazz frequently rocks historic Jack London Square. North of the square is the college town of Berkeley, where upscale shops and restaurants along Fourth Street somehow blend perfectly with the street vendors on Telegraph Avenue who hawk handmade jewelry, pottery, and tie-dyed sarongs. Still farther north of this street theater, in Vallejo, is the unique Six Flags Marine World.

On the other side of the Golden Gate Bridge from San Francisco, life is genteel. If you prefer not to drive, a short ferryboat ride past Alcatraz Island lands you in quiet Tiburon, a bayside bookend to bucolic Mill Valley with its boutiques, candlelit restaurants, and subdued bars. Meanwhile, on Bridgeway, Sausalito's main drag, families and couples drop in and out of art galleries or dine at any number of restaurants that look out on San Francisco Bay. A short drive north and east gets you into the Napa wine country, home to dozens of well-known vintners in Rutherford, Yountville, and St. Helena, which lie right on Highway 29. Sip and swirl to your heart's content here or at any of the wineries along a parallel route called the Silverado Trail,

© Robert Holmes / CalTour

home to Stags' Leap and Clos du Val, to name but a few.

Los Angeles: More than movies, Los Angeles offers a cultural diversity that is reflected in its museums, architecture, art and restaurants. Even the geography is diverse: Where else can you go snowboarding in the morning and catch a wave in the afternoon, or hike deep into the wilderness just off a busy freeway?

Los Angeles county stretches over 4,000 square miles, encompassing high deserts, sparkling beaches, snowy peaks, and meandering megalopolis that, since its inception, has inspired legions of dreamers - from de Mille to Steven Spielberg.

The greater Los Angeles area, which stretches from the Antelope Valley California Poppy Reserve in the north to Santa Catalina Island in the south, is the repository of every grandiose vision, no matter how extraordinary, that comes under the heading "California dream." This is where people come to liberate, stimulate, and even re-create their lives. Brunch at a beachside cafe in Venice and you can watch some of these individualistic spirits parade by on roller skates. It's also where they go for a night on the town, in places such as 2nd Street in Long Beach.

Other parts of the sprawling metropolis are equally soul-inspiring. Downtown you will find not one but two branches of the Museum of Contemporary Art. In between them is the ornate Bradbury Building, whose interior skylit lobby and creaking elevator set the mood for that quintessentially futuristic vision of Los Angeles in the movie Bladerunner. Moving west, one comes upon the stellar Hollywood Bowl, where on any given evening you might hear the booming cannons of Tchaikovsky's 1812 Overture or James Taylor crooning "Fire and Rain." And then there's the incomparable Getty Center, which sits perched over Brentwood like the modern-day temple to the arts that it truly is.

© Robert Holmes / CalTour

The county shows off its diversity gastro-nomically as well as culturally. There's a rich, vibrant Asian community in the San Gabriel Valley, where you can dine on the finest steamed pork cakes and salted duck eggs this side of Hong Kong. Portuguese heritage is celebrated in the little mom-and-pop cafes of San Pedro-longshoremen work-ing at adjacent Los Angeles Harbor fre-quently start their days off with linguica and scrambled eggs. And throughout the city, from Santa Monica to San Fernando, Pacoima to Pasadena, Mexican and Central American taquerias and antojito restaurants prove that tacos and tamales, the most con-ventional examples of Southern California cuisine, can be unconventional treats.

Los Angeles, you see, is a feast for the senses, so the only way to properly appreciate it is to sample a little bit of everything. Explore the city's roots along colorful Olvera Street, or go back even further in time with a stop at the La Brea Tar Pits, where sticky, bubbling tar trapped mastodons and other prehistoric creatures long before humans appeared on the scene. In Hollywood, celluloid history reigns along the legendary Walk of Fame, with its 1,800-plus speckled sidewalk stars, and at Mann's Chinese Theater, home of

© Robert Holmes / CalTour

countless famous hand- and footprints. And then a few blocks south are the palm-lined boulevards of Beverly Hills. The fashions along Rodeo Drive are as eye-popping as the price tags, but, hey, this is L.A., baby.

San Diego: California's heart and soul reside in San Diego. You can see it in the romantic architecture abounding in Balboa Park; in the whimsical red-roofed turrets of the Hotel del Coronado, known by locals simply as "the Del"; and in the vibrant mix of restored brownstones and handsome Victorian buildings housing pastel-tinted art galleries and jazzy restaurants in the Gaslamp Quarter. Sit under the stars taking in Shakespeare at the Old Globe, enjoy the mariachi band serenading diners at a Mexican restaurant in Old Town, and get eyeball-to-eyeball with gorillas at the World Famous San Diego Zoo. You could spend days, even weeks happily exploring the many faces of San Diego, but then you'd miss a number of surprises waiting farther afield- the north county's classic beach towns, a city made entirely out of LEGOs in Carlsbad, and the old-California beauty of Cuyamaca Rancho State Park and nearby Mt. Laguna.

Perhaps the best way to think of the San Diego County region is to picture it as a small state or an island, bounded by some of the best surfing beaches in California to the west, snowy mountainous peaks to the east, and an exotic neighbor-Mexico-to the south. Within these borders is the Wild Animal Park in Escondido, several California mis-sions dating from the 1800s, a small alpine town packed with hole-in-the-wall cafes (each selling homemade apple pie that claims to be "the best"), dense stands of ancient oaks and pine trees, splashing orcas at SeaWorld off Mission Bay, and coastal wetlands that every spring and fall attract hundreds of species of migratory birds-Canada geese, snowy egrets, and green-winged teals among them.

The people here are as diverse as the land-scape they live in. Pacific Beach attracts a laid-back surfing culture, while La Jolla attracts a more upscale crowd to its chic art galleries and fashionable shops. North of this village is a string of seaside towns that are known for their luxury resorts, challenging golf courses, and spectacular beaches. In Del Mar, the ponies have been running since Bing Crosby founded the Thoroughbred

© Robert Holmes / CalTour

Club in the 1930s, while flower fields are the attraction near Encinitas and Leucadia-go for blooming ranunculus in spring and poinsettias in December. On the island of San Diego County, there's something for everyone.

FLORIDA

No matter what your interests, you will find an attraction in Florida to enjoy. Mouse ears and the major theme parks of the Orlando area are what first come to mind as Florida attractions, but they are only the beginning. Wildlife and botanical attractions are among the most popular and include both large parks and zoos and small private gardens. Florida's rich history is reflected in museums, monuments, forts and homes throughout the state. For a cultural excursion, fine art museums have works from Dali to Rubens, sculpture and architecture by names such as Frank Lloyd Wright.

If you're looking to get away with your special someone, the Sunshine State surely has the place. Secluded hideaways and lively, bustling cities are perfect for a honeymoon, anniversary or special weekend escape. We have beautiful white-sand beaches, historic mansions, old-fashioned paddleboats and many other beautiful places to set the stage for romance.

Miami: In Miami and you're likely to hear the language and music of many cultures; dine in her restaurants and take a mini tour of the world. Although this sophisticated destination boasts miles of wide, white sand beaches, Miami offers much more. Visitors can have a cup of café con leche in Little Havana, Miami's Cuban community; stroll past art deco architecture in the city's artsy South Beach district (dubbed SoBe); explore trendy Coconut Grove; visit attractions such

© VISIT FLORIDA

as the Miami Seaquarium and the Miami Metrozoo, or take a cruise from the "Cruise Capital of the World." Nightlife is both sophisticated and varied here.

St. Augustine: Visitors escape to the past in St. Augustine, the nation's oldest continuously occupied European city. Visit the 17th-century fort Castillo de San Marcos, the reconstructed 18th-century Spanish Quarter, historic churches, and see colorful re-enactments of Colonial days complete with authentically costumed actors. Golfers won't want to miss the new World Golf Village with its World Golf Hall of Fame. Accommodations include charming B&Bs in the historic district and oceanfront hotels along the city's 24 miles of lovely beaches. Upscale Ponte Vedra Beach just north of St. Augustine is often described as Florida's "ritziest" destination because of its deluxe golf and tennis resorts. The Ponte Vedra Inn & Club offers first-class greens. Nearby, Marriott at Sawgrass is the official hotel of the Tournament Players Club (TPC), home of The Players Championship, and is the Association of Tennis Professionals (ATP) Tour International Headquarters.

Tampa: For a taste of life in the big city, visitors cross the bay to Tampa, where they encounter a glittering metropolis that's home to the region's top attractions -- Busch Gardens Tampa Bay, The Florida Aquarium and the Museum of Science and Industry (MOSI). Visitors will also discover a revitalized downtown waterfront, notable museums and an extraordinary performing arts and sports calendar. Ybor City, Tampa's historic Latin Quarter, is rich in Spanish and Cuban tradition and was once known as "the cigar capital of the world" and offers the area's liveliest nightlife. Much of the northern part of this area is rural, having been set aside as national, state and county parks and preserves.

The Florida Keys and Key West: The Florida Keys, tiny islands strung together first by nature, next by Henry Flagler's railroad and more recently by The Overseas Highway, seem to be in a time zone and attitude all their own. Visitors will find their worries disappear as they cruise U.S.1 - with its huge expanses of blue-green water, cer-

© VISIT FLORIDA

tainly one of the most scenic drives in the nation. Along the way, fishing villages, plush resorts, family-owned hotels and plenty of seafood restaurants dot the landscape. Throughout the islands, water activities top the list of things to do, though Key Largo, Big Pine Key and Looe Key (off the Lower Keys) are best known for diving and snorkeling; Islamorada and Marathon are most famous for fishing. The Lower Keys are the least developed in the island chain. Most visitors top off their Keys vacation with a trip to Key West, the eclectic end of the continent. This southernmost point of the United States embraces a fascinating mix of history, eccentricity and lush, island charm. Civil War-era forts, famous writers' homes, sidewalk cafés and outrageous folks add to the unique atmosphere of Key West.

Orlando: Besides the major attractions, there is so much more in the Orlando/Kissimmee area to spark the imagination. Orlando, the theme park capital of the world, is best known for its major attractions - Walt Disney World's Magic Kingdom, Epcot, Disney-MGM Studios and Animal Kingdom; Universal's Universal Studios and Islands of Adventure; and Sea

World's aquatic entertainment. Besides the parks, non-stop nightlife, plentiful shopping, dining and accommodations are throughout the Orlando and surrounding Lake Buena Vista, Kissimmee, Winter Park and Altamonte Springs. Just a short distance from the hustle and bustle of Orlando's attractions, several destinations offer back-to-nature experiences and small town charm. Travel to tiny, charming towns like Mount Dora and Bartow for antiques and other treasures. Mount Dora has often been called the "antiques capital of Florida," but it is also noted for its festivals.

LAS VEGAS

Entertainment Capital of the World... Images of the Rat Pack swilling martinis, showgirls in elaborate headdresses and Elvis impersonators are indelible in the minds of Las Vegas visitors. Today, Las Vegas' entertainment scene still has plenty of the old glamour, but it has evolved to include so much more. In addition to the classic staples, the destination offers a lineup of award-winning magicians, Broadway-caliber productions, world-renowned concert headliners and unique-to-Vegas production shows.

© The Las Vegas News Bureau

Luck Be a Lady... Nevada law permits a wide variety of gaming, including traditional card and dice games, race and sports books, slot machines, cashless slot machines, high-tech electronic gambling devices and international games of chance originating in Europe and Asia.

Las Vegas resorts offer an electronic version of virtually every type of casino game. Slot machines linked to statewide networks pay progressive jackpots in the millions. The jackpot grows each time coins drop into any of the more than 700-networked machines located in scores of casinos throughout Nevada. The statewide slot machine network, known as Megabucks, paid a record jackpot of more than $39.7 million in March 2003 to a 20-something bachelor from Southern California.

Attractions/Special Points of Interest: More than a thousand fountains dance to music ranging from Pavarotti to Sinatra at the Fountains of Bellagio.

Downtown Las Vegas comes to life nightly with a show featuring 2.1 million lights and 550,000 watts of concert sound at the Freemont Street Experience.

Neonopolis: Facility featuring an antique neon sign collection. 14 movie screens with auditorium style seating, digital sound, and

© VISIT FLORIDA

wall-to-wall screens. Shops, restaurants, and an art gallery are all found here.

Interact with live actors in a recreation of the USS Enterprise and battle aliens in a motion-simulator ride through space in Star Trek: The Experience.

The Volcano at the Mirage erupts every few minutes after dusk, spewing smoke and fire 100 feet above the water.

Bellagio Gallery of Fine Art: Home to touring exhibitions of art from around the world.

Over $5 million of the King's personal items are on display at the Elvis-a-Rama Museum. Automobiles, Las Vegas jumpsuits, and much more.

Hug, touch, and take pictures with more than 100 of your favorite stars at Madame Tussaud's Celebrity Encounter Wax Museum. Meet and mingle with Whoopi Goldberg, Nicolas Cage, John Wayne, Princess Diana, The Rock, Lucille Ball, and more, all masterfully portrayed in wax.

Shopping at the Forum Shops at Caesar's Palace: 110 shops and restaurants include Versace, Gucci, Escada, Volintino, Armani, FAO Schwartz, The Palm, Wolfgang Puck's Spago, Cheesecake Factory.

Nightlife: It's all about nightlife in Las Vegas. The following are just a small sampling of some of the clubs you'll find: Rain in the Desert offers the ultimate nightclub experience, with multiple VIP areas available in the form of sky boxes (with thumbprint-screening access for members), cabana areas, and water booths (where the patent-leather banquettes are actually filled with water.) Lavish special effects throughout the club include intelligent lighting and electrifying play of water, fire and fog.

Get in line early; the Rumjungle gets packed quickly. It is one of the

© The Las Vegas News Bureau

most popular clubs among visitors. It is a deliciously interactive new entertainment/dining experience. A dancing wall of fire is followed by volcanic mountains of rum rising in the illuminated bar.

Studio 54 features state-of-the-art sound, video, and lighting, live dancers and chart-topping music. Voted "Best Dance Club" by the Las Vegas Review-Journal, the 22,000-square-foot nightclub offers four dance floors and bars, an exclusive area on the second-floor for invited guests, and several semi-private lounges capable of holding up to 400 people.

Guests can party with a view at the VooDoo Lounge. Take the elevator upstairs to the 51st floor of the Rio and enjoy one of the VooDoo Lounge's award-winning cocktails. Surround yourself in ambiance and take in the extraordinary views of the Las Vegas Strip from our comfortable inside seating or outside on the terrace.

Accessible only by a dark, twisting staircase, Baby's décor is a mixture of 1960s modernism and 1970s chic. While standard club elements are plentiful, including waitress in zipper-top biker leather and translucent walls with images constantly projected on them, there's more than a few goodies (look for the underground lake) to make the experience memorable and worth repeating.

Scenic Getaways: Many travelers are drawn to the lights and excitement of Las Vegas, but too few are aware of the wonders of Mother Nature that surround them. Rugged mountains, red rock canyons and deep desert valleys offer stunning scenery and myriad outdoor recreational opportunities. The region's favorable climate makes outdoor activity around Las Vegas an attractive option year-round. The Grand Canyon, a true natural wonder, lies about 300 miles from Las Vegas, a 1 _ hour flight. Tours are available.

Spas: a Welcome Relief for Mind, Body and Soul Las Vegas and its surrounding areas feature more than 30 spa facilities, including the

© The Las Vegas News Bureau

newest treatments for mind, body and soul. Ranging from public facilities to those available to resort guests only, spas in Las Vegas are as varied as the resort hotels and casinos that house them.

Las Vegas is one of many destinations around the world embracing the growing spa phenomenon. According to the International Spa Association in 2001, there were more than 155 million visits to the nearly 10,000 spas throughout the U.S. The association says consumers no longer label spas as frivolous. Instead, many now consider spas a necessity to staying healthy.

Spa services offered in Las Vegas include sport, Shiatsu and Swedish massages to soothe tired muscles and smooth away kinks; body treatments including herbal baths, wraps, aromatherapy and reflexology; relaxing amenities such as steam rooms, saunas and whirlpools; and full-service salons offering manicures, pedicures, facials and hair styling.

Some resorts offer wellness centers, where professionally trained personnel offer advice on nutrition and healthy lifestyles, as well as innovative fitness facilities and equipment such as virtual reality bicycles and Cybex equipment.

Getting Married ...of course: On average, 150 couples tie-the-knot each day in Las Vegas.

From formal black tie affairs to renewing vows in front of a rhinestone-studded Elvis impersonator to cruising through a 24-hour drive-through chapel, with more than 100,000 couples obtaining licenses each year, Las Vegas is the marriage capital of the world.

WEDDINGS ON LOCATION

Marriage Requirements:
California: Both parties must apply together, in person for the mar-

© VISIT FLORIDA

© VISIT FLORIDA

riage license, which is good for 90 days. You must each present a driver's license and some counties require a certified birth certificate as well. The license costs $80 (at time of print) and many areas will only accept payment in cash, so be sure to contact the city clerk's office for specific requirements in your county. If either party has been married before, they must show proof of divorce, annulment, or death. The minimum age to be married in California, without parental consent, is 18.

Florida: Sun drenched beaches, cool ocean breezes, and numerous romantic hideaways make Florida an excellent spot for newlyweds to spend their honeymoon. For those exact reasons, the Sunshine State is a great place for a couple to begin their new life together by exchanging their vows.

Couples wishing to say "I do" simply need to visit any county courthouse in the State to obtain a marriage license. The ceremony can be performed the same day a license is obtained. Different requirements, such as a waiting period and premarital courses apply for state residents. However, these laws do not apply to out-of-state residents getting married in Florida. Non-Florida-resident couples simply pay the $88.50 license fee. There is no waiting period involved and counseling is not required.

So whether you're tying the knot at Fort Myers' Lovers Key, exchanging vows in Kissimmee, or being pronounced man and wife on Honeymoon Island in St. Petersburg, the Sunshine State is the place for romance.

Las Vegas: Neither blood tests nor waiting periods are required for couples wanting to get married in Las Vegas. Legal age is 18 for men and women (proof of age is required) and licensing fees are $55. Civil ceremonies can be performed at the Marriage Commissioner's Office at 309 South 3rd Street. Chapel fees vary. For a marriage license, call the Clark County Marriage License Bureau at 702-455-4415 (located in the Clark County Courthouse). Marriage License Bureau hours are 8am to midnight, Monday through Thursday. On weekends it is open around the clock from 8am Friday to midnight Sunday. On legal holidays, the bureau is open 24 hours.

LOCAL INFORMATION

Weather: California is so large that it has a wide variety of climate zones. Southern California tends to be temperate and warm year-round, though it can be rainy on and off from October to June. Near the coast in Northern California, it can be chilly, even during the summer. Inland, in the mountains, expect seasons as you'll find in the rest of the country, snowy in the winter and hot during the summer.

Florida's temperature varies depending on whether you're in the southern or northern areas of the state. In northern and central Florida, from November through March,

you can expect temperatures to be in the low forties to the high sixties/low seventies. The rest of the year, temperatures will generally fall from the mid-sixties to the low nineties. In southern Florida, from December through March, expect mid/high fifties to mid-seventies and the remainder of the year, mid-seventies to low nineties. It tends to be VERY humid.

Las Vegas weather tends to be hottest in June, July and August with temperatures soaring above 100 degrees F. It may not feel as hot due to very low humidity however, it is important to remember to drink plenty of water and wear sun protection outdoors. At night, them temperature will drop considerably, most notably in winter. Rain is not common although July and August hold threats of severe thunderstorms and flash floods. Winters are mild with snow fall virtually non-existent.

Peak Season :
California - is popular year-round due to its beautiful weather, though it tends to be busiest in the summer when other parts of the country get too hot.

Florida - is popular year-round, though it peaks during the winter, as it remains temperate while the rest of the east coast grows very cold.

© VISIT FLORIDA

Las Vegas - is located in the desert where the summers are hot and the winters are cool, making spring and fall the best times to visit.

Language: English

Currency: U.S. Dollars - USD

Standard Time Zone
California: UTC (Coordinated Universal Time/GMT (Greenwich Mean Time) – 8 hours: PST – Pacific Standard Time.

Florida: UTC (Coordinated Universal Time/GMT (Greenwich Mean Time) – 5 hours: EST (Eastern Standard Time)

Las Vegas: UTC (Coordinated Universal Time/GMT (Greenwich Mean Time) – 8 hours: PST – Pacific Standard Time

For more information, contact:
California:
California Tourism
Telephone: 916-319-5427
Website: www.visitcalifornia.com

Florida:
Visit Florida
Telephone: 850-488-5607 (X320 or 311)
Website: www.flausa.com

Las Vegas:
Las Vegas Visitor Information Center
3150 Paradise Road
Las Vegas, NV 89109-9096
Telephone: (702) 892-7575
Website: www.vegasfreedom.com

© Robert Holmes / CalTour

© C. Parent, P. Hurteau / Tourisme Québec

C A N A D A

Québec is divided into 20 tourist regions. From the Îles-de-la-Madeleine to the Far North, cover an immense territory of exceptional natural beauty. Each has its predominant feature the St. Lawrence River, virgin forests, lakes, streams, and mountains, and each reflects a different aspect of Québec, whose history, culture and geography are unique in North America.

Montréal: Like a precious work of art, Montréal is framed by Mont-Royal and the St. Lawrence River. Montréal has drawn on the combined strengths of its French and British roots to attract newcomers from around the world. This multicultural mix has fostered a fertile and vibrant cultural life. A broad range of movies, plays and shows draw large audiences, while bars, cafés and nightclubs rock until the early hours of the morning. Shopping in Montréal – a fashion capital – is another pleasure not to be missed. Montréal ...energizing, electrifying, amazing!

Québec City: Watch out, or you may fall under Québec City's spell ...the only fortified city in North America! As you explore the winding side streets, on foot or in a horse-drawn carriage,

© C. Parent, P. Hurteau / Tourisme Québec

the romance of the city will enrapture you. Curious about the past of this historical city? Stroll through its oldest neighborhoods, like Petit Champlain, Place-Royale and the Old Port. Even though this capital city is steeped in history, the year-round activities are truly up to date: world-class winter carnival and summer festival, theatre, exhibitions...and the accommodations and dining are topnotch!

Perched atop Cap Diamant, surveying the St. Lawrence River, Québec City is one of the landmarks of North American History. Québec City, the cradle of French civilization in North America, is today a busy seaport, an important centre of services and research, a cultural hot spot and of course the provincial capital. The remarkable parliament buildings (hôtel du parlement) are well worth a visit.

THINGS TO SEE AND DO

MONTRÉAL

Recreation: Montréal the metropolis has everything a big city can offer. But Montréal is also one-of-a-kind, a multicultural city that blends its French accent with that of over 80 other ethnic communities and charms visitors with its Euro-American ambiance. Montréal is also innovative and invigorating, offering a whirlwind of cultural creations, both traditional and modern. Its downtown bustles with life at the foot of its mountain, while history is rooted in the old quarters near the river.

With its year-round party atmosphere, Montréal beats to the rhythm of its festivals: jazz, comedy, cinema, fireworks and more! The city beckons you to discover its fashionable boutiques and famed cuisine, over 18 mi. of indoor pedestrian walkways, and its lively casino. Stroll through its colorful streets and typical neighborhoods representative of a mosaic of nations, take a ride along one of its many bicycle paths (over 400 mi. in the region), party in its inviting bars... Montréal? Oui, s'il vous plaît!

Special Points of Interest: Major attractions include: "Old Montréal", Notre-Dame Basilica, Olympic Park, Biodôme, Casino de Montréal, Montréal Botanical Garden, underground city, Saint Joseph's Oratory and Mont Royal.

Explore the old city. The "new" Old Port, entirely made over, is by far the most popular site with visitors. Its park and wharves buzz with activities and people all day long. You can take a tour boat, a ferry or even an amphibious bus for a ride on the St. Lawrence or around the Port, or challenge the Rapides de Lachine in a special jetboat.

Riding in a horse-drawn carriage around the XVIII and XIX century residences of Old Montréal, you will discover the imposing neogothic Notre-Dame Basilica, as well as museums that recount the past, such as the Pointe-à-Callière museum and the Centre d'histoire de Montréal. At the Old Port you will find the Montréal Science Centre, a vast complex dedicated to scientific culture that also includes an IMAX theatre. The Old Port is also the starting point for trips along the turbulent Lachine Rapids, at the western end of the island!

Île Notre-Dame and Île Sainte-Hélène are synonymous with vacationing fun. At Parc Jean-Drapeau, you'll have a ball at Québec's largest amusement park, La Ronde, and at the beach. At the Biosphère, in the former U.S. pavilion from Expo 67, you'll discover the secrets of water, while at the Stewart Museum, located inside an authentic fort, you'll learn about the history of the New World.

Nightlife: Find a vibrant nightlife on Crescent Street & St-Laurent Boulevard for all tastes. Unique to Montréal is the "underground city," a subterranean network of over 18.5 miles of office and apartment towers, major stores, hotels, restaurants, railway stations, parking garages, movie theatres, concert halls and much more, all connected by Montréal's clean, fast and convenient metro trains.

Glamorous places, magical places, the casinos of Québec propose to their visitors an exhilarating combination of entertainment, gastron-

© C. Parent, P. Hurteau / Tourisme Québec

omy and gaming. Not only must they be seen, they must above all be experienced!

Ten minutes from the heart of the city, the Casino de Montréal is linked by shuttle bus to the Centre Infotouriste. Built on île Notre-Dame, the Casino de Montréal boasts the city skyline as its vista. Located in facilities originally built for the 1967 World Fair (Expo 67), its structure is both amazing and impressive.

With its 120 gaming tables and 3,000 slot machines spread over five floors, it ranks among the largest casinos in the world. The Casino de Montréal has also become a required stopover for gourmets ever since its Nuances restaurant was awarded the coveted CAA/AAA's Five Diamond rating.

A less than two-hour drive from Montréal and a five-minute drive from downtown Gatineau (Hull), the Casino du Lac-Leamy offers a dramatic environment with its gaming areas surrounded by fountains, waterfalls and a bamboo forest. Sharing its site with the Hilton Lac-Leamy, a luxurious and ultramodern hotel, it definitely is a lively spot.

Dining: Dining in Montréal promises to be a memorable part of your trip. Renowned for its fine cuisine, French bistros and sidewalk cafés, the city offers an enormous variety of regional and international dining. Satisfy your craving for great food, Montréal-style.

Shopping: Montréal boasts an underground city comprised of a subterranean network of over 20 miles of office and apartment towers, major stores, hotels, restaurants, railway stations, parking garages, movie theaters, concert halls and much more, all connected by Montréal's clean, fast and convenient metro trains.

Museums: There are over thirty museums in Montréal. The Musée d'art contemporain exhibits the works of modern masters from Québec and beyond, while the Montréal Museum of Fine Arts regularly hosts major international shows.

The Canadian Centre for Architecture, the McCord Museum of Canadian History and the Musée d'archéologie et d'histoire Pointe-à-Callière are greatly appreciated by art and history lovers.

© C. Parent, P. Hurteau / Tourisme Québec

In Gatineau, the Canadian Museum of Civilization as an enviable reputation for the quality of its exhibits.

Parks & Gardens: Nature has always been part of Québec's cities, and Montréalers are particularly fortunate to have at their doorsteps Parc du Mont-Royal, a creation of Frederic Olmsted, the American landscape artist who also designed Central Park in New York. Its two lookouts offer glorious views over the city. The park is easily reached and explored via an extensive network of bicycle paths; like all green spaces in the city, it is truly designed to belong to everyone, as a public place of recreation and entertainment.

In Montréal, you will find some twenty gardens, as colorful and varied as a fresh-picked bunch of wildflowers. The Montréal Botanical Garden, one of the largest of its kind in the world, tops the must-see list. Founded in 1931, it today covers more than 185 acres. It features 10 exhibition greenhouses and some 30 outdoor thematic gardens, including an impressive Rose Garden (10,000 rose bushes). Among its jewels are the Chinese Garden (the largest outside of Asia), the Japanese Garden, the Arboretum (100 acres) and Tree House and the Insectarium.

Nature/Sightseeing: Summer is without a doubt the high point of the annual program of festivities. As soon as the warm weather arrives, the major cultural and sports events kick off: the Mondial SAQ, a dazzling pyrotechnical face-off; the Air Canada Grand Prix, a roaring, rubber-burning part of the

© C. Parent, P. Hurteau / Tourisme Québec

© C. Parent, P. Hurteau / Tourisme Québec

world Formula 1 championship; the immensely popular Festival international de jazz, which draws over one million music-lovers, and the Just for Laughs Festival, the Francofolies and the World Film Festival, popular with comedy fans and movie buffs.

QUEBÉC CITY

Recreation: In Québec, there is so much to do that you need at least four seasons to satiate the passions of nature lovers and outdoor enthusiasts! Air, earth, water… all of nature's elements come together to offer a dizzying range of sports and recreational activities for the most varied tastes.

Autumn arrives in an explosion of brilliant colors, as the curious at heart set off to watch the awesome landing of migratory birds at one of their favorite stopovers on the shores of the St. Lawrence and Outaouais.

What better time of year to journey into the forest or enjoy horseback riding over hill and dale! And imagine golfing or bicycling against the spectacular backdrop of changing shades of yellow, orange and red. It's no wonder cruise ships choose this season to sail up the river to Montréal and Québec City! This is also the best season to hunt for game.

The outskirts of Québec City are simply enchanting. In just a few minutes, you can find yourself deep in the countryside or in

the heart of one of the large natural parks. The Chute Montmorency alone (83 m / 272 ft. high) is a magnificent waterfall well worth the detour. Characterized by abrupt dips in the landscape, the Parc national de la Jacques-Cartier is sure to leave you speechless. Venture through the marshes at the Cap Tourmente National Wildlife Area to observe 300 species of birds up close, including the tens of thousands of snow geese that visit twice a year, in the spring and fall. This region is a sports lover's paradise both in summer and winter, with spectacular golf courses and majestic ski slopes like Mont Sainte-Anne and Stoneham.

This region, the birthplace of the province, features many ancestral villages all along the legendary Chemin du Roy, the first vehicular highway in Canada, and on Île d'Orléans, whose rural charm was so perfectly described in the songs of Félix Leclerc. On the edge of the downtown area, discover the traditions of the Huron-Wendat people in the village of Wendake at the Onhoüa Cheteke site. The Sainte-Anne-de-Beaupré Basilica is a pilgrimage site that attracts over one and a half million visitors each year.

Special Points of Interest: The old quarter of Québec City was declared a heritage site by UNESCO in 1985. This is the only fortified city north of Mexico, and from the top of its ramparts you can admire the maze of narrow, winding streets and sloping roofs.

It is said that the Château Frontenac is the most photographed hotel in the world. This proud and majestic building, an internationally renown symbol of Québec City, celebrated its hundredth anniversary in 1993. Right beside the Château is the Dufferin Terrace, which offers a magnificent view of the St. Lawrence River and the surrounding area. A funicular allowing visitors to quickly reach the Quartier Petit-Champlain and Place-Royale can be found at the easternmost point of the Terrace.

When New France was first being settled, people established themselves primarily along the shores of the St. Lawrence River in order to facilitate communication and transportation. The first Canadian roadway adapted to vehicular traffic, the Chemin Du Roy, or King's Highway, was built in 1734. It connected Montréal and Québec City, the two largest cities in the province.

The historical Île d'Orléans, connected to the North Shore by a bridge built in 1935, is located only 15 minutes from Old Québec. Stop at the island's tourist information office, which be reached at (418) 828-9411, and pick up tour guides, audio-guides for your car or maps for bicycle tours. These tools will make your visit to Île d'Orléans a truly memorable experience!

The Parliament Building, the premier historical monument in the province, is an imposing structure comprising four wings that form a square approximately 100m (310') per side. The Parliament is one of the rare examples in North America of a building whose architecture is inspired by 16th century French classicism. Here you can visit the National Assembly Chamber and the Legislative Council Chamber.

Located at the foot of Cape Diamant, Place-Royal, is one of the oldest neighborhoods in North America. Its narrow streets and stone-walled houses represent four centuries of history. During the summer, Place-Royale bustles with activity.

© C. Parent, P. Hurteau / Tourisme Québec

The Pont De Québec bridge was designated as an international historical monument by the Canadian Society for Civil Engineering and the American Society of Civil Engineers. The pont de Québec is formed by a 549 m (1702') suspended span located between two main pillars, which makes this bridge the longest cantilever bridge in the world. While the bridge was under construction, the suspended span collapsed on two occasions (in 1907 and 1916), killing many workers. Trains began using the bridge in 1917 while automobiles were only allowed on it in 1929.

This magnificently restored Quartier Petit-Champlain part of town resembles a quaint riverside village. Its narrow, romantic streets are lined with artisans' shops, and you can enjoy the shows given by the clowns, jugglers and other street performers. You can easily return to the Dufferin Terrace by taking the funicular in Old Québec, which is located at the intersection of rue Petit-Champlain and rue Sous-le-Fort.

Picturesque Rue Saint-Paul and the Old Port are located at the foot of Old Québec on its northernmost flank, near the confluence of the Saint-Charles and the St. Lawrence Rivers. Many antique dealers and craftsmen have set up shop along rue Saint-Paul, while not too far away, the Old Port has conserved the rich maritime history of Québec City.

Nightlife: A 90-minute drive from Québec City, nestled between the St. Lawrence River and the mountains, the Casino de Charlevoix distinguishes itself by its leisurely, relaxing atmosphere. In this somewhat private setting, 22 gaming tables and 800 slot machines are yours to discover. The Casino de Charlevoix is located on the site of the celebrated Manoir Richelieu, a luxurious resort renowned for its comfort and elegance. Superb food is to be enjoyed at any of its three restaurants, whether one feels like tasting gourmet delicacies or eating bistro fare. All this a stone's throw away from one of the country's most spectacular golf courses.

The Charlevoix region, a UNESCO World Biosphere Reserve, abounds in breath-taking landscapes and unique natural attractions. It is famous for its whale-watching cruises as well as its culinary creativity.

Dining: A veritable capital of fine cuisine, Québec City has more gourmet restaurants per capita than any other city on the continent. Local restaurateurs look to the seasons for inspiration and invite you to a celebration of flavors. Lobster season, hunting season and the much anticipated yearly arrival of von nouveau provide other occasions to discover our refined cuisine and locally produced delicacies of exceptional quality.

From maple products eaten in a sugar shack to fantastic meals savored in an XVIII-century residence, the Québec region is a veritable gourmet circuit!

Shopping: While strolling through the streets of Old-Québec, you will be unable to resist handicraft kiosks, renowned clothing designers' boutiques, art galleries and gourmet groceries… You will find real treasures at more that 1,000 boutiques throughout Québec!

Choco-Musée Érico chocolate shop and museum. Learn the history of chocolate from Mayan times to this day. Ancient and modern accessories, chocolate-making techniques (video and view of the kitchen) and more. For chocolate lovers: handmade chocolate, cookies, brownies, cakes, homemade ice cream.

Nature/Sight-seeing: In the summer, great bike paths will take you in and around the city to discover it on a different angle; swimming, camping etc. are readily available.

In the winter, the Carnaval de Québec is the biggest winter celebration of its kind in the world. Just minutes away from the city, great ski resorts offer ideal downhill & cross country skiing.

You can participate in a number of outdoor activities throughout the year in the Jacques-Cartier Valley, located only 40 minutes from downtown Québec City. Imagine...a valley whose microclimate supports an incredibly diverse natural environment, which is home to many animal species, including raccoons, Virginia deer and moose. You can enjoy a wide variety of outdoor activities here: canoeing, camping, fishing, snow-shoeing, nature walks and bird watching. Or you can simply come and take in the beautiful wilderness vistas found in this magnificent park.

WEDDINGS ON LOCATION

Marriage Requirements: It is indeed possible for foreign visitors to get married in Québec. First, complete and file the Marriage Civil form along with the two birth certificates. The future married couple will be summoned to an interview at which time the date of the marriage will be determined. Additional information is available at the courthouses (Montréal and Québec City addresses listed below) or by visiting the Ministry of Justice's web site at http://www.justice.gouv.qc.ca/english/publications/generale/maria-a.htm.

Montréal : Palais de justice de Montréal
Service des mariages civils
1, rue Notre-Dame Est, Bureau 3.150
Montréal (Québec) H2Y 1B6
Tél.: (514) 393-2113

Québec : Palais de justice de Québec
Service des mariages civils
300, boulevard Jean-Lesage, Bureau 1.24
Québec (Québec) G1K 8K6
Tél.: (418) 649-3501

LOCAL INFORMATION

Peak Season: May to October

Language: English is spoken in all major centers; however, in Québec the primary language is French.

Currency: Canadian Dollar - CAD. U.S. visitors benefit from an attractive exchange rate. The U.S. dollar buys at least 50% more. US$100 = CAD$150. And, there are no taxes on casino winnings in Québec.

Standard Time Zone: UTC (Coordinated Universal Time/GMT (Greenwich Mean Time) – 5 hours: EST (Eastern Standard Time)

Entry Requirements: Visitors from any country except the United States must carry a valid passport. American citizens need only proof of citizenship, such as birth certificate and a piece of identification which includes your photo, though a passport will still cover this. Visas are required for visitors from certain countries. It is always advisable to check with the Canadian consulate or embassy in your country before setting out for Canada.

Customs Regulations: Personal luggage not subject to any specific restrictions is tax exempt, but must be declared to Canadian customs, along with any plants and food products. Visitors 18 years of age and over may import 50 cigars, 200 cigarettes and 400g (0.88lbs) of tobacco. They may also bring in 1.14L (40 ounces) of spirits or wine, or 24 355-ml (12-ounces) bottles or cans or the equivalent of beer.

Safety: The province of Québec is a very safe destination. As in any other destination, visitors are encouraged to use common sense when traveling. Most hotels offer complimentary use of safety deposit boxes.

For more information, contact:
Province of Québec
Jean-Francois Niquette
Tourisme Québec
1010, rue Saint-Catherine Ouest, Bureau 400
Montréal (Québec) Canada H3B 1G2

Telephone: 1-877 BONJOUR
Website: www.bonjourquébec.com

© C. Parent, R. Bélanger / Tourisme Québec

welcome to
H A W A I I

© HVCB / Kirk Lee Ader

HAWAII - CLIMATE		
MONTH	HI	LO
JAN	80°	65°
FEB	80°	65°
MAR	82°	65°
APR	82°	66°
MAY	84°	70°
JUN	86°	72°
JUL	87°	72°
AUG	88°	74°
SEPT	88°	73°
OCT	86°	72°
NOV	84°	70°
DEC	81°	65°

Temperatures are provided in °Fahrenheit and based on averages.

H A W A I I

HAWAII - THE BIG ISLAND

What could possibly be more romantic than a full moon as seen through palm fronds? Moonlight reflecting off water maybe? Whatever magic is employed, it's working. And it's been working for as long as people in love have been coming to Hawaii.

And then there is the concept of aloha, a romantic-sounding word that means both hello and goodbye. It also means love. Because aloha is both prized and practiced, its warmth seeps into all the surfaces of Hawaii. It's Hawaii's unique gift.

THINGS TO SEE AND DO

Culture & History: To say Hawaii's history is fascinating would be an understatement. It is far more, and Hawaii's Big Island has been a large part of it. The Polynesians settled here long ago, and their rich history continues to this day with the unique and colorful concoction of cultures. The Polynesian culture of ancient Hawaii is welcomed and has absorbed countless traditions and art influences from Asia and Europe, and the rest is history.

Beaches & Watersports: The ocean is never out of view on Hawaii's Big Island. And here, there are all kinds of ways to have fun in, on, or under the warm, crystal-clear water. There are 266 miles of coastline and 47 beaches here with diverse sand colors from pristine white to green to rich volcanic black.

From mid-November through May, the great humpback whales make their annual visit to

© HVCB / Ron Dahlquist

Hawaii's Big Island. Keep your camera handy if you're on a whale watching tour; these gentle giants can take to the air at any moment.

Golfing: Bring your clubs. Hawaii's Big Island is known as the "Golf Capital of Hawaii." What could be more refreshing for your game than long days, perfect weather and challenging courses - spiced with panoramic ocean and mountain views? This is golfing at its finest.

Special Points of Interest: A must-see is Kilauea, the earth's most active volcano. It is said to be "the greatest show on earth." It's quite a feeling to witness the perpetual fiery birth of new land. A memory that will stay with you for a lifetime. Plan on a long day to tour Hawaii Volcanoes National Park. It's 218,000 acres from sea to summit that also includes Mauna Loa, the earth's largest active volcano. Other attractions include art centers, museums, and incredible drives like the 11-mile crater rim drive around the Kilauea caldera.

Nightlife: If romance is an emotional attraction or aura, then Hawaii's Big Island is romance itself. Walk along the beach hand in hand and gaze at a shimmering ocean reflecting the pathway of the moon. Tell someone you love them with a whisper that stirs the soft plumeria-filled air. Kiss under a rushing waterfall. Pop the question at a candle lit dinner overlooking a paradise garden, and don't forget to order champagne.

Dining: In the last hundred years, cuisine from around the world migrated to Hawaii's Big Island. Starting with the

Polynesians then flavored by an endless march of immigrants from Japan, China, the Philippines, Korea, U.S. mainland, and Europe; Hawaii's favorite foods are a carnival of compound tastes that are exciting and delicious. The result is called "Hawaii regional cuisine" and reflects the best of those places -- combined with the freshest locally grown, and often exotic, ingredients of Hawaii. Of course, this includes exceptional fresh-caught ocean fish like ahi, mahi-mahi, onaga, ono, opakapaka and opah.

Shopping: Browse treasures carved from local woods like Koa and Milo, such as bowls so thin that they're translucent. Find tropical wear for everyone in the family - at every level of fashion sophistication. Discover books and works of art reflecting Hawaii and the Pacific, along with Hawaiian quilts and pillows. And, don't forget to take home "made only in Hawaii" products such as fruit jams, Kona coffee, Hawaii Vintage Chocolate, macadamia nuts, and recipe books containing the secret ingredients and preparations of the Island's many exotic cuisines. They make wonderful gifts for friends, family, and co-workers who weren't lucky enough to come along.

Museums/Galleries: Pu'uhonua O Hona-unau National Historic Park is a 180-acre compound on the South Kohala coast, where defeated warriors, war victims, and law-breakers traveled to seek forgiveness and safety in ancient times. Pu'uhonua is surrounded by a large stone wall, which measures 1,000 feet long, 10 feet high, and 17 feet wide. The 180-acre site includes a fishpond, canoe landing, thatched hale (house), halau (a-framed large structure) and Hale O Keawa heiau (temple), an ancient temple surrounded by large ancient wooden kii (statue), which stand guard over the buried bones of 23 ali'i (Hawaiian royalty).

Nature/Sight-seeing: Some say the key to relaxing is getting active. Hawaii's Big Island makes it easy to get out and play. Here, you can discover a new outdoor adventure every day of the week.

The terrain on Hawaii's Big Island is a big temptation for bicycle riders. Gorgeous shoreline roads, rain forest trails, and long and winding

© HVCB / Ron Dahlquist

© HVCB / Kirk Lee Ader

backroad paths almost beg for riding. Explore them with the respect they deserve and they'll provide you the ride of a lifetime. Bike rentals are available as well as guided bike tours. For backcountry sightseeing sprinkled with awe-inspiring waterfalls, saddle up and explore the trails above Waipio Valley on horseback.

KAUAI

Kauai has a lush, rural feel and a laid-back lifestyle all its own. After all, Kauai is Hawaii's oldest island and, as first-born, has a legacy of paradise to uphold. And what a paradise! A trip around Kauai is a feast of green, tropical forest, cascading waterfalls, golden sand beaches and the time of your life. Your circumnavigation will be interrupted by one of the world's greatest natural wonders, the Napali Coast. Don't be daunted. Take to boat or helicopter to witness its 14 miles of vertical seamounts falling into a necklace of white surf spray.

THINGS TO SEE AND DO

Recreation: Kauai offers helicopter tours, windsurfing, deep-sea fishing, hang gliding, authentic rodeos, polo, and the PGA Grand Slam Golf. It's all good on Kauai. And it's all beautifully amazing. Which is probably why Kauai has been the film location site for more than 60 major motion picture and television films, including classics such as "South Pacific" and "Blue Hawaii" with Elvis Presley, and more recently "Jurassic Park," "Mighty Joe Young" and "Six Days/Seven Nights."

Beaches: On Kauai, you don't have to go far to find the kind of beach you're craving. There's more beach per mile of coastline here than on any other Hawaiian Island. Forty-three beaches in total, varying from quiet white-sand lagoons, to perfectly carved calm water bays, to expansive pounding ocean shores. Kauai is also Hawaii's water world. With rivers, waterfalls, and the deep blue Pacific, if it involves water, you'll find it here.

Golfing: Like the Hollywood filmmakers who shoot here, golfers go on location to Kauai for the spectacular scenic backdrops. Of course, they also enjoy a good challenge. Here, the courses are crafted by nature and helped along by some talented architects. The views could be considered an obstacle, as your mind may wander onto seaside cliffs, into forested hills, or smack-dab into the ocean. Just don't let your ball do the same.

Special Points of Interest: Take a fun and informative boat ride up Kauai'i's Wailua River to get to Kauai'i's oldest and most popular visitor attraction, Fern Grotto. The grotto is an unusual cave-like rock formation filled with giant cascading maidenhair fern.

The Kilauea Point National Wildlife Refuge is a 200-acre nesting refuge for albatross, frigate birds, red and white tropical birds, and red-footed boobies.

The Napali Coast is 22 miles of scenic coastline with 3,000-foot cliffs qualifying it as Hawaii's most remote wilderness accessible only by air, sea or foot. Getting to the coastline by foot requires an 11-mile overnight hike recommended for experienced hikers only. Less experienced hikers can try the two-mile hike to Hanakapiai Beach, a scenic hike. The beach is not recommended for swimming.

Nightlife: Imagine a balmy evening lit by a full moon and the sparkle of a thousand stars. Imagine a plumeria-scented breeze that caresses the skin like a gentle kiss.

© HVCB / Robert Coello

© HVCB / Ron Dahlquist

Imagine a brilliant double rainbow over jade-colored mountains. Settings like these were made for lovers.

Dining: On Kauai, like its people, you'll find a delightful cultural mix of foods - Chinese, Japanese, Italian, American, Filipino, Thai, Korean, Mexican and more. Pacific Rim cuisine is a favorite indulgence here, marrying the exotic flavors of Polynesia and Asia. Fresh fish, meats, and produce grown in the Islands are an inspiration for imaginative dishes that are so beautifully presented; they double as works of art.

Shopping: Shopping on Kauai is good laidback fun. Most of the retail stores you'll find here are the small, boutique-sized variety, so your experience is anything but hectic. You'll find treasure after treasure browsing through the tiny shops and casual shopping centers in Kapaa, Wailua, Poipu, Koloa, Hanapepe and Hanalei. The most common finds include hand-carved koa bowls and boxes, Hawaiian quilts, and fine art from paintings and sculptures to jewelry, ceramics and photography.

Museums/Galleries: Since Kauai is the oldest of islands in this Pacific chain, it's no surprise that it offers such a breadth and depth of cultural and environmental experience -- a magnitude that is unparalleled even by its

sister islands. Archaeologists speculate that the first "tourists" to Hawaii landed on Kauai perhaps as early as 500 A.D. The gentle Pacific Ocean trade winds that brought settlers from Marquesas, Tahiti, Samoa and other South Pacific islands were the same that eventually led Captain James Cook to make his first landing in Hawaii on the shores of Waimea, Kauai in 1778.

Nature/Sight-seeing: Plan a visit to Kauai's famed "Grand Canyon of the Pacific," Waimea Canyon. It's an impressive 3,567-feet deep and stretches 14 miles across the western end of the island. One look will take your breath away. Equally stunning are the 3,000-foot high mountain cliffs that rise from the ocean floor to form the magnificent, unspoiled Napali Coast. It's a must-see whether by air, land, or sea. State parks, wilderness preserves, wildlife refuges, taro fields, guava plantations, and botanical gardens are also attractions that are easy to come by, and not easy to pass up. Should you get tired, take a rest at the largest coffee plantation in Hawaii: the Island Coffee Company's 4,000-acre Kauai Estate Plantation.

MAUI

Maui No Ka 'Oi (Maui is the best) is what the locals say, and visitors couldn't agree more. The island weaves a spell over the more than 2 million people who visit its shores each year, and many visitors decide to return for good. The island was formed by two volcanoes that erupted long ago -- the extinct 5,788-ft Pu'u Kukui and the dormant 10,023-ft Haleakala (now the centerpiece of a national park). The resulting depression between the two is what gives Maui its nickname, the Valley Isle. Maui's volcanic history gives it much of its beauty. The roads around the island are lined with rich red soil, Central Maui is still carpeted with grassy green, and the deep blue of ocean and sky mingles with the red and green of Maui's topography. And the three planned resort communities along Maui's lee shore -- Kapalua, Ka'anapali, and Wailea -- offer self-contained environments of such luxury and beauty that the effect is almost surreal.

THINGS TO SEE AND DO

Culture & History: From the timeless grandeur of Haleakala crater to the historic charm of 19th century Lahaina, Maui offers a wealth of historic and cultural attractions that will captivate your imagination and reveal the extraordinary traditions of this magical isle.

The town of Lahaina is in fact a National Historic District, supplementing timeless charm with a variety of important historic sites and lovely period museums that take one back to the days when the town served as an important whaling port. History buffs will also find that the Lahaina-Kaanapali and Pacific Railroads provide an unforgettable journey into the area's romantic plantation past.

Recreation: Kaanapali Beach is four miles long and one of Maui's finest beaches. There is a paved beach walk that stretches the length and meanders past condominiums, hotels, restaurants and the Whaler's Village Shopping complex. One of Maui's best spots for snorkelers is a Kaanapali's doorstep fronting the Sheraton Maui. You can't miss "Black Rock." Below it, schools of tropical fish are in session all year long. At sunset, a cliff diver takes the plunge from high atop "Black Rock" into the waters below.

Special Points of Interest: Among the most popular diversions on Maui is driving the incredible "road to Hana." Drive the highway to heaven. It's 53 miles long, one lane wide, with 54 bridges to cross and

© HVCB / Ron Dahlquist

© HVCB / Robert Coello

617 curves to negotiate, but will lead you through misty rainforests, along lava cliffs, into sheer ravines, past waterfalls and fresh water pools, along hidden beach coves and into the heart of Maui's rainforests. Along the way, take in Twin Falls, Oheo Gulch and the Garden of Eden Arboretum and Botanical Garden. The coastal town of Hana is truly heavenly, green, lush and totally tropical. Hana, a sleepy little town that lies toward the end of the highway, is reminiscent of old Hawaii. Because of its green tropical location it's sometimes known as "Heavenly Hana."

Dining: Here, your dining options are as varied as Maui's multi-cultural population. From small cafés featuring Filipino, Thai, Chinese, and Portuguese specialties to lavish, five-star restaurants featuring the finest in European-inspired haute cuisine, Maui offers something to satisfy every appetite. No matter what type of food you prefer, be sure to enjoy a special meal of Hawaii Regional Cuisine - a style unique to the islands that features fresh island seafood, locally grown herbs and spices, and flawless presentation.

Shopping: No trip to Maui is complete without a little (or not so little) souvenir of your stay on this sensational island oasis. From charming boutiques of locally crafted creations to some of the world's most celebrated name brand stores, the sheer variety of shopping outlets is enough to satisfy the demands of the most avid shopping fanatic.

Museums/Galleries: Maui Nui Botanical Gardens is the only public botanical garden in the State of Hawaii which conserves, propagates and disseminates only native Hawaiian plants and trees of Maui Nui (Maui, Molokai, Lanai, and Kahoolawe.)

Maui Ocean Center: This is the best place to get nose-to-nose with 2,000 fish and even sharks that can be viewed safely through the clear acrylic tunnel of a 750,000-gallon tank. You can explore the stingray cove, turtle lagoon or get a hands-on encounter with a starfish, sea urchin, or sea cucumber in the "touch" pond.

Nature/Sight-seeing: Maui is the whale-watching capital of Hawaii. Humpbacks congregate in the warm offshore waters annually from

November through April. A full-grown whale can be more than 45 feet long and weigh more than 40 tons. McGregor Point is Maui's best viewing spot from land – spectators often say they see "smoke" rising from the water, but that's actually water vapor being exhaled by a whale's blowhole.

A popular dive spot, Molokini Island is a partially submerged, inactive volcano and nature preserve off the Maui coast. One of the best diving spots, Molokini's underwater life is home to kikakapu (lemon butterfly fish), puhi (eel), honu (sea turtle), hahalua (manta ray), mano (reef shark), orange cup coral and a whole lot of marine life. During winter months, scuba divers can hear the haunting sounds of the humpback whales.

OAHU

Oahu, the third largest Hawaiian Island, has an area of 608 square miles and a coastline of 112 miles. It reaches from sea level to 4,003-foot Mt. Ka'ala. This is the most populated island, where Honolulu is the Capital City, the principal port, the major airport, business and financial center, and the educational heart of the State. O`ahu is the military command center of the Pacific, and Waikiki

is the visitor center.

On Oahu, you will experience the diversity of an island paradise where cosmopolitan conveniences are surrounded by breathtaking scenery. Envelop yourself in the Aloha Spirit - a way of life in the islands that will leave you longing to return to Oahu, the heart of Hawaii. "Hang loose" at the world-famous Waikiki Beach or find your own secluded stretch of sand. A short drive out of town in any direction will bring you face to face with uncrowded beaches, natural wonders and beautiful scenery. The island of Oahu welcomes you to paradise found.

THINGS TO SEE AND DO

Recreation: Oahu has over 125 miles of awe-inspiring sandy shoreline. You are most likely familiar with world-famous Waikiki Beach, and you've undoubtedly heard of the big-wave north shore surf beaches Pipeline and Sunset. But you're in for a surprising treat when you discover the sandy wonderlands in between.

A world-famous strip of sand actually extends from the Hilton Hawaiian Village to Kapiolani Park on the Diamond Head side

© HVCB / Ron Dahlquist

of Waikiki. And although most people just call it "Waikiki Beach," it is actually a series of individual beaches, each with its own personality and attractiveness. Learn to surf off Waikiki's famous shoreline with the newest generation of surfing legends, the Waikiki "beach boys." Waikiki's gentle waves are perfect for the novice and you'll feel like royalty when you've mastered the surf historically known as the "surfing waters of the kings."

Golfing: Great golf is one of the main reasons Oahu is a favorite destination. There are more golf courses on Oahu than any other island. You can choose from more than forty public and private courses, ranging from casual municipal links to elegant resort courses. They offer not only superb challenges, but also spectacular vistas. Some call them "distractions," but make the game beautifully challenging.

Special Points of Interest: Oahu's combination of a thriving cosmopolitan city, exciting resorts, beautiful natural places, and quaint towns and neighborhoods offer tremendous diversity that the visitor and resident alike can enjoy. Things to do on Oahu are as varied as the island itself - from cosmopolitan Honolulu to the pristine shores of the North Shore.

Nightlife: Discover the magic of Oahu at night. With a bustling city and resort, Oahu offers a myriad of nightlife. From luau and Polynesian shows to cool clubbing and mar-

© HVCB / Kirk Lee Aeder

tini bar hopping to theater performances and comedy acts to romantic dining and the sounds of the ocean breeze and ukuleles, Oahu is a night lover's paradise.

Dining: Oahu is known for its eclectic and innovative fare, each with an exotic cultural background. The cuisine is as interesting and diverse as the people who live here. To "eat" your way through Oahu would literally take months, maybe longer. Its variety of ethnic foods and preparations are some of the most extensive in the world. So extensive in fact, you may never sample the same flavors twice. The assortment of Asian restaurants is truly astonishing, as is the seemingly endless venues for fresh seafood.

Shopping: Explore Oahu's malls with their unique blend of local stores and national chains. In one stop, pick up clothes for the kids, that long desired dress along with macadamia nuts and pikake scented lotion – only on Oahu. Find bargains at the swap meet and at the International Marketplace. Pick up t-shirts, lauhala placemats and dried tropical fruit - all at a steal. Discover Asian and Hawaiian surprises in Chinatown. Taste mango or li hing mui "seed," buy fresh fruit and don't forget to get those special leis to take back with you. Pick up a one-of-a-kind piece at the many craft fairs and at local shops around the island, such as up at the North Shore. Select a koa bowl, a Niihau shell necklace, a blown glass dolphin,

plumeria-shaped bowls, feather lei to go with your hat or poha berry jam that will remind you of the islands and wanting to come back. Oahu is a shopper's dream.

Museums/Galleries: Walk in the footsteps of history and delve into Hawaii's rich culture. Oahu has Hawaii's largest collection of museums. Be intrigued and fascinated by the voyaging Polynesians that first made Hawaii home, the missionaries that influenced the island's cultures, the reign of the Hawaiian monarchy, the Asian immigrant that came to work on the plantations, Pearl Harbor's involvement with World War II, and by Hawaii's entrance into Statehood. Learn more about the arts and culture at one of Oahu's many acclaimed art museums, theaters, and galleries. World-class exhibits and productions that generally are not seen elsewhere, can be found on Oahu.

Pearl Harbor and the Arizona Memorial : Pearl Harbor was originally a river, which early Hawaiians called Wai Momi or "river of pearl" because of its numerous oyster beds. Today, Pearl Harbor is Hawaii's largest harbor and the nation's only naval base designated as a National Historic Landmark with three significant memorials: the USS Arizona Memorial, honoring the 1,100 men of the Pearl Harbor attack; the Battleship Missouri Memorial, a living museum of the most celebrated and last-built battleship; and the USS Bowfin Museum, featuring a

© HVCB / Ron Dahlquist

World War II submarine, a Japanese mini submarine and extensive submarine history.

Nature/Sight-seeing: Test your wind stamina at Nuuanu Pali, where periodic wind gusts make it difficult for visitors to walk to the lookout point. Perched 3,000 feet above Windward Oahu, Nuuanu Pali is the site of the famous Battle of Nuuanu led by Kamehameha in 1795 when he drove hundreds of warriors over the cliff.

Diamond Head, Oahu's largest tuff cone, formed over 100,000 years ago by an active bubbling volcano. Nineteenth century British sailors nicknamed the crater Diamond Head when they mistook the calcite crystals for diamonds. A well-graded trail leads you up the 760-foot summit to a World War II bunker with a bird's eye view of Honolulu.

WEDDINGS ON LOCATION

Showcase your wedding on the beach beneath a lingering tropical sunset, with palm trees gently rustling in the trade winds. Or set the stage somewhere more remote with a cascading waterfall serving as background music. Choose a traditional Hawaiian luau wedding with sumptuous Island music and food. Or there's always the novel idea of having your wedding in a church. The Hawaiian islands offer abundant churches and temples of many different faiths, generally found in rural locales. Many of them are historical, all of them peaceful and beautiful.

Marriage Requirements: The first step to getting married in Hawaii is to obtain a

© HVCB / Kirk Lee Aeder

marriage license from an authorized agent. Once the license has been issued, there is no waiting period before the marriage can take place. No blood tests are required, and you do not need to be a citizen of the state. You must both appear, in person, before a marriage license agent.

You will need to provide proof of age (minimum age to marry without parental consent is 18) and an official application. The cost is $60.00, payable in cash only, and your license is issued at the time of application. The license expires after 30 days. A marriage certificate will be prepared and filed by your licensed marriage officiant or performer with the Department of Health. A newly married couple receives one certified copy of the certificate at no extra charge, upon payment of the marriage license fee, which will be sent to the couple by mail (60-120 days) after the marriage is performed.

Marriage performers must be duly licensed by and in the State of Hawaii to perform the marriage ceremony. More information on marriage licenses can be obtained by calling (808) 586-4545.

LOCAL INFORMATION

Climate: Year round in the Hawaiian Islands, the weather is wonderful. Because they're located at the edge of the tropical zone they really have only two seasons. In "summer," the average daytime high temperature is 85° F; in "winter," it's 78° F.

Ocean temperatures are always warm; trade winds keep the islands cool and the humidity comfortable. Beach-goers will be happy to learn that the temperature of Hawaii's near-shore waters stay comfortable throughout the year. The average year round water temperature is 74° F., with a summer high of 80° F. If you favor a dry and sunny destination, check out the leeward side of each island. (That's the region sheltered from the prevailing winds - generally the west and south.) If you want lush, tropical and wet, check out an island's windward side (the regions facing the prevailing winds - generally the east and north). But even to windward the showers usually last just long enough to create the legendary, blazing rainbows. And what would Hawaii be without them?

Peak Season: Unlike other destinations, Hawaii's "high" and "low" seasons aren't dictated by the weather here (it's always great), but rather the weather everywhere else. Expect premium rates during the winter months, mid-December through March. Family travel is most popular during the summer. Spring and Fall, while considered "low" season, offer great travel values and fewer visitors.

Language: While Hawaii is an exotic destination, it's still the 50th State in the United States and English is our official language. But our rich, multi-ethnic heritage means you'll hear echoes of Asia, Europe and South America in our delightful local "pidgin."

Currency: US Dollars - USD

Standard Time Zone: UTC (Coordinated Universal Time/GMT (Greenwich Mean Time) – 10 hours

Entry Requirements: No special requirements when traveling from the US.

Customs Regulations: Each family is required to fill out a customs form upon leaving Hawaii. No produce (other than certain items which you can purchase at the airport, such as pineapples and flower leis which have been specially inspected) may be brought out of Hawaii. If you attempt to bring fresh fruits and vegetables out of Hawaii, it will be confiscated and you may be fined.

Safety: Keeping safe in Hawaii is simple. Just follow the same common sense rules that you would follow anywhere. Lock your car and keep your valuables within sight and reach. Dialing 911 connects you to emergency assistance for police, fire and ambulance. In Hawaii, ocean safety is very important. Heed the international signage at local beaches, which alerts you to rough sea conditions, rip currents, jellyfish, and high surf. When hiking the wilderness, be sure to check in with park rangers first.

For more information, contact:
Hawaii Visitors and Convention Bureau
Waikiki Shopping Plaza
2250 Kalakaua Avenue, Room 502
Honolulu, HI 96815

Website: www.gohawaii.com
Telephone: 1-800-GO-HAWAII (464-2924)

© HVCB / Kirk Lee Aeder

welcome to

MEXICO

M E X I C O

ACAPULCO - CLIMATE		
MONTH	HI	LO
JAN	86°	70°
FEB	87°	70°
MAR	88°	70°
APR	89°	72°
MAY	90°	74°
JUN	90°	74°
JUL	91°	75°
AUG	91°	75°
SEPT	89°	76°
OCT	89°	75°
NOV	88°	73°
DEC	88°	70°

Temperatures are provided in °Fahrenheit and based on averages.

Mexico is an ideal place for a honeymoon. The country's enormous cultural and natural diversity means that it has something to offer newlyweds from anywhere in the world, from those seeking privacy and beautiful surroundings to those who would like to explore some of the country's cultural and natural attractions. Beginning your new life with a magical trip to Mexico will undoubtedly contribute to your future happiness.

ACAPULCO

Acapulco is the largest and most spectacular tourist resort in the Mexican Pacific. As a result of its stunning beaches, exuberant natural surroundings and wonderful climate, this port has been dubbed the Pearl of the Pacific. It is the most popular holiday resort in Mexico and Latin America, since its functional, modern infrastructure has had very little impact on its original beauty or attractions. Set in gorgeous natural surroundings, Acapulco offers an enormous range of attractions and activities. Calm, sunny beaches and exuberant vegetation that surrounds one of the loveliest bays in the Pacific blend seamlessly with major hotel complexes, superb restaurants and wonderful nightclubs.

THINGS TO SEE AND DO

Acapulco Bay has a score of delightful beaches. Some have gentle, friendly waves, like Caleta and Caletilla, others have moderate waves like La Condesa while still others have rough waves in the open sea like El Revolcadero, but all of them are extremely beautiful.

Acapulco is the favorite place for those who like fishing, and we're not talking about the type of fishing that involves sitting around for hours doing nothing in the middle of a lake. Fishing in Acapulco means the excitement of being on a boat out in the choppy, open sea and the rush of adrenaline you experience when a large sailfish pulls at your line. Your taste for excitement will also be fully satisfied when fishing for red snapper, sea bass, pompano or bonito. There are great facilities for renting the exact type of boat you require at either Puerto Marqués or in the Bay of Acapulco.

The transparent waters between the rocks and Icacos beach on the eastern side of Acapulco Bay are a great place for diving. Coralreefs and all sorts of fish can be seen at this spot. Other places where you can enjoy sea wildlife are Roqueta island and Caleta and Caletilla.

Special Points of Interest in Acapulco: There is a place in the surrounding mountains, about six kilometers north of Acapulco Bay, where there is a group of stones carved in the form of humans in many different positions. An Archaeological expedition like no other!

The San Diego Fort was rebuilt during the 18th century. Visitors can walk along the walls that defended the town from attacks by pirates who were after the treasures brought to Mexico on the Manila Galleon. There is a History Museum in the San Diego Fort where old maps of the port, religious objects and cloths that came over on the Nao de China (the ship from China) are on display. This museum shows the importance of the port of Acapulco for international trade.

Nightlife: Acapulco's nightlife has something for everyone, and its illuminated glass porches are now legendary. The discotheque, dance halls, and bars are designed for all sorts of people wishing to have a good time. Many of these establishments have a panoramic view of the bay.

Dining: Whether you're at a lively beachfront eatery along the boardwalk, a romantic hilltop restaurant, or one of the leading hotels, dining in Acapulco is a memorable experience. Even the most modest restaurant can offer fresh-from-the-sea fish and shellfish grilled to perfection, accompanied by ice-cold chelada – beer and lemon juice on ice, served in a salt-rimmed glass.

Acapulco specialties include ceviche-fish or shellfish marinated in lime juice and mixed with onion, tomato and cilantro; pescado a la talla -fish rubbed with spices and charcoal broiled; and pozole -a hearty stew made with chicken or pork and hominy that is traditionally found on Acapulco's restaurant menus Thursdays.

Shopping: Acapulco has modern shopping centers with all types of shops and boutiques. The port is the leader in top quality summer clothes. You can also find costume jewelry, silver, leather goods, perfumes and souvenirs made from seashells at the innumerable shops along the Costera (coast road).

Nature/Sightseeing: Laguna de Chautengo is located southeast of Acapulco, the Laguna de Chautengo lies between the sea and a natural sandbank. Boats can be hired to explore the mangrove swamps inhabited by herons, seagulls, and other sea birds.

Laguna de Coyuca is located 13 kilometers outside Acapulco on the way to Ixtapa-Zihuatanejo and its landscape contrasts sharply with that of Acapulco. The lagoon is an exotic estuary with lush tropical vegetation, wild fauna, and small islands.

La Condesa is an internationally renowned beach with medium slope and medium to strong waves. It is a favorite meeting place for young water sports enthusiasts.

A popular hiking location is the Canyon at the Papagayo River, a craggy canyon at the spot where the Papagayo River flows down the Southern Sierra Madre mountain range and joins the Omitlan River before it reaches the Pacific Ocean. The walls of the rocky canyon reach up to 60 meters high.

CANCÚN

Cancún has so much to offer! Its superb location, shaped like an island, its year-round mild climate, and its gorgeous, warm, sandy white beaches washed by the Caribbean sea are ideal for water sports. The waters of the bay sheltered by Isla Mujeres are calm and perfect for surfing, sailing, underwater diving and boat trips; those facing the open surf have stronger currents but are also suitable for fishing and snorkeling.

Cancún offers first rate services to tourists. The most famous hotel chains in the world have combined luxury and comfort with hospitality, and they all offer access to everything from tennis courts to relaxing spas.

Nightlife in Cancún's hotel zone is extremely varied. You will find some of the largest discotheque in the world and restaurants with some of the world's most famous chefs as well as fast-food outlets. If you are looking for a calmer atmosphere, there are jazz or piano bars, as well as those with traditional mariachi music.
 Cancún has fascinating Mayan remains, as well as a museum displaying pieces from this culture. Its excellent overland and air links will whisk you to some of the most impressive places in the Mayan World in both Quintana Roo and neighboring Yucatán.

THINGS TO SEE AN DO

One of the reasons why Cancún is a favorite among honeymooners from all over the world is that its makes you feel you're alone in paradise. Newlyweds arriving at its hotels and beaches feel they are on an island, yet with everything within easy reach: malls for souvenir shopping, superb restaurants for unforgettable dinners and lively discotheque or romantic nightclubs for slow dancing.

Recreation: The beaches at Cancún are the most popular among tourists of Quintana Roo. Their beauty is an irresistible invitation to a totally unique holiday. Some of the most outstanding among the many available options are: Las Perlas, Linda, Langosta, Tortugas, Caracol, Chac-Mool and El Rey, among others.

One of the best ways to enjoy the beaches and the Cancún surroundings is on horseback. The Rancho Loma Bonita is one of the most popular places for renting horses; the place itself also has a great riding area. It has paths through the jungle, mangrove swamps, pasturelands, and beaches that are ideal for riding horses. You can rent the horses right there.

Special Points of Interest: Cobá, located outside Cancún, is regarded as one of the most important archaeological sites because of the remains found there. Cobá has the highest pyramids found in the peninsula, the Nohoch Mul.

Cancún has vestiges of Mayan culture in places such as El Rey and El Meco. Cancún Museum, set in the Convention Center in the Hotel Zone, displays pieces from these and other archaeological sites in the state.

Cancún is just a short trip away from imposing Mayan centers such as Tulum and even San Gervasio, on Cozumel Island. Two hundred kilometers outside Cancún, in the state of Yucatán, stands Chichén Itzá, which can be reached by taking Hwy. 180 to Mérida.

Nightlife: Nightlife in Cancún is intense and goes on until dawn in its many discotheque and nightclubs. You'll find all kinds of music there as well as the finest Mexican and imported drinks. The bars are very entertaining and the waiters make sure there's always a lively atmosphere. Boats offering dinner with music and an open bar cruise around the bay and Laguna Nichupté.

Dining: You can enjoy a wide variety of succulent exotic dishes in Cancún. The exquisite dishes of Mayan origins are distinguished by their use of condiments found in the region. Fish of all sorts cooked in different ways, chirmole, papatz tzul, cocido, relleno negro and cochinita pibil are just some of the dishes you can try at restaurants in the state of Quintana Roo.

Shopping: Cancún is a cosmopolitan city with all facilities. There are many plazas and large shopping malls where one can acquire handicrafts from all over the country, leather articles, tobacco, and other imported goods in modern shops.

Museums: A great way to understand more

about the pre Hispanic history of the enigmatic Mayans in the state of Quintana Roo is through the museums. The Archeological Museum of Cancún has hundreds of objects found at the archeological sites of El Rey, Tulum, Coba, X'caret and Hel-ha on display. Similarly, you can visit the museum at the National Institute of History and Anthropology's Cultural center in the town that has displays of Mayan relics.

Parks & Gardens: The Xel-Ha park outside Cancún features underwater rivers, lagoons and limestone sinkholes ideal for swimming and snorkeling, and virtually unspoiled forest and archaeological remains

El Garrafon Submarine National Park is located on the southern tip of Isla Mujeres. Here you can dive freely at this beautiful coral reef rich in marine fauna and multicolored tropical fish.

Nature/Sightseeing:
The splendid beaches and archeological sites of Cancún are just a couple of the reasons why you should visit and enjoy everything it has to offer, including camping. This activity can be enjoyed at various spots in the state of Quintana Roo, including Puerto Juárez and Punta Sam, among others

Eco-tourism: Cancún is within easy reach of nature reserves such as Contoy Island and Sian Ka'an. The Riviera Maya has parks such as Tres Ríos and Xpu-Há offering cycling, walks and rowing facilities. It also has eco-archaeological parks such as Xcaret and Xel-há with a wide range of attractions.

LOS CABOS

When nature blends sky blue with navy blue, sculptures from the bottom of the sea come up to observe the spectacle and stay there for centuries, admiring the magnificent scenery. Los Cabos keeps watch over this gorgeous paradise that does everything in its power to help visitors enjoy the wonders of nature.

Los Cabos offers ultra-modern first-rate tourist services, including top quality hotels and condominiums, superb golf courses, marinas and restaurants. Wonderful facilities are available for fishing, swimming and sailing. Playa Chileno is ideal for diving, while the area between Cabo San Lucas and Cabo Pulmo is perfect for surfing.

THINGS TO SEE AND DO

Recreation: Los Cabos' main attraction is its natural surroundings, resulting from the warm Sea of Cortés meeting the colder Pacific Ocean. Its beaches offer incredible landscapes as well as facilities for all kinds of water sports.

Located on the Nautical Corridor, the beach of El Chileno includes an enormous strip of beach ideal for snorkeling.

Los Cabos is considered the world capital of marlin fishing. This sport can be practiced all year round, and boats of different sizes are available to take you to such places as El Chileno and Olamilla. These boats can be rented at several different places in the area. These two spots are particularly rich in marine fauna and offer great fishing possibilities.

Special Points of Interest: In wintertime, the western beaches of Cabo San Lucas are ideal for watching the arrival of whales in the Pacific, after they have swum for thousands of miles.

Located next to San Jose del Cabo, the San Jose Swamp is a salt and fresh water lagoon separated from the sea by a small sandbar. This body of water covers an area of 50 hectares and large numbers of palm trees surround it. It is also inhabited by various species of birds, reptiles, and mammals.

Nightlife: Los Cabos boasts a variety of nightlife, particularly in La Concepción, north of the Marina. Popular venues include Squid Roe, a dance club, and Kokomo's, a contemporary music bar on the Boulevard Marina.

Dining: As far as food is concerned, the Los Cabos Tourist Corridor offers everything from simple to gourmet food, as well as a wide range of seafood.

Nature/Sightseeing: Parque Nacional Cabo Pulmo is a paradise for diving enthusiasts, since it contains one of the largest coral reefs in the peninsula. It is a protected area outside San Jose del Cabo and attracts many colorful tropical fish and algae. With its vast size, you can dive without affecting the species living on the reef.

WEDDINGS ON LOCATION

Mexico is an ideal place for a honeymoon. The country's enormous cultural and natural diversity means that it has something to offer newly-weds from anywhere in the world, from those seeking privacy and beautiful surroundings to those who would like to explore some of the country's cultural and natural attractions. Beginning your new life with a magical trip to Mexico will undoubtedly contribute to your future happiness.

Marriage Requirements: All Mexican civil marriages are automat-

MEXICO

ically valid in the United States, however you may want to call ahead to your specific destination to be sure you are following the rules for that particular city and state. A religious ceremony can be had, but it isn't considered official. Your hotel can often arrange for a professional wedding planner to assist you with your preparations. It typically requires two to four days in Mexico to complete the arrangements, though having the assistance of a coordinator may shorten this.

Foreigners wishing to get married in Mexico must submit the following documents to the appropriate Mexican Registry Office, at least two days before the intended date of the ceremony. All foreign documents listed must be "apostilled" or legalized in their country of origin and translated into Spanish by a registered translator in Mexico.

- Current passports
- Certified copies of birth certificates
- Tourist cards or visas
- Names, addresses, nationalities, occupations and ages of both parties' parents
- Health certificates and blood tests performed in Mexico
- Four witnesses (each must have a photo id)

If either of you have previously been married, you will also need verification that at least a year has passed from the date of your divorce or the death of your spouse in the form of a certified copy of the divorce decree or a certified copy of the spouse's death certificate.

LOCAL INFORMATION

Climate: From May through October, Mexico has a rainy period, with hurricane season lasting through the summer.

Peak Season: Mid-December through April.

Language: Spanish, though English is sometimes spoken in touristy areas. Don't fear attempting to speak Spanish – Mexicans tend to be helpful and patient with those who try to speak their language.

Currency: Mexican Pesos - MXN

Standard Time Zone: UTC (Coordinated Universal Time/GMT (Greenwich Mean Time) –6 hours: CST Central Standard Time

Entry Requirements: Visitors from the U.S. need a valid passport or must present an original birth certificate and photo ID. After proof of citizenship has been presented, you will receive a free Mexican Tourist Card, which you must keep with you at all times when in Mexico. This permit must be given to officials on departure. If you lose your Mexican Tourist Card, you can obtain a copy or permission to leave the country from the local Immigration office.

Customs Regulations: Upon entering Mexico, you must fill out one customs form per family. The form will be given to you upon entry, by the crew of the ship or plane, or at the point of entry. It is important that you fill out the form correctly, as you may be subject to a random search. You may freely bring your personal luggage, 20 packs of cigarettes, 25 cigars or 200 grams of tobacco, and up to 3 liters of wine, beer or liquor. For more specific regulations, contact your embassy.

When you are returning after a trip of at least 48 hours, you may bring back $400 worth of duty-free merchandise (after that the next $1000 is subject to a 4% duty.) Perishable foods are not allowed into the United States. You can get more information from the US Custom Service at http://www.customs.gov.

Safety: The government of Mexico is working hard to improve safety throughout the country for both citizens and tourists. It is advisable not to carry lots of cash. Store any valuables in your hotel safe when possible, and keep a copy of your important document numbers in a safe place.

For more information, contact:
Mexico Tourism Board
Website: www.visitmexico.com
Telephone (From US): 800-929-4555
or 305-347-4338

w e l c o m e   t o

E U R O P E

© Daniel Thierry

F R A N C E

France offers enough diversity in landscape and culture to fill a lifetime of vacations.

The landscapes range from the coasts of Brittany to the hills of Provence, the canyons of the Pyrenees to the bays of Corsica, and from the valleys of the Dordogne to the peaks of the Alps. Each region, with its own local culture and style, has its own style of architecture, food, fashion and even its own dialect.

Whatever your fancy, France offers a place to make your honeymoon or vacation the trip of a lifetime!

Paris: Like all the world's greatest capitals, Paris lives at a fast pace, by day - by night and especially at rush hours. It is divided into 20 arrondissements that spiral out like a snail shell from the first, centered around the Louvre, of which certain quarters like the Montmartre, Montparnasse, and the Marais are real villages within the city. Paris is the world capital of art and culture because it has some of the most famous museums and monuments in the world like the Eiffel Tower, the Notre-Dame cathedral, and many more. With its history and architectural patrimony, Paris is living, moving, and evolving every day.

© Hubert Camille

Western France (Brittany, Normandy, Western Loire, Center Loire Valley, Poitou Charente): From magnificent Renaissance chateaux and soaring Gothic cathedrals to sleepy vineyards and sunbaked villages; from tender fresh oysters, tangy cheeses and fluffy crepes to elegant cognacs and the finest butter in the world, the five regions that make up "Le Grand Ouest" offer

PARIS - CLIMATE		
MONTH	HI	LO
JAN	42°	32°
FEB	44°	33°
MAR	50°	38°
APR	57°	42°
MAY	64°	49°
JUN	70°	54°
JUL	75°	56°
AUG	75°	56°
SEPT	70°	53°
OCT	60°	50°
NOV	50°	40°
DEC	45°	35°

Temperatures are provided in °Fahrenheit and based on averages.

a cultural and culinary odyssey as rich and varied as any in France.

Northern France (Nord Pas de Calais, Picardie): Just over the border from Belgium and a hop or a tunnel across the Channel from England lies the Nord/Pas-de-Calais region of Northern France, a picturesque land, which consists of contrasting forests, gentle meadows, and rolling hills dotted with windmills. Sandy beaches and imposing cliffs make up the 150-mile stretch of coastline. Visitors can cruise the network of canals and rivers and explore the wide countryside and nature reserves. There is almost always a fair, fete or festival going on.

The Picaderie region, with its calm woods, great forests, green pastures and quiet ponds blended with the peaceful, simple lifestyle of its people, is the birthplace of Gothic architecture with six cathedrals in the area. Senlis offers a true taste of an unspoiled French village. Prehistoric sites, Gallo-roman remains, abbeys, churches, castles and WWI battle sites bear vivid witness to this region's rich history. Pottery and lace are a very well known product of this region.

Eastern France (Lorraine, Alsace, Champagne, Franche - Comte, Burgundy): Eastern France offers a region filled with renowned museums and monuments, vineyards and gastronomic tables. No must-see site or happening is ever far off highways and picturesque bi-ways, always close by canals tailormade for drifting in hotel barges or self-piloted boats, and easily accessible from back roads and nature trails beckoning hikers and bikers. Life in the slow lane of this five-province region can be very nice indeed.

Central France (Limousin, Auvergne): The four departments which constitute Auvergne - Haute-Loire, Cantal, Puy-de-D&ocir-cme, Allier - form a striking province of sharp-peaked extinct volcanic mountains and sparkling crater lakes. A land of amazing geological diversity, webbed with little-traveled roads, Auvergne is dotted with castles, historic ruins and walled villages.

The Limousin region, on the western slopes of the Massif Central attracts visitors in search of unspoiled countryside. Hundreds of ancient village churches dot the landscape as well as more imposing abbey churches and fortresses. The many lakes and rivers of this area provide endless possibilities for canoeing, sailing, windsurfing and other water sports. Fishermen will also appreciate the abundant trout in the regions' streams and brooks.

Southern France (Corsica, Rhône-Alpes, Provence- Côte d'Azur, Languedoc-Roussillon, Riviera): Once described as "That mountain in the sea," the isle of Corsica, with over 600 miles of sandy beaches, and crested by 9,000 foot peaks, lies in the heart of the Western Mediterranean. Easily accessible by air and sea, Corsica is just 110 miles off the Southeastern coast of France and 50 miles from the shores of Italy. May/June and early fall are ideal times to explore this 3,500 square mile gem.

The Languedoc-Roussillon region, where the Pyrénées Mountains plunge into the Mediterranean, has begun to come into its own with a sparkling group of new yacht-port resorts. Long known as an area of abundant historic riches and distinctive Catalan cuisine and folklore, it has now also become a modern resort area whose stunning architecture gleams under the Mediterranean sun.

© Hubert Camille

The landscapes of Provence—Côte d'Azur (St-Rémy-de-Provence) inspired Van Gogh and Cézanne and changed the course of modern painting. Compressed within a few hundred miles' radius is scenery as varied and magnificent as anywhere in Europe. Vineyards of Gigondas, silvery groves in olive-capital Nyons, and lavender- scented hills from Valréas to Vaison-la-Romaine. The bold silhouettes of Provence encompass the monumental bald rock of Les Baux, and cypress and cedars blocked against azure skies at Arles.

Rhône-Alps. Springing from a glacier, the Rhône River flows south through France toward the sunshine of the Mediterranean. Its broad valley embraces thriving cities, Roman ruins and medieval castles, fabled vineyards and the snowy peaks of the French Alps.

Riviera (Haut-de-Cagnes): Just a bit back from the shore, a less publicized side of the Riviera offers a world of romantic hill towns and perched villages balanced on craggy peaks. Worn stone stairs and cobbled byways lead through modest hamlets crowding around ancient chateaux. Clusters of narrow-fronted houses, Roman ruins, modern museums and perfume centers cling to steep hillsides.

As long as anyone can remember, this French seaside Riviera was Europe's classic resort. Graced by palms, sub-tropical flowers, the well-named Azure Coast ranked for over a century as the preferred playground for those willing to settle for nothing less than first class. With the sheltering Alps as backdrop, calm blue Mediterranean at the door-step, France's glamorous southern coast was winter rendezvous for affluent elite who came to casinos, gala villa soirees and enjoyed the good life.

Only in comparatively recent times did the Riviera add the swinging summer scene - where the Bikini got its start and a whole new leisure life-style evolved. Mid-July to early September makes the high season, when film stars come for their quota of sun and sports from golf to race-track.

© Nicole LeJeune

FRANCE

THINGS TO SEE AND DO

Enjoy an original break in a friendly French holiday village, know as "Villages de Vacances". Everyone will enjoy a break in our comfortable holiday villages in their attractive settings. It's the ideal formula for anyone looking for freedom, authenticity, and friendliness.

Holiday villages are a good way of getting to know France at your leisure. They are close to beautiful countryside, where you can explore an unparalleled natural and cultural heritage and enjoy an authentic art of living. Spread over the 22 French regions, there are a total of almost 700 holiday villages, the great majority holding the Loisirs de France quality label.

Designed for a very wide public, both young and old, couples and families, groups and individuals, there are accommodation packages for every kind of holiday visitor. Depending on the destination, you can go full board, half board or self-catering (bungalows, apartments…). Most of these villages have rooms adapted for the disabled. As for catering, you can choose between the local inns and restaurants or typical dishes and menus provided by the village itself.

© Hubert Camille

© Hubert Camille

Integrated in special natural sites, at the seaside, in the mountains, or in the country, holiday villages also offer a wide range of leisure activities. When it comes to sports, you have mountain-biking, golf, kayak, tennis, archery, swimming, riding, sail-boarding, skiing…. If you prefer cultural pursuits, you can explore the local heritage and enjoy themed evenings and gastronomic events. Qualified entertainment and organizing personnel will be there to help you enjoy your stay.

Nightlife: Nightclubs are everywhere, in the remotest corners of France. Their style and music vary a lot from one place to another, but closing time is fixed at 5 o'clock in the morning.

Dining: Throughout France, you will find all sorts of restaurants, from simple, small, cozy ones to famous, gourmet restaurants, along with brasseries, inns, tearooms, etc. Bread and carafes of water are included in the price shown, as well as all service charges, even if it is usual to leave a tip.

Traditionally in France, there are three meals a day. Breakfast (a meal composed of a hot drink of coffee, tea, or chocolate, croissants and/or bread, butter, and jam); Lunch (the main meal usually consisting of a starter, main course, and/or a dessert usually finished off with an espresso); Dinner, usually starting around 8:00PM (typically not a large meal. A snack (around 4:00PM) is traditionally reserved for children, although some adults change it into tea and cakes.

The majority of restaurants serve food from 12.00pm to 3.00pm and from 7.00pm to 11.00pm. Some will welcome you even later – larger brasseries and those near to railway stations. In large towns, small grocery shops stay open until midnight. During the day, you can eat at any time in sandwich shops, fast-food restaurants, or again in some brasseries.

Shopping: Paris is one of the fashion capitals of the world. Go window-shopping at the great couturiers, along the Avenue Montaigne (Yves Saint Laurent, Christian Dior…), the Faubourg Saint-Honoré (Hermès, Gucci), the Place de la Madeleine, the Saint-Sulpice quarter or Sèvres-Babylone, between the Rues de Grenelle, du Cherche-Midi and des Saints-Pères (Versace, Sonia Ryckiel…).

Alongside these famous names, a number of designers have appeared: Agnès B. and

Claudie Pierlot (at Les Halles or Saint-Sulpice), Kenzo (Place des Victoires), Ventilo, Et Vous… in the Marais…

The department stores: Printemps, Galeries Lafayette, Bon Marché, Samaritaine or BHV, are Parisian institutions…some of which have branches in the regions. They provide numerous brand names and offer every sort of merchandise.

For bargain hunters, two large flea markets are held outside central Paris: Porte de Vanves and Porte de Saint-Ouen (the largest of all).

Another Parisian speciality – the booksellers with their stalls along the banks of the Seine around the Saint-Michel quarter. Antique books, all sorts of second-hand books, comic strips, post cards…You can find everything there at all prices. It is well worth strolling along! Markets: going to the market is a pleasure. Nothing surprising in that, there is always a happy mix of colors and smells. Paris has many and various markets: the flower market on the Ile de la Cité, bird markets, organic markets, and food markets in every quarter. A real walkabout in a good natured and typical Parisian atmosphere!

In the Regions, the town centre often has a number of clothes shops which are just as good as those in Paris. Some towns have second-hand clothes shops with keen prices or very trendy shops.

Every town or village in the different regions also has their weekly market; here you will find lots of regional products.

Parks & Gardens: In the last twenty years or so, France has been rediscovering its parks and gardens. This increasingly lively interest is perceived as a genuine social phenomenon. The fashion for the art of gardening is behind the creation of many new gardens and the restoration of historic gardens. The châteaux and monuments are the main focus of this interest. Medieval gardens, Renaissance gardens, formal or landscape gardens, contemporary or landscaped gardens: their style matches the style of the châteaux, museums and monu-

© Hubert Camille

ments. Each season, they host themed tours, exhibitions and sales of rare plants and festivals.

The medieval garden can be found at the Abbaye de Fontrevaud and at the Château d'Angers with beds of medicinal flowers and plants. The decorative elements of the Renaissance garden add colour to the flower beds of Cheverny. Straight lines mark out the formal gardens of Versailles, Chantilly, Saint-Cloud, Vaux-le-Vicomte, Fontainebleau and Pau. The landscape garden is developed at Champs-sur-Marne and Chantilly. The historic garden becomes landscaped at the Carrousel of the Louvre and at the Tuileries in Paris, but also at Chaumont-sur-Loire. At the turn of a path or encountering a vista, you are bound to be impressed by the orchards of Talcy, the orangery of Meudon and Versailles, or follies, such as the pagoda of Chanteloup.

Museums and Monuments: The towns and regions of France have all sorts of museums and monuments for visitors.

Museum opening times vary, but please note that municipal museums are closed on Mondays, and national museums are closed on Tuesdays (except the Musée d'Orsay in Paris, which is closed on Mondays).

The Association Intermusées offers The Paris museum pass which allows you to discover the extraordinary cultural and historical wealth

© Daniel Thierry

of the Ile-de-France region... and save money!

The carte musées-monuments gives unlimited access to over 60 museums and monuments in Paris and the surrounding region. Choice of three formulas : 1, 3 or 5 days (consecutive days only).

The pass provides unlimited and immediate admission to monuments and permanent museum collections. The pass has no expiry date; passes may be bought in advance and used at any time.

Each pass is issued with a brochure containing all the practical information on the museums and monuments involved in the plan (addresses, phone numbers, opening hours, days closed etc...).

WEDDINGS ON LOCATION

Because of France's strict requirements, it is not possible to marry there during a short stay. One of the parties must have lived in France for at least 40 consecutive days prior to the wedding. Banns must be posted at

least 10 days before the wedding, at least 30 days into the stay in France. The banns and civil ceremony must take place at the city hall in the area in which the party lives. Before having a religious ceremony, you must have a civil ceremony. The religious officiant will require proof that the marriage has already performed civilly. The 40-day period cannot be waived, no matter what.

You will receive a booklet which is an official document and in which all births, deaths, divorces and name changes are then recorded for your new family. You may also receive a marriage certificate by writing to the city hall in which your civil ceremony is performed, including a self-addressed envelope with the correct postage, the date of the marriage and the full names of both parties, including the wife's maiden name.

In order to be married, you must each present the following:

- A valid US passport or French residence permit

- A certified copy of your birth certificate

© Fabian Charaffi

less than 3 months old along with a sworn translation. You can find a list of sworn translators at the city hall where you will be married.

- An affidavit of marital status (certificate of celibacy) less than 3 months old. It can be done in the form of a notarized affidavit executed before an American Consular office in France.

- An affidavit of law and customs. It is a statement about US marriage laws, certifying that the American citizen is free to contract marriage in France and that the marriage will be recognized in the United States.

- A medical certificate less than 2 months old. The marriage banns cannot be posted until each party has obtained a pre-nuptial medical certificate attesting that the individual was examined by a doctor en vue de mariage.

- Two proofs of domicile (i.e. electricity or telephone bills, rent)

- If you wish to have a prenuptial contract, the French notary preparing the contract will give you a certificate which must be presented

Each city hall has its own requirements and may not require all of the above documents. Check well in advance with the city hall in which you plan to be married to be sure you have the correct documents.

© Hubert Camille

LOCAL INFORMATION

Climate: Usually, the temperature in Paris will range between 50-75° F from May - October. July and August are the warmest months.

Brittany in the far west is the wettest French locale, especially between October and November. May is the driest month for the Bretons.

In the South, the Mediterranean coast has the driest climate with any noticeable rain coming in spring and autumn.

Provence (in the southeast) occasionally plays reluctant host to le mistral, a strong, hot and dry wind that blows in over the winter for periods of only a few days up to a couple of weeks.

On the Atlantic Coast and in Bordeaux, (the region known as the Aquitane), the climate is generally mild with temperatures averaging 45° F in winter and 65° F in summer. There's no lack of sun. This region revels in warm, dry weather and receives an average of 170 days of sunshine a year. In fact, Parisians are known to say that Bordeaux has the best climate in France. With the days fresh and possibly damp in the spring and often sunny in the autumn, the climate is one of the most

important factors behind Bordeaux's high quality (as well as the wine it produces).

The weather in the French Alps varies from north to south. The northern Alps (the Savoy) are subject to oceanic influences resulting in abundant precipitation year round with low temperatures. During the warm season, winds blow along this region's wide valleys and by midday, warm air rises from the valleys, causing clouds to form around most mountain summits, indicating fine and steady weather. The heights can attract storms that are both violent and spectacular.

The southern Alps (Provence and the Cote D'Azur) enjoy a typical Mediterranean climate, with lots of sunshine, dry weather, clear skies and no mist or fog. Autumn is the best time of year in this region. Occasionally, violent storms may occur, but they are always followed by sunny spells with the air pure, light and invigorating.

Peak Season: Varies by region.

Language: The national language of France is French.

Currency: The national currency in France is the Euro - EUR. U.S. dollars are not accepted in most establishments; however, some hotels, shops and restaurants may

© Hubert Camille

accept U.S. dollars at an agreed upon exchange rate.

Standard Time Zone: UTC (Coordinated Universal Time/GMT (Greenwich Mean Time) + 1 hour

Entry Requirements: A valid passport is required for all US citizens and foreign nationals entering France. No visa is needed for American visitors staying less than 90 days, unless you are a student planning to study in France. For longer stays, you must apply for a temporary-stay visa, long-term visa, or residence card.

Customs Regulations: Returning US citizens who have been in France more than two days can return with $400 of merchandise duty-free. For those who wish to bring more of France back home with them, a flat rate of 10% is charged on the next $1000 worth of purchases (the duty-free limit in gifts is $100.) It's a good idea to retain the receipts from your purchases should they be requested by a Customs Inspector upon your return to the US.

For more information, contact:
French Government Tourist Office
444 Madison Avenue
New York, NY 10022-6903

Website: www.franceguide.com
Telephone (From US): 401-286-8310

© J.P. Gratien

G R E E C E

The territory of Greece stretches from the south Aegean to the Balkan countries. The historic sites of Greece span a time frame over four thousand years, leaving much for the curious traveler to discover.

Greece, as it is visited today, was born of diverse influences. Romans, Arabs, Latin Crusaders, Venetians, Slavs, Albanians, Turks, and Italians have all contributed to the landscape of modern Greece: from churches and monasteries to imposing castles. Most notably, the influence of four centuries of Ottoman Turkish rule contributed greatly to Greek music, cuisine, language and way of life.

Crete, the largest island in Greece, is the most popular vacation destination in all of Greece. It separates the Aegean from the Libyan Sea and marks the boundary between Europe and Africa.

The landscape of Crete ranges from majestic mountains to sandy beaches, connected by flowing streams. The built landscape contains many historic sites and relics; elegant pieces of architecture; world-class museums; ancient ruins, fortresses, castles and monasteries; and so much more. Culturally, you'll find an area filled with fellow travelers enjoying the wondrous sights, sounds and flavors that truly make Crete a popular Mediterranean destination.

THINGS TO SEE AND DO

CRETE

Recreation: Crete offers much to see and do. It is very popular for water activities, including windsurfing, snorkeling, diving and waterskiing. On land, vacationers enjoy hiking and bik-

GREECE	-	CLIMATE
MONTH	HI	LO
JAN	58°	48°
FEB	60°	48°
MAR	61°	50°
APR	68°	52°
MAY	72°	58°
JUN	80°	65°
JUL	84°	71°
AUG	83°	71°
SEPT	81°	68°
OCT	74°	62°
NOV	68°	58°
DEC	65°	52°

Temperatures are provided in °Fahrenheit and based on averages.

ing through the landscape's generous offering of breathtaking scenery, including tall mountains, deep gorges and a rugged southern coast. The less adventurous traveler, or those seeking leisurely-paced adventure, will enjoy guided tours of Crete's unique heritage sites, old farmhouses, monasteries and villages. There are also hundreds of outdoor cafes where one can people-watch while sipping a "sweat" or "medium" coffee, or a glass of "tsikoudia" (raki) while playing a game of cards or "tavli" (backgammon).

Special Points of Interest: A popular site in Crete is its capital, Iraklion. Here, the Archeological Museum proudly displays original artifacts such as statues, mosaics, pottery, jewelry and other artwork found at nearby archeological sites, notably Knossis and Festos, which are worth a visit while on the island. Knossis, once the capital of the ancient Minoan civilization, is in fact the most visited site on Crete. Knossos boasts ruins that date back to the 15th century BC. You can view ancient ruins in the same state and condition as they were uncovered as well as view the partially reconstructed Palace of King Minos with portions rebuilt to reflect how the palace looked originally, with authentic colors, copies of mosaics and other artifacts in their actual places.

The city walls still standing today are reminiscent of the Cyclopean walls of Tiryns and Mycenae. One can also see the remains of a small 1st c. B.C. temple of Demeter, a Roman theatre and enormous vaulted cisterns of the Roman.

In the District of Rethimno, visit Armeni, a Minoan cemetery with tombs carved out of rocks; Axos with finds from a big Greek-Roman city; Eleftherna where recent excavations held at the area brought to light important monuments from a Greek-Roman city; and Zominthos where a minion settlement has been discovered at the Nida plateau.

In the District of Heraklion, visit: Aghia Trias, with ruins of a royal villa, which most probably was the summer palace of the Phaistos rulers; Amnissos, where archaeologists found the Villa of the Frescoes of Amnissos, also called the Villa of the Lilies; Gortyn (Gortis), a city that flourished particularly during the Roman era boasting the distinctive monuments of the Praetorium (2nd c. AD.), the Nymphaion (2nd c. AD.) where the Nymphs were worshipped, the temple of Pythian Apollo the sanctuary of the Egyptian divinities, and the Odeon, where the famous inscription with the laws of Gortyn was found; and Kato Simi, Vianos, the Sanctuary of Hermes and Aphrodite dating from the Greek-Roman era.

In the District of Lassithi, visit Dreros (Driros), an archaeological site of this ancient Greek city comprises two acropolises with an Archaic agora between them; Gournia, the best preserved of the Minoan settlements, and one of the most noteworthy archaeological sites in Crete; Kato Zakros, the site of a luxurious Minoan palace, the fourth in significance on the island, which produced a number of important finds now in the Heraklion Archaeological Museum.

Nightlife: Greece is famous for its lively lifestyle. You will find lots of theatres, cafes, shops, music performances, cinemas, bars, casinos

and night clubs. Typically, night clubs open around 10.00p.m. and don't shut down until dawn. With your nights covered, it is also quite easy to find places for entertainment during the day.

Whether with fellow vacationers or seasoned locals, you will find something to suit your individual desire for entertainment and walk away an enriched person.

Dining: On Crete, you will find numerous tavernas and ouzeries serving tasty "meze", a specialty of the area: yogurt and honey, sweet tarts (kaltzounia), pies made of wild greens flavored with fennel, fried cheese (staka), rabbit stew, cheese pie from Hora Sfakion, cockles, boiled goat, fish, sea urchins, octopus and cuttlefish cooked on charcoal and fried squid to be tasted at seaside tavernas. And everywhere, the delectable Cretan wine is the perfect accompaniment to the tasty local fare. Every saint's feast day is celebrated with gusto at dozens of villages throughout the island, all of Crete throbbing to the sound of the Cretan lyre and the rhythm of the local dances, the pentozali and the sousta.

Greeks in all walks of life view evening dining as a pleasurable source of entertainment. Meals are often served late and dining outdoors is preferred. In most establishments that cater to Greek clientele, service is likely to be friendly and informal whereas in deluxe restaurants and resorts, service is likely to be more formal.

A meal in Greece is highlighted by a selection of hot and cold hors d'oeuvres (mezedes), which are served on small plates placed family style in the center of the table.

GREECE

Mezedes are comprised of such items as melitzanosalata (mashed eggplant with oil, lemon and garlic), taramosalata (Greek caviar spread), dolmadakia (meat or rice rolled in grapevine leaves), kalamarakia (deep fried squid), tyropitakia (cheese wrapped in strudel leaves), kolokithakia (deep fried zucchini) usually served with tsatsiki (cucumber, yogurt and garlic spread), keftedes (meatballs), stuffed peppers and tomatoes, pickled octopus and more.

The main course is typically a casserole or grilled meat or fish. Tasty meat, grilled cuts of meat and of course the well-known charcoal grilled lamb or pork called souvlaki are also quite popular.

Salad is usually ordered with the main course and is usually prepared with fresh vegetables or cooked dandelions (greens are boiled in water, drained and served with oil and lemon). Horiatiki, the usual Greek salad, consists of tomato slices, cucumber slices, olives and feta cheese dressed with oil and vinegar. All seasonal vegetables, such as artichokes, beans, peas, carrots, and zucchini are often cooked and served together in the casserole dishes rather than separately.

Greece produces a variety of cheeses. The most commonly offered in restaurants are feta (white semi-soft and salted), kasseri (yellow semi-soft), graviera (hard) and manouri (unsalted, creamy and fattening).

Desserts are a delectable treat, including baklava (consisting of strudel leaves and walnuts) and kataifi (nuts wrapped in shredded wheat with a honey syrup). In the summer, sweets give way to fresh fruit such as peaches, melon, watermelon, grapes and pears.

Shopping: Crete's rich tradition in handwoven fabrics, embroideries, wood-carvings and jewelry is readily seen in shops throughout Crete. Examples, old and new, can be found in the marketplaces of the large cities and also in the villages, where you may even have the opportnunity to see these age-old crafts being practiced.

In the shops of Sitia, Ierapetra and Anogia, you will be impressed by the spread out "patanies", traditional local woven fabrics in dazzling colors, and everywhere one sees skillfully crafted ceramics and leather goods. In the "Stivanadika" district of Chania (Skridlof St.) traditional boots (stivania) are

still made in the old-fashioned way, because though it may seem strange even today, there are Cretans who still wear their traditional costume. In Chania's only marketplace, every kind of food, fruit and vegetable produced in the fertile valleys, hot houses and mountain regions, is laid out on display. Exotic avocadoes, Belgian endive and bananas, juicy oranges and fragrant melons, succulent figs and tasty prickly pears, delicious grapes, sweet tomatoes, tender cucumbers, fresh-picked greens from the hillsides, snails, mouth-watering sardines, tempting lobster, kid from the islet of Gavdos, honey perfumed with thyme, and wonderful cheeses – graviera (gruyere), myzithra (ricotta) , fresh white cheese, and soft, luscious staka.

Museums/Galleries: Churches and Monasteries: Capital of the Roman province of Cyrenaica, Gortyn became the first Christian community in Greece in the year 65 A.D., after St. Paul appointed Titus as bishop, with a mission to convert the whole of Crete. In the 16th century, the Cretan School of painting, closely allied with Byzantine tradition, produced numerous painters of icons, both famous and unknown.

Crete is scattered with the ruins of countless frescoed churches dating from 961, when the Byzantines recaptured Crete from the Saracens, to 1204, when the island fell into the hands of the Venetians.

WEDDINGS ON LOCATION

Foreign nationals in Greece may be married either in a civil ceremony or a religious ceremony; both are recognize as legal under the laws of Greece.

Marriage licenses can be obtained from one's current place of residence, prior to coming to Greece, and are generally accepted by the Greek authorities. This only applies, however, if neither the bride nor the groom is resident in Greece.

Valid American Marriage Licenses are accepted in Greece provided that they do not contain restrictive statements. (For example, "This license is valid for county X" or "Marriage will take place in the state of California, etc." If these statements cannot be removed, the license should be amended by the issuing authority to include GREECE as one of the places in which the marriage can take place. It is also recommended that the marriage license be endorsed with the Apostle stamp, a special authentication for documents to be used outside the United States and can be obtained form your local State Secretary.

Marriage Requirements:

• A passport or other travel document.

• A certified copy of your birth certificate, along with an official translation. Official translations can be obtained at the Translation Department of the Greek Ministry of Foreign Affairs, 3 Voukourestious Street, 3rd floor in Athens. The translation may take up to a week to prepare.

• If applicable, documentary evidence (death certificate or final divorce decree) of the termination of a previous marriage (the most recent, if more than one), along with an official translation.

• Confirmation by an American Consular Officer that there is no impediment to the marriage (i.e. neither party is under 18 years o f age, there is no existing undissolved marriage, etc.). This confirmation is issued in the form of an Affidavit of Marriage signed under oath by the American citizen bride or groom before a Consular Officer in Athens or Thessaloniki. (For minors under 18 years of age, a court decision approving the marriage is required.) The affidavit must be completed in English and Greek. The Embassy's Notorial Unit and the Consulate General perform Notorial services. The fee for the affidavit is approximately US$10.00.

• A copy of the newspaper in which the wedding notice was published. Wedding notices should be published in one of the local newspapers in the Greek language (the names should be phonetically written in Greek and not in latin characters) before the application for a marriage license is submitted. In small towns where newspapers are not published, notices are posted by the mayor or president of the community at the City Hall or Community Office.

• Following the ceremony, the marriage must be registered at the Vital statistics Office (Lixiarcheio). This applies to all marriages, whether civil or religious, and must be done within 40 days following the ceremony. After 40 days, the marriage can only be registered with the payment of revenue stamps. After 90 days, the marriage can only be registered with the District Attorneys' authorization (addressed to the Registrar of the Office of Vital Statistics) and the payment of revenue stamps. Marriages can be registered by either spouse, or by a third party who is in possession of a power-of-attorney signed before a Greek Notary Public giving him/her authority to take all steps necessary to effect registration of the marriage. Marriages which are not registered have no legal validity.

LOCAL INFORMATION

Climate: The climate of Crete is one of the mildest in Europe. Greece enjoys mild winters and very hot, dry summers cooled by seasonal breezes, the meltemi, which moderate even the hottest months of July and August. Rainfall is rare during the summer months. Autumn is the mildest season, when temperatures are often higher than in spring. The mountains that run across the island act as a barrier to the weather, often creating different conditions in northern and southern Crete.

Language: The primary language spoken in Greece is Greek. English is spoken in hotels, most restaurants, department stores and by the "Tourist Police", who wear a badge on

their lapel depicting the English or American flags.

Currency: The official currency of Greece is the Euro - EUR.

Time Zone: UTC (Coordinated Universal Time/GMT (Greenwich Mean Time) +2 hours: EET (Eastern European Time)

Entry Requirements: US citizens require a passport valid for at least three months after the end of their stay. No visa is required but a return ticket is necessary.

Safety: Greece is considered a safe destination. True to all tourist areas, visitors are advised not to carry valuables on them.

For more information, contact:

Greek National Tourist Organization
Olympic Tower
645 Fifth Avenue, 9th Floor
New York, New York 10022

Website: http://www.greektourism.com

Telephone: (212) 421-5777

© Hotel Gritti Palace, Venice

I T A L Y

Italy is geographically divided into 20 regions (regioni). Of these regions, two of the most popular destinations with romantic travelers are Veneto (home to Venice) and Latium (home to Rome), and Tuscany (home to Florence).

© Italian Government Tourist Board

VENICE

Located in Northeastern Italy, Venice is arguably the most beautiful and romantic city in the world, unlike any other. It is entirely romantic and, as breathtaking it is in pictures and on film, positively dreamlike when visiting the real thing. Aside from the thousands of fellow visitors, Venice has a character as unique as the landscape it is built upon ...impressive architecture, exotic art, and romantic vignettes abound. The arts abound in Venice; from classic architecture lining the canals to modern art found in contemporary museums.

In spite of the undying allure of Venice, the city itself is in quite a state of turmoil. It is said that the city is sinking at a rate of 2 1/2 inches per decade. At the same time, the damp climate, pollution and occasional unpleasant smelling canals are further contributing to the city's decay. It is quite possible, that Venice will be nothing more than a legend within a few generations. The state of deca yis being studied with hopes of salvaging the world famous city. Until then, visitors will take in all there is to see and do while the gift of Venice still exists.

ROME	-	CLIMATE
MONTH	HI	LO
JAN	55°	38°
FEB	56°	39°
MAR	59°	42°
APR	64°	46°
MAY	71°	53°
JUN	78°	60°
JUL	83°	64°
AUG	83°	65°
SEPT	78°	60°
OCT	71°	53°
NOV	63°	46°
DEC	57°	41°

Temperatures are provided in °Fahrenheit and based on averages.

THINGS TO SEE AND DO

Venice is a city built entirely on water and comprised of more than 100 separate islands divided by roughly 150 canals and crossed by 400 bridges. The Grand Canal is the equivalent to Venice's Main Street. This waterway winds its way past awe-inspiring architecture in a medley of Renaissance, Gothic, Baroque and Rococo styles.

While the city has hundreds of bridges, the Grand Canal can only be crossed on foot at three points: Ponte degli Scalzi, near the train station (Ferrovia); Ponte di Rialto, at the Rialto; and at Ponte dell'Accademia. To view the Grand Canal in its full glory, you will want to hop aboard a water vessel. There are several options to choose from:

Vaporetto (water buses): Tickets cost about US$6 per trip but there are 24-hour, multi-day and weekly tickets that are less expensive per ride.

Traghetto (traditional gondola ferries): For a cheap, short ride across the canal (rather than going the length of it), try the traghetto, which embark from a half-dozen points between the railroad station and the Campo del Traghetto near St. Mark's Square.

Water Taxis: A short trip on the canal by water taxi can cost approximately US$80 to $100. Official water taxis have a black registration number on a yellow background, and can be hired at Piazzale Roma, Rialto, San Marco and the Lido.

© Italian Government Tourist Board

ly restored. In the 15th century, clerics found guilty of immoral behavior were suspended in wooden cages from the tower, sometimes forced to subsist on bread and water for as long as a year, other times left to starve.

Like Venice, Murano is made up of a number of smaller islands linked by bridges. It's known for its glassworks, which you can visit to see how glass is made. The houses are simpler than many found in other parts of Venice; as they traditionally were workmen's cottages. Just before the junction with Murano's Grand Canal -- 250 yards up from the landing stage -- is the Chiesa di San Pietro Martire, a 16th-century reconstruction of an earlier Gothic church that also has several works by Venetian masters, notably a Madonna and Child by Giovanni Bellini and St. Jerome by Veronese.

The first historical evidence of Carnevale (Carnival) in Venice dates from 1097, and for centuries the city has marked the days that precede quaresima (Lent), the 40 days of abstinence leading up to Palm Sunday, with feasting, concerts, street performances, parties and celebrations. Masked revelers fill the squares, and exclusive parties take place, in the city's palazzi for the 10 -14 days leading up to the start of Lent.

Nightlife: At first, it appears that Venice doesn't live much at night. As night falls, the noise and traffic quiets down, boat traffic slows and businesses shut down. Even most bacari (wine bars), which seem like natural spots for after-hours gathering, turn out the lights around 9 PM. But there is a night scene in Venice, subtly spread among many neighborhood locali (nightspots) that stay open until 1 or 2 AM. In these spots, you will often find good crowds enjoying live music.

Gondolas: Gondolas depart from St. Mark's Square, the Rialto, Piazzale Roma and the railway station. Each vessel carries up to six passengers and fares are set by a central agency at about $75 for 50 minutes. This is a minimum fee; gondoliers may demand more, but you can bargain for a shorter ride for less money. It may be to your benefit to book your ride in advance through local tour operators.

An opulent blend of Byzantine and Romanesque styles, Venice's gem, Basilica of St. Mark's (Basilica di San Marco), is laid out in the form of a Greek cross topped off with five domes. It was inaugurated in 1094 as the resting place of St. Mark the Evangelist. The basilica is famous for its 43,055 square ft of stunning mosaics; the earliest mosaics are from the 11th and 12th centuries; later ones were done as late as the 16th century. Tiny gold tiles were mounted at a slight angle to contribute to a shimmering glow cast by the light.

Piazza San Marco is the most famous piazza in Venice and its surrounding byways. Despite the heavy tourist crowds, you will see why Napoleon called this "the most beautiful drawing room in all of Europe."

Campanile. Venice's famous brick bell tower (325 ft tall, plus the angel) stood here for 1,000 years before it collapsed in 1912. It was rebuilt according to the old plan. Jacopo Sansovino's marble loggia below, dating from the early 16th century, was crushed and prompt-

© Westin Excelsior - Venice, Italy

Night nightspots will generally fall into three categories. The "osterie musicali" offer full meals, cicheti (little savory snacks), beer, inexpensive wine, and live music. Many of them also serve as galleries for local artists. Then there are the English and Irish style pubs, with beer on tap and occasional live music. These pubs tend to be especially popular with the younger crowd. Finally, there are the late-night cafes and piano bars that offer more late-night enjoyment.

Dining: The cuisine of Venice is based on fish and seafood – granseola (crab), moeche (small, soft-shelled crab), and seppie or seppioline (cuttlefish) all are prominently featured. It's usually priced by the etto (100 grams, or about _ pound) and can be quite expensive. Antipasti may take the form of a seafood salad, prosciutto di San Daniele (of the Friuli region), or pickled vegetables. As a first course, Venetians favor risotto, the creamy rice dish, prepared here with vegetables or shellfish. Pasta, too, is paired with seafood sauces. Pasticcio di pesce is pasta baked with fish, usually baccalà (salt cod). A classic first course here and elsewhere in the Veneto region is pasta e fagioli (thick bean soup with pasta). Bigoli is a local pasta shaped like short, fat spaghetti, usually served with nero di seppia (squid-ink sauce). Polenta, a creamy cornmeal dish, is another popular of regional cooking. It's often served with fegato alla veneziana (liver with onions).

Shopping: Alluring shops abound in Venice. You'll find countless vendors of trademark Venetian wares such as glass and lace. For There are also jewelers, antiques dealers, and high-fashion boutiques, on the same level of quality as those in Italy's larger cities but often maintaining a uniquely Venetian flair.

It's always a good idea to mark the location of a shop that interests you on your map; otherwise you may not be able to find it again in the maze of tiny streets. Regular store hours are usually 9-12:30 and 3:30 or 4-7:30 PM; some stores are closed on Saturday afternoon or Monday morning. Food shops are open 8-1 and 5-7:30, and are closed all day Sunday and on Wednesday afternoon. However, many tourist-oriented

© Westin Europa - Venice, Italy

shops are open all day, every day. Some shops close for both a summer and a winter vacation.

Museums: Hanging in the Accademia Galleries is unquestionably the most extraordinary collection of Venetian art in the world. Works range from 14th-century Gothic to the Golden Age of the 15th and 16th centuries, including oils by Giovanni Bellini, Giorgione, Titian, and Tintoretto, and superb later works by Veronese and Tiepolo.

ROME

Rome in the Latium Territory: The Latium region stretches from the western buttresses of the Apennines to the Tyrrhenian Sea. The landscape is varied and presents flatlands on the coastline and ridges and highlands inland. Latium has four very ancient volcanic distincts, where the craters of extinct volcanoes form the lakes of Bolsena, Vico, Bracciano, Albano and Nemi.

THINGS TO SEE AND DO

Rome's marvelous collection of piazzas make great resting places on your walks around the city. Vast and beautiful, Piazza Navona was laid out on the ruins of Domitian's stadium. It's lined with baroque palaces and holds three fountains: Fontana del Moro, Fontana di Nettuno and in the centre of the square Bernini's magnificent Fontana dei Fiumi. Traditionally, from the beginning of December till the Epiphany, this piazza is occupied by stalls selling sweets and toys.

Special Points of Interest: Michelangelo's Piazza del Campidoglio is the star attraction here. Designed in 1538, the piazza is a classic of Renaissance town planning. It's bordered by three palaces - the Palazzo dei Conservatori, the Palazzo dei Senatori and the Palazzo Nuovo - and formerly featured a bronze statue of Marcus Aurelius. The Conservatori and Nuovo now house the Museo Capitolino, just bursting with classic statues: Boy with Thorn ('in his side'), Dying Gaul and the Capitoline Venus. The Capitoline overlooks the Forum, and it was from here that ancient Rome was governed.

Piazza del Quirinale offers stunning views of Rome and St Peter's, while the Piazza Venezia is overshadowed by 'the Typewriter', otherwise known as the Victor Emmanuel Monument. Piazza Barberini features the fantastic Triton Fountain. Via Veneto was the place to be in the 1950s and '60s, when the truly astonishing Swedish import Anita Ekberg personified La Dolce Vita. It's a shadow of its former self today, but it still has fashionable pretensions. It's also home to a bizarre attraction that is definitely more morta than vita: the creatively decorated Santa Maria della Concezione dei Capuccini, with rococo decorations and pyramidal stacks created solely from the bones and skulls of the monks' long-departed fellows. The Campo de' Fiori is a lively piazza which is home to a daily (except Sunday) flower and vegetable market. The magnificent Renaissance Farnese Palace is just off the piazza.

© Hotel Danieli - Venice, Italy

The Forum is entered from the piazza leading from the Colosseum Columns rise from grassy hillocks, and repositioned pediments and columns aid the work of the imagination. Just some of the many must-sees include the Arch of Septimus Severus, the Temple of Saturn, the House of the Vestals, the Temple of Antoninus & Faustina and the Arch of Titus.

The Pantheon is an impressive example of the exquisite architectural technique of ancient Rome. It consists of a huge cylindrical body of equal height and width, covered by a great hemispherical dome. Important artists such as the painter Raphael are buried there, as well as the Italian Sovereigns of the period when Italy was a monarchy. Opposite to the Pantheon is Piazza della Rotonda with its beautiful fountain designed by Giacomo Della Porta.

Museums/Galleries: The Vatican. Arriving at St. Peter's Square, the visitor is immediately impressed by the size of the memorable square facing St. Peter's, surrounded by the magnificent four-row colonnade masterpiece of Gian Lorenzo Bernini. Only when one gets inside the basilica, slowly climbing up the sweeping three flights of steps designed by Bernini, one will be truly amazed by the size and splendor of the largest church in the world, the symbol of Christianity. It is possible to reach the top of the Cupola climbing 330 steps: once up there the view of the square below and of Rome is unforgettable. The church contains the masterpieces of important artists: the bronze baldachin by Bernini, the Pietà by Michelangelo, the tomb of Clement XIII by Canova and the mosaic of the Navicella by Giotto, located above the middle entrance to the Portico. Numerous and timeless works of art, mainly paintings, are kept in the Vatican Museums, which preserve the art of the most illustrious artists of all times. A visit to the Sistine Chapel, a milestone in the history of Italian painting, should not be missed.

The Colosseum owes its name to a colossal bronze statue, representing the Emperor Nero, more than 35 m. tall, that used to stand in this area. Symbol of Rome worldwide, the Colosseum was built by the emperors of the Flavian dynasty between 72-80 A.D., on the site once occupied by an artificial lake belonging to the magnificent Domus Aurea, a compound of buildings and gardens built by Nero now in ruins but with beautiful decorations which inspired Renaissance painters. As many as 100.000 cubic meters of travertine from the Tivoli quarries were used to build this amphitheater, the largest ever built in Roman empire. The Colosseum could hold more than 70,000 spectators who could watch the fights between gladiators, the hunting of animals and, at the very beginning, the naumachias: naval battles that took place in the arena that was flooded.

Dining: Roman cooking is predominantly simple; dishes rarely have more than a few ingredients, and meat and fish are most often baked or grilled. The typical Roman fresh pasta is fettuccine, golden egg noodles at their best with ragù, a rich tomato and meat sauce. Spaghetti alla carbonara is tossed with a sauce of egg yolk, guanciale (cured pork cheek) pecorino Romano cheese, and lots of black pepper. Pasta all'amatriciana has a sauce of tomato, guanciale, pecorino, and pepper. Potato gnocchi, served with tomato sauce and a sprinkling of

Parmesan or pecorino are a Roman favorite for Thursday dinner.

The best meat on the menu is often abbacchio (milk-fed lamb). Legs are usually roasted with rosemary and potatoes, chops are grilled a scottadito (eaten hot off the grill with your hands). Light Mediterranean fish such as spigola (sea bass), triglia (red mullet), and rombo (turbot or flounder) are other menu regulars.

Local cheeses are made from sheep's milk; the best known is the aged, sharp pecorino Romano. Fresh ricotta is a treat all its own. Rome is famous for carciofi (artichokes; in season from November to April), traditionally prepared alla romana (stuffed with garlic and mint and braised), or alla giudia (fried whole). Typical wines are those of the Castelli Romani, towns southeast of Rome. One of the great joys of a meal in Italy is that most restaurants will not rush you out. Service is relaxed and the bill (il conto) will not be brought until you ask for it. Almost all restaurants close one day a week (in most cases Sunday or Monday) and for at least two weeks in August. There was a time when you could predict the clientele and prices of

a Roman eating establishment by whether it was called a ristorante (restaurant), a trattoria, or an osteria (tavern). These names have since become interchangeable. A rustic-looking spot that calls itself an osteria may turn out to be chic and anything but cheap. Generally speaking, however, a trattoria is a family-run place, simpler in decor, cuisine, and service -- and slightly less expensive -- than a ristorante.

Shopping: Shopping in Rome is quite fun, no matter what your budget. The Italian flair for transforming display windows into stunning artistic still life scenes and whimsical theatrical tableaux makes window-shopping an aesthetic experience. If you're bent on buying, you're sure to find something that suits your fancy and your pocketbook. The best buys here are still leather goods of all kinds and silk goods and knitwear. Boutique fashions may be slightly less expensive in Rome than in the United States. Some worthy old prints and minor antiques can be found in the city's interesting little shops, and full-fledged collectors can rely on the prestigious reputations of some of Italy's top antiques dealers. Genuine

© Italian Government Tourist Board

Italian handicrafts aren't so easy to find these day but some shops still stock pottery and handwoven textiles made in Italy.

WEDDINGS ON LOCATION

Marriage Requirements: US citizens to be married in Italy must present the following documents:

• Passports

• Certified copies of each Birth certificate. A translation (certified by a Consular Officer) of each document into Italian is required as well as its Apostille. An Apostille is a seal affixed to a public record by the Secretary of State Notary Public of the State where the document was originated.

• If applicable, Final Divorce Decree, Annulment Decree or Death Certificate of previous spouse. A translation of each document into Italian is required as well as its Apostille.

• If under 18, sworn statement by parents or legal guardian consenting to the marriage. A translation of each document into Italian is required as well as its Apostille.

• To be legal in Italy, the translated documents must be given the Apostille Stamp

© Italian Government Tourist Board

by the Secretary of State in the state where each document was originally issued.

• Obtain an Atto Notorio from an Italian Consul in the United States. This is a declaration that according to US laws there is no obstacle to the marriage, and it must be sworn to by two witnesses.

Upon arrival in Italy, you will need to schedule appointments for:

• Another Declaration (Nulla Osta), sworn to by the US citizen at US Consulate in Italy stating that there is no legal impediment to his/her marriage under Italian Law and US Law.

• Legalization of the Nulla Osta must be done by the office of the Prefecture. There is one in every provincial capital.

• A waiver for a woman who has been divorced within the last 300 days must be obtained from the Procura della Republica (District Attorney), issued on presentation of a medical certificate that she is not pregnant.

LOCAL INFORMATION

Climate: Thanks to the moderating influence of the sea as well as the protection from the cold north winds given by the Alpine barrier from the cold north join together to bless Italy with a temperate climate. Nevertheless, the weather in any given area can vary considerably based on how far one is from the sea or the mountains. Typically, it is warm all over Italy in summer. The high temperatures begin in Rome in May, often lasting until sometime in October. Winters in the northern part of Italy are cold, with rain and snow, but in the south the weather is warm all year, even in winter.

Peak Season: In general, April/May/June and September/October are the best times to travel to Italy. Temperatures are comfortable and the tourist crowds are not too bad. July and August mark the busiest tourist time, even though temperatures are hotter and the air is muggier. In August, many Italians are on holiday themselves resulting in many hotels, restaurants and shops being closed.

© Italian Government Tourist Board

© Italian Government Tourist Board

Language: Italian is the language of the majority of the population but there are minorities speaking German, French, Slovene and Ladino.
Currency: The Euro - EUR is the official form of currency.

Standard Time Zone: UTC (Coordinated Universal Time/GMT (Greenwich Mean Time) +1 hours: CET (Central European Time)

Entry Requirements: You will need a valid passport to get into Italy, but will not be required to have a visa unless you are planning to stay in Italy for 90 days or more. All visitors must register with the police within 3 days of their arrival. This will be done for you by your hotel, but if you are staying in a private residence, you will need to apply in person at the local police station. If you have questions about this, call 461-950 when you arrive in Rome.

Customs Regulations: The limit on duty-free items you may bring back to the US is $400.00, and the goods must accompany you. For the next $1,000.00 worth of goods, a flat 10% rate is charged. Gifts may be sent home, however their value cannot exceed $50.00 to one person in one day. The package must be labeled with "Unsolicited Gift" and the contents of the package, and their value, must be declared.

For more information, contact:
Italian Government Tourism Board
630 Fifth Avenue
Suite 1565
New York, NY 10111

Telephone (From US): 212-245-5618
Website: www.italiantourism.com

welcome to

AUSTRALIA
& the
SOUTH PACIFIC

SYDNEY	-	CLIMATE
MONTH	HI	LO
JAN	80°	66°
FEB	79°	65°
MAR	77°	62°
APR	73°	57°
MAY	68°	50°
JUN	63°	46°
JUL	62°	43°
AUG	65°	45°
SEPT	68°	50°
OCT	72°	55°
NOV	75°	60°
DEC	78°	63°

Temperatures are provided in °Fahrenheit and based on averages.

A U S T R A L I A

Australia is an exciting country full of spirit, color and contrast: green, pristine wilderness, lush rainforest, blue skies, sparkling water, silver beaches and the red earth of the outback. Contrast is a way of life in Australia.

Australia itself is an ancient land as illustrated in its landscape. A good amount of the central and western portion of Australia is an arid, flat span of dry land. Yet, in contrast, its coastal cities boast a youthful buzz and energy …justified since most of which were founded as recently as the mid-nineteenth century.

It is this harshness of the interior landscape that has forced modern Australia to become a coastal country. Most of the population lives within 12-13 miles of the ocean. This metropolitan sector embraces the modern, values of materialism and self-indulgence while the beach climate is a playground for entertainment and socializing.

Buzzing cities, long sandy beaches, turquoise blue of the ocean, luxurious hotels, majestic landscapes and natural wonders, Australia has it all. Romance, adventure and paradise. Come and see for yourself.

THINGS TO SEE AND DO

Beaches: Australia boasts over 7,000 beaches - more than any other nation. With the reverse seasons of the northern hemisphere, Australia enjoys a largely temperate climate. Most of Australia receives more than 3,000 hours of sunshine a year, or an amazing 70 per cent of the total possible hours. Grab a hat and sunscreen and enjoy our delightful climate!

The Great Barrier Reef: Australia's most famous natural wonder, the Great Barrier Reef, will stun you with its magnificence. It's as big as the total combined area of the United Kingdom and Ireland, and contains more than 1,000 islands, from sandy cays to rainforest isles. The beauty of the waters and the prolific life it supports enraptures visitors. You can reach coral sites by air and water taxi and scuba dive or snorkel for intimate reef views. Or choose comfortable accommodations on a secluded reef island.

Special Points of Interest: A short walk from the Harbor Bridge, the Sidney Opera House is one of the world's premier performing arts centers. Taking almost 15 years to build, it was officially opened by Queen Elizabeth II in 1973.

Opened in 1932 and affectionately known as the 'coathanger,' the Sydney Harbor Bridge is slightly less than 1 mile long, weighs 58,200 tons, has six million rivets and needed almost 72,000 gallons of paint for its initial coat. Paint maintenance is a continual process. It takes 10 years and 8,000 gallons of paint before they start all over again!

Stretching 74.5 miles long and 6 miles wide, World Heritage listed Fraser Island offers vast white beaches, beautiful headlands and rainforests, and the best camping ever. You can mingle with kangaroos, wallabies and other unique animals, or stay in style at a resort!

Dramatic canyons, sheer valleys, thundering waterfalls and gum forests all make up Australia's most recent World Heritage area - the Blue Mountains

National Park. Also part of this latest listing is nearby Wollemi National Park - the home of the prehistoric Wollemi Pine.

Limited development has ensured an abundance of wildlife on Kangaroo Island located close to the tip of South Australia's Fleurieu Peninsula. Here sea lions, penguins, dolphins, koalas and of course, kangaroos, live in a protected natural environment. Pure air and clean water provide one of the last unspoiled wonders of the world.

The Tasmanian Wilderness World Heritage area is one of the largest conservation reserves in Australia, covering 1.38 million hectares. This stronghold of temperate rainforest and alpine vegetation provides pristine habitats for plants and animals found nowhere else in the world, including many rare and endangered species.

Dining: Fine wine and dining are now as characteristically Australian as warm sun and booming surf. Wherever your Australian travels take you, just as the sights and sounds of its marvelous landscapes will live on in your memory, its food and wine will resonate through your taste buds.

Australian cuisine is marked by its fresh, eclectic take on dishes gleaned from all the cultures of the world. The best Australian chefs are notable for their ability to blend influences without fear or favor. Australians like to eat and they eat well. They are very amenable to incorporating all sorts of culinary influences in their daily fare.

Glance in the window of one of the gourmet food stores scattered throughout Australia's capital cities and you'll be surprised. There's a huge variety available in every state – some examples are chevre from Queensland, prosciutto from Western Australia, brie and cold-pressed olive oil from South Australia, balsamic vinegars and snails from Victoria, milk-fed lamb from New South Wales, smoked salmon

from Tasmania, and mud crabs from the Northern Territory. It is only fitting that what Australia eats now comes from a collage of culinary influences that use a splash of olive oil with one hand while tossing in a handful of chopped chilies with the other.

There are many reasons for Australia's culinary success, including a diversity of micro-climates that allow it to produce mangoes as well as strawberries, custard apples, citrus fruits and coffee beans. Its lush coastal pastures are well suited to farmhouse cheeses; its native forests produce honeys of exceptional fragrance and flavor and its vast coastline yields succulent oysters, crayfish and tuna of tremendous delicacy.

Australian chefs have been quick to make the most of this natural bounty, experimenting with ingredients and drawing inspiration from the cultural cross-currents of modern Australia. Over the past 30 years, Australia has become one of the most ethnically diverse nations on earth, and when the present generation of chefs took over the restaurant kitchens, their cultural heritage seasoned the food. So successful have they become that Australia is now exporting its chefs to the wider world.

In addition to world class cuisine, Australia is ranked as the world's seventh-largest wine producer, and the finest Australian wines are among the best in the world - a judgment that is consistently reinforced at international wine shows.

Nightlife: Each of Australia's major cities has a nightlife attraction, whether it's an international-style casino with all the glitter of Las Vegas, a waterfront area where the barstools come with a view of yachts and dancing waves or an entire district that sparkles by night.

Shopping: Shopping is a part of any vacation, and a combination of fantastic shopping centers with a galaxy of goods found nowhere else

in the world will make sure you come home with something special. And after dark, the whole country comes to the party with a feast of entertainment.

Born to shop? If so, you'll be in your element in the major shopping complexes that are a feature of every major Australian city. As well as the best of the wider world, they'll tempt you with the fashions and souvenirs

Local markets are a great place to take the local pulse, and whether it's the city or the country, Australia has plenty to offer. At any one of these markets you'll be entertained, as well as intrigued by the goods on display, and of course there's the chance to go home with a souvenir bought straight from the maker.

New Age meets suburban chic at Sydney's favorite, fashion-conscious churchyard bazaar, Paddington Markets, where the range of goods includes crystals, tribal silver, plants or just slinky socks at knockdown prices.

Under siege from the surrounding rainforest, the north Queensland village of Kuranda has a flourishing market, Rainforest Market - the place to go for arts and crafts, fashions, and a range of exotic rainforest products.

Part country fair, part rock festival and part country show, the monthly Byron Bay Market combines music, spectacle, exotic fruit salads, ethnic finger-food and people skilled in basket weaving.

Held every Sunday, St Kilda's arts and crafts market is a browsers delight, with 220 stalls crammed with glass, books and clothes, drawing a colorful cast of characters to this bohemian beachside suburb.

Located on the wharf at Fremantle, Western Australia, the E Shed Market is one of the city's treasured institutions, the place to go for home furnishings, fabrics, garden ware and offbeat arts and crafts.

Salamanca Markets brings a dash of excitement to the historic stone warehouses on the Hobart waterfront every Saturday with a dazzling array of crafts by some of Australia's finest artisans.

Museums/Galleries: Australia's art and culture have a vitality that springs from youth and from the rich multicultural mix of its population. Whether you're looking for classical galleries, contemporary theatre, heritage buildings or Aboriginal artworks, you'll be fascinated, entertained and surprised by what's on offer.

Australia's contemporary architecture shows all the richness and complexity of a truly multicultural society in its ability to take the best of architecture and design from the wider world and adapt it to meet the special needs of the Australian environment - with a result that is distinctly Australian.

Every city in Australia boasts a major art gallery. Along with an appreciation for the visual arts of Europe and Asia - seen in the major touring exhibitions - Australia has a world-class tradition of its own in the art of its Aboriginal people, which has undergone a renaissance in the last 30 years.

Australia's museums provide the background reading to an astonishing continent. Australia's history, its plants and animals and its people are just some of the elements that make it unique, and Australia's museums turn the microscope on the richness and grandeur of the island continent.

Nature/Sight-seeing: The Tropical North Queensland Region is the ideal starting point for travelers wanting to explore the natural wonderland made up of the Great Barrier Reef, wet tropics rainforest, outback savannah plains and the vast wilderness of Cape York Peninsula. The natural values of this region are so great; much of it has been listed as World Heritage, to preserve the bio-diversity for future generations. Take a day tour to explore "nature's theme park" or immerse yourself totally with a longer stay.

Visit Tropical Volcanic Ranges where dramatically eroded volcanic features provide the landscape for the velvety green mantle of the Border Ranges. Stretching across the Queensland and New South Wales border, the ranges include the Nightcap and Mt Warning parks.

Australia's Top End – the tropical Northern Territory – is home to more than 20 wonderful national parks. There's Kakadu, Litchfield, Gregory, Katherine Gorge or Nitmiluk, to name just a few.

Visitors are struck by the beauty revealed within the boundaries Victoria's Grampians National Park. Sheer rock formations, dazzling waterfalls and great views; in spring, wildflowers burst into color.

Experience Australia's diverse population of birds and indigenous animals. Australia has around 800 species of bird, 400 of which are unique to this country. The wealth of bird life, from the boisterous laugh of the kookaburra, a large kingfisher, to the brilliantly plumed rainbow lorikeets, makes Australia a haven for bird lovers. As the Australian landmass separated from the other continents over 50 million years ago, indigenous animals have developed a range of individual and unusual characteristics in a unique habitat. The result is a wealth of wildlife not found anywhere else in the world.

In contrast to the red earth of the outback, Australia is a land of lush green, with forests alone covering five per cent of the landmass. Australia has beautiful and diverse green regions, many located close to major metropolitan areas. The distinctive smell of a eucalyptus forest shouldn't be missed!

WEDDINGS ON LOCATION
Romance requires a perfect backdrop, and when it comes to weddings and honeymoons, Australia's luxury resorts and grand country-house

hotels will bring an extra touch of sparkle to make them unforgettable occasions.

Before too long, you could be strolling hand in hand beside the Sydney Opera House, or sleeping in a "swag" in the Outback under the stars. Next you could be gliding down a tropical river, or being massaged by a waterfall as it plunges over sheer, red cliffs millions of years old.

Then there's the wildlife, the golden beaches, the Great Barrier Reef and the rainforests – plus the sophisticated cities, fantastic food and wine, world class entertainment and the fun-loving, friendly people.

And whether you stay in a five-star deluxe resort, a city hotel or a wilderness retreat, Australia's warm hospitality will ensure a perfect start to a new life together.

Marriage Requirements: Couples who wish to be married in Australia are required to submit a Notice of the Intended Marriage with their chosen celebrant. Civil and religious marriage celebrants are listed on the Attorney General's Commonwealth website, at http://www.law.gov.au/celebrants. The form must be submitted at least one month and one day before the marriage is to take place (and not more than 18 calendar month's notice of an intended date of marriage.) This form must be signed and witnessed either by an Australian Consular Official or Diplomatic Officer.

AUSTRALIA

Personal identification (such as a passport, birth certificate, etc.) is also required. Check with your celebrant to ensure you have the correct legal identification.

LOCAL INFORMATION

Australia's seasons are the reverse of those in the northern hemisphere. From Christmas on the beach to mid-winter in July, Australia's climate is typically mild in comparison with the extremes that exist in both Europe and North America.

Australia's seasons: Spring is September-November, Summer is December-February, Autumn (Fall) is March-May, Winter is June-August.

Australia also features a diverse range of climatic zones from the tropical regions of the north, the arid expanses of the interior and the temperate regions of the south. It's worth noting that the temperate regions have all four seasons, while those in the tropical zone have only two (summer 'wet' and winter 'dry').

Language: While it's common knowledge that Australians speak English, Australia also has a unique colloquial language that can confuse visitors when they first hear it. From 'fair dinkum' to 'cobber', our colloquial language is common throughout the land. Don't worry, you'll pick it up!

Currency: Australian dollars - AUD

Standard Time Zone: There are three time zones in Australia: Eastern Standard Time (EST), which includes New South Wales, Victoria, Queensland, Tasmania and the Australian Capital Territory; Central Standard Time (CST), which includes South Australia and the Northern Territory; and Western Standard Time (WST) - Western Australia. CST is Coordinated Universal Time/GMT (Greenwich Mean Time) +9:30 hours.

Entry Requirements: Travellers to Australia need a valid passport. Everyone, except travellers with Australian or New Zealand passports, requires a visa or an ETA

(Electronic Travel Authority) to enter Australia.

An ETA is equivalent to a visa, but there is no stamp or label in your passport and there is no need for you to visit an Australian diplomatic office to submit an application. If you are eligible, the ETA is issued electronically by a computer system operated for the Department of Immigration and Multicultural and Indigenous Affairs (DIMIA) of Australia. To make things easy for you the Australian Government has made it possible to arrange an ETA via the Internet - no application forms and no contact with an Australian visa office is necessary.

Customs Regulations: There are strict laws prohibiting or restricting the entry of drugs, steroids, weapons, firearms, protected wildlife and associated products. If you are unsure about anything declare it to Customs upon arrival.

For more information, contact:
The Australian Tourist Commission
2049 Century Park East, Suite 1920
Los Angeles CA 90067

Telephone: 310 229 4870
Website: www.australia.com

Amanwana © Amanresorts

B A L I

Temperatures are provided in °Fahrenheit and based on averages.

The Indonesian island of Bali has been widely known as an exotic heaven filled with unique arts and ceremonies. The people of Bali, a friendly and remarkably artistic people, living amid breathtaking panoramas, have created a dynamic society with unique arts and ceremonies, making Bali an island almost unreal in today's hectic and changing world. Terrace rice fields dominate the landscape, with rivers and small irrigation streams dissecting a luscious green landscape, filling the air with enchanting sounds of running water.

The island of Bali is one of over 17,000 islands that make up Indonesia's archipelago with a total population of more than 200 million, scattered over a land area of some 2.02 million square kilometers. Lying across a region of immense volcanic activity, Indonesia has some 400 volcanoes, with at least 70 still active.

Bali is an island divided by a string of impressive volcanoes running almost through the center of the island. Shrouded in mystery and magic, they stretch skyward in majestic splendor. Bali's main volcano is the still active and sometimes explosive Gunung Agung, which is considered sacred among local people as it is believed to be the center of the universe. Not just a few visitors leave with the same belief.

Art and culture are strongly bonded to Bali's unique form of Hinduism called "Hindu Darma." Classical dance dramas for example, are based on the old Hindu epics of the Ramayana and the Mahabarata, but contain an element of local folklore, peculiar to the island. The very soul of Bali is rooted in religion and is expressed in art forms that have been passionately preserved over the centuries.

Amanwana © Amanresorts

THINGS TO SEE AND DO

Indonesia is often referred to as the world's largest archipelago, a name which aptly represents its 17,000 or so islands which span more than 3,200 miles eastward from Sabang in northern Sumatra to Merauke in Irian Jaya. If you superimpose a map of Indonesia over one of Europe, you will find that it stretches from Ireland to Iran; compared to the United States, it covers the area from California to Bermuda.

There are eight major islands or island groups in the enormous chain of islands that make up the archipelago of Indonesia. The largest landmasses consist of Sumatra, Java, Kalimantan (Borneo), Sulawesi (Celebes) and Irian Jaya (the western half of Papua New Guinea). The smaller islands fall into two main groups: the Molluccas to the northeast, and the lesser Sunda chain east of Bali. Bali is a unique island, which for a number of reasons can be put into a class of its own.

Located between two distinct bio-geographic groups - Asia and Australia - the flora and fauna of the archipelago is also quite idiosyncratic. Species found nowhere else on earth have flourished in certain areas, including the famous Komodo dragon on the island of the same name. Also in abundance are rare flowers, including exotic orchids, unusual insects, birds of paradise and numerous indigenous spices such as cloves, nutmeg cinnamon, mace and many more.

Beaches: The beaches of Bali are, in one word, magnificent! From the stretch of sand in Kuta, fenced far in the South by the runway of Denpasar International Airport; the peaceful elegance of Nusa Dua; the mysterious quietness and somberness of Candidasa, as a temple dedicated to the sea goddess submerges; to the spectacular sunsets of Lovina in the North.

Practically on the opposite side of Sanur, the beaches of Kuta and Legian stretch on the southwestern side of Bali, again only about a 5 to 10 minute drive from Denpasar or the airport. Surfing is a major activity in these beaches. Shops, Kecak dance performances, pubs, and other facilities make Kuta a tourist mecca.

Jimbaran, directly south of the airport, on the way from Denpasar towards Nusa Dua, is a village on the narrow neck of the island of Bali, and thus it has two remarkably different beaches. On the west, Jimbaran Beach faces the Jimbaran Bay, recently lined by new luxurious resorts. On the east, the beach faces the body of water sheltered by Benoa Harbor.

Nusa Dua is a new luxurious resort area where the world's most sumptuous hotels gracefully integrate into the beautiful white beaches. Crystal clear water provides excellent snorkeling and diving, and the waves on the northern and the southern part of Nusa Dua allow for great surfing opportunities.

Near the northern tip of the island of Bali lies a stretch of villages by the Bali Sea, called Lovina Beach. It is well known as an excellent site for sunset watching, snorkeling, and diving. Night life activities also abound, as well as chartered boats to go out into the sea. If you like what Kuta offers but do not like the crowd, Lovina Beach is for you.

Diving and snorkeling: Diving and snorkeling are among major attractions in Bali. Divers can view various marine creatures, such as colorful tropical fish and coral reefs. The best time for diving here is

Amankila © Amanresorts

in the dry season that lasts from April to October, when warmer temperatures invite more fish and the objects can be clearly viewed.

Bali offers a lot of sites for beginners and professional divers, with some of them adjacent to the shore with abundant colorful hard and soft corals. Once you start diving, a wide variety of marine life, such as dolphins, rays, turtle, sea snakes and moray eels will greet you.

The locations for diving and snorkeling in Bali spread out along Bali's sea. The popular sites are located on the southern part: Sanur and Nusa Island (Lembongan and Nusa Penida); in the western part are Labuan Lalang, Menjangan Island, an uninhabited island with some of the best diving in Bali; in the north of the island is Lovina that will undoubtedly satisfy your diving needs. On the east coast are Amed where virgin nature can be enjoyed, Tulamben, Candidasa and Padang Bay also.

Surfing: Surfing can be done every day in Bali. Bali's magnificent surfing was discovered by Australian surfers at the end of 60's, and since then, Bali has become a paradise for surfers. Not just because of various choices for beaches and breaks, but surfing in Bali can be done everyday! Perfect waves to ride on are always available somewhere on this island. Kuta and Ulawatu are recognized for their magnificent surfing waves.

Outstanding reef breaks are found in Kuta and Sanur. Sanur reef is a real pleasure because here you will find a tube-forming waves that will carry you back to the seashore.

Whitewater rafting: After white water rafting that has gained popularity in Bali, comes offshore rafting or ocean rafting. The more adventurous sort of amusement has now become an alternative sport for tourists. Just try it. Your heart will beat faster, especially when your boat hits two meter-high waves at high speed but even so, just

Amankila © Amanresorts

like any other adventure sport, safety is the first priority. Meanwhile white water rafting is still a popular activity with trips on the Ayung, Telaga Waja, Unda rivers, etc. You can refresh your mind by watching beautiful scenery along the route.

Paragliding: If you do not want to push your heart so hard, paragliding is a good choice and an exciting way to see Bali from the air. If wind conditions are right, you can view Bali from a very different perspective. If you are a beginner, a professional instructor will accompany you to ride in tandem.

Golfing: Although this game is not so popular amongst Balinese, it doesn't mean that you cannot find international standard golf courses in this "morning world." And if you did not bring your clubs you can rent a set at most courses. Bali Golf and Country Club (BGCC) was named by Fortune magazine as one of the top five best courses in Asia in 1997. That course, together with Nirwana Golf and Country Club and the Bali Handara Kosaido championship courses, put Bali on the world-class golf course map.

Special Points of Interest: Bali is also blessed with beautiful nature. Endless sand

Amandari © Amanresorts

Amandari © Amanresorts

beaches envelope most of Bali's shores, where silvery waves come home to. Tall cliffs border the eastern shores. Volcanic mountains crown the center of Bali, home. Gunung Agung (Mount Divine), the sacred abode of the gods and the goddesses. Green forests stretch from east to west of the northern part of Bali, nurturing numerous flora and fauna that can only be found here.

Nightlife: Bali's best nightspots are in the south, a popular gathering place for young travelers looking to party. Legian has become the club town, with discos and after-hours bars that keep jumping until dawn. Kuta and Tuban, just south of Legian, offer 24 hours of dancing and music supplied by the local bars.

Ubud is the dance center of Bali. Hotels often provide shows, sometimes abbreviated in length and adapted for Western visitors. Performances held elsewhere around Ubud are more likely to reflect local culture.

Night life as commonly known in the West also exists in Bali, especially in Kuta. The cafés, pubs, and discotheques lining the streets of Kuta and Legian are definitely the place to be and to be seen. Pub crawls can require many nights, and the varieties beat even the wildest western college towns. So,

if your idea of fun consists of nightly pub crawls and daily sun bathing to cure the hangover, simply stay in Kuta, day and night. You won't be disappointed.

Up North near Singaraja, Lovina Beach also has its own collection of pubs, restaurants, and discotheques. The environment is nice, friendly, and relaxed, certainly not as hectic as Kuta.

Dining: Your visit to Bali is not complete unless you also partake in a delightful gastronomical tour of the food and fruit of Bali. In fact, the multitude of sensations titillating your taste buds and olfactory senses upon seeing, smelling, and eating Balinese food and fruit should be enough of a reason to visit Bali.

Some suggestions include Paradise UN'S Restaurant, serving a selection of refined European cuisine and Indonesian specialties in an unforgettable setting of romantic candlelight. The Arak Bali Restaurant & Pub combining fun dining with live entertainment in Nusa Dua. The Bali Bamboo Restaurant and Guest House offers special Balinese gourmet dishes, like Balinese Smoked Duck, in a comfortable Ubud setting.

Check out New Café Luna, open since 1986, considered among Kuta & Legian's Top Places to go. If you want to taste real Balinese seafood, visit Teba Café on Jimbaran Beach, located just before the Four Seasons Resort and just five minutes from the International Airport. If it's romance you crave, you will find a romantic atmosphere at Warung Mina where you can enjoy the freshest seafood cooked in traditional Balinese style. Or, for a faster-paced, exotic experience, step forward to the hustle of Kuta, into a world of pleasure found at Raja's Bar & Restaurants, serving an exclusive range of selected international and Indonesian cuisines, wine and cocktails.

Shopping: Shopping in Bali is not simply walking into a shop, picking something from a shelf and paying for it. Shopping is an art. In every traditional market and art shop around Bali, bargaining is a must.

This traditional way makes shopping in Bali a fun time, where you can feel the warmth of human value in every transaction. Before you begin your shopping tour on this island, please obtain cash because most places do not accept credit cards.

Even if you are not a seasoned negotiator, be prepared to enjoy the bargaining process. It is a fun activity, be patient and you will get the "best (and maybe even local) price." In some places you can bargain until you get as much as 50% off. Always go in at less than a third of the price (maybe even a quarter), bargain some more and maybe even walk away, hold out until you get the price you want.

As the capital of Bali, Denpasar is the center of "market" activity for local people. The biggest traditional market stands near Badung's river, Kumbasari market. It can give you an insight into the traditional Indonesia market where local people do their daily shopping. Fruit, vegetables and meat can be found in the basement; on the second level is the place for spices and dried goods; while household wares, clothing, art and craft is on the third level. Here you can get a very good price if you're smart in bargaining. In the eastern part is

Amanjiwo © Amanresorts

Sulawesi Street, the place for all kind of fabrics on its both sides with some shops providing household ware in between. The area here is very colorful with all types of material from the traditional 'songket' (cloth woven with strands of gold or silver) to modern day stretchy and shiny material.

As an international village, almost all of the shops and restaurants in the Kuta area are geared towards tourists. You can find handicrafts, clothing, jewelry, CDs, furniture and leather crafts on each side of the road. But you can also see many street hawkers with their various offerings along the road. The street hawkers can get fairly aggressive; if you make eye contact or sometimes even just look at their offerings, they may follow you along the street and pester you to buy something.

The shopping center in Sanur is on Jalan Danau Tamblingan where the situation is almost the same as Kuta but with very few hawkers. Many products are sold in established shops and nice restaurants.

The Batubulan area, on the border of Denpasar and Gianyar, is the home of stone sculptures. You can find various kinds of style here, from traditional to modern, small to large. The craftsmen can make up your order and even arrange to ship it to your address back home.

Nature/Sightseeing: The wild forests of Bali can be found mostly in the Bali Barat National Park, dedicated to the preservation of

Amanusa © Amanresorts

wildlife. And the tropical climate of Bali endows it with a rich flora. In the forests, tall tropical trees reach for the sky, nursing a variety of wild orchids to grow on their branches. Pine trees carpet the mountains. Ever protective, waringin trees faithfully stand at the center of every village. Flowers beautifully punctuate little gardens in every house, and most importantly, spreading their sweet fragrance into the midnight air and completing offerings to the gods and goddesses.

Bali tigers (Panthera tigris balica) used to roam these forests, but now you can only find deer or wild boars. Bali Barat National Park is also reestablished as the new habitat for Bali Starling (Jalak Bali), a sweet, white bird that has inspired many a painter. Sea turtles, another protected species, can play-fully accompany you when you go snorkel-ing in the the waters of Nusa Dua.

The resort area Bedugul is on the shore of Lake Bratan. It also houses the temple Ulundanu. Gitgit, famous for its waterfall, is located just slightly north of Mount Catur.

The most revered and the highest peak in Bali, Mount Agung stands tall at over 3100 meters. The Balinese consider Mount Agung to be the center of the world, and all temples in Bali point towards Mount Agung.

WEDDINGS ON LOCATION

The Indonesian island of Bali is known as the island of the Gods. It offers tremendous spirituality in a tropical environment and is a fabulous destination in which to celebrate a spiritual event as special as a wedding or even honeymoon.

Celebrating a wedding in Bali offers you so very much as the Balinese people are natu-rally friendly, warm and welcoming. They are talented musicians, dancers and artists and can add an enormous amount to your special day. Your wedding in Bali can be as quiet and simple or as elaborate as you desire. It can take place on a beach, in a gar-den, in a resort or villa, even in a royal tem-ple. There is little that is not possible when holding a wedding on Bali.

Amanwana © Amanresorts

To qualify as a legal marriage in Indonesia, the service has to be performed according to the laws of the respective religious beliefs of the parties concerned.

All couples who marry in Indonesia must declare a religion. The Civil Registry Office can record marriages of persons of Islam, Hindu, Buddhist, Christian-Protestant and Christian-Catholic faiths. Agnosticism and Atheism are not recognized. Marriage part-ners must have the same religion; otherwise one partner must make a written declaration of change of religion. The US has a Consular Representative in Bali that can offer assis-tance to you.

A Christian, Hindu or Buddhist marriage is usually performed first in a church or temple ceremony. After the religious ceremony, every non-Islamic marriage must be record-ed with the Civil Registry (Kantor Catatan Sipil). Without the registration by the Civil Registry these marriages are not legal. Recording by Civil Registry officials can be performed directly at the religious ceremony for an additional fee.

All persons of non-Islamic faith are required to file a Notice of Intention to Marry with the Civil Registry Office in the Regency where they are staying as well as a "CNI" (Certificate of No Impediment to Marriage) obtained from their consular representatives. A CNI is simply a letter from your Consular Representative or Embassy Representative in Indonesia stating that there is no objec-

Amandari © Amanresorts

tion for you to get married in Indonesia. Contact the Consular Representative of your country for details well before your intended date of marriage. The US Consular Representative in Bali can be reached at 62-361-233-605.

The Civil Registry office has a Mandatory Waiting Period of 10 working days from the date of filing. This waiting period may be waived for tourists presenting a guest registration form (Form A).

All Marriage Certificates (except Islamic Marriage Certificates) will be issued by the Civil Registry usually on the same or next day. A sworn English translation of the marriage certificate should be obtained for use abroad. It is not necessary for the marriage certificate or translation to be registered by your Consular Agency. However, it might prove beneficial to have the sworn translation of the marriage certificate verified or a special translation made by the Consular Agency of your home country.

Most hotels and resorts can offer assistance with your arrangements for getting married in Bali. Many resort wedding packages include necessary arrangements for religious and legal ceremonies, rental of bridal dresses, hair styling, make-up, photography, cake, etc. There are also many packages catering to couples celebrating their honeymoon.

Amanusa © Amanresorts

LOCAL INFORMATION

The climate in Bali is tropical - hot and humid all the time! There are two seasons, dry and hot (April - September), and rainy (October - March). The timing of these seasons has varied considerably in the past few years, however, due to El Niño and other climatic interference. Temperatures range from 21 to 33°C in the low lands, but it can get quite chilly at night in the highlands of Central Java. Bring a jacket if you intend to do any volcano climbing.

Language: Bahasa Indonesia is the official language. English is frequently used in commerce.

Currency: Indonesian Rupiah - IDR. Exchange facilities for the main foreign currencies are available in banks or at authorized money changers in major cities of Indonesia. Rupiah comes in denominations of 100,000, 50,000, 20,000, 10,000, 5000, 500 and 100 in bank notes, and 1000, 500, 100, 50, 25, 10 and 5 coins.

Time Zone: UTC (Coordinated Universal Time/GMT (Greenwich Mean Time) +8 hours

Entry Requirements: It is not necessary to obtain a visa prior to traveling to Bali if you are traveling from the US.

Amanusa © Amanresorts

Customs Regulations: On entry to Indonesia, each adult is allowed to bring in tax-free a maximum of one liter of alcoholic beverages and 200 cigarettes or 50 cigars or 100 grams of tobacco.

Cameras, video cameras, portable radios, cassette recorders, binoculars and sport equipment are admitted provided they are taken out of the country on departure. They must be declared to Customs. Prohibited are firearms, narcotics, pornography, Chinese printing and medicines, and many electronic devices.

Safety: The people of Indonesia are, by nature, an extremely friendly and welcoming people.

In light of recent events that have harmed foreign tourists in Indonesia, including US citizens, you should read and follow any travel advisories issued by the US government informing US citizens of potential threats and/or dangers.

For more information, contact:
Indonesian Consulate General
3457 Wilshire Blvd. Floor 4
Los Angeles, CA 90010

Telephone: 213-383-5126
Website: www.indony.org

© The Fiji Visitors Bureau

F I J I

Bula! (Welcome) Sunny, unique and unspoiled, the Fiji Islands are one thousand miles of pristine white sand beaches, fabulous coral gardens and azure lagoons. More then anything else, Fiji is an exotic destination. It's the exhilaration of a dolphin arching high into the air beside your boat; the long gliding swoop of an orange dove through the rainforest; the smiles of excited children performing in unison to the beat of a hollow log drum.

Fiji's 333 islands can sizzle with excitement or murmur with the quiet calm of pristine nature. Where else can you swim with huge, harmless manta rays congregating by the shore, snorkel over giant rainbow gardens of soft coral, or scuba dive the White Wall and famous Astrolabe Reef. Fiji is where the Cloud Breaker, the incredible six-metre wave found offshore at Tavarua, draws surfers from around the world. It is also where you can float in the calm, quiet waters of a turquoise lagoon at sunset or walk alone through lush rainforest. It is where the sun shines almost everyday and when it does rain, people rush outside for a rain bath in the warm, brief downpour of a tropical shower which ends as quickly as it began. This is where life is lived for the joy of it all, where rushing is rude, and the name of a new friend is never forgotten. Fiji is where people wear flowers tucked in their hair, not to impress visitors, but because they like to.

© The Fiji Visitors Bureau

The Fiji archipelago is at the cross roads of the South Pacific. In the days of sailing ships it was known as The Cannibal Isles and carefully avoided by mariners because of its fierce warriors and treacherous waters. However, in the age of jumbo jets and global travel, Fiji has become the central hub of the exotic South Pacific. More than 85 flights land at Nadi on the main island of Viti levu every week. From there it is only a quick seven minute hop to one of the offshore island resorts, or less than an hour of flying time to Vanua Levu or Taveuni, the second and third largest islands, where the outside world is quickly left behind.

For those who like to keep their feet on the ground once they arrive, the big island of Viti Levu offers a wealth of tropical scenery, from rushing mountain rivers and waterfalls in the depths of the rainforest, to palm-fringed beaches where time seems to stop. This is where you can fish from the reef in the morning, picnic at the edge of a waterfall plunging into a rocky jungle pool at midday and eat native food cooked in an earth oven in the evening, and then dance to the beat in a swinging discotheque until long after midnight. Along with its pristine tropical beauty, Viti levu offers several large towns and the bustling capital of Suva, a shopper's paradise, and you will never have to travel more than a few hours to get anywhere on the island.

THINGS TO SEE AND DO

Fiji is famous for the variety of activities available. These include snorkeling over shallow reefs close to shore, diving, which offers a full range of a underwater experience, riding in a jet boat, trekking in the tropical rainforests, swimming in the crystal clear waters of a rushing river, even visiting a sacred cave. Take a full or half-day shopping tour of Suva, or a special week-long excursion around the major island where you can pilot a raft through raging rapids, sail through the magnificence of the Yasawa island chain or safari into the highlands.

Recreation: Fiji, "the Soft Coral Capital

FIJI	-	CLIMATE
MONTH	HI	LO
JAN	87°	75°
FEB	86°	74°
MAR	86°	74°
APR	85°	73°
MAY	82°	71°
JUN	80°	70°
JUL	79°	69°
AUG	79°	68°
SEPT	80°	69°
OCT	81°	70°
NOV	83°	71°
DEC	85°	73°

Temperatures are provided in °Fahrenheit and based on averages.

of the World," is rated as one of the top 10 dive destinations in the world. It is well deserved.

Fiji's vast, varied and colorful underwater playgrounds boast something spectacular for divers at every skill level... breathtaking hard and soft corals, wall dives, caves, grottos and shipwrecks. Fiji is truly a diver's paradise where the daily menu is so diversified that it is sometimes difficult to believe you are in the same country.

Fiji's remarkable marine life embodies all the elements that make Fiji's reefs so exceptional: drama and diversity, brilliant lavish panoramas, deep water rich with food and hiding places... Fiji's marine realm is as dynamic and splendid as nature can be.

Many operators employ multilingual dive masters and instructors to cater to Japanese, Korean, and European divers who wish to learn about diving in their native tongue. Live aboard charter fees include all diving (often unlimited), meals, accommodations and transfers for the duration of the voyage. All the major training agencies such as PADI. NAUI and SSI are represented in Fiji. Most diving services have full snorkeling and scuba equipment for rent.

For the avid snorkeler – Fiji is wonderland! Shallow reefs harbor beautiful corals, reef fish, turtles and any number of awesome marine creatures big and small. Any of the operators would be able to organize a try-a-dive or Discover Scuba Diving. You might try out the Scuba equipment in a pool or a wonderful warm, blue, fish-filled, shallow lagoon.

Special Points of Interest: As exciting as you would want, there is much to choose from: visits to an old colonial capital city, motor tours through the highlands, the serenity of Fiji's wilderness to explore.

© The Fiji Visitors Bureau

© The Fiji Visitors Bureau

Island Cruises, both day or half-day, are available from Nadi area to Mana, Plantation, Beachcomber, Castaway Island or a combination of these islands in the Mamanuca group. Choose your mode of transport-Catamaran, Schooner, motor-sailor or Ketch! Once you've landed, each island offers water sports, entertainment and dining.

Cultural River Cruises provide daytime excursions from Sigatoka jetty upriver visiting a traditional Fijian village, a kava welcoming ceremony, and pottery making demonstration. Then head downriver to Sigatoka Sand Dunes to a historic village of original Fijian ancestors, lovo feast and shopping for Fijian crafts.

Fiji Museum at Thurston Gardens (Suva) hold the world's largest collection of Fijian artifacts as well as actual relics from H.M.S. Bounty! The guided Suva City Tour of Fiji's capital city will take you to Government House, Fiji Museum, Albert Park, Botanical Gardens, University of the South Pacific, Laucala Bay, The Fijian handicraft Centre, Moslem mosque, Hindu Temple, Roman Catholic Cathedral and our main shopping district. And don't forget the open-air market on Saturday.

Go 'Flight Seeing' on Island Hoppers helicopters, Turtle Airways seaplanes or South Seas Cruises float planes. Your view of the islands, mountain ranges, rainforests, hilltop and valley villages is a photographer's dream.

Dining: Dining in Fiji offers a multiethnic culinary experience. Whether dining at your hotel, island resort or "in town," you'll find a palate painted by flavors from India, China, Korea, Japan, Italy and the best of Europe as well as Australia, New Zealand and the South Pacific waters.

Restaurants run the gamut from five star international to 24-hour air-conditioned coffee shops. Steaks and local seafood can be found in most restaurants as can the specialties of our own Fijian cooking heritage. Most hotels and resorts also offer specific culinary themed nights, magiti (Fijian feasts), beach or poolside BBQ's, as well as Fiji's best known and pervasive outdoor cooking experience-the lovo, an underground oven of heated rocks cooking a variety of foods wrapped in banana leaves, covered with earth and coming out after several hours of cooking with a faintly smoky flavor. Lovos produces succulent, tender meats, chicken, seafood, and given the proper occasion, a whole suckling pig!

You shouldn't leave Fiji without having experienced other traditional Fijian dishes. Kokoda, Fiji's most popular specialty, is portions of fresh fish marinated in lime juice and served in a half coconut in lolo - a word that sounds as sweet as it taste- made from the sweet cream of the coconut, a staple in Fijian cooking. Or savor a palusami, meat wrapped in taro (dalo) leaves and cooked in lolo.

Shopping: Most stores are open 8am to 5pm or 6pm, sometimes later at hotels and resorts. Most stores are closed on Sundays. All of your major credit cards are widely accepted.

© The Fiji Visitors Bureau

© The Fiji Visitors Bureau

Some popular items to bring home for friends, family and business associates to enjoy include Fijian inspired designer T-shirts, carved tanoa bowls, from which the "national drink yaqona" (kava) is mixed and served, Fijian replica war clubs, "cannibal forks" and Fijian combs. Handicraft like woven baskets and mats, masi (tapa cloth), animal wood carvings and pottery items are best sellers. And, for international fashion buffs, the ubiquitous sulu for men and women is Fiji's all-purpose, one-size-fits-all garment. Women wear them 100 different ways from a beachside wrap to an evening dress while men in business and government wear them as a day skirt.

Beyond the hotels and resorts, in our towns and cities, you'll find a wide assortment of shops frequented by locals. Shops offering glittering displays of gold jewelry along with cottons and silks are popular among and often owned by our Indian compatriots.

And, if you really love the age-old practice of bargaining, head for Cummings Street in Suva where it has reached the highest art form!

Shop the markets - Fiji style. There is no chrome shelving. Point of sale signs are mostly hastily hand-rendered on bits of cardboard and the muzak is a background hub-bub of Hindustani, Chinese and Fijian.

Nature/Sightseeing: Fiji's rainforests are unique in that they have no harmful animals or insects. Here one can enjoy serene contemplation of nature in complete safety. Multi-hued birds flit from the trees, and if you are lucky you may spot several varieties of Fiji's tiny wild parrots. While the forest can be thick and impenetrable, you will find pathways used by the Fijians who know the jungle as well as you know your own living room. Because of the mountainous nature of the islands, there are numerous streams and waterfalls, often with a cool pond in a rocky basin beneath the falls. One of the most famous is the sacred Bouma Falls on the Island of Taveuni, seen by the world in the motion picture "Return to the Blue Lagoon." Here you will also find a natural waterslide, also featured in the movie, where local residents have enjoyed themselves for centuries. Fiji has no leeches or crocodiles, and wild streams and brooks are crystal clear and unpolluted.

One of the fascinating aspects of general tours available in Fiji is their wide range of options and level of accessibility. Tours abound, from cultural and scenic tours of a localized area to the larger excursions such as week-long river and bamboo rafting tours to interior villages. The airlines also provide flight-seeing by seaplane over Fiji's picturesque mountain and coastal areas.

WEDDINGS ON LOCATION

You can choose from modern international resorts or smaller more intimate islands because this tropical paradise has a resort just right for you. Some resorts will help you arrange your wedding either in traditional Fijian style or the white wedding of your dreams.

Are you stressing out with all your wedding plans? Wouldn't it be great, once the hectic schedule of your wedding is over, to arrive at a place which is so mellow and unhurried that you probably don't even have to wear a watch anymore?

Fiji … an idyllic and relaxing tropical paradise, a haven for the about-to-be weds, newly weds and the romantic at heart. Getting hitched in Fiji has become quite a trend in this century, to the extent that many resorts, hotels and even cruises, are offering fabulous wedding and honeymoon packages to suit every couple's needs.

Choices range from luxurious private hideaways to more modest options. Enjoy lush tropical surroundings, feel the waves lapping beneath your feet, or even partake of a unique underwater ceremony.

Marriage Requirements: There is neither a residence requirement nor a minimum period of stay required for marriage in Fiji.

• Birth certificates of the couple to be married. (Minimum marriageable age for girls is 16 years; for boys is 18.) Birth certificates must either be originals or copies certified by and bearing the seal of the issuing authorities.

• If either was previously married, legal proof of termination of the

© The Fiji Visitors Bureau

© The Fiji Visitors Bureau

prior marriage(s). Death and/or divorce certificates must either be originals or copies certified by and bearing the seal of the issuing authorities

• U.S. passport if either/both party(ies) U.S. citizen.

• Two witnesses over the age of 21 years.

• If either party is under the age of 21 years, a written notarized consent is required from the father; the consent may be signed by the mother only if the father is deceased or cannot be located. If the parent(s) unreasonably refuses to consent, a written consent from a Court Magistrate will suffice.

Fees: Currently approximately US$10.00. For a Special License, it costs approximately US$8.00 and applicants must marry within 28 days from date license issued.

Other Important Information: District Officers and Registrars may perform marriages without a marriage license. After the ceremony, it may take 15 working days to obtain the marriage certificate: 10 days for the Minister or District Officer's document to reach the Registrar General and 5-6 days for the Registrar to search its records and issue the certificate.

A Special License is required if the marriage ceremony is to be performed by a Minister of Religion or performed at a venue other than the Registrar-General or District Offices. If you decide to have a civil ceremony, it is advisable to make an appointment either a day or two in advance.

A marriage performed in accordance with the legal requirements of the country in which it takes place is recognized as valid in the United States. For specific information, consult an attorney in the jurisdiction where you reside.

The two main offices of the Registrar-General in Fiji are located in Suva and Lautoka: Suva = Tel: (679) 315-280), (Lautoka = Tel: (679) 655-132)

LOCAL INFORMATION

Climate: Fiji enjoys an ideal South Sea tropical climate and can get hot in the summer but seldom reaches above 96°F. Trade winds from the east southeast bring year long cooling breezes late afternoon and early evening.

Fiji sits far enough from the equator to have relatively mild summer heat but close enough to have warm balmy winters too! The 'dry' season in Fiji is May to October,

'wet' season is November to April. But Fiji's weather varies greatly geographically. The leeward (west) sides of the major high islands including Viti Levu and Vanua Levu are protected from the prevailing south east trade winds and receive less rainfall than the windward sides of the islands.

Peak Season: June to October.

Language: Fiji is an English speaking country.

Currency: The Fijian dollar - FJD. Approximately 2 Fiji dollars equals 1 US Dollar.

Standard Time Zone: UTC (Coordinated Universal Time/GMT (Greenwich Mean Time) +12 hours

Entry Requirements: Fiji welcomes visitors, and everything has been done to make the process of entry as pleasant as possible. A valid passport for at least three months beyond the intended period of stay and a ticket for return or onward travel is required. Entry visas are granted on arrival for a stay of up to 4 months or less for nationals of the United States.

© The Fiji Visitors Bureau

Customs Regulations: Fiji Customs operates a Dual Channel System - the Red and Green Channels - for expeditious clearance of air travelers.

If you have any prohibited or restricted goods, or dutiable goods exceeding your duty/VAT free concessions, you should seek Customs Clearance.

If you do not have any prohibited, restricted or commercial goods, or dutiable goods exceeding your Duty/VAT concessions, you should proceed.

Safety: Fiji has one of the world's lowest crime rates, but prudence dictates that if carrying valuables, you check them in hotel/resort room safes or safe deposit boxes.

Fiji is free from malaria, yellow fever and major tropical diseases that are endemic to most tropical countries. It has an effective medical system in place although local people still believe in the efficacy of age-old herbal remedies. Fresh water in Suva, Lautoka and the other major towns has been treated and is safe to drink from the tap. This also applies to hotels and resorts. Some resorts use artesian water for bathing, but provide drinking water separately. If this is the case, visitors will be advised.

For more information, contact:
Fiji Visitors Bureau Offices
Thomson Street, GPO Box 92, Suva

Toll Free: 1-800-YEA-FIJI
Fax: (679) 330 0970
Website: www.BulaFiji.com
Email: infodesk@fijifvb.gov.fj

© The Fiji Visitors Bureau

© Tahiti Tourisme

FRENCH POLYNESIA

FIJI	-	CLIMATE
MONTH	HI	LO
JAN	86°	74°
FEB	86°	74°
MAR	87°	73°
APR	87°	73°
MAY	85°	72°
JUN	83°	70°
JUL	82°	69°
AUG	82°	69°
SEPT	83°	69°
OCT	84°	71°
NOV	85°	72°
DEC	85°	73°

Temperatures are provided in °Fahrenheit and based on averages.

Tahiti and Her Islands comprise an area officially known as French Polynesia. The Islands are scattered over four million square kilometers (one and a half million square miles) of ocean in the eastern South Pacific.

The total land area of these 118 islands and atolls adds up to only 4,000 square km. (1,544 square miles), and consists of five archipelagos: the Society Islands, Austral Islands, Marquesas Islands, Tuamotu atolls and the Mangareva Islands.

Tahiti is the largest island in French Polynesia. Its capital city, Papeete. In the last few years, Papeete has grown into a very modern city boasting a variety of new public facilities: shopping centers, boutiques, restaurants, night clubs and bars, travel agencies and airline offices, art galleries and museums.

© Tahiti Tourisme

The population of French Polynesia is an amalgam of Polynesian (75 percent), Chinese (10 percent), and European (15 percent). Among these racial categories exists every conceivable mixture. It would not be unusual to encounter a Tahitian of Chinese, American, Polynesian and French ancestry.

THINGS TO SEE AND DO

French Polynesia offers many exciting recreational activities. You can find a new activity to suit your sense of adventure each day and every of your vacation.

Get a sense for the "local color" by registering for

a circle island tour. These bus tours, which are available on selected islands in French Polynesia, visit the small villages, fields, hills and plantations of the region, giving tourists a feel for every day Tahitian life.

To thrill-seekers looking for a pulse-quickening experience, helicopter tours offer a bird's-eye view of Tahiti and her islands. Soar above velvety green volcanic peaks, past sprawling crystalline waters and sparkling sands.

Rent a bicycle or scooter and see French Polynesia up close and personal. Rentals are an excellent way for curious visitors to mix with the natives, take in the sights, and customize their vacation experience.

The International Golf Course of Atimaono, located on Tahiti's west coast some 25 miles from Papeete, is one of the most contemporary and beautiful courses in the South Pacific, and is open to visiting golfers.

The campgrounds of French Polynesia are popular with backpackers, students, and other visitors who enjoy "roughing it." Campgrounds are always private and there are no facilities in parks or other public areas.

There's something about the notion of hiking through French Polynesia that appeals to the explorer in visitors. Trails are numerous on the islands, and it's a good idea to seek out a guide to ensure against getting lost.

Examining the mountains, hills, valleys and volcanic peaks on horseback is a marvelous way for visitors to commune with nature. The Tahitian islands are home to some of the finest riding stables in Polynesia.

Outriggers, or racing canoes, are popular in French Polynesia. Some hotels and rental agencies around the island offer outriggers, and visitors can even sign up for Outrigger tours.

Tahiti and her neighboring islands are renowned for their superb dive sites. Here you'll find plenty of curiously shaped coral, a rainbow assortment of fish, and astounding undersea plant life. The underwater attractions vary from island to island and many guests choose to take in a number of dive sites.

There is no better way to explore French Polynesia than by yacht. Navigation is generally easy throughout the archipelagos. Steady trade winds and an abundance of anchorages make this region one of the great destinations of the seven seas.

In recent years, an increasing number of visitors have discovered the excellent surfing opportunities in French Polynesia. Though conditions are good throughout the islands, the best surf can be found around Tahiti, Moorea, Raiatea, and Huahine.

Tahiti and her islands are a shopper's dream, featuring a mind-boggling array of handicraft merchandise – exquisite, one-of-a-kind black pearl jewelry; decorous, hand-crafted garments; gorgeous, woven goods; and stunning carved items.

BORA BORA

Bora Bora's main island sits like a jewel in the center of its legendary multi-colored lagoon, which is surrounded by off-shore islets inside a protective necklace of coral. Bora Bora's guided tours bring visitors closer to the people, sites and history of this world-famous island. Knowledgeable guides can tell you all about the island's environment and ancient culture, as well as its strategic importance during World War II.

© Tahiti Tourisme

© Tahiti Tourisme

Special Points of Interest: Few watering holes are so mythic that they merit inclusion on a list of historic sites, but Bloody Mary's bar/restaurant is an exception. It's a Bora Bora institution, thanks to the many international celebrities who have passed through the doors. The restaurant's most famous patrons are listed on a prominent sign inside the bar. Reservations are strongly recommended.

The Mount Pahia, a majestic volcanic peak, is greatly admired for its imposing beauty. Depending on the weather and the time of day, visitors can see brilliant contrasts in light and color between the great peak and the ever-changing lagoon that surrounds it.

Situated on the island's east coast, Mount Otemanu is the highest point on Bora Bora. Made of ominous black rock, this ramrod-straight peak dwarfs nearly everything on the island.

Nightlife: When night falls on Bora Bora, the city slows to a quiet crawl. But the island is so beautiful that even a mundane activity like walking takes on wondrous new resonance. Take a night stroll along one of white-sand beaches, or relax over drinks at a beachfront resort. Though the island offers relatively little in the way of wild revelry, you can take in a night show at the Club Med resort or dance at Le Recif, the island's only disco and after-hours club.

Dining: Recently a number of quality, budget-priced eateries have broken ground on Bora Bora, making the island's dining scene even more exciting and diverse. When it comes to dining on Bora Bora, the choices are many. Naturally, there is an abundance of Polynesian eateries on the island, which prepare tempting and exotic seafood dishes. You'll also find American, Chinese, French and Italian cuisine here, as well as Polynesian variations on the aforementioned themes.

Shopping: From small-ticket items to costly crafts and souvenirs, visitors can easily get their shopping "fix" on Bora Bora. The island boasts an assortment of boutiques, stocking such budget mementos as T-shirts and pareos, to expensive gifts like hand-crafted jewelry, carvings and woven goods. Several boutiques sell the unique Tahitian black pearl.

The boutiques in the resort hotels are well stocked with vacation needs, souvenirs and black pearls, while the smaller hotels carry such items as T-shirts, suntan lotion and film.

If you happen to be on the eastern side of the island, be on the lookout for the small, outdoor vendors who set up shop around Anau Village. The wares here make for great souvenirs, such as shell leis and green (drinking) coconuts.

Nature/Sightseeing: Imagine spending the day on your very own island. The resort hotels in Bora Bora can arrange to take you and a loved one to a private motu (islet) for a secluded picnic. This is a true Tahitian experience that is not to be missed.

French Polynesia is known the world over as an aquatic Neverland, but the waters around Bora Bora are exceptional even by Tahitian standards. Bora Bora's lagoon is home to the

© Tahiti Tourisme

large manta ray, which makes this area popular among divers. Indeed, many of the island's most popular diving sites are named after the creatures, including Manta Bay, Manta's Reef, Manta Ray Channel and Manta Ray Pit. Mantas aren't the only sealife on Bora Bora. Divers can also see Moray eels, turtles, barracuda, and grey sharks.

A popular attraction with both locals and tourists, Matira Point is a pin-shaped parcel of land that is home to one of Bora Bora's finest public beaches.

MOOREA

Often likened to James Michener's mythical island of Bali Hai, Moorea is marked by volcanic peaks reflected in the tranquil waters of its two signature bays. Take a crash course in the culture and geology of Moorea by signing up for one of the many guided tours offered on the island, which can be organized through your hotel's activities desk. You'll be astounded by Moorea's fertile plantations and gorgeous vistas, not to mention its friendly people.

Special Points of Interest: Get ready for a quest of discovery that spotlights Polynesian culture and some of Moorea's fabulous natural resources. Meet stingrays and exotic tropical fish. Learn dolphin training tech-

niques and participate in the daily care of these amazing animals.

Indulge your inner explorer and take in a Moorean submarine excursion. Plunge as low as 200 feet deep and marvel at the island's undersea flora and fauna.

Old Polynesian charm blends with quaint European style at this curious guest house. Chez Pauline is a great place to purchase souvenirs and relics, including grinding stones, prehistoric stone tikis, and wooden artifacts culled from around Moorea's Afareaitu Village.

Perhaps Moorea's most spectacular scenic overlook, Belvedere Point provided the setting for the film saga "Return of the Bounty," featuring Mel Gibson and Anthony Hopkins. As the locals will tell you, the Point offers an awe-inspiring panoramic view of the Opunohu Valley. From your perch on the crater's ridge, you will enjoy a superlative vista of the Cook and Opunohu Bays.

The Opunohu Valley has yielded many ancient remnants over the years, most notably the stone "marae" temples and archery platforms which were used by Polynesian royalty in pre-Christian days (archery was a sacred sport in ancient Tahiti).

© Tahiti Tourisme

Star your excursion by hiking through the Paopao Valley, and conclude your journey in Opunohu Bay.

Unlike many of Moorea's historical sites, Tiki Theatre Village is actually a recreation of a pre-colonial Tahitian village. A massive tiki-like sculpture greets visitors at the entrance. The Tiki Theatre Village dance troupe performs four times weekly, and their kinetic shows must be seen to be believed.

Nightlife: Moorea eases into nighttime like a cavalier might ease into his smoking jacket. Indeed, once the sun sinks in Moorea, the atmosphere becomes laid back and relaxed. In place of celebrational frolic, Moorea nightlife centers around cultural and social activities. Visitors can take in a dance performance at the Tiki Theater Village or savor a repast at one of the island's hotels.

Dining: Colorful food-vans are legendary around Moorea for good reason – Les Roulottes provide delectable, fast food at reasonable prices. It's a Moorean custom for locals to mingle with visitors at the various Les Roulottes around the island. Meals range from barbecue steaks, chicken and shish-kabob to pizza cooked in a wood-burning stove or freshly cooked delicacies from the provinces of China.

If you're fed up with the steak-and-potatoes routine, break the habit at Moorea's diverse and exciting restaurants and grocers. Continental is the keyword here, with plenty of patisseries, brasseries, and seafood eateries to serve you. You've never tasted French, Italian or Chinese cuisine like they serve on Moorea. The island's chefs cook with a decidedly Polynesian passion and flair.

Shopping: If you want to take home some fine indigenous crafts, then you should plan a visit to the boutiques, shops and art galleries of Moorea.

In keeping with the island's proud heritage, merchandise on Moorea has a decidedly Polynesian feel. Visitors can select from an array of

© Tahiti Tourisme

goods, including black pearl jewelry, paintings, pottery, sculpture, wood carvings and woven artifacts. Moorea's laid-back lifestyle is chronicled in the work of many of the island's local artists.

Nature/Sightseeing: Take a guided hike through the luscious rainforest of Le Col des Trois Cocotiers (Pass of the Three Coconut Trees).

Witness the undersea wonders of Moorea with a deep-sea fishing expedition. Half- and full-day excursions are available, as well as trolling off-shore Moorea. Picnic and drinks are often included in expedition deals.

Moorea Lagoon Beach, Temae Beach & Village Faimano are three beaches that offer exquisite vistas, plenty of swaying palms, gentle surf, and prime swimming and snorkeling.

TAHITI

Often called "The Queen of the Pacific," Tahiti is the largest of the islands. Home to mountain waterfalls, beautiful beaches and the capital city of Papeete, its effect on visitors is magical. Whether by air, land or sea, you can learn more about Tahiti through one of the many tours offered on the island. From breathtaking aerial tours to leisurely sightseeing explorations via boat or all-terrain vehicle, there are countless ways to savor the splendor of Tahiti. Most tours can be arranged by hotels.

© Tahiti Tourisme

Nightlife: Get lucky at one of three hotel casinos in Tahiti. The Pacifica, Prince Hinoi, and Royal Papeete hotels now offer private, 24-hour gambling casinos. Spin the roulette wheel or try your hand at blackjack or poker.

Toss off your inhibitions – and your shoes – and dance the night away at one of Tahiti's many clubs. They provide an excellent opportunity for visitors to mingle with the locals. Some of Tahiti's clubs boast a ballroom ambiance, while others jump to the driving rhythms of disco beat or rock and roll.

Tahiti's local bars possess an almost mythic quality. Packed with revelers, these no-nonsense, smoke-filled nightspots present a great opportunity for visitors to mix with the locals.

Dining Les Roulottes are colorful food-vans that provide good, fast food at reasonable prices, and every evening hundreds of Tahitians and visitors gather to eat, laugh and enjoy the end of the day. Meals range from barbecue steaks, chicken and shishkabob to pizza cooked in a wood-burning stove or freshly cooked delicacies from the provinces of China.

The mixture of Polynesian and French cultures has resulted in a fertile culinary environment. There is a variety of splendid foods available in Tahiti ranging from traditional Tahitian fare to fine French cuisine, and tempting combinations thereof. The Tahitian diet consists mostly of fish, shellfish, breadfruit, taro, cassava, pork, yams, chicken, rice and coconut.

Visitors will also find any number of Italian, Vietnamese and Chinese restaurants of various price categories and quality. For Americans accustomed to fast-food, Papeete and some of the outer islands serve hamburgers, steaks, fries and similar staples.

Shopping: Tahiti's premier marketplace, Le Marche, is a great place to pick up handicrafts and souvenirs. Shoppers will find an assortment of jewelry, hats, skirts, carvings, mats and weaving here, as well as small cafes and vendors offering tempting fruits, vegetables and fish.

Situated directly across the waterfront, the Vaima Center, a four-level, block-square shopping center, has everything from airline bureaus, banks and boutiques, to book stores, travel agencies and restaurants.

© Tahiti Tourisme

Nature/Sightseeing Teeming with footpaths where visitors can view its acres of well-cultivated plants, the Harrison W. Smith Botanical Garden of Papeari feature bamboo, bananas, palms, hibiscus, and mapes (an indigenous chestnut tree).

Tahiti's only real lake, Vaihiria is a vast reservoir for rain and the river water that plunges down the outer wall of the Papenoo crater. Surrounded by luxuriant, green mountains, the Vaihiria Lake area is popular for its large eels and nearby banana plantations.

The fern-covered caverns in Maraa Fern Grotto, have become a must-see destination for Tahiti visitors. The site actually features three grottos.

WEDDINGS ON LOCATION

Unless you are a French National, getting married in French Polynesia is very complicated, and requires a minimum of one months residency. All legal weddings are basic civil ceremonies, which are carried out at the Town Hall in front of the Mayor.

Sentimental Wedding Ceremonies: For couples wishing to renew their vows, or lovers looking for a unique and legally non-binding way to express their feelings, the traditional Tahitian wedding ceremony is a fun way to say "I do." Couples are bedecked in pareus, flowers and shells, and the groom approaches the beach in an outrigger canoe. The bride, who is carried in on a rattan throne, awaits her groom on a white sand beach. A Tahitian priest performs the ceremony and gives the couple their Tahitian names.

© Tahiti Tourisme

LOCAL INFORMATION

The temperature averages about 79 degrees (F) year round, both air and water. It is a tropical destination blessed with lots of sun and enough rain to keep the waterfalls flowing and the flowers growing. The summer is from November through April, when the climate is slightly warmer and more humid. Winter is from May through October, the climate is slightly cooler and dryer.

Peak Season: July and August

Language: Official languages are Tahitian and French, but Paumotu (language of the Tuamotu Islands) and Mangarevan (spoken in the Gambiers) are also native tongues.

Currency: French Pacific Franc - CFP, though US dollars and credit cards are common. (At time of pub, approx. 125CFP to the US Dollar), Notes: 500, 1000, 5000, and 10000; Coins: 1, 2, 5, 10, 20, 50, 100

Standard Time Zone: UTC (Coordinated Universal Time/GMT (Greenwich Mean Time) –10 hours

Entry Requirements: Foreigners wishing to visit French Polynesia must have a valid passport, which, depending on the nationality of the visitor, contains a valid visa. Such visitors must also have an airline ticket back to their resident country or to at least two more continuing destinations. Visitors must also have a sufficient amount of funds to cover their planned stay in the territory. Citizens of the US are exempt from all consular visa requirements for stays of one month or less.

Customs Regulations: In addition to personal effects, the following are allowed into Tahiti duty-free: 200 cigarettes or 100 cigarillos or 50 cigars or 250 grams of smoking tobacco, 50 grams of perfume, 500 grams of coffee, 100 grams of tea and 2 liters of spirits.

To import plants and flowers, special permission is necessary from the Service of Rural Economy, P.O. Box 2551, Papeete, Tahiti, Tel. 50.44.55. All passengers importing plants, flowers, fruits or vegetables, must be in possession of an international certificate.

© Tahiti Tourisme

Safety: While this is one of the safest parts of the French empire, there is still some street crime (pick-pocketing, etc.) Always make extra copies of important documents, such as passports.

There are no snakes, poisonous spiders or fearsome animals in these islands. Hotels and dispensaries on each tourist island and atoll keep first aid supplies on hand to treat coral cuts, sunburn and the extremely rare case of poisoning, when the barefoot swimmer steps on the toxic spines of the stonefish. All the islands maintain hygienic controls to combat potential epidemics of tropical diseases, such as the dengue fever.

Tap water in the hotels and restaurants is safe to drink. Local mineral waters and all sorts of French mineral waters are available.

For more information, contact:
Tahiti Tourism Board
123 Main Street
New York, NY 01917

Telephone: 888-555-1234
Website: ww.tahiti-tourism.com

© Tahiti Tourisme

© Andrea Pohlman

M A L D I V E S

MALDIVES	-	CLIMATE
MONTH	HI	LO
JAN	86°	78°
FEB	86°	78°
MAR	87°	78°
APR	88°	79°
MAY	87°	79°
JUN	86°	78°
JUL	86°	77°
AUG	86°	77°
SEPT	86°	77°
OCT	86°	77°
NOV	86°	77°
DEC	85°	77°

Temperatures are provided in °Fahrenheit and based on averages.

A string of pearls scattered over the deep blue Indian Ocean - The first glimpse you get of this fascinating atoll- formation confirms two unique aspects of the Republic of Maldives. Not only does it consist of the most beautiful tropical islands, but 99% of its area is covered by the sea. Of the 1,190 total coral islands, 202 are inhabited and 87 are exclusive resort islands.

Island Resorts …the ultimate concept and a totally unique experience. Imagine having your own little island as your vacation home. A short barefoot walk from your bungalow takes you to every little corner of the island, whether it be the restaurant, bar or the dive school. A single resort occupies the whole island. While the rooms are individual or semi-detached bungalows built around the island facing the beach, or built over water in the shallow lagoon that surround the island, the restaurants and the bars, game rooms, gymnasium, spas and swimming pool may be built in a centralized area or scattered around the island to give each an individual and unique feel. What surprises many is that in all of these resort islands the only inhabitants other than the guests are the resort staff.

Accommodations range from detached individual cottages to over water bungalows. All resorts have deserted white sandy beaches and translucent clear lagoons enclosed by rich house reefs. Every island has its individual charm, character and ambience. The facilities and service offered on the resorts vary widely.

One way to discover the secrets of this Indian Ocean hideaway is to choose one of the liveboards that cruise across the atolls. Ranging from small cabin sailing to bigger cabin cruise ships, the on-board facilities and services vary from rather basic to exclusive.

© Andrea Pohlman

The origins of the Maldivian people are shrouded in mystery. The first settlers may well have been from Sri Lanka and Southern India. Some say Aryans and some archeological evidence suggests the existence of Hinduism and Buddhism before the country embraced Islam in 1153 A.D. Not surprisingly, the faces of today's Maldivian display the features of various faces that inhabit the lands around the Indian Ocean shipping and maritime routes. The Maldives has long been a melting pot for African, Arab and South East Asian mariners.

Nearly 50% of the population is under 15 years old, which you will see as children swarm the streets on their way to school. Maldivians are friendly, hospitable and peace-loving people, at the same time reserved and in control of their emotions.

THINGS TO SEE AND DO

Every resort offers a variety of excursions and a selection of evening entertainment. The excursion could be a day long trip or a half-day trip out to fishing villages, resorts and uninhabited desert islands. In the evenings there is usually a weekly disco, the popularity of which often depends on the composition of guests on the island at the time. Fishing enthusiasts can enjoy fishing expeditions' big game fishing, trolling or night fishing, which is a relatively relaxing option. Snorkeling is quite popular in all the resorts. It is easily accessible, relaxing, and no prior training is necessary.

Recreation: Swimming, Scuba Diving and Snorkeling. A visit to Maldives is incomplete without experiencing the realms of the underwater world. If you thought the aerial view was breathtaking, exchange your sunglasses for a mask, and take a glimpse underwater. This is where the real treasure of the Maldives is hidden.

Most visitors enjoy the lagoons as the natives do, swimming and snorkeling in the warm, turquoise waters, or canoeing, sailing, wind surfing, parasailing, deep sea fishing, jet skiing and water skiing. You can go on a shark feeding/ whale shark watching expedition, where you're in the water with hungry reef sharks that are being hand-fed by a guide. You can also charter a yacht, perhaps with a captain and chef, to sail among the islands.

The Maldives is famed for its rare underwater beauty. The profusion of psychedelic colors and the abundance and variety of life underwater have fascinated divers and snorkelers since Maldives was discovered as a diving destination. The highest level of visibility that one could expect- sometimes exceeding 50 meters - and warm temperatures throughout the year makes diving in the Maldives a delight you would want to experience over and over again. The Maldives has some of the best dive sites in the world and many visit the Maldives repeatedly for the sole purpose of diving. All resorts in the Maldives have professional dive schools with multi-lingual instructors and conduct courses for beginners as well as the advanced. Many of the resorts have excellent house reefs.

You don't have to be a diver to enjoy the fascinating underwater world of the Maldives. A snorkel mask and fins is your passport to enrich your holiday experience and to encounter different species of playful fish, turtles and other curious creatures that may be residing in the house reef.

Fishing is not only the lifeblood of the Maldivian economy; it is also

© Yassin Hameed

a popular pastime among locals as well as visitors. Maldivians enjoy a variety of different types of fishing. The most popular among these is night fishing. The boat leaves the island and anchors at a reef before the sun sets and darkness sets in. The lines are tethered with hooks and sinkers and dropped overboard from both sides of the dhoni. If the fishing is good it gives a lot of excitement to everyone. If not, it gives you an excellent opportunity to relax under the night sky as the boat gently rocks with the waves.

Morning fishing or big game fishing involves trolling, usually outside the atoll along the reef. Fishing enthusiasts may prefer to bring their own equipment. Almost all the resorts organize night fishing trips at least once a week. Big game fishing or morning fishing, if not included in the resort's weekly program, may be organized upon request.

Surfing: Maldives is fast establishing itself as a destination for surfers. Surfing is relatively new to the Maldives, especially compared to more established activities such as scuba diving. However, the recent O'Neil Deep Blue Contest has placed Maldives firmly on the world's surf map. While most of the recognized surf breaks are in Male' Atoll, there is certainly more to be discovered. For resort-based surfing it is advisable to choose one of the resorts on the eastern side of North Male' Atoll where there is access to a number of excellent breaks.

Special Points of Interest: Male', the capital of Maldives, would certainly count as one of the smallest capitals in the world in terms of its physical size. A third of the country's population lives in Male'. Different from any other island in the country, Male' is a city of high-rise buildings and paved roads. The main streets are lined with shops and offices. In the old bazaar area which still houses the country's hub of wholesale and retail trade, the lanes are so narrow that a single vehicle would find it difficult to navigate through, especially with its throngs of busy people.

© Yassin Hameed

MALDIVES

Male' is green and pleasant. The streets in the residential areas are shaded with trees, at places forming an arch overhead. A fair number of main streets are lined with big trees providing shade on both sides. Even a stroll around it would offer interesting sites and shots for the memories; the fish market and the local market at the northern waterfront, the new harbor in the south-west corner and the 400-year old Friday Mosque, to name a few.

Take a stroll around the residential areas or shopping streets, or simply sit down and relax at one of the small parks dotted around the capital and just observe the pace of life. Huskuru Miskiiy: Built in the 17th century, the Huskuru Miskiiy or Friday Mosque served the population of Male' as their main mosque for almost four centuries, until the Islamic Centre and Grand Friday Mosque took over the function in 1984. Built by Sultan Ibrahim Iskandhar in 1656, the mosque is a masterpiece of coral curving and traditional workmanship - probably the best display of coral curving anywhere in the world. The walls of the mosque are hewn together with blocks of filigree-curved coral blocks. Heavy wooden doors slide open to the inner sanctums with lamp hangings of wood and panels intricately curved with Arabic writings. The area surrounding the

© Yassin Hameed

mosque is a cemetery with a legion of intricately curved coral headstones. The Munnaaru or minaret in front of the mosque, used to call the faithful to prayer, was built in 1675 by the same Sultan.

Mulee-aage: Right in front of the Hukuru Miskiiy is Mulee-aage, a palace built in 1906 by Sultan Mohamed Shamsuddeen III, replacing a house dating back to the mid-17th century. The palace, with its wrought iron gates, fretwork friezes on its roof edges, and well-kept garden, was intended for his son, but the Sultan was deposed. During World War II vegetables were grown in its garden to help relieve food shortages. It became the President's Official Residence when Maldives became a republic in 1953 and remained so until 1994, when the new Presidential Palace was built. At present Mulee-aage houses the President's Office.

Entertainment: Bodu Beru is the most popular form of music and dance in the country, enjoyed by the young and the old, men and women. There is a Bodu Beru troupe in almost every inhabited island, and it is regularly performed at special functions and festivals.

The musical instruments used in Bodu Beru consist of three or four drums and a variety of percussion instruments. The drums are made from hollowed coconut wood and covered on both ends with manta ray skin or goat hide. A lead singer chants the lyrics and a chorus of 10 to 15 follows as they clap to the beat of the drums. The rhythm build as the song continues until it reaches a frenzied crescendo.

As the rhythm picks up, dancers come out from amongst the troupe swaying to the rhythm. As the beat becomes faster the dancers leap and jerk to the beat as if in a trance. Onlookers join in the clapping and dancing. Old men suddenly catch a stray rhythm and throw themselves into the arena. To wild applause from the crowd they gyrate and grimace in their dance, passing on to the young what they have learned from their forefathers. According to some historians Bodu Beru was introduced to the country in the early 19th century by African slaves. During the reign of Mueenuddeen I these slaves were liberated and sent to Feridhoo in Ari Atoll. It is believed that bodu beru spread out from there to become one of the most popular forms of entertainment in the country.

© Andrea Pohlman

Thaara also holds a special place in local entertainment. Two lines of men attired in white sit on the ground and sing to beating hand drums while others dance between them. Thaara is believed to have been introduced from the Middle East in the seventeenth century. Today Thaara is only played at national events.

Dhandijehun is another form of entertainment, which is popular throughout the country. This is mostly performed to celebrate festive events such as Eid and other national occasions.

Bandiyaa Jehun is a more popular form of dance performed by young women. The women carrying metal water pots stand in two lines facing each other. They sing and dance to melodious tunes while tapping the rhythm on the pots with rings worn on the fingers.

Although western pop and Indian music is quite popular today, traditional forms of music and song that have been passed down to us by our ancestors survive. Raivaru, farihi and bandhi are all unique styles of singing that are still practiced by people around the country.

Shopping: The Local Market, just a block away from the Male' Fish Market on the northern waterfront, is divided into small stalls. Here the pace is slower and the atmosphere peaceful, compared to the hectic activity in the rest of this neighborhood. Each stall is filled with a variety of local produce mainly from the atolls. Here you will find different kinds of local vegetables, fruits and yams, packets of sweetmeat, nuts and breadfruit chips, bottles of homemade sweets and pickles, and bunches of bananas hanging from ceiling beams. Another building just next door sells smoked and dried fish.

It is not difficult to find your way around Male', especially if you carry a map with you. After all it is only two square kilometers. The main street, Majeedhee Magu, runs right across the island from east to west. Chaandhanee Magu on the other hand runs from north to south. Most souvenir shops line the northern end of Chaandanee Magu, earlier known as the Singapore Bazaar for its many imports

© Andrea Pohlman

from Singapore. Guides and vendors speaking in English and other foreign languages patiently wait to serve the visitors. These shops are stocked with an ample supply of gifts and souvenir items. Best buys include the 'thudu kuna,' the Maldivian mat woven with local natural fibers. Attractive too are the wooden miniature 'dhonis'. When shopping for souvenirs, do keep in mind that export of products made of turtle shell, black coral, pearl oyster shell and red coral is prohibited.

Museums/Galleries: The National Museum is housed in the only remaining building of the former Sultan's Palace, which is now the Sultan's Park. It is an Edwardian colonial-style building of three storeys and fairly low key from the outside compared to the amazing collection inside. The articles on display range from thrones and palanquins used by former sultans to the first printing press used in the country, the rifle used by Mohamed Thakurufaanu in his fight against the Portuguese in the 16th century, ceremonial robes, headgear and umbrellas used by Sultans to statues and other figures dating from 11th century, excavated from former temples. A variety of artifacts from times past would give an idea of the unique and rich culture and history of this island nation. A visit to the museum gives an instant insight to the wealth of history most visitors never suspect existed. No longer will you think of the Maldives solely in terms of a tourist destination.

LOCAL INFORMATION

Climate: The Maldives has a tropical climate with warm tempera-

© Andrea Pohlman

tures year round and a great deal of sunshine. The warm tropical climate results in relatively minor variations in daily temperature throughout the year. The hottest month on average is April and the coolest, December. Average temperature is around 84 – 89 degrees Fahrenheit. The weather is determined largely by the monsoons.

There is a significant variation in the monthly rainfall levels. February is the driest with January to April being relatively dry; while May and October record the highest average monthly rainfall. The southwest monsoon or hulhangu from May to September is the wet season. Rough seas and strong winds are common during this period. The northeast monsoon iruvai falls between December to April. This is a period of clear skies, lower humidity and very little rain.

The Maldives is in the equatorial belt and therefore severe storms and cyclones are extremely rare events.

Peak Season: January through April

Language: Dhivehi is the language spoken in all parts of the Maldives. English is widely spoken by Maldivians, and visitors can easily make themselves understood around the capital island. In the resorts, a variety of languages are spoken by the staff, including English, German, French, Italian and Japanese.

Currency: Rufiyaa and Laaree (1 Rufiyaa = 100 Laarees) (Coins: MRf. 2, 1, 50 larees, 20, 10, 5, 2, and 1 laaree; Bills: 5, 10, 20, 50, 100 and 500 Rufiyaa.) US dollars are commonly used, though not everyone will accept them.

Standard Time Zone: The Maldives are 10 hours ahead of Eastern Standard Time.

Entry Requirements: A 30-day visa is granted free of charge. You must present your passport for entry. You may be asked where you are staying, so it is important to book your hotel in advance.

All baggage is screened electronically. Be sure not to lock your baggage as security will

© Andrea Pohlman

break the lock if they are required to inspect it. It is prohibited by law to import alcoholic beverages, pornographic materials, and idols of worship. Strict penalties apply to those attempting to import illegal drugs into Maldives. If you are bringing in a lot of photographic or diving equipment, it is advisable to inform your resort of the details prior to your arrival, or to bring a list with details (i.e. serial numbers of equipment) to avoid delay at the airport upon arrival. You will be expected to take all such equipment back with you. Import duty is payable for any items left behind.

Safety: The most common problems tourists encounter are sunburn and dehydration. Drink plenty of water during the day to prevent dehydration. Use sun creams of a high factor especially during the first few days. A variety of sun creams and lotions are available in all shops and boutiques.

Be careful where you eat and drink when in the Maldives. Registered outlets are usually safe. Avoid raw fruit and vegetables from dubious sources or of unknown nature without consulting someone you can trust.

For more information, contact:
Maldives Tourism Promotion Board
4th Fl, Bank of Maldives Building
Male 20-05, Republic of Maldives

Telephone: 960-32-3228
Website: www.visitmaldives.com

© Andrea Pohlman

WORLD'S BEST

WEDDING & HONEYMOON

DESTINATIONS

Hilton Maldives Resort & Spa - The Maldives

The following resorts were selected for their quality of service, ideal
location, outstanding facilities and beautiful surroundings.

• at a glance

Location: Anguilla, British West Indies
Mailing Address: CAP JULUCA P.O. Box 240 Maunday's Bay, Anguilla Leeward Islands, British West Indies
Reservations: 888-858-5822
Fax: 305-466-0926
Web Site: www.capjuluca.com
Size of Property: 179 acres
Meeting Space: 600 square feet
Accommodations: 18 beachfront villas
Range of Rates: $325 - $5725

about the area

Currency: U.S. Dollars
Weather: Tropical
Languages: English
Nearest Airport: St. Maarten's Julianna

• nearby attractions

Private shopping charters, golf charters, gaming charters, deep sea fishing trips, horseback riding, snorkelling trips and scuba diving. 100 restaurants on Anguilla from haute cuisine to basic beach bar.

Cap Juluca

LEEWARD ISLANDS, ANGUILLA

Consider a world that's secluded, peaceful, sophisticated luxurious. Imagine it on 179 acres of a 35-square mile northern Leeward island wrapped by Caribbean and Atlantic coral reefs. Add breezy trade winds yielding average 80F temperatures and refreshingly low humidity.

Fringe this world with soft, sifted-sugar, powder-white sand on two miles of crescent-shaped beaches protected by coral reefs. Surround it with 12,000 neighbors, island residents who prefer seclusion to the beaten path.

Bring in imaginative architecture - arches, domes, parapets and turrets in Moorish white embellishing 18 very private two-story beachfront villas that shelter 58 spacious luxury rooms and junior suites, seven suites and six pool villas.

Pure, stark white sand plays against bright white archways as the brilliant turquoise blue sea plays against blue sky. Textured interiors that combine Moorish and Caribbean motifs, leather, stoneware, inlaid mirrors, Brazilian walnut, Moroccan rugs and Italian tile all play against the tropical colors of the flora in the gardens.

Cap Juluca's guests, more than 50 percent of whom are repeat guests, find unexpectedly spacious accommodations. The six three- and five-bedroom pool villas have up to 3,500 square feet of luxury space; the 72 rooms and suites range in many configurations up to 2,200 square feet.

All rooms and suites have private, walled terraces with sea views and king-size beds. All rooms are air conditioned and have ceiling fans, safes, complimentary mini-bars and refrigerators. Louvered doors and windows of Brazilian walnut complement the cool tiled floors. Sumptuous bathrooms are of Italian Travertine marble and tile, some even have a lounging banquette. Many have double sinks

• onsite facilities

Three restaurants - Romantic waterside Pimms and Kemia, casual beachfront George's. Tennis, aqua golf driving range, croquet, nature trail, numerous watersports, fitness centre and a large selection of spa and holistic services

• wedding services

6 Gem of a Wedding programs. All programs include an engraved silver chalice, cost of the marriage license, officiant, transportation and photographs. Tie the knot on the beach, in a seaside gazebo, or in a private beachside villa.

and bathtubs for two with double headrests which look out to a private sunning terrace. All have glass-enclosed showers, bidets and dressing areas and twice-daily service to freshen the towels. Beachfront pool villas have private full-size, freshwater swimming pools in flower filled courtyards and sundecks within the suite areas.

The amenities of the resort are in keeping with the island's leisurely pace. Guests can windsurf, sail, kayak, waterski and snorkel. All water sports are complimentary and excellent instruction is available. Nearby, scuba diving and deep sea fishing can be arranged.

Guests can make day trips by air or sea to the neighboring islands of Saba, St. Martin, St. Barts, and Nevis. They can also play tennis on three omni- turf surface courts along with a tennis professional.

Cap Juluca is unique in that it brings its 'spa to the people'. Guests can luxuriate in their very private rooms or on their terraces whilst participating in the numerous spa and holistic services that are offered. Yoga takes place every morning around the pool, and for one week every month the hotel offers 'the second generation of spa services', the Mind, Body and Spirit program that includes Astrology, Shamanic Healing, Transpersonal Services and Regression Therapy.

There are three restaurants, the romantic waterside Pimms and Kemia, and the casual beachside George's. At Pimms, guests sample an imaginative seafood-based menu marked by French, Asian and Caribbean influences, in a setting that can only be described as breathtaking. Pimms is situated on a coral outcrop directly overlooking the Caribbean, inspiring what is now one of Cap Juluca's most charming traditions: colorful fish, turtles and rays that are waiting for crumbs, get fed as guests toss bits of bread into the moonlit water.

Along the beach, and strategically placed, beach bars provide complimentary bottled water and other tropical drinks and alert beach attendants deliver cold refreshment to quench the beach-goers thirst. And at night, guests return to their rooms wooed by a soft, romantic flickering candlelit lantern that awaits them.

What guests discover at Cap Juluca is a softer, slower, sweeter world that's as remarkable for its absence of high tech stress as it is for sheer beauty and luxury. Cap Juluca is the ultimate for wedding and honeymoon beauty, comfort, elegance, service, privacy, romance, relaxation and rejuvenation.

· ROMANTIC FEATURES ·

Cap Juluca, Anguilla, one of the most romantic, luxurious and private hotels in the world,offers many romantic touches through its 'Gem of a Wedding' program. Tie the knot in this fairy-tale setting, whether on the powder white crescent of Maundays Bay beach, beneath the white Moorish arches of a villa, or under a gazebo perched on a sand dune looking out to the setting sun, the sea and the mountains of St. Martin, a wedding at Cap Juluca makes a very special event even more special and memorable.

Romance is also in the air for honeymooners on a Romantic Rendezvous program - imagine a massage for two nestled side by side on your beachfront terrace, or having a glass of champagne in a double bathtub whilst looking up at the stars!

· wedding regulations

In order to be married in Anguilla, you need to be on the island for at least two working days prior to your wedding date. A valid passport is also required.

· 2003 Awards

Best Caribbean Resort Hideaway Report Readers Survey 2003 #1 Hotel in the Caribbean, Worlds Best Awards 2003 - Travel & Leisure #1 Resort in the Caribbean 2003

CuisinArt Resort & Spa

ANGUILLA, BRITISH WEST INDIES

CARIBBEAN

• at a glance

Location: Anguilla, British West Indies
Mailing Address: Resort Information
P.O. Box 2000 Rendezvous Bay
Anguilla, British West Indies
Reservations: 800-943-3210
Fax: 212-515-5669
Web Site: www.cuisinartresort.com
Size of Property: 40 acres
Meeting Space: Maximum of 25 people
Accommodations: 93 rooms and suites
Range of Rates: $325 - $4,000

about the area
Currency: U.S. Dollars
Weather: Tropical; Avg. mid-80's
Languages: English
Nearest Airport: Wallblake Airport

• nearby attractions

Shoal Bay East offers over a mile of white sand and clear waters, superb for snorkeling and scuba diving. "Scilly Cay," a tiny coral-based island in the middle of the Island Harbour's bay, is a popular spot for snorkeling and diving.

Tucked into a crescent curve of Rendezvous Bay, CusinArt is an oasis of Mediterranean villas crowned with brilliant cerulean blue domes. Each of the 93 rooms and suites offers extraordinary sea views ranging from 950 to 10,000 square feet.

Vibrant Italian fabrics and furniture imported from around the world create a distinct elegant charm in the guestrooms and suites. Large bathrooms are set in soft-toned Italian marble and feature deep bathtubs complimented by custom designed gentle bath amenities.

The 8,000 square foot Venus Spa was the first full-service luxury resort spa on the island.

Fresh is redefined in the world's first resort-based hydroponics farm. Guests feast on exquisite cuisine, much of it complemented by the resort's healthy fresh-picked produce, in all three of CuisinArt's superior restaurants.

Enjoy all of this and more while you are surrounded by two miles of the pearliest, white beach in the world.

• onsite facilities

Our three restaurants offer tasty selections for breakfast, lunch and dinner. Hydroponic farm tours and cooking classes are also available to guests. An 8,000 square foot full-service spa provides endless ways to pamper yourselves.

· ROMANTIC FEATURES ·

Create the wedding of your dreams and slip into the rhythm of Caribbean life. Anguilla is as serene as it is breathtaking. Your wedding is one of the most treasured moments of your life. Let CuisinArt help you savor every minute of it.

We take care of all the details so that you can be a guest at your own wedding and truly savor the memories you are about to create.

Whether you envision reciting your vows on the beach at sunset, on a shell-strewn terrace overlooking the blue Caribbean, or in a private courtyard surrounded by bougainvillaea-draped columns, our Wedding Planners will show you how easy creating your dream wedding on a tropical island can be.

• wedding services

CuisinArt Resort offers destination weddings without the work for busy brides and grooms who want a memorable day but don't have the time to pull it together. Cuisinart Resort is the perfect place to begin your new life together.

Sandals Antigua Resort & Spa

ANTIGUA

• at a glance

Location: Antigua
Mailing Address: Dickinson Bay PO Box 147 St. John's, Antigua
Reservations: 1-800-SANDALS
Fax: 305-667-8996
Web Site: www.sandals.com
Size of Property: 19 acres
Meeting Space: 1,334 square feet
Accommodations: 193 rooms and suites
Range of Rates: $305 - $545

about the area

Currency: U.S. Dollars
Weather: Tropical
Languages: English
Nearest Airport: V.C. Bird International

• nearby attractions

Champagne Sunset Cruise • Cades Reef Cruise • Horseback Riding • Jolly Roger Pirate Cruise • Bird Island Cruise • Tropikelly Trails • Circumnavigation Cruise • Shirley Heights Lookout • Estate Safari • Prickley Pear Experience

S et on breathtaking Dickenson Bay, the island's best and most

famous beach, this 5 Star Diamond awarded resort offers the charm of a quaint Caribbean village accompanied by the refined luxuries of a world-class all-inclusive that has been voted World's Leading Honeymoon Resort for seven years in a row. Here you can engage in every land and water sport such as water skiing, scuba diving and an impressive fitness center. Then relax at our full-service spa. When it comes to dining, there are five extraordinary restaurants to choose from. Discover Sandals Antigua and rediscover each other.

No other resort in the world with 193 rooms can offer as many as 4 exceptional dining choices - more than any other resort in Antigua. The flash of a knife reflects exotic Teppanyaki cuisine. Sophisticated international dishes are served by candlelight with Sandals signature white-gloved service.

• onsite facilities

Tennis, fitness center, volleyball, lawn chess, croquet, pool tables, European spa, scuba, snorkeling, sailing, paddle boats, windsurfing.

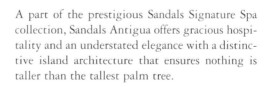

• ROMANTIC FEATURES •

A part of the prestigious Sandals Signature Spa collection, Sandals Antigua offers gracious hospitality and an understated elegance with a distinctive island architecture that ensures nothing is taller than the tallest palm tree.

Sandals has married the wedding and the honeymoon and has created the ultimate new romantic tradition....The WeddingMoon. One beautiful package, one perfect price. Best of all, we take care of everything, so all you have to think about is the magical time the two of you will have at Sandals.

A Sandals wedding can be as intimate as a ceremony for two under a gazebo or as a custom made extravaganza elsewhere on the resort.

• wedding services

Free Wedding with minimum 5 nights. Package includes: document preparation, certified copies of marriage license, announcement cards, wedding reception, champagne and hors d'oeurves, wedding cake, honeymoon candlelight dinner, bouquet, and boutonniere.

Atlantis, Paradise Island

PARADISE ISLAND, BAHAMAS

CARIBBEAN

• at a glance

Location: Paradise Island, Bahamas
Mailing Address: P.O. Box N4777, Nassau, Bahamas
Reservations: 800-ATLANTIS
Web Site: www.Atlantis.com
Size of Property: 60 acres
Meeting Space: 100,000 square feet
Accommodations: 2,317 rooms, suites and villas
Range of Rates: $240 - $25,000 (seasonal)

about the area
Currency: U.S. Dollars
Weather: Tropical
Languages: English
Nearest Airport: Nassau International Airport

• nearby attractions

Atlantis offers excursions that range from tranquil to thrilling. Among the possibilities, guests can swim with dolphins, ride a carriage through Historic Nassau, soar above the island on a helicopter tour, snorkeling, or relax on a catamaran.

• onsite facilities

Royal Towers guest rooms are elegantly appointed in a contemporary Atlantean theme. All guest rooms feature a variety of amenities such as full or french balconies, sitting areas, and service bars kept fully stocked on a daily basis.

• wedding services

For a couple planning a wedding, choosing the setting is half the fun. Atlantis offers some of the most breathtaking sites for an unforgettable ceremony. Wedding packages at Atlantis can be arranged and booked through Seashells Weddings.

Come and explore the wonders of Atlantis. Time spent here is relaxing, exciting, invigorating and inspirational. With experiences to suit everyone, no matter what your desire, visitors are sure to have every wish fulfilled.

From world class luxury to moderately priced comfort, Atlantis gives you a wide range of choice to suit your needs. Regardless of which accommodations you choose from our large selection, you will have all the experiences of Atlantis at your disposal.

The magnificent Royal Towers are the crown jewel of Atlantis. The architecture and decor are stunningly original, featuring unique murals, sculptures, and fountains. The most elegant accommodations at Atlantis, the Royal Towers are noted for impeccable service, sumptuous rooms and suites, and sweeping views. The Great Hall of Waters lobby, with its ceiling a dome of golden shells soaring 70 feet into the air, opens on one side to the Marina.

• ROMANTIC FEATURES •

Atlantis offers endless water features. Eleven pool areas and miles of white sand beach provide both adventure and relaxation. For those seeking excitement, seven different water slides and rides are guaranteed to let guests experience the thrill of a lifetime. Rivaling the legendary Marina of Monte Carlo, The Marina at Atlantis is the premier facility in The Bahamas. This luxury yacht harbor accommodates vessels up to 220 feet. The Marina also offers a variety of charter services. Guests of the Marina enjoy all of the services of Atlantis. The Mandara Spa at Atlantis offers a full menu of massages, facials, body treatments, aromatherapy treatments, and salon services.

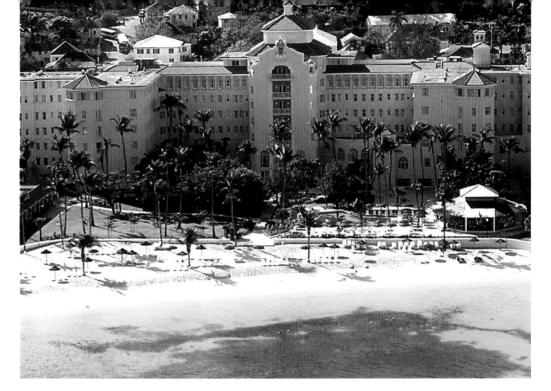

- **at a glance**
Location: Nassau, Bahamas
Mailing Address: Number One Bay
Street P.O.Box N-7148 Nassau, Bahamas
Reservations: 242-322-3301
Fax: 242-302-9010
Web Site: www.hiltoncaribbean.com/nas-sau
Size of Property: 8 acres
Meeting Space: 7,500 square feet
Accommodations: 291 rooms and suites
Range of Rates: $120 - $250

about the area
Currency: USD - Bahamian Dollar
Weather: Tropical; Avg. 80 degrees
Languages: English
Nearest Airport: Nassau International
Airport

- **nearby attractions**

Beautiful white sand beaches; the Straw
Market; unlimited duty-free shopping; Fort
Fincastle; Adastra Gardens and Zoo;
National Arts & Cultural Museum; and the
Arawak Cay Fish Fry.

British Colonial Hilton

NASSAU, BAHAMAS

Situated on the site of old Fort Nassau, the British Colonial

Hilton is the oldest building in downtown Nassau and an architectural masterpiece, which remains a part of Bahamian history. After its recent $68 million renovation in October 1999, this 291 room oceanfront property has evolved into a classic and luxurious leisure and business hotel that maintains a tropical, Colonial feel. Centrally located in downtown Nassau, it is in close proximity to all the happenings and activities on and off the island, from unlimited duty free shopping on Bay St., golfing and casinos, to diving with the dolphins. Guests can enjoy the dazzling sun and ocean waves at our freshwater pool. Just off our private beach, kayaking and snorkeling are popular diversions.

Each room and suite is beautifully furnished in Colonial decor with modern conveniences. There are 2 restaurants and 3 bars on property, as well as nightly entertainment in the upscale Blue Note Jazz Club.

· ROMANTIC FEATURES ·

Host an event as picture perfect as the Caribbean! The property offers an intimate and relaxed atmosphere, with private lounge areas throughout the hotel as well as beautiful gardens and private beach areas that are perfect for relaxing or having a wedding. The hotel has an experienced staff of meeting professionals on hand and can cater any number of special themed dinners or receptions, from grand events to small and intimate affairs. They can assist with the little details or help you plan the entire event from decor to location.

Guests can indulge in a variety of services at the Azure Spa, including aromatherapy, couples massages, body wraps, facials, hydrotherapy bath, or simply relaxing in a hammock in our lush tropical gardens.

- **onsite facilities**

Guests can relax on the private beach, in the lush tropical gardens, or in the outdoor freshwater pool. Non-motorized watersports, kayaking and paddleboats available, along with an on-site snorkeling facility and a full service spa and gym.

- **wedding services**

Our team of on-site wedding coordinators can arrange the ceremony, officiant, flowers, photography, decor, ideal location, and marriage license. The wedding cake, music and styling can be arranged, if needed, as well as airport transfers.

One&Only Ocean Club

PARADISE ISLAND, BAHAMAS

CARIBBEAN

• **at a glance**
Location: Paradise Island, Bahamas
Mailing Address: P.O. Box N-4777
Nassau, Bahamas
Reservations: 1-800-321-3000
Fax: 1-242-363-2424
Web Site: www.oneandonlyresorts.com
Size of Property: 500 acres
Meeting Space: Executive Boardroom
seats 20 people
Accommodations: 105 rooms, suites
and cottages
Range of Rates: $450 - $1,250

about the area
Currency: U.S. Dollars
Weather: Tropical
Languages: English
Nearest Airport: Nassau International
Airport

On an island called paradise is a legendary oasis, One&Only Ocean Club. Within the sanctuary of this exclusive resort, sapphire skies and turquoise waters conspire in idyllic perfection, complimented by the old-world charm of Versailles-inspired gardens. One&Only Ocean Club has emerged at the turn of the 21st century as one of the most elegant luxury resorts in the Americas.

Intimate in size, placing the highest priority on pampering, the resort offers a wide range of accommodations in gracious colonial Bahamian style, with round-the-clock butler service and little luxurious touches like champagne and strawberries in the afternoon and icy sorbet served on the beach. A spa facility that easily rivals any in the Caribbean and perhaps the world, One&Only Spa features serene, lush surroundings with private spa villas that can be shared by couples. Ocean Club Golf Course, created by pro golfer Tom Weiskopf, offers seaside green and tee settings, with expansive views of the azure sea. ❧

• ROMANTIC FEATURES •

One&Only Ocean Club offers the highest level of pampering, perfect for our honeymoon guests. A host of superlative touches at the pool and/or beach include five-minute foot massages, frozen grapes, cool lemonade, cold towels, and a selection of CD's and portable CD players. Guests can also get a personally-drawn bath with rose petals and votive candles in their rooms, special dining arrangements under the stars or on the beach, and the resort's signature champagne and chocolate-covered strawberries delivered every afternoon. To attend to guests' every need, One&Only provides around-the-clock butler service so you always receive the pampering that you deserve. ❧

• **nearby attractions**

Set sail on a catamaran cruise. Swim with the dolphins or discover an underwater world teeming with colorful reef fish on a snorkeling or SCUBA adventure. Tour historic Nassau in a romantic horse-drawn carriage.

• **onsite facilities**

Fresh-water Pool; Family Pool; Six Har-Tru tennis courts; Fitness Center; Golf Course; aquacat sailing, kayaking, and snorkeling. Traditional gardens; Spa and salon; Dune, a critically-acclaimed signature restaurant.

• **wedding services**

One&Only Ocean Club is graced by a spectacular terraced garden, modeled in the fashion of the grounds of the Château de Versailles in France. These formal gardens feature elegant statues and are an idyllic setting for a wedding ceremony.

Sandals Royal Bahamian Resort & Spa

NASSAU, BAHAMAS

• **at a glance**

Location: Nassau, Bahamas
Mailing Address: P.O. Box 39-CB-13005
Cable Beach, Nassau, Bahamas
Reservations:1-800-SANDALS
Fax: 305-667-8996
Web Site: www.sandals.com
Size of Property: 16 acres
Meeting Space: 11,000 square feet
Accommodations: 405 rooms and suites
Range of Rates: $335 - $750

about the area
Currency: U.S. Dollars
Weather: Tropical
Languages: English
Nearest Airport: Nassau International

• **nearby attractions**

Botanical Gardens, Dolphin Encounter, Horseback Riding, Submarine Dive, Deep Sea Fishing, Powerboat Adventures, Blue Lagoon Excursion, Shipwreck Adventure, Catamaran Cruise, Hartley's Undersea Adventure.

Quietly nestled on Nassau's famed Cable Beach, every facet of the celebrated Sandals experience reaches new levels of luxury at Sandals Royal Bahamian. As the recipient of the prestigious Five Star Diamond Award, this monument to regal elegance combines the grandest of European sophistication with the seductive passion of the Caribbean. You'll revel in the grandeur of our colonnaded pool. As our pampered guest, you'll dine on dazzling delicacies at your choice of eight gourmet restaurants.

Savor sumptuous Northern Italian cuisine at colorful Casanovas to the knife-flashing flare of exotic Teppanyaki fare at Kimonos. Classic French cuisine awaits you at Baccarat with its Art Nouveau inspired interior. Masterpiece cuisine is served in white-glove splendor in The Crystal Room, the most stunning dining room in the islands. From a Southwestern grill to authentic Mediterranean and Caribbean cuisine, Sandals Royal Bahamian is an incomparable passport of excellent taste for the world's most discerning palates.

• **onsite facilities**

Private offshore island includes pool, swim-up pool bar, 2 beaches and seafood restaurant. European spa, fitness centers, volleyball, basketball, tennis, scuba, snorkeling, sailing, windsurfing.

• ROMANTIC FEATURES •

Sandals Royal Bahamian Resort & Spa – a rhapsody of elegance and romance.

Sandals Royal Bahamian brings an unsurpassed level of luxury and personalized attention to an outstanding range of accommodations, ensuring that your selection is your perfect private palace. Over half of this extraordinary resort is comprised of magnificent suites, some as large as private villas.

• **wedding services**

Free Wedding with minimum 5 nights. Package includes: document preparation, certified copies of marriage license, announcement cards, wedding reception, champagne and hors d'oeurves, wedding cake, honeymoon candlelight dinner, bouquet, and boutonniere.

Sheraton Grand Resort
Paradise Island

NASSAU, BAHAMAS

• **at a glance**

Location: Nassau, Bahamas
Mailing Address: Sheraton Grand Resort Paradise Island, 1200 South Pine Island Road Suite 700 Plantation, FL 33324
Reservations: 1-800-GRANDFUN
Fax: 954-476-7226
Web Site: www.sheratongrand.com
Meeting Space: 8,500 square feet
Accommodations: 340 rooms and suites
Range of Rates: 4-day/3-night packages from $550 per person. Other packages available.

about the area
Currency: U.S. Dollars
Weather: Tropical
Languages: English
Nearest Airport: Nassau International

• **nearby attractions**

Next to the Atlantis Casino. Walking distance to duty-free shopping and nightlife. Near championship golf and downtown Nassau. Parasailing, jet skiing, waterskiing, deep-sea fishing, windsurfing, snorkeling, scuba diving all available.

• **onsite facilities**

Three miles of beach, fitness center, lighted tennis, activities center, beachfront pool, 4 restaurants, 4 bars, bicycle rentals, beauty salon, Bahama Divers scuba shop, gift shop, tour desk, business center, event and meeting space.

• **wedding services**

With 2 Certified Wedding Planners, we provide the minister, license, affidavits, flowers, music, limo and bus service, photographer, champagne breakfast, and a variety of indoor and outdoor settings, including the beach! Packages available.

The Sheraton Grand Resort in the heart of Paradise Island is located along three miles of white-sand beach, one of the most beautiful in The Bahamas. Lie in the sun. Swim with the dolphins. Try your luck at the Atlantis Casino next door. Breakfast at the oceanfront Verandah. Lunch at the Sundeck Bar & Grille. Dine at the oceanfront Rotisserie or at Julie's Ristorante Italiano. Every guestroom features a private balcony and guaranteed ocean view, cable TV, minibar, coffeemaker, hairdryer, iron and ironing board, safe, and direct-dial phone with voicemail and data-ports. The real magic of the 340-room Sheraton Grand is in our staff. From our knowledgeable and helpful Guest Services Director to our restaurant staff to our front desk personnel, you can depend on a level of service unmatched in the islands. Those are just some of the reasons the Sheraton Grand has been named one of the Top 25 resorts in the Caribbean/Atlantic region by Condé Nast Traveler magazine in its 2003 Readers' Choice Awards.

• ROMANTIC FEATURES •

The Sheraton Grand Resort offers you honeymoon and wedding plans and festivities you'll never forget - in a setting as perfect as your one true love. If you're planning a wedding or a honeymoon, our casually elegant island setting and decor make the Sheraton Grand splendid for just such occasions. What's more perfect than a marriage made in Heaven and celebrated in Paradise? Our Certified Wedding Consultants handle everything from the minister to the music, the ceremony to the cuisine. We provide a variety of locations, including the beach, Penthouse Suite and Grand Ballroom. We offer a variety of honeymoon and wedding packages we're sure will add to your grand romance.

Cobblers Cove

ST. PETER, BARBADOS

• at a glance

Location: St. Peter, Barbados
Mailing Address: Cobblers Cove Road View, St Peter, Barbados, West Indies
Reservations: 246-422-2291
Fax: 246-422-1460
Web Site: www.cobblerscove.com
Size of Property: 5 acres
Accommodations: 40 suites
Range of Rates: $340 - $2,650

about the area

Currency: BBD - Barbadian Dollars
Weather: Tropical
Languages: English
Nearest Airport: Grantley Adams International

• nearby attractions

The Barbadian People • St Nicolas Abbey • Original Plantation House Orchid World • Beautiful gardens with a focus on orchids • Harissons Caves • Dramatic underground caves • Rum distillery tours • Jeep safaris into the interior of Barbados

Cobblers Cove, Barbados One of the Caribbean's most renowned

and loved hotels, set amidst lush tropical gardens on the waters edge of the Caribbean Sea. Cobblers Cove, a member of coveted Relais & Chateau, epitomizes the perfect balance of peace, tranquility and comfort coupled with unobtrusive service, Cobblers exudes a special club-like atmosphere. Complimentary afternoon tea is served daily between 4 and 5pm in the Drawing Room.

The 40 suites are nestled around the original pink Planters' house, the focal point of the property, housing two of the most stunning suites in the Caribbean, the Camelot and Colleton.

Suite rates include unlimited water sports such as waterskiing, sunfish sailing, windsurfing and snorkeling. There is also a gymnasium and an all-weather tennis court on property.

For those who adore small private and intimate hotels, Cobblers Cove is one not to miss. ❧

• onsite facilities

All suite property • Air-conditioned bedrooms • Small kitchenette • Library of best selling novels in each suite • Complimentary watersports • Gymnasium • Tennis • Fresh water pool

• wedding services

Coordination of entire wedding, providing a bespoke experience • Ceremony with Minister or registrar • Administration of certificates • Transfer to and from the ministry • Wedding cake • Champagne • Bouquet • Boutonniere • Decorations

· ROMANTIC FEATURES ·

Peaceful, intimate beach resort. Camelot and Colleton, with their private pools, are a haven for those who just want to disappear into the depths of luxury. ❧

The Fairmont Glitter Bay

PORTERS, ST. JAMES, BARBADOS

CARIBBEAN

• at a glance

Location: Porters, St. James, Barbados
Reservations: 800-441-1414
Fax: 246-422-3940
Web Site: www.fairmonthotels.com
Size of Property: 19 acres
Meeting Space: 2,400 square feet
Accommodations: 83 suites and pent-houses

about the area
Currency: BBD - Barbadian Dollars
Weather: Tropical
Languages: English
Nearest Airport: Grantley Adams International

• **nearby attractions**

Access and transportation to exclusive championship golf courses; unlimited duty free shopping; nearby to Folkestone Underwater Park and Museum, and 8 miles from the capital, Bridgetown.

• **onsite facilities**

Half mile of white sand beach, outdoor pool; tennis courts; complimentary watersports - snorkeling, waterskiing, and windsurfing; Fitness & massage center; hair salon. Guests also enjoy the amenities at our sister property, Royal Pavilion.

• **wedding services**

From an indoor reception to an event under the stars, our wedding and catering coordinators work to ensure an atmosphere of romantic sophistication. From flowers and cake selection to wedding licenses, let us design the day of your dreams.

O n the legendary Platinum Coast, nestled in its own nineteen-acre private oasis, you'll find a historic resort that blends the charm of yesteryear with the beauty of the Caribbean. This is Glitter Bay, a magnificent tropical hideaway, where Caribbean warmth and British tradition graciously offer a luxurious and unique escape. Paralleled with a half-mile of white sand beach, ocean breezes flow freely through the luxurious guest rooms and suites, offering your very own piece of heaven.

By day a host of complimentary watersports

awaits you: from windsurfing or sailing, to luxuriating in the cool clear waters of the brilliant sea, or simply exulting in a massage.

Later, treat yourself to the refined pleasure of a traditional afternoon tea, or browse the specialty shops and art gallery. By night, savor the Caribbean's finest cuisine under the stars. All of this plus many other exciting things that we have to offer, make The Fairmont Glitter Bay your key to a Barbadian paradise.

• ROMANTIC FEATURES •

Take a relaxing break following your special day and celebrate your honeymoon with us. Let the seductive sea breezes caress your soul as you surrender to the breathtaking luxury and impeccable service that our resort has to offer. Gourmet dining, a gracious staff and enchanting ambiance make Fairmont Glitter Bay the only place to celebrate your love! Enjoy the best of the Caribbean with a romantic package for you and your sweetheart and sail on a catamaran over lunch, or see one of the spectacular Caribbean sunsets.

Whether celebrating your wedding or joining us for a relaxing honeymoon, you will always remember that special place where your life together began.

CARIBBEAN

• at a glance

Location: Porters, St. James, Barbados
Reservations: 800-441-1414
Fax: 246-422-3940
Web Site: www.fairmonthotels.com
Meeting Space: 1,167 square feet
Accommodations: 72 oceanfront rooms,
1 villa
Range of Rates: $249 - $4,350

about the area

Currency: BBD - Barbadian Dollars
Weather: Tropical
Languages: English
Nearest Airport: Grantley Adams
International

• nearby attractions

Beaches; watersports; access to exclusive championship golf courses; parks and gardens; scenery and natural wonders; wildlife and nature; historic sites; museums; sightseeing; nightlife; scenic tours; and unlimited duty free shopping.

• onsite facilities

2 most sought-after dining venues on the West Coast; tennis courts; outdoor pool; complimentary watersports including snorkeling, waterskiing, and sailing; health club; massage therapy; beauty salon; and exclusive boutiques.

• wedding services

From an indoor reception to an event under the stars, our wedding and catering coordinators work to ensure an atmosphere of romantic sophistication. From flowers and cake selection to wedding licenses, let us design the day of your dreams.

The Fairmont Royal Pavilion

PORTERS, ST. JAMES, BARBADOS

On the eastern edge of the Caribbean Sea exists a

place of enchantment. A magical oasis of luxury where the sand is white and pink, the sea and sky cornflower blue, the people warm and friendly, and the hospitality fit for sophisticated travelers. The Fairmont Royal Pavilion, a AAA Four-Diamond resort, has been described as 'The Jewel in the Crown of Barbados' - an elegant retreat where you can golf exclusive courses, play tennis, snorkel, sail, water ski and revel in the sun. An oasis of luxury and tranquility beneath gently swaying palm trees.

Re-opened in October 2003, Royal Pavilion has undergone a complete renovation undertaken by the world-renowned design firm, Wilson & Associates. Each luxurious room features DVD players and 27" flat screen television sets, as well as a 112 square foot balcony with breathtaking views of the sapphire Caribbean Sea. The adult-only policy has created one of the most intimate resorts on the island with the atmosphere of a Barbadian plantation home.

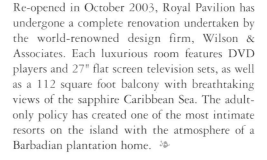

· ROMANTIC FEATURES ·

Rising above the gardens of fragrant lily and spectacular bougainvillea, The Fairmont Royal Pavilion graciously invites you to spend your honeymoon amongst the magnificence of its Barbados surroundings. Every beautifully appointed room offers sweeping ocean views and gentle trade winds that lull you into a state of romanticism. We will personally meet you at the airport and bring you to The Fairmont Royal Pavilion where champagne, orchids, and chocolate covered strawberries await your arrival. Then spend your days splashing in the sparkling waters of the Caribbean and your nights sailing on a catamaran or sharing one of our spectacular sunsets and candle light dinners on your private terrace.

Le Méridien L'Habitation - Le Domaine

ST. MARTIN, FRENCH WEST INDIES

CARIBBEAN

• **at a glance**
Location: St. Martin, French West Indies
Mailing Address: BP 581 Anse Marcel,
Saint Martin, French West Indies 97150
Reservations: 590-0-590-87-67-67
Fax: 590-0-590-87-67-88
Web Site: www.lemeridien.com
Size of Property: 30 acres
Meeting Space: 5297 quare feet
Accommodations: 396 rooms and suites
Range of Rates: $200 - $1200

Le Méridien L'Habitation - Le Domaine share the same

idyllic site on the beautiful island of St. Martin and combine European sophistication with Caribbean relaxation. Designed in Colonial style elegance, they are situated on one of the island's most beautiful beaches and are nestled in lush tropical plantation gardens.

Decorated with French Creole flair and style, Le Méridien St. Martin offers seclusion and relax-

ation in truly exceptional surroundings. Its bedrooms and suites are charmingly scattered around a tropical garden, while its white sandy beach tempts even the least enthusiastic of sunbathers. The hotel's tastefully decorated bedrooms and suites are complemented by four restaurants, three bars, a sports center, two swimming pools and a marina.

With Grand Case Village, Orient Beach, and the capital of French St. Martin, Marigot, only a few minutes away, Le Méridien St.Martin is in the ideal location for guests who love to experience the sights and sounds of foreign cultures.

• ROMANTIC FEATURES •

The tastefully decorated bedrooms and suites are set in a contemporary Creole style. Each room is dipped in the bright, fresh colours of a Caribbean palette, with luxury bedding, throw pillows, drapery treatments and artwork. A private terrace or balcony opens to the beckoning breezes, luring guests to al fresco refreshment.

La Belle France, one of four restaurants, serves French Creole cuisine and gourmet à la carte. Theme is French colonial / local tradition. The restaurant is decorated with pastel colours and designs, with seating for up to 70 guests.

about the area
Currency: U.S. Dollars
Weather: Temperate
Languages: English
Nearest Airport: Princess Juliana International

• **nearby attractions**

Surrounded by mountains, the hotel is nestled amid tropical gardens. Nearby attractions include the charming French Capitol - Marigot, with its colourful market and a total of 37 beaches with soft white sandy beaches and crystal clear water.

• **onsite facilities**

The resorts offer numerous activities including a fitness center, tennis courts, water sport rentals, volleyball, squash, racquetball, deep sea fishing, a scuba/snorkel center, jetski wave runner tours, and sunset cruises.

• **wedding services**

Le Méridien St Martin is the perfect venue for your wedding celebrations. The Hotel can cater for up to 300 guests in our air-conditioned Amiral Suite, or alternatively, dine under the stars in our extensive gardens.

Raffles Resort

CANOUAN ISLAND, THE GRENADINES

CARIBBEAN

• **at a glance**
Location: Canouan Island, The Grenadines
Mailing Address: 440 Park Avenue, 5th floor New York, NY 10022 USA
Reservations: 1-877-CANOUAN
Fax: 1-312-565-9930
Web Site: www.raffles.com
Size of Property: 300 acres
Meeting Space: 3,500 square feet
Accommodations: 156 rooms and suites
Range of Rates: $345 - $1,365

about the area
Currency: U.S. Dollar, XCD - Eastern Caribbean Dollars
Weather: Tropical
Languages: English
Nearest Airport: Canouan International

• **nearby attractions**

Located in The Grenadines, pristine Canouan Island is only 20 miles from Mustique. Day trips to nearby Tobago Keys and other picturesque islands of the Grenadines are easy to arrange.

• **onsite facilities**

Pamper yourselves at the exotic Amrita Spa, or opt for an in-room treatment. Savor gourmet cuisine in four world-class restaurants. Enjoy excellent watersports, boating and an 18-hole championship-grade golf course.

• **wedding services**

Canouan Island has a beautiful, reconstructed, non-denominational, 12th Century English church that's ideal for romantic weddings. We have a wedding coordinator on staff to make sure your special day is everything you dreamed it would be.

For a fortunate few, the Caribbean sun is about to shine a little brighter. July 15, 2004 will mark the unveiling of what will be the ultimate convergence of luxury and romance.

On the shores of the Caribbean's pristine Canouan Island, some of the most respected names in luxury and hospitality will come together on 1,200 secluded acres, to create the premiere resort property in the western hemisphere, Raffles Resort at Canouan Island.

Imagine a championship-grade, 18-hole golf course designed by Jim Fazio; European-style gaming at the Villa Monte Carlo managed by

Trump; a cliff-side luxury Amrita Spa; private yacht moorings operated by The Moorings, Ltd.; the largest swimming pool in the Southern Caribbean, and seaside recreation on a picture-perfect white sand beach—all brought together by Raffles, an internationally renowned hospitality company whose name is synonymous with the Asian commitment to unparalleled personal service.

· ROMANTIC FEATURES ·

It's hard to imagine a more perfect honeymoon destination than Raffles Resort at Canouan Island. With only 156 ocean-view accommodations, couples have the rare opportunity to retreat into a paradise all their own.

Of course, when you do decide to emerge, the ultimate luxury experience awaits. Four world-class restaurants let you wine and dine as if touring the cuisine capitals of Europe. Pamper yourself with any number of exceptional indulgences at the Amrita Spa—or opt for a special in-room massage for two.

Spend the day basking on an immaculate, crescent white sand beach, then return at night for moonlight stroll, the gentle Caribbean Sea lapping at your feet. It is romantic, indeed.

The Caves

NEGRIL, JAMAICA

• **at a glance**
Location: Negril, Jamaica
Mailing Address: The Caves, P.O. Box 3113, Light House Road, Negril, Jamaica, West Indies
Reservations: 1-876- 957-0269
Fax: 1-876- 957-4930
Web Site: www.thecavesresort.com
Size of Property: 2 acres
Accommodations: 10 units, 12 rooms
Range of Rates: $445 - $1000

about the area
Currency: JMD - Jamaican Dollars
Weather: Tropical
Languages: English
Nearest Airport: Montego Bay - International

The Caves Hotel in Negril, Jamaica is an organic interpretation of romance. Designed by Greer-Ann and Bertram Saulter, each of its 10 hand-crafted cottages is planted in a garden on the edge of the sea. It's the perfect choice for guests who value spirituality, privacy, romance and verdant beauty.

The Caves is a very sensual place. Its two seafront acres hide many secrets—sundecks and nooks, even grottos in the cliff itself. One of these grottos is designed for dining—lit with candles and strewn with flowers. The Aveda Mini-Spa looks out on deep blue water. The high-ceiling cottages are made of wood and stone with thatched roof. The Caves is the perfect choice for a romantic getaway or a personal retreat.

The Caves is located on Lighthouse Road in the West End of Negril, a resort town in western Jamaica. Staying at The Caves puts you in the center of a lush, serene environment — with easy access to the nightlife and legendary beaches of Negril. ❧

• ROMANTIC FEATURES •

This is a unique hotel as the houses are built around the natural caves and fossilized reef. Watching dolphins swim whilst eating breakfast is a common occurrence. Enjoy our Aveda Spa and jacuzzi. Complement the treatments with a rousing cliffside jump! The Caves has many repeat visitors who have expressed a serious wish to be part of the property. As a result we now have a Model House ready for viewing. Each of its 10 cottages is planted in a garden on the edge of the sea. It is the perfect choice for guests who value spirituality, privacy, romance and verdant beauty. It is a very sensual place. Enjoy treatments in the Aveda Mini-Spa as you look out onto the deep blue waters. ❧

• **nearby attractions**

Negril is not only a pastime - it is a lifestyle. Please check with our staff for the most suitable charters, rentals, fun bars and restaurants. Mayfield Falls, Palm Reserve, YS Falls, horseback riding, Bluefields and many more.

• **onsite facilities**

The rooms at the Caves are cozy and romantic. They are airy and spacious and designed with verandas and other elements such as outdoor showers that enhance the sense of openness.

• **wedding services**

WEDDING PACKAGE: (Bride & Groom only) Minister, license, bouquet, boutonniere, bottle of premium champagne, photographer. Cost: $800, plus prevailing room rates. 3-night minimum stay required.

Half Moon, Montego Bay

MONTEGO BAY, JAMAICA

• at a glance

Location: Montego Bay, Jamaica
Mailing Address: Half Moon
P.O. Rosehall, Montego Bay
St. James, Jamaica
Reservations: 1-800-339-9728
Fax: 876-953-2731
Web Site: www.halfmoon.com.jm
Size of Property: 400 acres
Meeting Space: 26,000 square feet
Accommodations: 419 rooms and suites
Range of Rates: $240 - $1,190

about the area

Currency: JMD - Jamaican Dollar
Weather: Tropical
Languages: English
Nearest Airport: Montego Bay Airport

• nearby attractions

Enjoy a range of activities; birding/garden tours, hiking, shopping and spa experience, horseback riding and more. Some places to go; Rosehall Great House, Rum Jungle Night Club, Dunn's River Falls, The Fern Gully and more...

• onsite facilities

The most Complete Caribbean Resort offers you a full experience of our Dolphin Lagoon, Golf Putting Green or Championship Golf Course, Fitness Center, Tennis Facilities, Shopping Village, Horseback Riding, Spa, Restaurants and More...

• wedding services

Whether It's an intimate ceremony for Two or a lavish extravaganza, Half Moon offers a variety of magical settings to make your dream wedding come true. A team of professionals will coordinate every detail of your once in lifetime event.

Half Moon Offers over two miles of intoxicating crescent-shaped beaches dotted with palm trees, and more than 50 cool, freshwater pools that summon guests in for a quick dip or a languorous swim. For those craving rejuvenation, the resort's exclusive spa facility is a welcome haven. The Robert Trent Jones Sr. designed championship golf course and tennis facilities are world-class. If you prefer, you can swim with the dolphins, exclusively for Half Moon's guests. A variety of dining options allow guests to follow their whims and choose gourmet Italian one night, a casual beach barbecue the next night or bask in the moonlit settings of The Sugarmill Restaurant.

At Half Moon, you will find an unhurried, relaxed atmosphere and a friendly, well-trained staff who cater to your every wish. At Half Moon, we are proud of our heritage and are committed to preserving our beautiful piece of paradise.

• ROMANTIC FEATURES •

Romance fills the air at Half Moon, the Caribbean's most popular and most gracious honeymoon destination.

By taking advantage of the resort's picture-perfect seaside location, lush landscape and warm tropical breezes, brides can design the ultimate one-of-a-kind wedding that will be cherished by all who attend. Choose our lavish Lily Pond Wedding Gazebo, with majestic palms and the Caribbean Sea as your backdrop. Or perhaps a wonderful tropical garden is more your style. For something intimate, a century-old sugar mill waterwheel will provide the perfect ambiance for saying "I do." Or for the more adventurous, how about tying the knot on horseback?

With professional wedding coordinators at your service, your wedding can be a dream come true.

Renaissance Jamaica Grande Resort

OCHO RIOS, JAMAICA

S tay in "Grande" style in Ocho Rios Jamaica.

An island of intoxicating natural beauty, from lush rain forests and mountainous terrain, to spectacular waterfalls and beautiful beaches.

A haven for nature-lovers, Jamaica is also a paradise for fun-seekers. No resort on the island puts the two together more dynamically than the Jamaica Grande. Here, guests enjoy the excitement and grandeur of Jamaica's most complete

resort, offering offering the all-inclusive experience.

Located within walking distance of Ocho Rios, the 720-room hotel provides guests with the best of both worlds. There's excellent sightseeing such as Dunn's River Falls and a colorful straw market. Everything for the vacation of a lifetime is right at your doorstep. Exotic location. Timeless romance. Unrivaled personal service…the honeymoon of a lifetime starts at the Renaissance Jamaica Grande Resort. All of this leading to an unforgettable moment of unbridled happiness.

• ROMANTIC FEATURES •

Imagine walking down the aisle on one of the world's most beautiful islands. Imagine one special moment that stays with you forever. Imagine the most important day of your life with nothing to worry about at all. Let your imagination go, because a Jamaica wedding at the All-Inclusive Renaissance Jamaica Grande Resort is truly a magical event. Beautiful weather. Opulent ceremony locations. Fragrant flowers. All leading to an unforgettable moment of unbridled happiness. And since we take care of every detail, you are free to bask in the magic of romantic sunsets, candlelight dinners, and lazy days in the Jamaican sun.

CARIBBEAN

• at a glance

Location: Ocho Rios, Jamaica
Mailing Address: Main Street, Ocho Rios, St. Ann, Jamaica, West Indies
Reservations: 876-974-2201
Fax: 876-974-2289
Web Site: www.renaissancehotels.com
Size of Property: 22 acres
Meeting Space: 30,000 square feet
Accommodations: 720 rooms, 15 luxury suites
Range of Rates: $190 - $440

about the area
Currency: U.S. Dollars
Weather: Tropical
Languages: English
Nearest Airport: Montego Bay

• nearby attractions

The island's physical attractions include jungle mountaintops, clear waterfalls, and unforgettable beaches; its tourist areas are grouped around the northern and western coastlines.

• onsite facilities

Wouldn't it be nice if your All-Inclusive resort didn't just include everything, but the best of everything? At the Renaissance Jamaica Grande Resort, that's exactly what you'll discover.

• wedding services

The Renaissance Jamaica Grande Resort offers special Jamaica "I DO" wedding packages that include the ceremony and other expenses. Full-time wedding coordinators are available to plan and organize intimate weddings for two or 1,200.

Royal Plantation
Spa & Golf Resort

OCHO RIOS, JAMAICA

Some say the lush northern coast of Jamaica, where the rolling

hills sweep down to the pristine white beaches, is one of the most beautiful places on earth. Flawlessly set amidst this tropical paradise, Royal Plantation Spa & Golf Resort is a splendid seclusion for those who are serious about

taking life easy, yet desirous of every refinement. Offering just 80 luxurious suites, all with stunning ocean views, it has the intimacy of an elegant private villa and the panache of a world-class resort of the highest caliber.

Step across the threshold where British-inspired elegance is touched by the exotic allure of the tropics. Reminiscent of aristocratic manors, all 80 suites possess mesmerizing ocean views and an amazing attention to refinements.

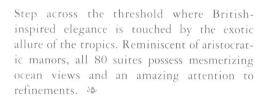
· ROMANTIC FEATURES ·

A truly romantic and unique one bedroom suite located on the first through third floors of the East wing. Enter your suite through the living room; to your right is the entrance to your bedroom which features a four-poster king-size bed, a balcony and a marble master bath. To the left, an entrance to your private Roman tub spa with French windows overlooking the East Beach, the Cove and the Caribbean. The Royal Plantation is a sophisticated and romantic hide-a-way like no other in the world!

• at a glance
Location: Ocho Rios, Jamaica
Mailing Address: Main Street, P.O. Box 2, Ocho Rios, St. Ann, Jamaica
Reservations: 1-888-48-ROYAL
Fax: 305-667-8996
Web Site: www.royalplantation.com
Size of Property: 8 acres
Meeting Space: 1,848 square feet
Accommodations: 80 suites
Range of Rates: $405 - $1,510

about the area
Currency: U.S. Dollars
Weather: Tropical: Avg. 82 degrees
Languages: English, Spanish
Nearest Airport: Sangster International

• nearby attractions

Complimentary tour of Dunn's River Falls, Port Antonio River Rafting, Port Antonio Highlight, Luminous Lagoon, Sun Valley / Firefly, Kingston Tour, Martha Brae River Rafting, Black River Safari, Sightseeing & Shopping, Coyaba / Fern Gully and many more.

• onsite facilities

Royal Plantation is a peaceful sanctuary, abundant with treasures that clarify the mind and lift the spirit. Here, you're as close to two pristine beaches as it's possible to be.

• wedding services

Free Wedding with minimum 5 nights. Package includes: document preparation, certified copies of marriage license, announcement cards, wedding reception, champagne and hors d'oeurves, wedding cake, honeymoon candlelight dinner, bouquet, and boutonniere.

Sandals Dunn's River Golf Resort & Spa

OCHO RIOS, JAMAICA

Inspired by the great Italian Renaissance period... and named

after the world-famous waterfall located minutes away... this breathtaking resort combines Mediterranean elegance with Jamaican charm, creating Caribbean luxury on a grand scale.

From a stunning lobby with soaring columns and winding staircase reminiscent of an Italian palazzo...to the rippling waters of Jamaica's largest freshwater pool, highlighted by a cascading waterfall that mirrors the image of its famous namesake.

As part of Sandals Spa Collection, this impressive resort offers the ultimate in elegance, refined ambiance, and elevated services. Enjoy luxurious accommodations including sumptuous suites with the dedicated pampering and special privileges of our exclusive Suite Concierge program.

To accommodate you in the luxurious manner you so richly deserve, we offer 256 of the Caribbean's finest rooms and suites in eight categories.

· ROMANTIC FEATURES ·

Sandals Dunn's River is a romantic paradise that is home to flawlessly friendly service amidst every world-class amenity, all set on the most beautiful stretch of white-sand beach in Ocho Rios.

Relax in the clear blue water of the island's largest pool with a cascading waterfall. Or make all sorts of waves with windsurfing, sailing, kayaking and water-skiing. Sandals is always about fun and exciting choices. Land lovers love scoring at tennis, racquetball and outdoor chess featuring life-size pawns. Play world-class golf at the nearby Sandals Golf & Country Club.

CARIBBEAN

• at a glance

Location: Ocho Rios, Jamaica
Mailing Address: PO Box 51, Mamme Bay, Ocho Rios Jamaica, WI
Reservations: 1-800-SANDALS
Fax: 305-667-8996
Web Site: www.sandals.com
Size of Property: 25 acres
Meeting Space: 1,596 square feet
Accommodations: 250 rooms and suites
Range of Rates: $270 - $675

about the area
Currency: U.S. Dollars
Weather: Tropical
Languages: English
Nearest Airport: Sangster International

• nearby attractions

Dunn's River Falls, Coyaba River Garden & Museum, Port Antonio, Blue Mountain, Bicycle Tour Blue Mountain Trek 52', Catamaran Cruise, Sunset Cruise, Prospect Plantation, Shopping Tour, Deep Sea Fishing, Horseback Riding, Martha Brae River Rafting.

• onsite facilities

2 impressive freshwater pools with swim-up bars, sailing, snorkeling, scuba, windsurfing, pitch & putt course on property, challenging 18-hole course at nearby Sandals Golf and Country Club, tennis, fitness center, European spa.

• wedding services

Free Wedding with minimum 5 nights. Package includes: document preparation, certified copies of marriage license, announcement cards, wedding reception, champagne and hors d'oeurves, wedding cake, honeymoon candlelight dinner, bouquet, and boutonniere.

• at a glance
Location: Negril, Jamaica
Mailing Address: P.O. Box 12 Negril, Jamaica, W.I.
Reservations: 1-800-SANDALS
Fax: 305-667-8996
Web Site: www.sandals.com
Size of Property: 21 acres
Meeting Space: Capacity: 20 persons
Accommodation: 223 rooms and suites
Range of Rates: $300 - $650

about the area
Currency: U.S. Dollars
Weather: Tropical
Languages: English
Nearest Airport: Sangster International

• nearby attractions

Dunn's River Falls, Ricks' Cafe, Horseback Riding, Deep Sea Fishing, Negril Hi-Lite Tour, Montego Bay Hi-Lite Tour, Wild Thing Cruise, Rafting Negril, Lighthouse Anancy Park.

Sandals Negril Beach Resort & Spa

NEGRIL, JAMAICA

A midst a pristine tropical setting, this world-class beachfront
resort combines a laid-back atmosphere with refined elegance. Spanning the longest and best stretch of Jamaica's famous seven-mile beach, this hotel won the coveted Green Globe Award and the CHA Green Hotel of the year, emblematic of its environmentally friendly ambiance.

Where even the architecture has been designed to be lower than the highest palm trees. At Sandals Negril, kicking back and doing nothing is considered a native art form...and doing everything is "no problem." Discover why Sandals Negril is perfect...for an ocean of reasons. To accommodate you in the luxurious manner you so richly deserve, we offer 223 of the Caribbean's finest rooms and suites in eight categories. Unparalleled luxury is evident in the lavishly appointed beachfront rooms ...stunning new grand luxe honeymoon rooms and honeymoon suites...as well as the two story loft suites showcasing spiral stairs that lead to panoramic ocean views.

• ROMANTIC FEATURES •

The sensational 2 story suites are almost directly on the beach. The first floor is the living area, leading out to your private patio or balcony. A romantic spiral staircase takes you upstairs to the loft and your sleeping area.

Enjoy Kimono's exotic Teppanyaki fare prepared with a theatrical flair or light spa cuisine enjoyed directly on the beach at The 4C's. Fine dining is complemented by unmatched selection of unlimited premium brand drinks and wines.

• onsite facilities

Sports Complex: racquetball, squash, tennis, basketball, fitness center, European Spa Watersports: waterskiing, scuba, snorkeling, sailing, windsurfing, kayaks, paddleboats, hobie cats.

• wedding services

Free Wedding with minimum 5 nights. Package includes: document preparation, certified copies of marriage license, announcement cards, wedding reception, champagne and hors d'oeurves, wedding cake, honeymoon candlelight dinner, bouquet, and boutonniere.

• **at a glance**
Location: Ocho Rios, Jamaica
Mailing Address: Sans Souci Resort,
P.O. Box 103, Ocho Rios/St.Anne
Jamaica
Reservations: 1-876-994-1206
Fax: 1-876-994-1544
Web Site: www.SansSouciJamaica.com
Size of Property: 27 acres
Meeting Space: 3,000 square feet
Accommodations: 146 suites
Range of Rates: $170 - $320 per person

about the area
Currency: U.S. Dollars
Weather: Tropical
Languages: English
Nearest Airport: Montego Bay

• **nearby attractions**

Ocho Rios is a popular seaport town and stopover for numerous cruise ships, with plenty of native shopping opportunities. Other attractions include horseback riding at Chukka Stables, Dunns River Waterfalls and Blue Mountain Biking Tours.

• **onsite facilities**

On site facilities include two beaches, 4 pools, tennis courts, full-service spa, fitness/aerobics center, water sports facilities with scuba, snorkeling, sailing and kayaking, four restaurants, three bars, and duty free gift/jewelry shops.

• **wedding services**

Ceremonies can be performed in a variety of breathtaking locations on the property, including a picturesque gazebo perched atop a lush hillside overlooking the ocean, an intimate tropical garden, and an alcove adorned by fresh-cut flowers.

San Souci Resort and Spa

OCHO RIOS, JAMAICA

Situated along the majestic emerald cliffs of Jamaica's northern coast, the exclusive, four-diamond, all-inclusive Sans Souci Resort & Spa encompasses a unique 27-acre property unparalleled in natural beauty, history and legend.

Located just a short distance from the fabled town of Ocho Rios, the property where the Sans Souci Resort & Spa now resides has been sought outfor centuries by travelers because of its fabled natural mineral spring and pristine beaches. Today this beautiful landscape is coupled with a true world class resort and spa and has aptly been coined the "Jewel of Jamaica."

Sans Souci Resort & Spa is built entirely around a natural mineral spring that has historically been acclaimed with restoring health, wellness, energy, and even love. Legend calls it a "fountain of love." Dating back to the mid-1600's, stories have been told of a Spanish maiden and an English naval officer who shared a forbidden love in the grottos beneath the cliffs. Risking everything, the couple would steal away under a canopy of stars to the spring's bubbling grottos. Because of their unbridled love, said to still linger in the hidden grottos, the legend attests that couples who soak in the mineral spring together will awaken hidden passion.

Local history books also tell of generations of nearby residents who lined up every Sunday to take their turn bathing in the natural mineral spring, believing it to heal minor ailments, skin conditions, and arthritic pains.

Today guests at the resort learn that not only is the natural mineral spring at the Sans Souci Resort & Spa without comparison, but also without peer is the individual hospitality and pampering that the staff provides to every guests.

Moreover the scenery is divine. Winding pathways through lush greenery, an elaborate labyrinth of small bridges, breathtaking vistas, four pools, two beaches, outdoor Jacuzzis, hilltop gazebos and secluded hammocks for two barely begin to describe the relaxed beauty of the resort. Thoughtfully arranged activities include sailing, windsurfing, water-skiing, hydra-biking, kayaking, scuba diving, snorkeling, volleyball, basketball, tennis, golf, and bocce ball. Nearby there is also golf at the prestigious Upton Links (green fees are free) and plenty of sightseeing opportunities and recreational pursuits from white water rafting, to mountain biking, shopping and swimming with the dolphins at Dolphin Cove. One beach is even "clothing optional."

A new favorite pastime at the Sans Souci Resort & Spa is getting pampered at the full-service professionally staffed tropical-style spa. Here guests may choose from a long menu of treatments performed in private cabanas, perched above the melodic hum of the Caribbean waters. Included in the stay, the resort has handpicked an assortment of services for each guest to ensure everyone receives an ample amount of bodily indulgence. Guests can lounge in the original grottos of the spring or in the resort's eco-friendly additions.

Whether relishing under the warm sun while listening to the whispering breeze, reinventing oneself in the resort's state-of-the-art fitness pavilion, dining at one of the resort's four award-winning restaurants, or sipping premium cocktails at one of the five distinctively themed bars, every guest at the Sans Souci Resort & Spa will find what they're looking for. And for those who prefer intimate privacy, the resort provides 24-hour in-suite dining in any of the elegant oceanview suites .

• **wedding utopia**

Few places in the world can compare to Sans Souci Resort & Spa as an elegant seaside wedding utopia. A place of great beauty, it has inspired lovers for hundreds of years.

• **wedding services**

In addition to providing the most unforgettable and photographically perfect setting, Sans Souci offers complete wedding packages with a wide array of complimentary services.

> ### • ROMANTIC FEATURES •

Weddings at the Sans Souci Resort & Spa are nothing short of magical. Couples can practically breeze into their own fairytales. Because each detail of the wedding is virtually free and handled by a complimentary professional wedding coordinator, couples can relax and enjoy every moment of their time together.

Sans Souci Resort & Spa will help each couple to grant each wedding wish. Many couples elope to the Sans Souci Resort & Spa, and more are decidedly choosing the resort to have a destination wedding, surrounded by intimate friends and family.

Horned Dorset Primavera

RINCON, PUERTO RICO

The Horned Dorset Primavera Hotel is an eight-acre hillside property overlooking the sea on Puerto Rico's secluded west coast. Oceanfront buildings rest on a large stone retaining wall. Hillside villas have panoramic sea views. Many of the suites have private pools and all have either a private balcony or terrace. Our rooms and suites surround you in luxurious comfort with antiques, exotic woods and marble baths.

Our poised and dedicated staff is the core of the Horned Dorset Primavera experience. Each member is a reflection of our high standards and commitment to excellent service and cuisine.

The Horned Dorset has recently undergone an expansion and renovation. Twenty-two new deluxe suites were recently added to their existing 33 rooms. A restaurant "The Blue Room" is also newly opened, directed by the Primavera's world-class chef Aaron Wratton. Other additions include an infinity pool (the third major pool on the property) on the hillside, overlooking the sea. ❧

• ROMANTIC FEATURES •

The Cuisine at the Horned Dorset follows the cycle of the tropical day; Breakfast is served al fresco in The Verandah, on the Terrace of the Blue Room, or in the privacy of your suite. Room service is available for light, cold snacks throughout the day, and the beach and pool areas are fully staffed so that a Puerto Rican Rum Punch is never too far away.

After watching the setting sun from the terrace overlooking the Caribbean Sea, guests may dine either soothed by the Steinway, crystal, and silver of the Formal Dining Room, or surrounded by the vivid colors and bistro flavors of the Blue room and its romantic outdoor terrace at the edge of the sea before retiring for the night. ❧

CARIBBEAN

• at a glance

Location: Rincon, Puerto Rico
Mailing Address: Apartado 1132 Rincon, Puerto Rico 00677
Reservations: 800-633-1857
Fax: 787-823-5582
Web Site: www.horneddorset.com
Size of Property: 7-acre seaside property
Accommodations: 53 suites and junior suites
Range of Rates: $440 - $740 MAP

about the area

Currency: U.S. Dollars
Weather: Tropical: Avg. 82 degrees
Languages: Spanish, English
Nearest Airport: Mayaguez, Aguadilla

• nearby attractions

There are many recreational activities in our area including wonderful snorkeling and sea kayaking directly in front of the hotel on the Caribbean Sea. The nearby island of Desecheo offers clear water and sheer underwater cliffs for diving.

• onsite facilities

Conceived in 2001 as a small village adjoining the sea front suites of the original hotel, these 1400 square feet, two-story, king-bedded town house suites all have private terraces and plunge pools facing the endless horizon.

• wedding services

WAll assist in organizing service, planning reception and menus by award-winning chef. Special arrangements for groups who reserve the entire property. Facilities range from formal dining room to open air terrace by the sea.

• **at a glance**
Location: Rio Grande, Puerto Rico
Mailing Address: 6000 Rio Mar
Boulevard Rio Grande, PR 00745-6100
Reservations: 800-4 RIO MAR
Fax: 787-888-6600
Web Site: www.westinriomar.com
Size of Property: 500 acres
Meeting Space: 48,000 square feet
Accommodations: 600 rooms and suites
Range of Rates: $399 - $3,950

about the area
Currency: U.S. Dollars
Weather: Tropical: Avg. 82 degrees
Languages: English, Spanish
Nearest Airport: San Juan
International

• **nearby attractions**

Beaches, Golf Courses, Water Activities, Tennis, Shopping, El Yunque Caribbean National Rain Forest, Hiking and Horseback Riding, Historical Tours of Old San Juan, Bacardi Rum Distillery, Camuy Caves and more.

• **onsite facilities**

12 restaurants, lounges and entertainment venues, Two Championship Golf Courses, Two Beachfront Pools, Spa, Beauty Salon & Fitness Center, On-site casino, Dive Shop & Water Activities, Specialty Shops and Boutiques, Westin Kids Club.

The Westin Rio Mar Beach Resort & Golf Club

RIO GRANDE, PUERTO RICO

Located on the spectacular Rio Mar Beach, in the shelter of lush mountains, Westin presents the Caribbean's premier beachfront vacation and golf resort - The Westin Rio Mar Beach Resort & Golf Club.

Nestled in a lush hideaway on the "Island of Enchantment," The Westin Rio Mar Beach Resort & Golf Club was created to pamper and impress. Its breathtaking ocean views are rivaled only by the elegant tropical decor of its splendid 600 guest rooms and superbly appointed suites. Each room and suite surrounds you in the comforts of home with Westin's signature Heavenly Bed® and Heavenly Bath®.

Two world-class golf courses and superior facilities are just a couple of characteristics that make The Westin Rio Mar Beach Resort & Golf Club a one-of-kind experience. A mile of palm-lined beach, two oceanfront swimming pools, endless water sports, a 13-court Tennis Center, spa, salon and complete fitness center, 12 superb restaurants and lounges, an on-site casino and award winning service. ❧

• ROMANTIC FEATURES •

Host an event as picture perfect as the Caribbean itself. Look to our staff for assistance with weddings, rehearsals and receptions. Let us plan an unforgettable event complete with gourmet banquet and catering options. The Westin Rio Mar Beach Resort & Golf Club enriches every event with stunning surroundings and the consummate skill of banquet and catering artisans. Our staff will manage all the details for your once-in-a-lifetime event. Only the best of banquet and catering services await for your Caribbean dream wedding. Contact our wedding planner today for more information. ❧

• **wedding services**

Our Wedding Coordinator will help you choose: Location, Reverend/Judge Service, Music, Food and Beverage, Cake, Decor, Flowers.

Anse Chastanet Resort

ST. LUCIA, WEST INDIES

• at a glance

Location: St. Lucia, West Indies
Mailing Address: P O Box 7000
Soufriere St. Lucia, West Indies
Reservations: 758-459-7000
Fax: 758-459-7700
Web Site: www.ansechastanet.com
Size of Property: 600 acres
Accomodations: 49 rooms
Range of Rates: $220 - $918

about the area

Currency: XCD - East Caribbean Dollars
Weather: Temperate
Languages: English, Creole
Nearest Airport: Hewannora
International-UVF

• nearby attractions

St.Lucia's spectacular scenery offers many sightseeing attractions. The most dramatic ones such as The Sulphur Springs, St.Lucia's famous walk-in volcano, the Louis XVI Mineral Baths, the Tropical Rain Forest and the famous Twin Pitons are within a short distance away.

• onsite facilities

2 Restaurant/Bars, 2 boutiques, full service spa, art gallery, tennis court, SSI/PADI scuba diving, snorkeling, windsurfing, sunfish sailing, kayaking, mountain biking.

• wedding services

Weddings are the unique and individual affair they should be, and every ceremony is organised in personal consultation with the bride and groom. There is no dedicated "wedding chapel", the bride and groom choose their own special location.

Voted one of the World's Top Ten Most Romantic Resorts by A&E television, Anse Chastanet Resort is in one of the most scenically spectacular settings that the Caribbean, if not the world, has to offer.

Enjoy the romance, tranquility and adventure of our 600 acre lush historical estate bordering on two soft, sand beaches, with pristine coral reefs just off shore. Relax in 49 individually designed hillside and beachside rooms and suites, decorated with original artwork by local and visiting international artists. Let the full service spa pamper you.

Go diving or snorkeling with the Resort's professional scuba operation, "Scuba St. Lucia". Go hiking or jungle biking on one of the 12 miles of private resort trails. Do nothing. Float and watch the sunset. Take a stroll on the beach after your candle lit gourmet dinner. Take our Stairway to Heaven. 🪸

• ROMANTIC FEATURES •

Anse Chastanet's spectacular scenic location, its unique setting and special ambiance has firmly ensconced the Resort as one of St. Lucia's foremost honeymoon vacation spots.

This position has been further cemented by the many romance awards Anse Chastanet has been proud to receive. Readers of Caribbean Travel and Life magazine have repeatedly voted Anse Chastanet to be one of the Caribbean's Most Romantic Resorts and A&E television voted Anse Chastanet to be one of the world's top ten most romantic resorts based on a vote by travel industry leaders and journalists. 🪸

- **at a glance**

Location: Gros Islet, St. Lucia
Mailing Address: .P.O. Box G.I. 2247
Gros-Islet, St. Lucia, W.I.
Reservations: 1-800-SANDALS.
Fax: 305-667-8996
Web Site: www.sandals.com
Size of Property: 17 acres
Meeting Space: 20,000 square feet
Accommodations: 284 rooms and suites
Range of Rates: $340 - $825

about the area
Currency: U.S. Dollars
Weather: Tropical
Languages: English
Nearest Airport: Vigie Airport

- **nearby attractions**

Soufrière Day Sail, Soufrière by Land & Sea, Deep Sea Fishing, Dolphin & Whale Watching, Jeep Rainforest Safari, Maria Island, The Jungle Trai, Marquis Plantation, Horseback Riding, Shopping Shuttle, Waterfall Bike Ride.

- **onsite facilities**

European Spa, Golf, 4 pools, 4 whirlpools, lawn chess, tennis, volleyball, fitness center, basketball, scuba, snorkeling, sailing, waterskiing, windsurfing, paddle boats.

Sandals Grande St. Lucian
Spa & Beach Resort

GROS ISLET, ST. LUCIA

O n an island so "simply beautiful" the French and British fought

over it for over 150 years, lies a Five Diamond resort considered the Caribbean's grandest new addition. Set on its own spectacular peninsula surrounded by the sea on both sides, the resort offers breathtaking vistas of the bay and the mountains on one side and the island of Martinique's distant shores on the other. Sandals Grande St. Lucian Spa and Beach Resort, where the views will steal your soul and the staff will steal your heart.

There are 284 luxurious rooms and suites to choose from, each custom appointed with large private verandas and designer baths - all with mesmerizing water views. For guests in search of something truly unique, there are 24 spectacular Lagoon Pool Rooms that allow you to swim right up to your patio.

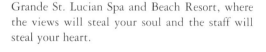
· ROMANTIC FEATURES ·

Built in the style of a British palace where majestic stone archways lead through a three-story open-air lobby, Sandals Grande St. Lucian is framed by spectacular mountain views and edged by the island's most dramatically perfect beach - an endless stretch of sparkling white sand. Indulge in everything aquatic, from scuba-diving to swimming, in a choice of four impressive pools - including a creative lagoon pool, which allows guests to swim right up to their rooms. There's hiking at neighboring national parks and golfing at the nearby Sandals Regency St. Lucia. Best of all, everything is yours merely for the asking - without compromise.

- **wedding services**

Free Wedding with minimum 5-night stay. Package includes: document preparation, certified copies of marriage license, announcement cards, wedding reception, champagne and hors d'oeurves, wedding cake, honeymoon candlelight dinner, bouquet, and boutonniere.

Sandals Regency St. Lucia
Golf Resort & Spa at La Toc

CASTRIES, ST. LUCIA

CARIBBEAN

• **at a glance**
Location: Castries, St. Lucia
Mailing Address: P.O. Box 399 Castries,
St. Lucia, West Indies
Reservations: 1-800-SANDALS
Fax: 305-667-8996
Web Site: www.sandals.com
Size of Property: 210 acres
Meeting Space: 1,800 square feet
Accommodations: 327 rooms and suites
Range of Rates: $220 - $825

about the area
Currency: U.S. Dollars
Weather: Tropical
Languages: English
Nearest Airport: Vigie Airport

• **nearby attractions**

Soufrière Day Sail, Soufrière by Land & Sea, Deep Sea Fishing, Dolphin & Whale Watching, Jeep Rainforest Safari, Maria Island, The Jungle Trail, Marquis Plantation, Horseback Riding, Shopping Shuttle, Waterfall Bike Ride.

• **onsite facilities**

3 freshwater pools plus scuba pool, 4 whirlpools, 9 hole golf course on property, basketball, volleyball, lawn chess, tennis, scuba, snorkeling, waterskiing, hobie cats, canoes, kayaks, sailing.

• **wedding services**

Free Wedding with minimum 5 nights. Package includes: document preparation, certified copies of marriage license, announcement cards, wedding reception, champagne and hors d'oeurves, wedding cake, honeymoon candlelight dinner, bouquet, and boutonniere.

Set along a half-mile crescent-shaped beach, this 210 acre

Five Star Diamond resort, that is part of Sandals Signature Spa Collection, takes you to the height of glamour. Where the service is rendered by a staff who is genuinely pleased to have you as their guest. No detail has been spared to bring you an infinitely romantic gateway on an exotic island that boasts the world's only drive through a volcano. Amenities such as the largest freshwater pool in the Eastern Caribbean, our own rolling fairways and the magnificent new Villa Suites on Sunset Bluff bring Sandals Regency St. Lucia Golf Resort & Spa to the pinnacle of perfection.

Every personalized comfort is provided in 13 different accommodation categories. Refined appointments highlighted by a cheerful island decor include custom-made four-poster mahogany beds and designer styled baths.

· ROMANTIC FEATURES ·

From beachfront rooms... to expansive honeymoon suites with a private plunge pool... to water's edge suites with split-level living rooms, Sandals Regency St. Lucia is the lover's retreat of a lifetime. For those who want to put themselves on the leading edge of luxury, Sandals Regency St. Lucia offers the Villas Suites on Sunset Bluff. Lavish one and two-story suites perched atop a magnificent coral bluff with unforgettable panoramic ocean views and private plunge pools.

• at a glance

Location: Providenciales, Turks & Caicos
Mailing Address: P.O. Box 186 Lower
Bight Road, Providenciales, Turks &
Caicos Islands, B.W.I.
Reservations: 1-800-BEACHES
Fax: 305-667-8996
Web Site: www.beaches.com
Size of Property: 125 acres
Meeting Space: 2,500 square feet
Accommodations: 453 rooms & suites
Range of Rates: $335 - $1,250

about the area
Currency: U.S. Dollars
Weather: Tropical
Languages: English
Nearest Airport: Turks & Caicos
International

• nearby attractions

Sunset Sail Island Getaway, Half-Day
Cruise, Glass Bottom Boat, French Cay,
Deep Sea Fishing, Middle Caicos Caves,
and a Conch Cruise.

• onsite facilities

6 freshwater pools, 4 with swim ups, scuba
pool, kids pool, 3 whirlpool, European Spa,
waterslides, state of the art video game
center, fitness center, volleyball, tennis,
basketball, scuba, snorkeling, windsurfing,
kayaks.

Beaches Turks & Caicos Resort & Spa

PROVIDENCIALES, TURKS & CAICOS

Anyone looking for the rare and exotic will find this destination the crystal clear choice. The waters are the most transparent you'll ever see and aglow with more shades of turquoise than you could ever count. People are outnumbered by the infinite variety of tropical fish. And there are moments you'd swear that time stands still. Beaches Turks & Caicos... a getaway for those who prefer to separate themselves from the crowd.

Beaches Turks & Caicos is your invitation to limitless gourmet dining inspired by the world's most celebrated cuisines.

From Caribbean hot to Continental haute, nine restaurants cater to your culinary cravings in a variety of enticing settings. So you can dine casually or formally, indoors, outdoors, even under the stars overlooking the serene sea...blissfully ordering as much as you want - whenever you want.

• ROMANTIC FEATURES •

Beaches Turks & Caicos is designed not only to fulfill your every waking fantasy but your bedtime ones too. Tucked into the heart of the resort, luxurious ocean view rooms and suites offer a refined elegance with breathtaking views of the turquoise sea. You'll find a variety of accommodations, each showcasing a unique mood and ambiance. Quaint bungalow villas in soothing pastels provide a charming island-style retreat. Within The French Village, chic rooms and suites with French doors and wrought iron railings overlook formal gardens.

• wedding services

Free Wedding with minimum 5 nights.
Package includes: document preparation,
certified copies of marriage license,
announcement cards, wedding reception,
champagne and hors d'oeurves, wedding
cake, honeymoon candlelight dinner, bouquet, and boutonniere.

Westin St. John

GREAT CRUZ BAY, ST. JOHN, USVI

• at a glance
Location: Great Cruz Bay, St. John, USVI
Mailing Address: P.O. Box 37
St. John, USVI 00831
Reservations: 1-888-627-7206
Fax: 340-779-4500
Web Site: www.westinresortstjohn.com
Size of Property: 47 acres
Meeting Space: 10,000 square feet
Accommodations: 282 rooms, suites and townhouses
Range of Rates: $399 - $1,755

about the area
Currency: U.S. Dollars
Weather: Tropical: Year-round 85°
Languages: English
Nearest Airport: St. Thomas Airport

• **nearby attractions**

Located on St. John, US Virgin Islands. 2/3's of the island is U.S. National Park with spectacular beaches & crystal clear waters, hiking trails, historical ruins and underwater snorkel trail at world renowned Trunk Bay. Watersports abound.

• **onsite facilities**

1/4 acre fresh water pool, white sand beach, a state-of-the-art fitness club, full service spa, six lighted tennis courts, shopping complex, Marina Watersports desk, 4 dining venues, 10,000 square feet of meeting space, banquet/catering services.

• **wedding services**

Ceremony packages are available as well as a Honeymoon Romance Package. Wedding Coordinators will help plan & organize all aspects of the nuptials. Enjoy an elegant beachside Gazebo ceremony or a romantic ceremony on the beach. Call 349-714-6070 for more information.

S et on a crescent-shaped beach surrounded by 47 lush, tropical acres and tucked into the green hills of tranquil St. John, the Westin offers 282 guest rooms, suites, and townhouses decorated in delightful island pastel colors with bamboo furniture, balconies or patios, air-conditioning, marble baths, Westin's signature Heavenly Beds, Heavenly Showers, voicemail and dataports. There are an additional 67 fully equipped vacation villas, many with private waterfall pools.

For dining and entertainment, there are four distinct venues, 24-hour room service and seasonal entertainment. The Spa at The Westin St. John Resort provides facials, body treatments and massages by a certified and caring staff. Activities abound with six lighted tennis courts, snorkeling, diving, sailing, windsurfing, kayaking, parasailing, fishing, a full-service fitness center, jeep rentals, and hiking in St. John's extensive Virgin Islands National Park. Golf is available on St. Thomas, shopping & dining in Cruz Bay.

• ROMANTIC FEATURES •

For those who desire romance, the brilliant blue skies, shimmering turquoise sea, lush tropical gardens, extraordinary service and gracious amenities all await you at The Westin St. John Resort & Villas—a Four Diamond Resort.

Indulge yourself in our spacious suites with luxurious Heavenly Beds™, spa baths and balconies or terraces. Sunset sails and romantic open-air gourmet restaurants heat up the nights while your days are filled with watersports, action and fun on the Caribbean Sea and shore.

Explore St. John, the most pristine and exclusive US Virgin Island or discover the Baths in the BVI. Pamper yourself at our state-of-the-art Fitness Club & Spa, shop the boutiques, laze around the pool. The ways to play here are endless…

Frenchman's Reef & Morning Star Beach Resort

ST. THOMAS, U.S. VIRGIN ISLANDS

• at a glance
Location: St. Thomas, U.S. Virgin Islands
Mailing Address: P.O Box 7100, St. Thomas, USVI 00801-0100
Reservations: 800-223-6388
Fax: 340-715-6191
Web Site: marriottfrenchmansreef.com
Size of Property: 22 acres
Meeting Space: 60,000 square feet
Accommodations: 504 rooms
Range of Rates: $155 - $1,500

about the area
Currency: U.S. Dollars
Weather: Tropical
Languages: English
Nearest Airport: St. Thomas (STT)

• nearby attractions

The Adventure Center Tour Desk arranges sightseeing excursions, including tours of St. Thomas, St. John, Coral World - an underwater observatory, Magen's Bay Beach, shopping tours, tram rides and other popular attractions and activities.

• onsite facilities

From meeting your specific catering needs to meeting details for your wedding, we'll provide the elements that support your event. Our facilities have the flexibility to accommodate everything from large banquets to intimate dinners.

• wedding services

Have you ever dreamed of getting married on a tropical island on the picture perfect day with a soft ocean breeze blowing in from the sparkling, blue Caribbean standing above a glistening beach? Weddings In Paradise can make it happen.

Crowning the Southern tip of St. Thomas, overlooking beautiful Charlotte Amalie Harbor, the majestic Marriott Frenchman's Reef & Morning Star Beach Resort offers the perfect Caribbean experience for vacations and honeymoons.

This award-winning resort offers a total of 504 guest rooms, including Morning Star's exclusive enclave of 96 rooms nestled at the water's edge, just steps away from the white sugary sand of our quarter mile beach. A variety of dining options are available, including a gourmet convenience market and Coco Joe's "off de beach bar." Enjoy any one of our 3 expansive pools, or pamper yourself at our Reef Health Club, featuring a variety of spa services. With fragrant breezes wafting through Marriott Frenchman's Reef, little is left for you to do other than relax. Our gracious staff will indulge you. The well-appointed guest rooms will comfort you. The activities and spa services will pamper you. And the dining choices will delight you throughout each day.

• ROMANTIC FEATURES •

Marriott Frenchman's Reef & Morning Star Beach Resort "Weddings In Paradise™" offers four different wedding packages and a full service staff to plan everything, from flowers to photography, and coordinate all necessary legal requirements to ensure a stress-free event. Couples recite their vows in a charming "Gazebo by the Sea" perched in a garden setting on a bluff overlooking the blue waters of the Caribbean Sea, making the entire experience a picture-perfect occasion. For couples wishing to combine their wedding with a honeymoon at one of the fabulous Marriott Beach Resorts, we have a "Honeymoon in Paradise" which includes your choice of weddings, along with a 6 day/5 night stay. Please call 1-800-FOR-LOVE for more information.

Arizona Biltmore Resort & Spa

PHOENIX, ARIZONA, USA

K nown throughout the world as the "Jewel of the Desert," the

Arizona Biltmore Resort & Spa provides a restful oasis of 39 acres covered with lush gardens, glistening swimming pools, and Frank Lloyd Wright-influenced architecture. Set in the heart of Phoenix, the Arizona Biltmore Resort & Spa has been a favorite of celebrities and U.S. presidents throughout its colorful history.

The Biltmore features 730 guest accommodations, including 78 one- and two-bedroom villas, eight swimming pools, seven tennis courts, an 18-hole putting course, and a full-service. European spa, salon, and fitness center. The adjacent Arizona Biltmore Country Club offers two 18-hole PGA golf courses: the Links and the Adobe. The Arizona Biltmore Spa is more than just a relaxing destination. It is an intoxicating journey that provides an escape from all aspects of daily life. ﾞ

· ROMANTIC FEATURES ·

The Arizona Biltmore offers more that 40,000 square feet of unique ceremony and reception space. Each ballroom and ceremony site embodies the Frank Lloyd Wright-inspired architecture, complete with ornate decor, historic antique accessories, manicured gardens and views of Squaw Peak Mountain. Embrace a long history of refinement, impeccable taste and a standard of entertaining that is synonymous with grace and style. Our wedding services are an extension of the Resort's international reputation as a place of stately beauty, flawless service and luxurious amenities. Events held at the resort are filled with a sense of exclusivity and singular charm, tempered with the romance of a grand hotel. ﾞ

U.S & CANADA

· at a glance

Location: Phoenix, Arizona USA
Mailing Address: 2400 E. Missouri
Phoenix, AZ 85016 USA
Reservations: 800-950-0086
Fax: 602-954-2571
Web Site: www.arizonabiltmore.com
Size of Property: 40 acres
Meeting Space: 100,000 square feet
Accommodations: 738 luxury accommodations
Range of Rates: $195 - $1760

about the area
Currency: U.S. Dollars
Weather: Desert
Languages: English
Nearest Airport: Sky Harbor
International

· nearby attractions

Whether it be booking a Grand Canyon tour or Hot Air Balloon ride or simply making a reservation with a member of our recreation department for a fitness class or a hike up Squaw Peak Mountain, your recreation needs are met.

· onsite facilities

Events here are filled with a sense of exclusivity and charm, tempered with the romance of an ageless grand hotel. From intimate weddings to grand celebrations, the ambiance of the Resort lends a dreamlike quality.

· wedding services

Embrace a long history of refinement, impeccable taste and a standard of entertaining synonymous with grace and style. Our wedding services are an extension of the Resort's international reputation as a place of beauty & flawless service.

• **at a glance**
Location: Tucson, Arizona, USA
Mailing Address: 10000 North Oracle
Road, Tucson, AZ 85737 USA
Reservations: 800-325-7832
Fax: 520-544-1222
Web Site: www.hiltonelconquistador.com
Size of Property: 500 acres
Meeting Space: 100,000 square feet
Accommodations: 428 guest rooms
Range of Rates: $129 - $490

about the area
Currency: U.S. Dollars
Weather: Desert
Languages: English
Nearest Airport: Tucson International

El Conquistador Golf and Tennis Resort

TUCSON, ARIZONA, USA

• **nearby attractions**

Imagine beautiful horseback rides, hiking and biking trails, and incredible sunsets. Now combine them with 45 holes of championship golf, a new $3.5 million pool with hot & cold springs and waterslide, 31 lighted tennis courts, and a spa.

" **T**ruly A Diamond Among The Rough" in the tranquil high

desert of Southern Arizona sits 500 acres of paradise where the views are breathtaking, the facilities elegant, the service exceptional and the recreation is endless. Fill your days with fun and relaxation at a true destination resort. This luxury full-service resort is inspired by the beauty of its pristine natural canyon views and lush desert surroundings. Imagine the luxury of gorgeous rooms and suites (over 100 suites) - all with remarkable views and private balconies. Each room comes standard with a king or two queen beds, and all rooms have been recently remodeled in a territorial style fashion reflecting the charm of Tucson living. Each guest room offers spectacular views of the mountains, lush desert, or pool view. Finally, experience the exquisite tastes of the Southwest in five delightful restaurants, including our own Last Territory Steakhouse and Music Hall with live can-can shows on the weekends. ⁙

• **onsite facilities**

Our atmosphere and award-winning service bring out the best in any event, including weddings. Exceptional catering gives you a wide variety of delicious dining options, and our expertise will make even the toughest decision easy.

• ROMANTIC FEATURES •

A Luxury Destination Resort, Hilton Tucson El Conquistador Golf & Tennis Resort is set in the breathtaking Catalina Mountain range in Tucson, Arizona. This luxury full-service resort is inspired by the beauty of its pristine panoramic views and lush desert surroundings, making it a perfect destination for either an unforgettable wedding, a romantic getaway or just winding down after the wedding of the century. Relax and rejuvenate at the Desert Springs oasis while enjoying fabulous weather year round. Partake in our luxurious spa treatments in a beautiful desert mountain setting. Golf on one of our three scenic golf courses. The El Conquistador will make your stay unforgettable. ⁙

• **wedding services**

Our space, atmosphere and award-winning service bring out the best in any event, large or small, including corporate meetings, trade shows, weddings and special gatherings. For special and memorable weddings, call our event planners.

Clift San Francisco

SAN FRANCISCO, CALIFORNIA, USA

U.S & CANADA

• at a glance

Location: San Francisco, California USA
Mailing Address: 495 Geary Street San Francisco, CA 94102 USA
Reservations: 800-652-5438
Fax: 415-441-4621
Web Site: www.ianschragerhotels.com
Size of Property: 17 floors
Meeting Space: 6,000 square feet
Accommodations: 363 rooms, including 26 suites
Range of Rates: $220 - $1,800

about the area

Currency: U.S. Dollars
Weather: Temperate
Languages: English, French, Japanese
Nearest Airport: 25 minutes to SFI Airport

C lift, Ian Schrager's premiere hotel in San Francisco, is a template breaking tour de force that promises to change forever the notion of what it means to be a luxury hotel . Elegant and sophisticated, yet in a total modern way, Clift takes the conventional hotel philosophy and turns it on its head!

While bearing some of the hallmarks of the traditional luxury hotel, such as exemplary service and amenities, what makes Clift truly special-and what sets it apart from the rest-is the unique energy created by its daring and brilliant juxta-positions. The hotel reads like a surrealists' manifesto: a desire to bridge the gap between fantasy and reality, the pairing of seemingly unrelated objects and a desire to return to the innocence of childhood, where a free-wheeling "down the rabbit hole" approach to life is embraced. Clift is a wonderland for today's daring traveller of any age. ✺

• nearby attractions

Located in heart of the theatre district, close to Union Square, (largest downtown shopping district), China Town, Cable Car rides, Nob Hill, Fisherman's Wharf, SOMA museum, gallery district and restaurants. One hour to Napa & Sonoma Valley.

• onsite facilities

The event rooms at Clift recapture the elegance of a by-gone era. High-ceilinged rooms accommodate up to 200 guests. The Spanish Suite on the 15th floor features hardwood floors, a fire place, two terraces and soaring panoramic city views.

• wedding services

Wedding Ceremonies up to 175 guests and Wedding Receptions up to 225. The Clift offers a comprehensive wedding referral service, including floral, entertainment, wedding coordinators, wedding cakes and more.

• ROMANTIC FEATURES •

The 363 rooms at Clift are generously scaled and beautifully appointed. Outfitted in tranquil and warm shades of ivory, grey and lavender, they exude a sensual softness that is a welcome counterpoint to the hustle and bustle of urban life. The room's beautifully crafted and detailed furniture include a massive English sycamore sleigh bed positioned on a polished chrome base. 400 threadcount Italian bedding complement the room's muted elegance.

Each room has two large frameless mirrors positioned on opposite walls, creating a mesmerizing "infinity" effect of unbounded dimension.

Lush silk curtains frame the mirrors and project a warm metallic glow throughout the room. ✺

• **at a glance**
Location: La Jolla, California USA
Mailing Address: 9700 North Torrey
Pines Road, La Jolla, CA 92037
Reservations: 858-550-1000
Fax: 858-550-1001
Web Site: www.estancialajolla.com
Size of Property: 9.5 acres
Meeting Space: 29,681 square feet
Accommodations: 199 rooms and 11
suites
Range of Rates: $229 - $750

about the area
Currency: U.S. Dollars
Weather: Temperate
Languages: English
Nearest Airport: San Diego
Lindbergh Field

• **nearby attractions**

Walk to beautiful Black's beach and Torrey
Pines State Park. The beaches of Del Mar
and La Jolla, famous Torrey Pines Golf
Course and the shops of La Jolla Village
are just 5 minutes away. Close to Del Mar
Race Track and San Diego attractions.

Estancia La Jolla Hotel & Spa

LA JOLLA, CALIFORNIA, USA

Luxurious amenities, exquisite surroundings and impeccable service define the essence of Estancia La Jolla Hotel & Spa. Whether you are searching for a quiet spa weekend, or the excitement of ocean water sports, we offer glorious vacation and getaway experiences you are sure to treasure.

A romantic California coastal retreat where time stands still, Estancia La Jolla features wrought iron railings, arched doorways, and picturesque clay tile roofs among lushly landscaped gardens. From the moment you arrive, the open-air arcades and garden courtyards create a tranquil setting that provides a sense of intimacy. Built on the former Black Family Equestrian Estate, our location in La Jolla provides the perfect climate for our world class spa, featuring tranquil indoor and outdoor treatment rooms.

Estancia La Jolla is located just minutes from the beautiful beaches of La Jolla and Del Mar, and only 14 miles from San Diego International Airport.

· ROMANTIC FEATURES ·

Stroll hand in hand through Estancia La Jolla's beautifully landscaped courtyards and gardens, including our signature Rose Garden.

Experience a sensational California sunset on one of our outdoor patios. Enjoy a margarita or glass of wine next to one of two outdoor fireplaces or in the Library, an intimate, gracious room adjacent to the Bodega Wine Bar.

Indoor and outdoor dining rooms will showcase local flavors and provide a variety of culinary delights as our Chef presents some of San Diego's finest culinary tastes, in an atmosphere of warm sophistication.

Couples can spend a relaxing and memorable day together at The Spa with "His & Hers" massage or body treatments.

• **onsite facilities**

Enjoy a cabana by the pool, a massage in our full-service spa, or relax in one of our three jacuzzis. Indoor and outdoor seating at both restaurants. Bodega Wine Bar features wines from California's eclectic vineyards. 24-hour in-room dining.

• **wedding services**

From small intimate occasions to the most lavish affair, our full service wedding planning is provided by one of our catering professionals. Custom menu selections and elegant decor assure that your celebration will be one of a kind.

Le Merigot, a JW Marriott Beach Hotel and Spa

SANTA MONICA, CALIFORNIA, USA

In the timeless tradition of the very finest hotels of France's Cote D'Azur, Le Merigot blends European elegance with the casual lifestyle of Southern California. Located at the beach in the city of Santa Monica, Le Merigot offers its guests luxurious accommodations combined with a full-service, European-style spa and superb cuisine.

Le Merigot's spacious guest rooms offer tranquil ocean views, absolute comfort and the finest amenities, including oversized desks and access to high speed Internet data ports.

The suites and rooms at Le Merigot have been designed with an eye towards distinctive style

and ultra-comfort. Informal, yet elegant, room furnishings combine our exclusive "Cloud Nine Beds" ™, dressed in Frette Linen, down duvets and feather pillows with plush, oversized upholstered chairs, couches and marble baths. Deluxe accommodations, boast spectacular views of the ocean and feature large patios overlooking the Hotel's Spa terrace and the aqua blue Pacific. ⌘

· ROMANTIC FEATURES ·

Santa Monica combines the historic and the hip in a way few Southern California towns can match. The ocean breeze keeps the climate comfortable; accordingly, the area attracts locals and visitors alike to its expansive beaches and vital downtown. The famous Santa Monica Pier, with its Ferris Wheel and attractions has been popular for generations.

Restaurants and shops, hiking and biking paths, historic buildings and modern architecture are all within walking distance of Le Merigot. Over the last few years, the 3rd Street Promenade, a multi-block pedestrian mall lined with stores and eating places and festooned with street artists and vendors has become a very popular gathering place. ⌘

U.S & CANADA

· at a glance
Location: Santa Monica, California USA: Near Historic Santa Monica Pier
Mailing Address: 1740 Ocean Avenue • Santa Monica, California 90401 USA
Reservations: 800-228-9290
Fax: 310-395-9200
Web Site: www.lemerigothotel.com
Size of Property: 200 yards along the boardwalk
Meeting Space: Over 10,000 square feet
Accommodations: 175 luxurious rooms
Range of Rates: $199 - $479

about the area
Currency: U.S. Dollars
Weather: Mild
Languages: English
Nearest Airport: L.A.X.

· nearby attractions

Just a short stroll from the famous Santa Monica Pier as well as downtown Santa Monica and the popular 3rd Street Promenade, Le Merigot is the perfect destination for business or a romantic and relaxing luxury vacation.

· onsite facilities

Cézanne is LeMerigot's fine dining restaurant. Le Troquet features an impressive selection of fine liquors, premium wines, appetizers and cigars. A complete health spa and outdoor pool with private access to the beach are also on site.

· wedding services

Over 10,000 square feet of meeting rooms have been specifically designed to accommodate weddings or corporate needs, and the hotel's comprehensive planning and banquet services insure outstanding events.

Le Parker Méridien Palm Springs

PALM SPRINGS, CALIFORNIA, USA

U.S & CANADA

• **at a glance**

Location: Palm Springs, California, USA
Mailing Address: 4200 E. Palm Canyon
Drive Palm Springs, CA 92264 USA
Reservations: 800-543-4300
Fax: 760-324-2188
Web Site: www.parkermeridien.com
Size of Property: 13 acres
Meeting Space: 9,500 square feet
Accommodations: 117 rooms and villas
Range of Rates: $189 - $350

about the area

Currency: U.S. Dollars
Weather: Temperate
Languages: English, Spanish
Nearest Airport:: Palm Springs
International

• **nearby attractions**

Located 10 minutes by car from charming downtown Palm Springs. · Offering world-class golf nearby on over 100 championship courses. · Just 100 miles east of Los Angeles and 150 miles northeast of San Diego.

• **onsite facilities**

Two indoor and two outdoor heated swimming pools, six tennis courts, lush gardens, exercise facility, three Jacuzzis. The spa has been rated as one of the top 5 spas in Condé Nast. We offer pilates, yoga and tennis classes.

• **wedding services**

Unique ceremony options • Fabulous photo spots throughout the hotel • Dedicated wedding planning professionals • Large bridal suites • LPM - Palm Springs Spa Voted Condé Nast Travelers' 2003 "Top Five" Spa Scenes.

Are you ready to disconnect? To reconnect with life.

Take a dip, go for a hike, get in a round-it's all to be found at the desertsmart Le Parker Méridien Palm Springs. Located only 10 minutes from charming downtown Palm Springs, home to the stars of the Silver Screen since the 1920's. Just 115 miles east of Los Angeles and 145 miles northeast of San Diego, Palm Springs offers world-class Golf on over 100 championship courses. All rooms feature a large desk, data ports for computer hookup, three telephones with two lines, in-room safes, spacious marble vanities in all bathrooms, iron and ironing boards and 27" televisions. Villas have king beds, showers, separate living rooms and wet bars, and private patios with lounge furniture. Rooms feature spacious king beds or two double beds. Bring the outdoors into your next event in our gardens or choose one of our indoor chateaus. Perfect for any function, Le Parker Méridien Palm Springs is sure to please. For more information on planning your next event, please call 760-321-4608.

· ROMANTIC FEATURES ·

Le Parker Méridien Palm Springs with its 114 rooms and villas gives you a desertsmart escape in the Southern California sun. Stretch out to unwind. Get laid back, soak up some rays, play hard or dance until dawn. Put the ahhh in spa at one of Condé Nast Traveler's 2003 "Top Five" spa scenes. Get pampered, scrubbed or covered in mud, wrapped up in seaweed or find release with Shiatsu. Choose alfresco dining at La Terrasse, or for that quick bite, be seen at Le Barre. Our poolside rooms offer direct patio access to the pool and private seating areas. From the mountains to the picturesque pools to the sprawling landscapes this desert flower will stimulate all 6 senses.

Manchester Grand Hyatt

SAN DIEGO, CALIFORNIA, USA

Manchester Grand Hyatt San Diego, a perfect marriage of Grandeur and Service. Enjoy superb food, spectacular bay-views and surroundings in the highest tradition of elegance.

Clearly defining San Diego's dynamic skyline, Manchester Grand Hyatt San Diego is located on the water's edge in downtown San Diego, in close proximity to the city's most noted attractions.

Newly expanded, the hotel's resort-like setting is compromised of two stylish buildings, the 40-story harbor building and the new 33-story seaport building which are connected by a rooftop pool and a 25,000 sq. foot sun deck that overlooks the San Diego Bay and Coronado Island. The hotel's main entrance, an elegant porte-cochere, creates a sense of arrival and sets a tone of prestige. Inside the hotel is adorned with chic chandeliers complimenting exaggeratedly high ceiling and rich appointments throughout.

Luxurious guestrooms, exceptional food and impeccable service are found everywhere at Manchester Grand Hyatt San Diego.

• ROMANTIC FEATURES •

This is the one event for which there are no dress rehearsals. You can rely on the artistry of the master chefs and wedding consultants at the Manchester Grand Hyatt.

We specialize in providing quality catering in surroundings of elegance customized to fit your personal taste. Teams of event coordinators work closely with you to assure all the details of your special occasion are perfect.

Whether your event is simple and elegant or a festive celebration, you can count on the impeccable service at the Manchester Grand Hyatt.

U.S & CANADA

• at a glance
Location: San Diego, California USA
Mailing Address: One Market Place San Diego, CA 92101 USA
Reservations: 800-233-1234
Fax: 619-233-6464
Web Site: www.manchestergrand.hyatt.com
Size of Property: 33 & 40-story towers
Meeting Space: 125,000 square feet
Accommodations: 1,625 rooms
Range of Rates: Contact Hotel For Rates

about the area
Currency: U.S. Dollars
Weather: Avg. 72 degrees
Languages: English
Nearest Airport: San Diego International

• nearby attractions

The hotel's prime waterfront location is a brief walk from the Convention Center, Seaport Village, and the Gaslamp Quarter which hosts over 100 restaurants and nightclubs. Located near beaches, Sea World, the San Diego Zoo, and more.

• onsite facilities

Zagat-endorsed Laels Restaurant; fitness center; tennis courts; rooftop pool with sun-deck overlooking San Diego Bay; full-service day spa & salon featuring Aveda hair and body treatments as well as Epicuren skin care products.

• wedding services

Our coordinators can assist with every detail of your wedding, from creative menus and wedding cakes, to entertainment and floral designs. Breathtaking views from all of our banquet areas offer picture perfect settings for photographs.

Montage Resort & Spa

LAGUNA BEACH, CALIFORNIA, USA

• at a glance

Location: Laguna Beach, California USA
Mailing Address: 30801 South Coast
Hwy Laguna Beach, CA 92651 USA
Reservations: 1-866-271-6953
Fax: 1-949-715-6100
Web Site: www.montagelagunabeach-
weddings.com
Size of Property: 30 acres
Meeting Space: 14,500 square feet
Accommodations: 262 rooms and suites
Range of Rates: $495 plus per night

about the area

Currency: U.S. Dollars
Weather: Tropical
Languages: English
Nearest Airport: John Wayne Airport

• nearby attractions

Whether it's shopping, art tours, water
sports, beach activities, or spa treatments,
at Montage Resort & Spa, there are endless opportunities to enjoy the natural habitat and attractions of the Laguna Beach
area.

• onsite facilities

Oceanfront opulence abounds at Montage.
With lush landscaping and pristine white
sand beaches, this is a retreat unlike any
other-offering elegant accommodations, a
beachfront spa, three sparkling swimming
pools and distinctive dining.

• wedding services

Our creative wedding experts customize
your special day to exceed your every
wish. From flowers to menus, we coordinate every detail so your celebration is a
treasured memory that lasts a lifetime

Nestled along the stunning coastline of Laguna Beach,

Montage Resort & Spa is an intimate seaside retreat that reflects the culture and heritage of Southern California. It's a place where every luxurious room offers sweeping ocean views. Where art and life blend seamlessly, and intimate sand beaches encourage quiet contemplation.

Here, memories and traditions are created for each bride and groom. Spontaneity and imagina-tion are encouraged. Beauty and romance prevail, making every wedding a dream come true.

Ballrooms are adorned in silk fabric wall cover-ings, crown molding & wainscoting. Fine Bausher China, Riedel Crystal, Frette linens, Christofle flatware, & glass beaded chargers evoke classic sophistication.

From its gracious craftsman-style architecture to the rugged coastline views to a multitude of serv-ices and amenities, this world-class resort offers a masterful mix of nature, art and luxury.

• ROMANTIC FEATURES •

Start the rest of your life at Montage with our "Splendid Honeymoon" package. Enjoy a 6-night/7-day luxury honeymoon in an Ocean Suite. Your first night, watch the moon glisten off the ocean as you enjoy a candle light dinner in your guestroom, followed by a soak in the over-sized tub filled with a botanical bath drawn by our "Romance Artist." The next morning, enjoy breakfast in bed before experiencing true honey-moon bliss with a relaxing massage for two in Spa Montage's romantic couple's suite. Enjoy the rest of the week lounging by the pool, on the beach or experiencing the variety of activities in Southern California. End your honeymoon with a romantic dinner in The Loft.

U.S & CANADA

- **at a glance**

Location: Beverly Hills, California USA
Mailing Address: 9291 Burton Way,
Beverly Hills, CA 90210
Reservations: 800-800-2113
Fax: 310-278-8247
Web Site: www.lermitagehotel.com
Size of Property: 1 acre
Meeting Space: 5,200 square feet
Accommodations: 123 rooms and suites
Range of Rates: $345 - $3,800

about the area
Currency: U.S. Dollars
Weather: Temperate
Languages: English
Nearest Airport: LAX

- **nearby attractions**

Walk to famous Rodeo Drive and the unique boutiques and galleries of Beverly Hills. Minutes to Century City, The Getty Museum, Museum of Tolerance, LACMA, The Petersen Automotive Museum and the beach towns of Malibu and Santa Monica.

- **onsite facilities**

Pool terrace: 1,600 sq ft of rooftop privacy. Rooftop terraces: north & south, hosts 120 in sit-down elegance. Raffles suite: 1,000 sq ft & club-like. RafflesAmrita Spa: offers complete spa services. The rooftop pool; southern California.

- **wedding services**

The pool terrace and the rooftop terraces come with views to forever, providing the perfect backdrop for an above it all ceremony & wedding reception. Up to 120 guests. Complete Wedding packages are available.

Raffles L'Ermitage Beverly Hills

BEVERLY HILLS, CALIFORNIA, USA

Has again received the prestigious Five-Diamonds & Five-Stars.

Most 5 star, 5 diamond hotels are surrounded by office towers and businesses, so you will be delighted to discover this 5 star, 5 diamond, Beverly Hills gem on a beautiful tree-lined residential street. Close enough to make Rodeo Drive (with its shops, boutiques and galleries) a few minutes walk. Far enough away to create a golden sense of privacy. Travel+Leisure's readers voted it one of their "Favorite Places to Stay and Zagat rated it the 4th best hotel in America.

With the latest in in-room-technology (DSL internet, private phone lines, a 40 inch TV, DVD &

CD players with Bose speakers & a substantial library), a Singapore inspired Spa (RafflesAmrita), fine dining in restaurant JAAN, a quintessential California roof-top pool with views to forever, you may vote never to leave.

Featuring 24-hour flexible check-in, Raffles L'Ermitage Beverly Hills continues to exemplify excellence in luxury service and accommodations. ❧

• ROMANTIC FEATURES •

RafflesAmrita Spa, a mystical oasis, provides a range of spa and skin care services, cutting-edge facilities, private label aromatherapy products and signature RafflesAmrita Spa cuisine. The Amrita name is derived from the ancient Sanskrit legend, where Hindu deities searched for "Amrita," an elixir that promised eternal youth. This legendary assurance of renewal will be a commitment delivered to every guest.

The rooftop pool boasts a view of the beautiful Bel Air and Hollywood Hills while exclusive poolside cabanas offer a comfortable option for those guests wanting more privacy. Exceptional service and delectable cuisine and "His & Hers" massage or body treatments are available to cabana and pool guests alike. ❧

Rancho Valencia

RANCHO SANTA FE, CALIFORNIA, USA

Rancho Valencia is a secluded hideaway offering privacy,

relaxation, and recreation on an intimate scale. Sport enthusiasts will enjoy the 18 tennis courts and our "Top 10 in America" tennis program, heated outdoor pool, 2 whirlpool spas, croquet lawn, fitness center and nearby golf courses. Spa treatments are available in the privacy of each suite.

The Rancho Valencia Restaurant is located off a mission-style courtyard and, using the freshest local ingredients, serves California-Eurasian cuisine for breakfast, lunch, and dinner daily, as well as brunch on Sundays. Dine in the restaurant or

al fresco on one of the many terraces or courtyards.

Set amidst 40 acres of rolling hills and lush landscaping, our forty-nine richly appointed suites offer privacy and luxury in a tranquil setting. Rancho Valencia boasts state of the art banquet facilities and a full range of event planning services, from weddings and social events to corporate events.

The resort was rated number 2 out of the top 75 North American Resorts in the 2003 issue of Condé Nast Traveler.

· ROMANTIC FEATURES ·

Tucked in a private canyon in Rancho Santa Fe, the resort is just minutes from the seaside towns of Del Mar and La Jolla.

Acres of year-round flowers and lush landscaping surrounds 49 luxurious suites. Suites start at 850 square feet and are either studio or one-bedroom, and all offer fireplace, private garden patio, spacious bathroom with walk-in closet, wet/mini-bar. Some suites offer private whirlpool spas on the patios as well as steam shower and jetted tub. The Mediterranean-Spanish decor features open-beamed ceilings, plantation shuttered windows and terra cotta tile floors.

U.S & CANADA

· at a glance
Location: Rancho Santa Fe, California USA
Mailing Address: P.O Box 9126, Rancho Santa Fe, CA 92067-4126
Reservations: 800-548-3664
Fax: 858-756-0165
Web Site: www.ranchovalencia.com
Size of Property: 40 acres
Meeting Space: 20,000 square feet
Accommodations: 49 luxurious suites
Range of Rates: $470 - $5,000

about the area
Currency: U.S. Dollars
Weather: Temperate
Languages: English
Nearest Airport: San Diego International

· nearby attractions

San Diego Zoo, Sea World, Wild Animal Park, Beach Communities, Disneyland, Universal Studios, Legoland, Local Vineyards.

· onsite facilities

Reminiscent of early California haciendas, each suite features custom furnishings, cathedral ceilings, hand painted tiles, fireplaces and private garden patios shaded by an array of trees.

· wedding services

With breathtaking views, private terraces and authentic decor, Rancho Valencia is suitable for Bridal Showers, Rehearsal Dinners, Wedding Ceremonies and Receptions.

The Regent Beverly Wilshire
A Four Seasons Hotel

LOS ANGELES, CALIFORNIA, USA

• at a glance

Location: Los Angeles, California USA
Mailing Address: 9500 Wilshire
Boulevard Beverly Hills, CA 90212 USA
Reservations: 310-275-5200
Fax: 310-274-285
Web Site: www.regenthotels.com
Size of Property: One full city block
Meeting Space: 18,250 square feet
Accommodations: 395 rooms, 122 suites
Range of Rates: $399 - $3,950

about the area

Currency: U.S. Dollars
Weather: Mild
Languages: English
Nearest Airport: LA International

• nearby attractions

LA. The City of Angels. Tinseltown. This fabled metropolis - famous for its celluloid history - is part reality, part dream. Four thousand square miles comprise Los Angeles County, from the beaches to museums to theme parks.

• onsite facilities

The hotel is comprised of two unique environments: the historic Wilshire Wing has a classic distinction and features 147 rooms on 10 floors, while the Beverly Wing is elegantly contemporary with its 248 rooms on 14 floors.

• wedding services

From engagement to vows to glorious honeymoon, Four Seasons makes every moment unforgettable. Whether you travel across town or across the world, discover everything in one place: superb settings, award winning cuisine and meticulous, personalized support.

The Regent Beverly Wilshire is an oasis of elegance, warmth and impeccable service at one of the world's most famous intersections - Rodeo Drive and Wilshire Boulevard. Accented by Four Seasons intuitive, personal service and style, its splendor is further enhanced by an impressive renovation - perfectly blending tradition and trend with a dignity that only comes with experience. The hotel features spacious guest rooms with luxurious appointments, award winning restaurants, lively entertainment, unparalleled meeting facilities, and a complete health spa.

The hotel is comprised of two unique environments: the historic Wilshire Wing has a classic distinction and features 147 rooms on 10 floors, while the Beverly Wing is elegantly contemporary with its 248 rooms on 14 floors.

The Regent Beverly Wilshire also has a variety of special one and two-bedroom suites that are truly one of a kind, including The Veranda Suite with its private staircase and rooftop terrace, and the Ambassador Suite with its bath side, bay window views of Beverly Hills. ᔑ

• ROMANTIC FEATURES •

For those who desire romance, the Romantic Escape package includes a bottle of champagne and strawberries upon arrival along with roses, soothing aromatherapy bath salts and two personally monogrammed terry bathrobes. A deep-soaking tub, magnificent marble bathrooms and the stylish elegance of a Regent Suite offered at $650 per night is all the more reason to celebrate and get away. The Regent Beverly Wilshire offers award-winning California cuisine with Italian accents. The elegant decor complements the exquisite food, fine wines, soft piano music and unsurpassed service. The restaurant serves breakfast, lunch and dinners. The Health Spa offers shiatsu, Swedish and reflexology massage. ᔑ

The Westin St. Francis

SAN FRANCISCO, CALIFORNIA, USA

U.S & CANADA

• **at a glance**

Location: San Francisco, California USA
Mailing Address: Union Square, 335 Powell Street, San Francisco, CA 94102 USA
Reservations: 1-800-WESTIN1
Fax: 415-403-6865
Web Site: www.westinstfrancis.com
Size of Property: One City Block
Meeting Space: 45,000 square feet
Accommodations: 1195 rooms & suites
Range of Rates: $129 - $2,700

about the area
Currency: U.S. Dollars
Weather: Temperate
Languages: English/Multilingual
Nearest Airport: SFO

T his enduring legend continues to welcome travelers from around the world just as it did nearly a century ago...

Located in the heart of the city, facing Union Square, it has maintained its preeminence as San Francisco's center of social, theatrical, and business life since first opening in 1904.

As one of the last survivors of colorful, turn-of-the-century San Francisco, The Westin St. Francis is as modern as tomorrow – with a proud past – a collecting place of history and legend.

Isn't it time that you came to experience The Westin St. Francis?

Considerable care has been taken throughout the ongoing restoration programs to reflect the original ambiance of The St. Francis -- travertine marble, oak columns, gilded ceilings, crystal chandeliers and three magnificent murals in the Tower Lobby.

Starwood Hotels & Resorts Worldwide, Inc. is one of the leading hotel and leisure companies in the world with more than 740 properties in more than 80 countries. ॐ

• ROMANTIC FEATURES •

At the turn of the century, the guardians of the Charles Crocker family announced plans to build the finest hotel on the Pacific Coast. Their vision was to make San Francisco the "Paris of the West." After studying all of Europe's grand hotels – from those in Berlin, Vienna, and Monaco to Claridge's in London to The Ritz in Paris – construction on the original St. Francis Hotel began. Two years and $2.5 million later, on March 21, 1904, the doors of The St. Francis opened. By seven o'clock that evening, a line of carriages and automobiles three blocks long waited in line to approach the brightly lit towers of the St. Francis. ॐ

• **nearby attractions**

From it's location on Powell Street, The Westin St. Francis is perfectly situated to provide easy access to the region's most popular points of interest, including: Lombard Street, North Beach, Fisherman's Wharf and the Golden Gate Bridge.

• **onsite facilities**

Each of our guest rooms has been transformed and impeccably appointed with new furniture, including our famous Heavenly Beds™, Heavenly Baths™, wall and floor coverings, in-room safes, and state-of-the-art safety upgrades.

• **wedding services**

The catering expertise of The Westin St. Francis is legendary. If you are planning a wedding, our catering staff provides the uncompromising quality and service you would expect from The Westin St. Francis.

The Gant

ASPEN, COLORADO, USA

U.S & CANADA

- **at a glance**
Location: Aspen, Colorado USA
Mailing Address: 610 S. West End St.
Aspen, CO 81611
Reservations:1-800-345-1471
Fax: 1-970-925-6891
Web Site: www.gantaspen.com
Size of Property: 5 acres
Meeting Space: 5,052 square feet
Accommodations: 123 rooms and suites
Range of Rates: $150 - $900

about the area
Currency: U.S. Dollars
Weather: Temperate
Languages: English
Nearest Airport: Aspen Airport

- **nearby attractions**

Aspen offers 300 restaurants, shops, and nightclubs. There is something for everyone with virtually every outdoor activity, dozens of art galleries, performing arts, historical sites, and a world class Spa.

- **onsite facilities**

Guests of The Gant can enjoy two heated outdoor swimming pools, three jetted hot tubs, locker rooms with dry saunas, five tennis courts, and on-site exercise facility. Shops, bars and restaurants all within short walking distance.

- **wedding services**

Bring everyone together for a memorable stay at The Gant. And our distinctive conference center and outdoor deck offer the perfect setting for a relaxed rehearsal dinner or next day brunch for family and friends.

The Gant is "Aspen's finest condominium resort," ideally located at the foot of Aspen Mountain, just three short blocks from the downtown area. Five beautifully landscaped and maintained acres include 120 one, two, three, and four bedroom condominiums with outstanding facilities and balconies for the enjoyment of our guests. Each condominium is individually owned and decorated, making the guest experience not unlike a stay in a private home. Guests at The Gant also enjoy a level of service more like that of a fine hotel than a typical condominium property. Serene and attractive reception with comfortable sitting area for entertaining guests. Experience pristine mountain views in a quiet residential area at the edge of the resort, close to the base of Aspen Mountain. Enjoy the freeform pool with beautiful terrace surrounded by sun loungers and two Jacuzzis fringed by rows of aspens. Free courtesy transportation around Aspen provided on request. ༄

༄ ROMANTIC FEATURES ༄

Bring everyone together for a memorable stay at The Gant. They'll feel right at home in one of our many luxurious condominiums. It's like hosting your guests in a private home with dozens of bedrooms. And our distinctive conference center and outdoor deck offer the perfect setting for a relaxed rehearsal dinner or next-day brunch for family or friends. When you gather at The Gant, the celebration goes well beyond the ceremony. Events from the simple to the sublime, we exceed expectations of our guests time after time. At The Gant, our objective is always to exceed the expectations of meeting planners and guests alike while helping you obtain your goals to create a perfect wedding weekend. ༄

• at a glance

Location: Telluride, Colorado USA
Mailing Address: 119 Lost Creek Lane
Telluride, CO 81435 USA
Reservations: 888-601-5678
Fax: 970-728-7953
Web Site: www.innatlostcreek.com
Size of Property: 5 acres
Meeting Space: 1,560 square feet
Accommodations: 32 rooms and suites
Range of Rates: $195 - $1,295

about the area

Currency: U.S. Dollars
Weather: Seasonal
Languages: English, Spanish, French
Nearest Airport: TEX, MTJ

• nearby attractions

Telluride Ski Resort: skiing, snowboarding, nordic. Telluride Golf Club: 18 holes, views of 13,000 foot peaks. Telluride Historic District: hiking, 4 wheeling, mountain biking, summer festivals. Free gondola. Beautiful scenery.

Inn at Lost Creek

TELLURIDE, COLORADO, USA

You'll find yourself lost in elegance and charm at the Inn at Lost Creek. Renowned for award-winning design and distinctive service, Inn at Lost Creek features 32 exquisitely designed suites and acclaimed 9545 Restaurant. Luxury suites include stone fireplace, marble baths with jetted tub, steam shower, sleep system beds, balconies with French doors, and beautiful mountain views. You'll be treated to spa services, privately reserved hot tub, nightly turn-down and full concierge service. From sunset concerts on the lawn in summer and ski-in, ski-out trails in winter, you'll enjoy the superb location of the most romantic boutique hotel in the Colorado Rockies. The Inn is located in the center of Telluride Ski and Golf Resort and connected by a free gondola system to the quaint, historic town of Telluride. Perfectly situated amid the towering rugged peaks of Southwest Colorado's San Juan Mountains, Telluride is famous for stunning scenery, summer festivals, skiing, and fine restaurants. ❧

• onsite facilities

Sundeck • Great Room • Individually designed suites • Spa services • Ski-in, ski-out access. 100 yds from free gondola connecting Inn to historic town of Telluride. Ski, golf, valet. Roof-top spas.

• ROMANTIC FEATURES •

Exquisitely designed suites with magnificent mountain views and custom furnishings add an aura of romance and elegance to your bridal suite and wedding. Romantic pleasures include private reservations at our roof-top spas with strawberries and champagne, breakfast served in the privacy of your suite, and massage services. Your personal concierge will accommodate requests for flowers, candles, and romantic amenities. You'll sleep in ultimate comfort in our Euroflex sleep system beds with light, downy, allergy free comforters and duvets, and soft fluffy pillows. Terry cloth robes and slippers are provided for your spa indulgences. ❧

• wedding services

Planning assistance for nearby or on-site ceremony location, photographer, catering, and other wedding details. Receptions, brunches, private parties at 9545 Restaurant, Great Room, outdoor terrace. Wedding Night amenities. Group rates.

U.S & CANADA

• at a glance

Location: Englewood, Colorado USA
Mailing Address: 200 Inverness Drive
West Englewood, CO 80112 USA
Reservations: 800-346-4891
Fax: 303-799-5874
Web Site: www.invernesshotel.com
Size of Property: 13 acres
Meeting Space: 60,000 square feet
Accommodations: 302 rooms, 18 suites
Range of Rates: $89 - $289

about the area

Currency: U.S. Dollars
Weather: Temperate
Languages: English
Nearest Airport: Denver International

The Inverness Hotel and Conference Center

ENGLEWOOD, COLORADO, USA

At The Inverness Hotel and Conference Center, wedding specialists make your wedding an experience unlike any other. Our catering team designs masterful menus, cakes and settings to provide the perfect place for your event. With an elegant collection of on-site services from restaurants for rehearsal dinners to an in-house florist and bakery, just about every detail for your wedding can be coordinated through your wedding specialist. Over 20,000 square feet of breathtaking indoor and outdoor space provide an exceptional location for your wedding ceremony and reception. The Inverness also provides complete catering services as well as luxurious accommodations overlooking either the majestic Rocky Mountains or our championship golf course. Our amenities, which will keep all of your guests entertained, include an 18 hole PGA golf course, three tennis courts, jogging trails, indoor and outdoor pools and massage services. We look forward to creating a unique and beautiful experience to celebrate the joy of your wedding.

• ROMANTIC FEATURES •

Call us hopeless romantics, but when it comes to affairs of the heart, we make sure your getaway is personalized and memorable. Your choices abound. Relax and enjoy the view from a suite on our Club Floor, featuring a sunken living room, private balcony, upgraded amenities including oversized towels and robes and access to our exclusive Mountain View Lounge serving continental breakfast and evening hors d'oeuvres. Golf on our 18 hole championship golf course, dine in one of our five dining and entertainment venues, enjoy a soothing massage or shop at Park Meadows Retail Resort, just five minutes away. But then again, you may wish to do something entirely different. And that's perfectly fine with us. After all, when do you get a chance to do anything you wish? Or, absolutely nothing at all.

• nearby attractions

Park Meadows Retail Resort with over 100 shops and restaurants and Fiddler's Green Amphitheater are just minutes away. The Inverness is 30 minutes south of downtown Denver where you can enjoy major league sports teams, shopping and museums.

• onsite facilities

With five incredible outdoor venues, several well-appointed banquet rooms, and five dining and entertainment venues, The Inverness has the perfect setting for your event - whether it is a quiet romantic wedding or an event for 500.

• wedding services

The Inverness has extensive menu selections, an in-house florist, a bakery that will create a designer wedding cake, a preferred vendor list and expert Wedding Specialists to help you with every step of your wedding plans.

The Little Nell

ASPEN, COLORADO, USA

Guests choose the Little Nell when they want to experience

absolute comfort and luxury. The Little Nell is uniquely situated at the base of Ajax Mountain in the very heart of Aspen, just seventeen steps from the Silver Queen Gondola taking guests to the summit of 11,212 feet, and within a few blocks of Aspen's finest shops, restaurants, nightlife and year-round activities. Aspen's only Five-Star/Five-Diamond luxury hotel, The Little Nell blends the virtues of a country inn with the personalized service and amenities of a grand hotel. Dual concierge teams assure that no boot is unwarmed, no ski unwaxed, no reservation unchecked and no special request denied, all for the pleasure of our guests. The Little Nell has been recognized by the Zagat Survey in its 2002 Guide to Top US Hotels, Resorts & Spas in the category of Small Resorts & Inns and holds the prestigious Relais & Chateaux affiliation. The Little Nell's magnanimous approach to service keeps guests coming back for more. ❧

• ROMANTIC FEATURES •

Decorated in rich Aspen colors, including red, gold, burgundy and blue, comfort abounds at every nook, from the cozy gas-burning fireplaces to the deluxe goose-down stuffed sofas and chairs. Oversized beds with fluffy down duvets and pillows create a romantic setting for couples ready to relax after a day on the slopes. Guests come from around the world to stay at the Little Nell, where unparalleled skiing amid comfort and splendor is the name of the game in the fall and winter, and outdoor sports and cultural activities entertain the rest of the year. Offering the perfect combination of relaxed ease and gracious prompt service, the Little Nell will make you feel as if you have entered a private home. ❧

• at a glance
Location: Aspen, Colorado USA
Mailing Address: 675 East Durant Avenue Aspen, CO 81611 USA
Reservations: 888-843-6355
Fax: 970-920-4670
Web Site: www.thelittlenell.com
Meeting Space: 2,500 square feet
Accommodations: 92 rooms and suites
Range of Rates: $250 - $4,400

about the area
Currency: U.S. Dollars
Weather: Temperate
Languages: English
Nearest Airport: Aspen Sardy Field

• nearby attractions

Uniquely situated at the base of Aspen Mountain, The Little Nell is Aspen's only ski-in and ski-out resort. Seemingly carved into the mountain, The Little Nell complements its environment with its charming, peaked, wooden rooftops.

• onsite facilities

With 92 accommodations, each room at The Little Nell is designed for maximum comfort. The Little Nell also features a complete health club, a nearby gondola ride to The Aspen Mountain Club and The Sundeck for special events.

• wedding services

The Montagna Restaurant and Bar at The Little Nell offers Aspen's finest American Contemporary cooking, featuring fresh regional ingredients and a spectacular presentation. The Grand Salon is an intimate setting for wedding receptions and rehearsal dinners.

Mountain Lodge Telluride

TELLURIDE, COLORADO, USA

Nestled in the heart of Southwestern Colorado's San Juan Mountains, just a breathtaking gondola ride from historic Telluride, is true paradise.

Telluride, a National Historic Landmark District, rests at the base of the Telluride Ski Mountain. Victorian homes, historic buildings and a rich assortment of boutiques, art galleries, bookstores and gourmet restaurants characterize this delightful town.

Featuring breathtaking alpine views, Mountain Village offers contemporary lodging, stylish boutiques, sophisticated dining and a championship golf course.

The Mountain Lodge at Telluride offers a variety of accommodations, all richly furnished in a Western motif with soft leather furniture, pine cabinetry, granite countertops, flagstone accents and designer touches throughout. Dazzling views of the rugged, 14,000-foot peaks of the San Juan Mountain Range will complete your Mountain Lodge at Telluride experience.

· ROMANTIC FEATURES ·

The Mountain Lodge at Telluride is the perfect destination for exquisite weddings, family reunions and other celebrations. Our on-site facilities provide a scenic backdrop for smaller, private functions, and the nearby Telluride Conference Center has the capacity to handle events up to 400 people. The town of Telluride is nestled in a box canyon enveloped by majestic peaks of the San Juan Mountains. Just eight blocks wide and twelve blocks long, this historic district is peppered with colorful Victorian homes, clapboard storefronts, boutiques, art galleries, bookstores, gourmet restaurants and historic buildings. Romance is in the air at the Mountain Lodge!

U.S & CANADA

· at a glance
Location: Telluride, Colorado USA
Mailing Address: 457 Mountain Village Blvd Telluride, CO 81435 USA
Reservations: 866-3MTN-TOP
Fax: 970-369-4317
WebSite:
www.mountainlodgetelluride.com
Meeting Space: 500 - 3,500 square feet
Accommodations: 126-lodge rooms, condos and cabins
Range of Rates: $100 - $2,000

about the area
Currency: U.S. Dollars
Weather: Temperate
Languages: English
Nearest Airport: Telluride, Montrose

· nearby attractions

Enjoy skiing, snowshoeing, snowboarding, snowmobiling, snow tubing, mountain/road biking, fly fishing, ice/rock climbing, jeep tours, sleigh/carriage rides, dog sled tours, paragliding, hot air balloon rides, spa, hot springs, and golf.

· onsite facilities

Concierge services, outdoor deck with heated pool & Jacuzzi, valet parking, exercise room, steam room, men's and women's locker rooms with showers, general store, heated underground parking, daily housekeeping, and grocery shopping services.

· wedding services

Full planning services - Perfect venue for receptions and rehearsal dinners. The Mountain Lodge at Telluride provides your guests with lodging that is distinctively Telluride and sits at the edge of the slopes and lifts of the ski mountain.

• at a glance
Location: Orlando, Florida USA
Mailing Address: 5800 Universal Blvd.
Orlando, FL 32819 USA
Reservations: 1-800-232-7827
Fax: 407-503-2010
Web Site:
www.universalorlando.com/hardrock
Size of Property: 26 acres
Meeting Space: 5,600 square feet
Accommodations: 650 rooms and suites
Range of Rates: $219-$269

about the area
Currency: U.S. Dollars
Weather: Tropical: Avg. 82 degrees
Languages: English, Spanish
Nearest Airport: Orlando
International

• nearby attractions

Hard Rock Hotel® is located inside Universal Orlando® Resort. Two amazing theme parks, Universal Studios® and Universal's Islands of Adventure®, plus amazing nightlife at Universal CityWalk® are all a short walk or water taxi ride away.

• onsite facilities

The Palm Restaurant, 12,000 sq ft beach pool with underwater stereo, fitness center with steam rooms and sauna, Hard Rock Merchandise Store, supervised children's activity center, game room, 5,600 sq ft of meeting and function space.

• wedding services

A variety of wedding packages are available, from small to large in size. Three and Five Day Honeymoon Packages are available to choose from with amenitis to enjoy all the hotel and resort have to offer.

Hard Rock Hotel®
at Universal Orlando® Resort

ORLANDO, FLORIDA, USA

Vacation like a rock star at the 650 room Hard Rock

Hotel® at Universal Orlando® Resort, the coolest hotel on earth. This AAA Four Diamond Award winner will make you feel like rock 'n' roll royalty with impeccable accommodations, a wealth of recreation and personal service and attention fit for "The King."

Designed in California mission-style architec-

ture, the Hard Rock Hotel® embodies the soul, spirit and attitude of rock. It's lively, yet laid back. Classy, yet casual. You'll be surrounded by music, from the CD player in every guestroom, to the rare rock 'n' roll memorabilia throughout the public areas, to the underwater music of the huge palm-lined swimming pool.

Each guest room also includes an in-room safe suitable for laptop computers, two dual-line telephones, a mini bar and separate bath and vanity area.

· ROMANTIC FEATURES ·

Universal Orlando® Resort has an array of fine dining restaurants including Emeril's at Universal CityWalk®, Emeril's Tchoup Chop at the Royal Pacific Resort, a Loews Hoel, Delfino Riviera, and Mama Della's Ristorante at Portofino Bay Hotel, a Loews Hotel.

Hard Rock Hotel® also offers poolside cabanas for anyone needing a little extra privacy. Guests can indulge and be pampered at Mandara Spa located in the Portofino Bay Hotel. Enjoy moonlit strolls via the private walking paths around the resort. Enjoy a drink at the cool Velvet lounge. And of course, breakfast in bed!

The Inn at Fisher Island

FISHER ISLAND, FLORIDA, USA

• **at a glance**
Location: Fisher Island, Florida USA
Mailing Address: 1 Fisher Island Drive
Fisher Island, FL 33109 USA
Reservations: 305-535-6026
Fax: 305-535-6003
Web Site: www.fisherisland.com
Size of Property: 216 acres
Meeting Space: 5,288 square feet
Accommodations: 67 rooms
Range of Rates: $325 - $2,170

about the area
Currency: U.S. Dollars
Weather: Tropical
Languages: English, Spanish
Nearest Airport: Miami International

• **nearby attractions**

For health and beauty advocates, The Spa Internazionale, rated among the top ten spas in the western world by Town & Country Magazine, pampers residents in luxurious privacy. For discriminating diners, try one of Fisher Island's fine restaurants.

• **onsite facilities**

Guests of The Fisher Island Club reside in faithfully restored Vanderbilt-era Cottages, luxurious one-bedroom Villa Suites with sitting rooms, private patios and hot tubs, and spacious one-and two-bedroom Seaside Villas.

• **wedding services**

Experience the pinnacle of romantic getaways at the Fisher Island Club. This tropical haven offers the ultimate in privacy, while providing a myriad of tempting diversions: the Spa, Tennis, Golf, soft white beaches, and much more.

Welcome to Fisher Island. This private 216-acre oasis between sunrises over the Atlantic Ocean and sunsets into Miami's Bay and Skyline offers a unique lifestyle that combines the security, beauty and tranquility of island living with luxurious accommodations and the finest amenities and services. At Fisher Island you'll find privacy, not isolaton. In fact, Fisher island offers an ideal location that places you minutes from all the charms of south Florida, although it seems a world apart.

The dream of creating an island paradise took hold when developer Carl Fisher purchased the land that now bears his name in 1919. Fisher was friends with William Kissam Vanderbilt and was often invited to social gatherings aboard Vanderbilt's luxurious yacht named the "Eagle" of which Fisher was more than fond. In 1925, Vanderbilt proposed a trade to his friend: Fisher Island for the "Eagle." Fisher gladly accepted. Grace and grandeur were Vanderbilt's pleasure and Fisher Island continues with the tradition for its members, residents and guests. Guests of The Fisher Island Club reside in faithfully restored Vanderbilt-era Cottages and luxurious one-bedroom Villas.

• **ROMANTIC FEATURES** •

Grace and grandeur were William Vanderbilt's pleasure. In the same tradition that Vanderbilt held lavish and extravagant affairs for his guests, the Fisher Island Club hosts an active schedule of sports tournaments, theme parties and cultural events throughout the year.

Dance the night away at one of our fun-filled theme nights. Choose from Latin Night, Disco Night and a bevy of others. Is live music more your thing? The Fisher Island Club has hosted intimate concerts with such international stars as opera singer Katherine Battle, baritone Dmitri Hvorostovsky and the Florida Philharmonic, just to name a few.

Little Palm Island Resort & Spa

LITTLE TORCH KEY, FLORIDA, USA

Little Palm Island is graced with a beautiful, natural white sand beach. Visitors can enjoy precious 'Do Nothing' time around the island and by the pool. There are also limitless water sport amenities, exceptional Deep Sea and Back Country fishing and sailing adventures. Indulge in the peace and tranquility of the SpaTerre. Enjoy the privacy of your own veranda, visit the wonderful library in the Great Room, bask on a white sandy beach, engage in a life-size game of chess or meditate in the Zen Garden. Swim in our fresh water pool with waterfall, visit the Island Boutique and Gift Shop, get in a workout in our new Fitness Center, or indulge yourself in the SpaTerre. Enjoy meals in our oceanfront dining room and celebrate nightly sunsets in the Monkey Hut Lounge. We offer Eco Tours to the Great Heron Wildlife Refuge as well as challenging Deep Sea and Backcountry Flats fishing excursions. Cruise the crystal clear waters of the Atlantic on a sailing charter. ❧

· ROMANTIC FEATURES ·

With names like Osprey, Snowy Egret, and Ibis, the 28 thatched-roof Bungalow Suites and two Island Grand Suites offer the ultimate privacy with interior décor inspired by nature. Discreetly nestled throughout the island amid hundreds of Jamaican coconut palm trees, each bungalow houses two handsomely appointed one-bedroom suites with private sundecks and ocean views.

All bungalows feature a comfortable living room and an expansive bedroom with a king-sized bed, and a sitting area furnished with exquisite British colonial pieces. Little Palm Island is an elegant, friendly oasis for seafarers traversing the Gulf and Atlantic. ❧

• at a glance
Location: Little Torch Key, Florida USA
Mailing Address: 28500 Overseas Hwy
Little Torch Key, FL 33042 USA
Reservations:1-800-343-8567
Fax: 305-872-4843
Web Site: www.littlepalmisland.com
Size of Property: 6 acre private island
Accommodations: 30 one-bedroom suites
Range of Rates: $595 - $2,295

about the area
Currency: U.S. Dollars
Weather: Tropical
Languages: English
Nearest Airport: Key West International., 28 miles

• nearby attractions

Little Palm Island is graced with a beautiful, natural white sand beach. Visitors can enjoy precious 'Do Nothing' time around the island and by the pool. There are also limitless water sport amenities, exceptional Deep Sea and Back Country fishing and sailing adventures. Then indulge in the peace and tranquility of the SpaTerre.

• onsite facilities

With names like Osprey, Snowy Egret, and Ibis, the 28 thatched-roof Bungalow Suites and two Island Grand Suites offer the ultimate privacy with interior décor inspired by nature. SpaTerre indulges guests in the ultimate spa experience.

• wedding services

It has always been your dream... an intimate wedding ceremony in a lush tropical garden or on a white sandy beach at sunset. All you do is choose the package, and our Wedding Coordinator will do the rest. We will make your dreams come true.

U.S & CANADA

• **at a glance**
Location: Orlando, Florida USA
Mailing Address: 5601 Universal Blvd. Orlando, FL 32819 USA
Reservations: 800-232-7827
Fax: 407-503-1010
Web Site: www.universalorlando.com /portofino
Size of Property: 49 acres
Meeting Space: 43,000 square feet
Accommodations: 750 rooms and suites
Range of Rates: $249 - $309

about the area
Currency: U.S. Dollars
Weather: Tropical: Avg. 82 degrees
Languages: English & Spanish
Nearest Airport: Orlando International

Portofino Bay Hotel, A Loews Hotel

ORLANDO, FLORIDA, USA

B ienvenuto... Welcome, to the legendary seaside village

Portofino the jewel of the Italian Riviera. Today, the ambiance of this famed European getaway has been re-created at the luxurious Portofino Bay Hotel at Universal Orlando®, A Loews Hotel.

You'll feel yourself transported to the sunny Mediterranean at this AAA Four Diamond

Award® winner, named to Condé Nast Traveler magazine's 2001-2003 Gold List of the "World's Best Places to Stay" and the only Orlando hotel named to Travel + Leisure magazine's 2002 list of Top 100 Hotels in the U.S. and Canada.

Here at Portofino, every detail from Italy has been reproduced, right down to the cobblestone streets and outdoor cafés.

Portofino Bay Hotel is flagship hotel of Universal Orlando® Resort, offering superior Loews service, outstanding recreation and world-class accommodations.

• **nearby attractions**

Portofino Bay Hotel is located inside Universal Orlando® Resort. Two amazing theme parks, Universal Studios® and Universal's Islands of Adventure®, plus amazing nightlife at Universal CityWalk® are all a short walk or water taxi ride away.

• **onsite facilities**

Three themed swimming pools, scenic jogging paths, bocce ball courts, and the 12,300 sq. ft. Mandara Spa. Enjoy a variety of hotel activities from live music to cooking demonstrations to wine tastings and eight restaurants and lounges.

• ROMANTIC FEATURES •

The perfect marriage of elegance and excitement - enjoy moonlit strolls on the piazza, followed by a fun and exciting day at the theme parks. Enjoy an array of fine dining options at Universal Orlando® Resort including Emeril's at Universal CityWalk® and Emeril's Tchoup Chop at the Royal Pacific Resort a Loews Hotel, The Palm Restaurant at Hard Rock Hotel® and Delfino Riviera at Portofino Bay. Portofino Bay Hotel also offers poolside cabanas for anyone needing a little extra privacy. Indulge in a couples massage and be pampered at Mandara Spa located onsite.

• **wedding services**

A variety of wedding packages are available -from small to large in size. Three & Five Day Honeymoon Packages available to choose from with amenities to enjoy all the hotel and resort has to offer.

South Seas Resort

CAPTIVA ISLAND, FLORIDA, USA

On enchanting Captiva Island, South Seas Resort is nestled among lush mangroves with more than half of the plantation-style resort a dedicated wildlife preserve and estuary. World-renowned sailing and fishing, Gulf-edged golf and discovering storied barrier islands, such as Useppa and Cabbage Key are among the unforgettable experiences of a South Seas guest.

Dotted with mansions and the private retreats of celebrities and captains of industry, it's not surprising that the pristine beauty of South Seas Resort captured filmmakers' attention for Sweet Home Alabama and Blue Sky.

Offering more than 600 accommodations ranging from hotel rooms and villa suites to three-bedroom beach homes and cottages, South Seas Resort features 10 cuisine outlets, a full-service yacht harbour and marina, on-site naturalist and Captiva Kids Club.

Re-connect at South Seas Resort, call (888) 2-CAPTIVA.

· ROMANTIC FEATURES ·

Couples rekindle romance while learning to sail with the pleasures of "Ocean Dreams."

Romantics are greeted beachside with tiki torches, a pair of adirondack chairs and choice of wine complimented with cheese and crackers or bubbling champagne and chocolate covered strawberries upon arrival. They then receive five half-day sailing lessons by a certified world-renowned Steve Colgate Offshore Sailing School captain. Following half-days of sun-soaked sailing, couples return to South Seas Resort Yacht Harbour to enjoy soothing in-room spa treatments. As a finale, couples toast the sunset on a farewell cruise.

• at a glance

Location: Captiva Island, Florida USA
Mailing Address: 5400 Plantation Road Captiva Island, FL 33924 USA
Reservations: 888-2 CAPTIVA
Fax: 239-472-754
Web Site: www.south-seas-resort.com
Size of Property: 330 acres
Meeting Space: 28,000 square feet
Accommodations: 600 hotel rooms, villas, suites and homes
Range of Rates: $250 - $12,000

about the area

Currency: U.S. Dollars
Weather: Tropical: Avg. 82 degrees
Languages: English, Spanish
Nearest Airport: SE Florida International

• nearby attractions

J.N. "Ding" Darling National Wildlife Refuge is part of the largest undeveloped mangrove ecosystem in the U.S., providing over 600,000 acres of preserved subtropical barrier island habitat for Florida's native wetland with biking and hiking.

• onsite facilities

Sailing School • Yacht Harbour • Marina • Nature Center • Golf Course • 18 Tennis Courts • 21 Fresh Water Pools • Captiva Kid's Club • Resort boutiques • Resort Spa Services

• wedding services

Personal Wedding Coordinator can arrange pristine beachside weddings or lawn ceremonies amidst stunning sunsets or in elegant function halls.

Universal's Royal Pacific Resort

ORLANDO, FLORIDA, USA

Sail away to a tropical paradise of swaying palm trees,

authentic Asian cuisine and a lagoon-style pool. It's the closest you can get to experiencing the splendor of the tropics without traveling halfway around the world.

A dramatic bamboo forest and terraced rice paddies mark your entrance. Sparkling waterfalls and swaying palm trees point the way to your room.

A serene orchid court where flowers are always in bloom soothes your spirit. The warm sand beach of a lagoon-style swimming pool tempts you to shed your shoes   - and your cares - forever. And a grand staircase with carved mahogany leads you to a world of tropical delights.

This luxury resort is unquestionably Orlando's most exotic, and one of three spectacular on-site hotels at Universal Orlando Resort. ❧

· ROMANTIC FEATURES ·

The perfect marriage of elegance and excitement - enjoy moonlit strolls on the resort's walking paths, followed by a fun and exciting day at the theme parks.

Enjoy an array of fine dining options at Universal Orlando including Emeril's at Universal CityWalk and Emeril's Tchoup Chop at the Royal Pacific Resort, The Palm Restaurant at Hard Rock Hotel and Delfino Riviera at Portofino Bay.

Royal Pacific Resort also offers poolside cabanas for anyone needing a little extra privacy. Indulge in a couples massage and be pampered at Mandara Spa located at the nearby Portofino Bay Hotel. ❧

• at a glance
Location: Orlando, Florida USA
Mailing Address: 6300 Hollywood Way
Orlando, FL 32819 USA
Reservations: 800-232-7827
Fax: 407-503-3010
Web Site:
www.universalorlando.com/hotels
Size of Property: 53 acres
Meeting Space: 85,000 square feet
Accommodations: 1,000 rooms and suites
Range of Rates: $189 - $219

about the area
Currency: U.S. Dollar
Weather: Tropical
Languages: English
Nearest Airport: Orlando International

• nearby attractions

Royal Pacific Resort is located inside Universal Orlando. Two amazing theme parks, Universal Studios Florida and Islands of Adventure, plus amazing nightlife at Universal CityWalk, are all a short walk or water taxi ride away.

• onsite facilities

Emeril's Tchoup Chop, spectacular authentic luaus in the Wantilan Luau Pavilion, 5,000 sq ft fitness center, lagoon-style pool, steam room and sauna, game room, 85,000 sq ft of meeting and event space, supervised children's activity center.

• wedding services

Choose from a variety of wedding packages and Three or Five Day Honeymoon Packages including amenities to enjoy the hotel and the entire resort.

Westin Grand Bohemian

ORLANDO, FLORIDA, USA

• at a glance

Location: : Orlando, Florida USA
Mailing Address: 325 South Orange
Avenue Orlando, Florida 32801 USA
Reservations: 866-663-0024
Fax: 787-888-6600
Web Site: www.grandbohemianhotel.com
Size of Property: 15-Story Highrise
Meeting Space: 9,600 square feet
Accommodations: 250 rooms snd suites
Range of Rates: $139 - $459

about the area

Currency: U.S. Dollars
Weather: Sub-Tropical
Languages: Interpreters Available
Nearest Airport: Orlando
International

• nearby attractions

Please contact our Concierge for area
attraction information. Activities range from
visits to cultural attractions such as the
Orlando Museum of Art, to everyone's
favorite parks such as Walt Disney World,
Universal Studios and SeaWorld.

• onsite facilities

Restaurant, Lounge, Concierge, Outdoor
Heated Pool, 24-Hr. Room Service, Golf &
Tennis Nearby, 24-Hr. Fitness Center, Bell
Services, Currency Exchange, Gift/Sundry
Shop, Art Gallery, In-Room Massage
Treatments, Live Entertainment, Valet.

• wedding services

Receptions for up to 150. Packages
include tuxedo attired hotel maitre d' at
your personal disposal, hospitality suite
during reception, complimentary suite for
bride & groom on wedding night and 1-year
anniversary, and referral services.

At first glance, The Westin Grand Bohemian will bring you back in time to a place that existed nearly 100 years ago. European Bohemia, the present day Czech Republic is known to history as the center for art and music. Home to Prague, the Bohemian art movement is a mix of old and new, classic and contemporary.

Today, The Westin Grand Bohemian is Orlando's "Experience in Art and Music." A unique showcase of rare art, classical and contemporary music, luxurious accommodations, and personalized service. The lobby of The Westin Grand Bohemian greets its visitors with its barrel vaulted ceiling decorated in red and gold mosaic Smalti Italian tiles, and is a masterpiece of culture and vision. Designed in turn-of-the-century Secession style of architecture, the hotel offers 250 guest rooms, including 36 guest suites, and first class amenities.

• ROMANTIC FEATURES •

Unique furnishings that combine dark Java wood with brushed silver accents are hallmarks of the richly appointed guest rooms at The Westin Grand Bohemian. Lush velvets in jewel tones are featured throughout, and the tall headboards on the all-white Westin Heavenly Beds are upholstered in iridescent fabrics.

We can help you plan a perfect romantic getaway. Sip iced champagne and nibble on tuxedo strawberries while you indulge in a relaxing Aromatherapy Bath in the oversized Jacuzzi tub in one of our suites. Snuggle up in our signature bathrobe while you listen to CD's on your in-room stereo system. Order a late night meal or breakfast in bed with our 24-hour room service.

The Drake Hotel

CHICAGO, ILLINOIS, USA

• at a glance

Location: Chicago, Illinois USA
Mailing Address: 140 E Walton Place
Chicago, IL 60611 USA
Reservations: 800-55-DRAKE
Fax: 312-787-1431
Web Site: www.thedrakehotel.com
Meeting Space: over 30,000 square feet
Accommodations: 537 rooms and suites
Range of Rates: Varies by season

about the area

Currency: U.S. Dollars
Weather: Temperate
Languages: English, Multilingual
Nearest Airport: O'Hare/ Midway

• nearby attractions

Located across from Oak Street Beach, overlooking Lake Michigan, and on the Magnificent Mile in downtown Chicago, The Drake Hotel puts its guests in the center of Chicago's exciting shopping, nightlife, culture, and dining experiences.

The Drake Hotel is a Chicago landmark and has been a symbol of white glove elegance for over 80 years. The pride of Chicago, the hotel has been the first choice of celebrities and heads-of-state since its opening in 1920. The Drake Hotel is perfectly located in the heart of the Gold Coast, overlooking Lake Michigan, across from Oak Street Beach, and right on the Magnificent Mile in downtown Chicago. The Drake Hotel puts its guests in the center of Chicago's exciting shopping, nightlife, culture, and dining experiences.

Since 1920, whether traveling to Chicago for business or pleasure, The Drake Hotel combines tradition with elegance and style to accommodate all the needs of our hotel guests. The hotel's 537 elegant rooms, including 74 luxurious suites, many with Chicago views, offer an array of modern amenities.

With unparalleled acclaim for arranging the finest banquets in the world, The Drake Hotel is the place to hold your Chicago event.

• onsite facilities

Located in the Gold Coast, The Drake Hotel is the ideal Chicago venue. Its 18 meeting rooms and over 30,000 square feet of meeting space are individually designed to cater to every type of event, from eight VIPS to 600 delegates.

· ROMANTIC FEATURES ·

For over 80 years, The Drake Hotel has made fantasy weddings a reality. Whether you choose the opulent Gold Coast Room overlooking Lake Michigan, or the circa 1920s Grand Ballroom with the balcony and grand staircase, your guests will be enchanted by our historic splendor, polished service, and spectacular cuisine.

A historic landmark, The Drake is well known as Chicago's most romantic hotel. From the moment you enter you can see why so many brides and grooms have chosen to dance their first dance in The Drake's Ballrooms, begin their honeymoons in our luxurious suites, and return to celebrate their 1st and 50th anniversaries.

• wedding services

A symbol of white glove elegance for over 80 years, The Drake Hotel is internationally renowned for its large, impressive weddings and smaller more intimate gatherings. Your event is in the hands of our award winning catering team.

The Sutton Place Hotel

CHICAGO, ILLINOIS, USA

Chicago Hotels do not come any better. The AAA Four Diamond

rated Sutton Place Hotel, noted for its striking architecture, contemporary design, and original Robert Mapplethorpe floral photography, brings you thoughtful service, exceptional cuisine and luxurious amenities. With its key location in the heart of Chicago's famed Gold Coast neighborhood, you could say that even our location is a luxury! Take a stroll along Lake Michigan, spend the day shopping on Michigan Avenue or enjoy a night on the town in one of the city's hottest restaurants/clubs; it's all just steps away from The Sutton Place Hotel entrance.

Rande Gerber's famed Whiskey Bar & Grill, within The Sutton Place Hotel, provides an outstanding dining and nightlife option. Our unique meeting venues and excellent private dining staff make it easy to plan memorable private events.

• ROMANTIC FEATURES •

Whether it's your wedding night, a return stay to celebrate your anniversary, or just a romantic night away from the everyday routine, The Sutton Place offers a unique mixture of style and serenity in the middle of the bustling Chicago lifestyle. The spacious guest rooms offer plush accommodations and modern amenities. Enjoy fine cuisine through room service as you view the romantic city skyline. After dinner, pamper yourself in the oversized soaking tub, pop in a CD from our offered selections and snuggle under the down comforter. Sweet dreams are sure to follow!

U.S & CANADA

• at a glance
Location: Chicago, Illinois USA
Mailing Address: 21 East Bellevue Place Chicago, IL 60611 USA
Reservations: 312-266-2100
Fax: 312-266-2103
Web Site: www.suttonplace.com
Meeting Space: 7,000 square feet
Accommodations: 246 rooms
Range of Rates: $189 - $900

about the area
Currency: U.S. Dollars
Weather: Temperate
Languages: English
Nearest Airport: O'Hare International Airport

• nearby attractions

The Sutton Place Hotel is located in the heart of the Gold Coast and steps away from world class shopping on Michigan Avenue and Oak Street. The Sutton Place is also surrounded by the city's hottest dining and nightlife.

• onsite facilities

The Sutton Place Hotel offers a unique mix of style and serenity in the middle of the bustling Chicago lifestyle. We offer plush guest rooms with modern amenities and unique banquet spaces with views overlooking the city.

• wedding services

Each detail of your wedding - menus, music, table settings and guest rooms, will receive the personalized attention & care of our catering representative. We specialize in events from 50-150, but will help you tie the knot with only 10 guests.

U.S & CANADA

• at a glance

Location: Chicago, Illinois USA
Mailing Address: 320 North Dearborn
Street Chicago, IL 60610 USA
Reservations: 800-WESTIN-1
Fax: 312-527-2650
Web Site: www.westinchicago.com
Meeting Space: 28,000 square feet
Accommodations: 424 rooms and suites
Range of Rates: $149 - $2,500

about the area

Currency: U.S. Dollars
Weather: Seasonal
Languages: English
Nearest Airport: O'Hare & Midway
Airports

• nearby attractions

The heart of the theatre district & many great
restaurants and nightlife. The Westin
Chicago River Nortth is within walking distance from the best shops in the world & surrounded by fabulous museums sure to cap-
ture everyone's interest.

• onsite facilities

Overlooking the Chicago River, we offer
424 luxurious guest rooms & suites, a fully
equipped health club with personal trainers, massages, a full-service business center, restaurant, lounge and sushi bar.

• wedding services

More than just exquisite facilities - we
extend to you our high standards of personalized service and individualized attention. Every arrangement, every detail, is
tailored to make your special wishes come
true.

The Westin Chicago River North

CHICAGO, ILLINOIS, USA

Located in Chicago's vibrant River North district, The Westin

Chicago River North provides a four-star experience for visitors to one of North America's most
dynamic cities. The Westin overlooks the scenic
Chicago River and offers quick access to the city's
many cultural attractions.

Elegant accommodations and 424 spacious guest
rooms and suites provide the ultimate in comfort
and luxury. All rooms feature Westin's signature
Heavenly Bed® and Heavenly Bath® and
amenities like terry-cloth robes, lavish toiletries,
refreshment center and Starbucks Coffee.

Our stunning ballrooms are ideal for any social
gathering, including the Astor Ballroom with
one of the most impressive settings in the city.
Our on-site wedding specialists will ensure the
success of every event - from the smallest dinner
- to the most lavish reception.

Not far from The Westin Chicago River North
lobby doors are Chicago's theatres, museums, and
the premier shops of Michigan Avenue - the
famed Magnificent Mile. ❧

• ROMANTIC FEATURES •

Overlooking the Chicago River, The Westin
Chicago River North offers three beautiful ballrooms. The exquisite Astor Ballroom, with it's
neo-classical design, is luxuriously appointed
with handmade Italian murano crystal chandeliers, rich wood paneling and custom patterned
carpets in tones of brown and gold... the perfect
room for an intimate wedding celebration.

The more contemporary Grand Ballroom is decorated with warm, inviting colors and accommodates up to 600 guests. The ballroom reception
area features glass doors that lead to a dramatic
outdoor terrace with its breathtaking views.

Enjoy your day, your way, at our romantic,
award-winning, downtown hotel. ❧

W Chicago Lakeshore

CHICAGO, ILLINOIS, USA

A distinguished hotel for an equally distinguished city,

W Chicago Lakeshore, AAA Four Diamond hotel, is the only hotel in Chicago that directly overlooks Lake Michigan providing easy access to the beach itself. If the sand is not to your liking, enjoy the sunshine and cocktails at Wet (aka pool) from noon until sundown.

Inside, discover a Zen-like shelter for body and soul. Asian influences are seen in the grand entrance of Chinese tiles, a mahogany-lined grotto, and the zen-spired fountain. The fierce

Chicago winters are kept at bay with the warmth of dark woods and a welcoming hearth.

Wave - W Chicago Lakeshore's plush new signature restaurant is getting raves from Chicago's restaurant reviewers. This water-inspired dining experience brings innovative cuisine in an ultra-contemporary, visually stunning atmosphere. By night, Wave transforms into a sexy lounge.

Whether it's a quiet getaway or the social event of the season, W Chicago Lakeshore has everything to make it happen. ❧

· ROMANTIC FEATURES ·

W Chicago Lakeshore is more than a place to spend the night. The service, the style, the overwhelming sense of well being...every aspect was designed with your comfort in mind. Relax in one of our 549 deluxe guestrooms made to appeal to all your senses. Sink into our W signature beds that include pillow top mattresses, feather beds, 100% goose down duvets and pillows, and 250 thread-count Egyptian cotton sheets. Toast your occasion in our intimate and comfortable living room or enjoy an exquisite dinner for two at Wave. End the evening with a nightcap at Whiskey Sky and enjoy the breath taking views of the glittering Chicago night skyline. ❧

· at a glance

Location: Chicago, Illinois USA
Mailing Address: 644 N Lakeshore Drive Chicago, IL 60611 USA
Reservations: 877- WHOTELS
Fax: 312-255-4456
Web Site: www.whotels.com
Size of Property: One acre
Meeting Space: 12,500 square feet
Accommodations: 549 rooms and suites
Range of Rates: $209 - $800

about the area

Currency: U.S. Dollars
Weather: Seasonal
Languages: English
Nearest Airport: O'Hare or Midway Airport

· nearby attractions

Just steps away from the beaches of Lake Michigan and Navy Pier. Walk to the city's best attractions: the Theatre District, Sears Tower, Museums, Galleries, and the premier shops along Michigan Avenue, the famed Magnificent Mile.

· onsite facilities

Restaurant; Bar; Indoor Pool; Beach Access; Fitness Center; In-room massage; 24-hour room service; Meeting and event facilities, including revolving banquet room with changing panorama of Lake Michigan and the skyline.

· wedding services

Enjoy a number of personalized wedding services including premium bar service, passed hors d'oeuvres, champagne toast, three course dinner with wine service, changing rooms and special room rates for your out-of-town guests.

Algonquin Hotel

NEW YORK, NEW YORK, USA

Located in the heart of Manhattan, the Algonquin is the hotel

preferred by those who best appreciate New York -- a true landmark, with a tradition of elegance that began a century ago. Superb accommodations and a gracious atmosphere make the Algonquin an oasis of polished sophistication amid the hustle and bustle of the city.

Situated on prestigious Club Row – 44th Street between Fifth and Sixth Avenues—the Algonquin Hotel is in the heart of Midtown Manhattan. Guests find themselves within walking distance of New York's famous Broadway

Theaters, fashionable shopping on Fifth and Madison Avenues, the Empire State Building, the Museum of Modern Art, Rockefeller Center, Radio City Music Hall and Times Square.

Every room features a remote control color TV with HBO, pay-per-view movies, clock radio, dual line speakerphones with data ports, high-speed Internet access, voice mail, room service, hair dryer, robes, in-room safes, smoke alarms, iron and ironing board, and Aromatherapy.

· ROMANTIC FEATURES ·

It is never difficult to find exceptional food and entertainment in New York. As a guest at The Algonquin, you find it easier still. Without leaving the hotel, you can enjoy some of the city's finest hospitality. Cocktails and hearty pub fare are served at the Blue Bar. Enjoy coffee and conversation in the Lobby, where the famous walk.

Experience the glamour and sophistication of "New York's Best Cabaret" at the legendary Algonquin. Spend a magical evening at the acclaimed Oak Room enjoying a stellar cabaret performance, dining on exquisite "Café Society" fare, and then retire to your sumptuous deluxe queen room.

U.S & CANADA

• at a glance

Location: New York, New York USA
Mailing Address: 59 W. 44th Street, New York, NY 10036 USA
Reservations: 888-304-2047
Fax: 212-944-1618
Web Site: www.algonquinhotel.com
Meeting Space: 2,500 square feet
Accommodations: 174 rooms and suites
Range of Rates: $179 - $309

about the area
Currency: U.S. Dollars
Weather: Temperate
Languages: English
Nearest Airport: LGA, JFK, EWR

• nearby attractions

The Algonquin is in the center of Midtown Manhattan, within walking distance of many of New York's attractions: the theatres of Broadway, the midtown business district, the city's finest shopping and and the world's best restaurants.

• onsite facilities

Guest rooms at the Algonquin recall an era when comfort and elegance were not subject to compromise. Handsome, understated furnishings are designed to be as restful to the eye as the body, while modern amenities ease the burdens of 21st Century travelers.

• wedding services

A wedding at the Algonquin is much like the hotel itself: possessed of a unique charm and appeal available nowhere else. With four thousand square feet of meeting space, the hotel can accommodate all manner of events.

Hotel Plaza Athenee

NEW YORK, NEW YORK, USA

• **at a glance**

Location: New York, New York USA
Mailing Address: 37 East 64th Street at Madison Ave New York, NY 10021 USA
Reservations: 212-734-9100
Fax: 212-772-0958
Web Site: www.plaza-athenee.com
Size of Property: 240 acres
Meeting Space: 1,400 square feet
Accommodations: 150 rooms and suites
Range of Rates: $299 - $660

about the area

Currency: U.S. Dollars
Weather: Temperate
Languages: English
Nearest Airport: La Guardia International Airport

• **nearby attractions**

Within walking distance from Madison Avenue's designer shops, Central Park, Metropolitan Museum of Art, The Whitney Museum and The Frick Museum. Shop Bloomingdale's, Barney's, and Bergdorf Goodman. An Upper East location, close to Midtown.

• **onsite facilities**

Our reception room is one of the most romantic rooms in New York City. The cuisine is modern French and Zagat-rated. Some suites have balconies and glass-enclosed indoor terraces. Bar Seine lounge is one of the trendiest venues in the city.

• **wedding services**

We can cater to your needs for ceremonies and wedding receptions, bridal showers, rehearsal dinners, high tea, brunch, and offer luxuriously romantic honeymoon suites.

Nestled among the residences and quiet tree-lined street of the fashionable East Side of Manhattan, this charming, boutique hotel is just a stroll away from Central Park, Madison Avenue shopping, museums and midtown. This elegant European-style hotel, known for providing the ultimate in personalized service, offers 115 guest rooms and 35 suites, some with glass enclosed indoor terraces and outdoor balconies.

Beautifully decorated surroundings make the Hotel Plaza Athenee the address of choice for weddings and special events. The hotel's reception room is one of the most romantic rooms in New York City and is decorated in gold and Murano glass splendor. Zagat 2004 says, "A

'beautiful' 'way to escape the hustle-and-bustle' is this 'elegant' East Side 'quiet oasis' in the Hotel Plaza Athenee, where the 'delicate', 'delicious' French cuisine is served..."

An on-site wedding coordinator specializes in receptions, rehearsal dinners, high tea and brunch events.

• ROMANTIC FEATURES •

Charming and intimate, Hotel Plaza Athenee is home to one of the most romantic rooms in New York City.

"Arabelle", the hotel's stylish new restaurant and reception area, features a contemporary, exciting cuisine where the food is as creative as the decor.

"Le Trianon," the hotel's ceremony space, is elegantly appointed in natural earth tones with six windows overlooking the residences of East 64th Street. Double doors connect to a parlor Suite for increased ceremony seating.

Spend your wedding night in an elegant honeymoon suite. Some, with glass enclosed atriums and terraces, are perfect for an intimate in-room dinner. Rose petal turn down and chocolate covered strawberries await you at the end of the day.

Le Parker Méridien New York

MIDTOWN MANHATTAN, NEW YORK, USA

• **at a glance**

Location: Midtown Manhattan, New York USA
Mailing Address: 118 West 57th Street New York NY 10019-3318 USA
Reservations: 800-543-4300
Fax: 212-708-7471
Web Site: www.parkermeridien.com
Size of Property: 240 acres
Meeting Space: 9,000 square feet
Accommodations: 730 rooms and suites
Range of Rates: $250 - $3,000

about the area

Currency: U.S. Dollars
Weather: Temperate
Languages: Spanish, French, Japanese
Nearest Airport: La Guardia

• **nearby attractions**

Just two blocks south of Central Park the prime Manhattan address has its own upscale perks: quick walking access to Carnegie Hall and Fifth Avenue shopping, as well as the Times Square Theatres and hundreds of other midtown attractions.

• **onsite facilities**

Gourmet Catering Provided • An Exclusive Setting – Just one wedding at a time • A variety of ceremony and cocktail options • Newly refurbished modern decor • Norma's Award Winning Breakfast, all day every day • Gravity Spa & Fitness Center

• **wedding services**

Unique Ceremony Options • Fabulous Photo Spots throughout the Hotel • Dedicated Wedding Planning Professional • Large Bridal Suite Included in Package • Outdoor Penthouse Terrace • A dance among the clouds.

Hip and dysfunctional are out. Style and function are in.

Surround yourself with breathtaking views in the chic, fully renovated Estrela Penthouse, complete with dramatic outdoor terrace, high atop the fashionable Le Parker Méridien. Begin your lives together with a dance among the clouds expertly organized by the pros at Le Parker Méridien. Innovative cuisine prepared by our French culinary team is sure to WOW even the toughest critic. The hotel's 730 ergonomically inspired rooms and suites surround you with luscious cherry and cedar woods. These sleek rooms have a 32" television, CD/DVD player, air-conditioning, hairdryer, minibar, iron, ironing board, three phones, and free high speed internet. Many with fantastic views of Central Park and the Manhattan skyline. Indulge yourself with New York's "Best Breakfast" at NORMA'S or enjoy a touch of Paris at Seppi's Bistro open until 2AM. Come and experience the newyorksmart© difference of Le Parker Méridien New York. ❧

· ROMANTIC FEATURES ·

A swim among the clouds, an enchanting walk in the park or a cozy carriage ride is within easy reach at Le Parker Méridien New York. Put the "ahh" in spa at gravity fitness and spa or hit the famous shops of Madison and Fifth Avenues. Snuggle up in your window seat overlooking Central Park and really get to know the object of your affections. Our suites come complete with separate sitting area, an incredible king-size bed, cedar-lined bath, and a shower big enough for two. You could move in and live happily ever after. Be in the heart of it all with your sweetheart on West 57th Street steps away from Central Park, Times Square, Carnegie Hall, Broadway theatres and all that famous shopping. ❧

U.S & CANADA

• **at a glance**

Location: New York, New York USA
Mailing Address: 995 Fifth Avenue New York, NY 10028 USA
Reservations: 212-650-4721
Fax: 212-650-4705
Web Site: www.stanhopepark.hyatt.com
Meeting Space: 2,855 square feet
Accommodations: 185 rooms and suites
Range of Rates: $269 - $495

about the area
Currency: U.S. Dollars
Weather: Moderate
Languages: English
Nearest Airport: LaGuardia

The Stanhope Park Hyatt New York

NEW YORK, NEW YORK, USA

The Stanhope is a small, elegant hotel located on Manhattan's

prestigious Upper East Side. Situated on Museum Mile at Fifth Avenue and 81st Street, across from the Metropolitan Museum of Art, The Stanhope Park Hyatt New York is in the heart of the city's cultural center. The Cooper-Hewitt, Frick, Guggenheim and Whitney museums, art galleries and designer boutiques on Madison Avenue are just blocks away.

Just beyond the heart of Midtown, this refined cosmopolitan hotel blends old-world elegance with American warmth and hospitality. Since its debut in 1926, discriminating business and leisure travelers alike have been drawn to this stylish hotel.

A state-of-the-art workout room is equipped with stairmaster, lifecycle, treadmill, one-line 3500 Vectra weight station, free weights and sauna. A personal trainer and massage therapy may be arranged by appointment through the concierge.

· ROMANTIC FEATURES ·

A peaceful oasis amidst the hustle and bustle of an urban pulse. A sparkling jewel at the center of a lush landscape. Welcoming European hospitality embraced by cosmopolitan savvy...

The Stanhope Park Hyatt offers perhaps the most desired address in the Upper East Side. Our Intimate reception salons overlooking Fifth Avenue and the Metropolitan Museum of Art are ideally suited for Bridal Teas, Rehearsal Dinners and Traditional Wedding Receptions for up to 80 guests.

Make your day memorable with the understated elegance and beauty of a luxury boutique hotel.

• **nearby attractions**

The Stanhope Park Hyatt New York is a small elegant hotel located on Fifth Avenue within Manhattan's prestigious Upper East Side. Located directly across from the Metropolitan Museum of Art and Central Park and just steps from Madison Ave.

• **onsite facilities**

A state-of-the-art workout room is equipped with stairmaster, lifecycle, treadmill, one-line 3500 Vecra weight station, free weights and sauna. A personal trainer and massage therapy may be arranged by appointment through the Concierge.

• **wedding services**

The Stanhope Park Hyatt offers perhaps the most desired address in the Upper East Side. Our Intimate reception salons overlooking Fifth Avenue are ideally suited for Bridal Teas, Rehearsal Dinners and Wedding Receptions for up to 80 guests.

• at a glance

Location: New York, New York USA
Mailing Address: 130 East 39th Street
New York, NY 10016 USA
Reservations: 212-685-1100
Fax: 212-889-0287
Web Site: www.whotels.com
Meeting Space: over 3,200 square feet
Accommodations: 198 rooms and suites
Range of Rates: From $199

about the area

Currency: U.S. Dollars
Weather: Four Seasons
Languages: English
Nearest Airport: JFK or La Guardia
Airport

W New York - The Court

NEW YORK, NEW YORK, USA

• nearby attractions

The pulse of the world thrives just beyond the lobby door- the heart of midtown Manhattan. Find museums, the theatre district.and more. The East side offers charming restaurants, and transportation to the Hamptons. Go everywhere. Go wild.

Amid the bustling skyline of midtown Manhattan, W New York - The Court rests on a tree-lined street in the heart of the city's vibrant and historic neighborhood between Lexington and Park Avenues.

This intimate hotel just recently underwent a number of renovations to make sure everything from the carpets to the pillowcases had a softer, more comfortable feel. This splendid property, which is known for its residential ambiance,

indulges our guests with spacious rooms, sophisticated amenities, and unbeatable service. Enjoy all the comforts of home, and then some. Oversized wooden desks, down cushioned chaise lounges, luxurious pillow-top beds, luxurious bath products, and DVD players.

This charming retreat radiates warmth from the sizzling scene at Wetbar to the sultry, satisfying dishes of Icon by famed restaurateur Drew Nieporent. Live in style at one of W New York - The Court's 155 deluxe rooms and 43 one-bedroom suites.

The amenities? Unparalleled. The service? Impeccable. ❧

• onsite facilities

24-hour in-room massage, Restaurant, Concierge Service, W cafe and bar for quick meals, Fitness center, Spa, Video Conferencing Services, Meeting and Event Facilities.

• ROMANTIC FEATURES •

Guest rooms and spacious suites that feel like home. Framed black and white photos of New York leaning on a picture rail, a glass water carafe by the bed, and an upholstered chaise lounge.

Wrap yourself in luxury. Or in our snugly chenille blanket. We've come up with the ultimate bed for the dreamiest sleep-a firm, pillow-top mattress with soft, 250-thread count linens, a fluffy goose down comforter with pillows to match. Nestle in and leave the world behind. ❧

• wedding services

Our savvy knowledgeable staff can handle every detail. Your only job is to show up on time. W will take care of the rest.

The Greystone Inn

LAKE TOXAWAY, NORTH CAROLINA, USA

Conveniently located on the shores of Lake Toxaway, the largest private lake in North Carolina, this intimate, historic, resort inn combines the lure of its panoramic mountain setting with the comfort of modern luxuries and exceptional cuisine. At all turns, our guests enjoy warm, friendly, and personal service. In fact, owners Tim & Boo Boo Lovelace often join the guests on the Sun Porch for Afternoon Tea, followed by a daily champagne cruise on the lake. Whether searching for a tranquil visit full of spa services, relaxing boat rides, and romantic candlelit dinners, or an active visit with golf, guided hikes and waterskiing, the Greystone Inn has it all. 🔊

· ROMANTIC FEATURES ·

Our lakeside hammock, relaxing Champagne Cruise and tranquil mountain lake setting begin the process of restoring your mind, body, and spirit. Our Spa at the Greystone Inn is the best medicine for a busy, high - pressure filled life.

The Spa is a place to be pampered. You will have reduced stress, relieved tension, and an increased sense of well being.

Enjoy the relaxing music, the warmth of our sauna, and the caring touch of our professional staff. The Spa at The Greystone Inn provides an experience you will savor. Whether for a half hour or the entire day, our Spa offers a wonderful escape from the hectic pace and pressure of everyday life. This experience is something you owe to yourself. 🔊

• at a glance

Location: Lake Toxaway, North Carolina USA
Mailing Address: The Greystone Inn Greystone Lane Lake Toxaway, NC 28747 USA
Reservations: 828-966-4700
Fax: 828-862-5689
Web Site: www.greystoneinn.com
Size of Property: 10 acre peninsula
Meeting Space: Elegant 800 square feet meeting room
Accommodations: 33 rooms and suites
Range of Rates: $265 - $500

about the area
Currency: U.S. Dollars
Weather: Temperate
Languages: English
Nearest Airport: Asheville, Greenville

• nearby attractions

Biltmore Estates • Pisgah National Forest • Great Smokey Mountain Railway • Craft & Antique Shopping • (Brevard/ Cashiers/ Highlands)

• onsite facilities

Historic Mansion • Award winning spa • State-of-the-art Fitness Center • Lakeside Dining Room • Full service marina (included in rate) on private lake • Elegant mahogany 26 passenger boat.

• wedding services

Intimacy of a small luxury inn with list of amenities that matches the largest of resorts. Perfect for a wedding weekend full of activities for all, including bridal luncheons aboard mahogany boat.

The Grove Park Inn Resort & Spa

ASHEVILLE, NORTH CAROLINA, USA

Located just minutes from scenic downtown Asheville, The Grove Park Inn Resort & Spa is much more than an ordinary hotel. It is a landmark with a celebrated history dating back to 1913. It's a four-star, 510-room resort, where guests can enjoy swimming, championship golf, sports like racquetball and tennis, and a spectacular Spa. And it's a place where you can indulge in exceptional dining and shopping, without ever leaving the resort's grounds.

Then there are the claims to charm and distinction to which no guidebook can do full justice: The views that encompass an entire horizon line of the Blue Ridge Mountains. The high, stone fireplaces that invite our guests to linger fireside. The rows of rocking chairs that illustrate how since the beginning, we have stood as a place that resists hurry and rush.

Here you'll feel worlds away, in a place where mountains, water and sky combine to feel like heaven.

• ROMANTIC FEATURES •

Built from massive mountain stone, our historic Inn presents a dramatic picture as soon as you drive up. Yet our striking exterior is just one of the ways our resort is like no other: 14-foot stone fireplaces, mountain views and a rich historic ambiance make us a favorite getaway for couples.

Our resort is large enough to allow you to personalize your wedding; choose from a number of wonderful settings, such as our Norman-style Country Club. Our exclusive Club Floor makes for a luxurious stay, for a wedding or honeymoon. And while you're here, a host of modern amenities, such as our Spa, golf, and Sports Complex, make for an experience that's as fun-filled as it is deeply romantic.

U.S & CANADA

• at a glance
Location: Asheville, North Carolina, USA
Mailing Address: 290 Macon Avenue
Asheville, NC 28804 USA
Reservations: 800-438-5800
Fax: 800-374-7432
Web Site: www.groveparkinn.com
Size of Property: 149 acres
Meeting Space: 50,000 square feet
Accommodations: 510 rooms, including 12 suites
Range of Rates: $110 - $930

about the area
Currency: US Dollars
Weather: Temperate, mild seasons
Languages: English
Nearest Airport: Asheville Regional

• nearby attractions

The resort overlooks the Blue Ridge Mountains, with hiking, biking and rafting. The Biltmore Estate, the country's largest privately owned home, is minutes away. Chimney Rock Park offers a 404-foot waterfall and spectacular views.

• onsite facilities

This four-diamond resort is home to a world-class Spa, a Sports Complex and a Donald Ross championship golf course. Also enjoy four restaurants and a gallery of inviting shops. The resort easily accommodates groups from 10 to 1,000.

• wedding services

Our seasoned team of professionals are trained to handle all the details of your special day. We offer complete planning, floral, catering and ceremony set-up. We also offer a variety of intriguing locations for your special event.

Pinehurst

PINEHURST, NORTH CAROLINA, USA

Pinehurst Resort is a place of timeless golf traditions

and incomparable experiences - and it's yours to explore. We invite you to take a closer look as we detail our superior service, world-class accommodations and renowned amenities. We know you'll understand why, once you've seen it for yourself. Nothing compares to Pinehurst.

No matter what you do by day in Pinehurst, we know you expect a soft pillow at night and the

comfort of home with all the luxury and service befitting a four-star, four-diamond resort.

Pinehurst's award-winning accommodations will pamper you in a setting that combines modern convenience with incomparable service. Over 500 sleeping rooms (including suites) in five different venues await you: our signature Carolina hotel, the newly-restored Holly Inn, the quaint Manor Inn, four-bedroom Villas, and Condominiums. ॐ

· ROMANTIC FEATURES ·

Step in from the everyday, into a cocoon of pure relaxation. The world will wait outside. Step into the Spa at Pinehurst, and you'll enter a world where aches and pains, cares and concerns, are dropped like baggage at the door. Your room awaits. There are slippers and robes, warm waters and soothing music. You're not here just for a one-hour massage. You're here for an experience. An escape. And the Spa at Pinehurst delivers. Over 28 treatment rooms, a lap pool, cascading whirlpools are yours to explore. Over 40 treatments - from baths to body wraps - are yours to choose. Work out in the fitness center. Let the professionals work magic on your hair and toes. This is luxury. ॐ

· nearby attractions

Pinehurst is the place to experience golf. Come see our eight courses - five originating from the Main Clubhouse, three on the resort perimeter. Let each of the 144 holes challenge you, delight you, make you think.

· onsite facilities

Hotel accommodations at the Carolina, Holly Inn, The Manor, and the Villas offer nightly turndown service, in-room mini bar, bell staff, room service, express checkout and data ports for Internet usage.

· wedding services

Enjoy your first night as Husband and Wife, or stay a few days and enjoy the splendor of this award winning resort. The "Romance in the Pines" Honeymoon Package includes a taste of all that Pinehurst is famed for, from golf to spa.

Litchfield Plantation

PAWLEYS ISLAND, SOUTH CAROLINA, USA

Imagine entering through wrought iron gates and traveling a

quarter-mile avenue lined with live oak trees shrouded in Spanish moss leading to a gorgeous plantation house. As you wander through the 600 private estate acres of this once prosperous rice plantation, it's another time, another world.

Litchfield Plantation, member of Small Luxury

Hotels of the World, is a one of a kind romantic destination providing superb service with professional attention given to quality and detail. Chosen as one of the "Top 10 Most Romantic Inns" by American Historic Inns, you can be confident that your romantic getaway will be an unforgettable experience.

Accommodations are individual in decor and atmosphere and range from the historic Plantation House and six-bedroom Guest House Mansion to private villas. ✿

· ROMANTIC FEATURES ·

Chosen as one of the "Top 10 Most Romantic Inns" by American Historic Inns, you can be confident that your wedding or honeymoon, intimate to grand scale, will be an unforgettable experience. When we plan your Litchfield Plantation wedding/honeymoon, you will receive our exclusive room upgrade on arrival through our wrought iron gates with a bottle of champagne in your suite. Why not be married in a one-of-a-kind destination? Horse drawn carriage, sunset reception, picturesque surroundings...you can make this vision a true to life experience. ✿

U.S & CANADA

• at a glance

Location: Pawleys Island, South Carolina, USA
Mailing Address: P.O. Box 290, Kings River Road, Pawleys Island, SC 29585 USA
Reservations: 800-869-1410
Fax: 843-237-1041
Web Site: www.litchfieldplantation.com
Size of Property: 600 acres
Meeting Space: 3,000 square feet
Accommodations: 38 rooms and suites
Range of Rates: $150 - $620

about the area
Currency: U.S. Dollars
Weather: Temperate
Languages: English, German
Nearest Airport: Myrtle Beach

• nearby attractions

Brookgreen Sculpture Gardens, Atlantic Ocean, Historic Sights/Tours, over 100 area golf courses. Located just thirty minutes from Myrtle Beach, offering shopping, entertainment and sightseeing opportunities.

• onsite facilities

Accommodations range from the historic Plantation House and six-bedroom Guest House to private villas. Amenities include full breakfast daily, private beach clubhouse, tennis courts, marina, heated pool, concierge, newspaper, & turndown.

• wedding services

Our professional hospitality staff provides a beautiful destination for your wedding, from intimate to grand scale, including wedding services and all banquet catering services for rehearsal dinners, receptions, bridal luncheons and more.

Wild Dunes Resort

ISLE OF PALMS, SOUTH CAROLINA, USA

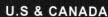
• at a glance

Location: Isle of Palms, South Carolina, USA
Mailing Address: 5757 Palm Blvd, Isle of Palms, SC 2945 USA
Reservations: 800-845-8880
Fax: 843-886-2140
Web Site: www.wilddunes.com
Size of Property: 1,600 acres
Meeting Space: 18,000 square feet
Accommodations: 468 rooms, villas and homes
Range of Rates: $125 - $750

about the area
Currency: U.S. Dollars
Weather: Temperate
Languages: English
Nearest Airport: Charleston International

O n the tip of Isle of Palms, a barrier island off South

Carolina, Wild Dunes Resort is a 1,600-acre oceanfront paradise just 20 minutes from the charm and grace of historic Charleston. The resort offers two world-renowned, Tom Fazio designed golf courses, top 10 ranked tennis center, the nation's top 5 ranked recreation program, extensive banquet facilities for groups up to 400, and over two miles of pristine beach. Four restaurants and 2 lounges complement the resort. At the heart of the resort, the Four Diamond Boardwalk Inn offers 93 guest rooms, luxurious suites and 3 unique function rooms. In addition, there are 375 villas and luxurious homes. Historic Charleston, voted one of the most romantic cities in the United States, features fine dining, unique shopping and true Southern hospitality. Visitors enjoy the many historic homes, charming carriage rides and extensive historic sites. Year long, the region enjoys a temperate climate, glorious sunshine and extensive outdoor recreation. ❧

• nearby attractions

Wonderful shopping and dining in nearby Historic Charleston; Boone Hall Historic Plantation; Harbor Cruises; Ghost Tours; S.C. Aquarium; Spoleto USA Festival; Historic Forts; Charleston Riverdogs; Family Circle Cup Tennis; and the USS Yorktown.

• onsite facilities

Two Tom Fazio designed golf courses; award winning tennis instruction and recreation program; pools; miles of pristine beach and marshlands; 4 diamond-rated Boardwalk Inn and 375 luxury homes and villas with full kitchens.

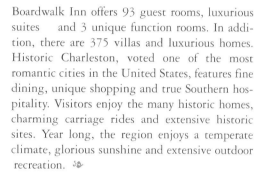

· ROMANTIC FEATURES ·

We want to make your time with your special someone as unique as the two of you. From two miles of pristine, white sand beach, sunset cruises, seaside picnics, sports clinics, and in-room spa services, you're sure to revel in romance and recharge your relationship. Enjoy romantic fine dining at the Sea Island Grill, located in the award-winning Boardwalk Inn. Just across the street, the walking village offers the Sports Pavilion, home to the Top 10 rated Tennis Center, Bike Shop, Harbor Course golf shop, Dunes Deli & Pizzeria, and the Swim Center. Wild Dunes' unique island location offers a multitude of choice outdoor settings, perfect for any number of catered events. ❧

• wedding services

Professional catering service for receptions and full meals. Beautiful outdoor venues with ocean and resort views. Wedding planning services including decor, flowers, etc. Luxury homes for events as well as overnight accommodations.

Woodlands Resort & Inn

C H A R L E S T O N ,   S O U T H   C A R O L I N A ,   U S A

O ne visit to Woodlands Resort & Inn provides a clear

understanding of why the resort's hometown of Summerville, South Carolina has been considered a restorative retreat since 1886, and why the resort continues to receive awards for both dining and lodging. The area provides the perfect backdrop to a resort that offers an exceptional experience.

The Inn is an impeccably restored 1906 classical revival mansion set amidst 42 acres of parkland grounds, right outside historical Charleston, SC. It is an elegant estate that draws its guests and visitors into a special sanctuary of southern hospitality, superb dining and exceptional experiences.

- Member Relais & Chateaux and Relais Gourmand.
- AAA Five Diamond and Mobil Five-Star for the Inn & Dining Room.
- "The only perfect food score in North America" and "Among the Top Ten Hotels for Service in the World," Condé Nast Traveler, Gold List.
- "Getaway – Old South hospitality meets New South luxury," Instyle Magazine.
- "Grand Award Winner," Andrew Harper.

· ROMANTIC FEATURES ·

"Couples can lose themselves at Woodlands," says general manager Marty Wall. " There's plenty to do on or near the property, from croquet to tennis to first-class golf, but this is also the kind of place where you take walks in the woods, linger for hours over lunch or dinner in a quiet corner of the dining room, or just stay in bed all day and listen to the cardinals, mockingbirds, and a host of other songbirds sing." He adds that Charleston -- long known as one of the most romantic cities in America, with its storybook houses, its glorious gardens, and its past full of pirates and planters and aristocrats, is just down the road.

• at a glance

Location: Jackson Hole, Wyoming USA
Mailing Address: 1535 North East Butte Road, Jackson Hole, Wyoming 83001 USA
Reservations: 656-887-3337
Fax: 656-887-3338
Web Site: www.amanresorts.com
Accommodations: 40 suites
Range of Rates: $700 - $1,200+

about the area
Currency: U.S. Dollars
Weather: Temperate
Languages: English
Nearest Airport: Jackson Hole, Wyoming, USA

• nearby attractions

Amangani is located at the southern end of the Greater Yellowstone ecosystem, a huge expanse of mountain and meadow, sage flats, rivers, national forests, wildlife refuges and two national parks – Grand Teton and Yellowstone.

Amangani

JACKSON HOLE, WYOMING, USA

Amangani, or "peaceful home," is set on a crest 7,000 feet above sea level with views of the snow-capped Grand Tetons in the distance and the Snake River and valley below. Built of Oklahoma sandstone blocks and Pacific redwood, the three-story, 40-suite resort evokes an atmosphere of the native west with its woven cowhide chairs, faux wolf cushions, deep fireplaces and Native American wall hangings.

There are two distinct seasons at Amangani. In summer, wildlife safaris in the surrounding wilderness areas of Grand Teton and Yellowstone National Parks are amongst the attractions, along with fishing in the Snake River, horseback riding and golf. In winter, wintersports at the ski resort of Jackson Hole, just 20 minutes away are a highlight. Skiing, snowmobiling, snowshoeing, dogsledding, crosscountry skiing and heliskiing are some of the activities on offer. Amangani also offers a spa, 35-meter swimming pool and whirlpool, exercise studio, gym and library for lounging. ✒

• onsite facilities

Amangani's 35-meter outdoor swimming pool is finished in frost-colored quartzite tiles and linked to a whirlpool. Both are heated in winter and enjoy magnificent mountain views, especially at sunset.

· ROMANTIC FEATURES ·

Air-conditioned suites include a living room and spacious bathroom and overlook the magnificent mountain scenery. The living area consists of a king-size platform bed and fireplace. Furnishings include a redwood-frame day bed for lounging, a black resin-and-terrazzo dining table and woven cowhide chairs in faux wolf fabric. Suites also offer a CD player and TV/VCR. Living-area walls are decorated with back-lit cedar planks and sliding glass doors lead to a sun deck, with mountain and valley views. A deep soaking tub with a window view highlights the large bathroom, and the twin vanities and shower room are trimmed in slate. Our staff will manage all the details for your once-in-a-lifetime event. ✒

• wedding services

Ceremonies can be held in the library with its cozy and inviting ambience and floor-to-ceiling panoramic windows or alfresco on the patio. An alternative might be poolside, overlooking the mountain vistas.

The Fairmont Chateau Lake Louise

LAKE LOUISE, ALBERTA, CANADA

Surrounded with snow-frosted Rocky Mountain peaks...

secluded next to a legendary lake... showcased by a majestic glacier...in a land of storybook endings, The Fairmont Chateau Lake Louise awaits your arrival. Escape to a haven of inviting splendor. Indulge yourself with tantalizing cuisine from Canada, and around the globe.

Elegant and polished yet relaxed and inviting, the Chateau's accommodations strive to live up to the natural wonder with whom we share our name. Unwind where the luxury of a bygone era has been perfectly preserved. Hide away here as

Fairbanks and Barrymore, Monroe and Hitchcock once did. Discover why snow worshippers, nature lovers and polished travelers all call this Chateau "The Diamond in the Wilderness."

Nothing complements a Diamond better than "Gold." The Chateau's exclusive Fairmont Gold floor is designed to pamper you from the moment you arrive at a private 7th floor check-in...because you deserve to be pampered.

· ROMANTIC FEATURES ·

The Fairmont Chateau Lake Louise is naturally graced with all the elements of a magical celebration. Embraced by mountains frosted with white wedding cake snow, glittering glaciers and a sparkling lake, our setting will add inspiration to one of the most important days of your life. The Chateau blends a mood of grandeur with a sense of ease, accented by fine cuisine and thoughtful service. Each detail of your wedding will receive the personalized care and attention of our Catering Team.

Simple or traditional, festive or formal, intimate or grand, in a ballroom, by a picture-perfect window, or overlooking the lakeshore, The Fairmont Chateau Lake Louise is always the perfect venue. ♨

U.S & CANADA

• at a glance
Location: Lake Louise, Alberta, CA
Mailing Address: 111 Lake Louise Drive, Lake Louise, Alberta, Canada T0L 1E0
Reservations: 800-441-1414
Fax: 403-522-3834
Web Site: www.fairmont.com/lakelouise
Meeting Space: 36,000 square feet
Accommodations: 550 rooms, including 72 suites
Range of Rates: Approx. $155 - $2,000

about the area
Currency: CAD - Canadian Dollars
Weather: Seasonal
Languages: English, French
Nearest Airport: Calgary

• nearby attractions

Mother Nature has created a destination unlike any other. A mountain playground for all seasons. As refreshing as taking a guided walk to a secret spring. As thrilling as floating through bottomless quantities of the finest powder on earth.

• onsite facilities

We're making room in our new wing with a spectacular ballroom accommodating 500 guests, 6 generous salons and our inspiring Heritage Hall. Additionally, our 1912 Victoria Room will evoke the grandeur of your 400 guests as it did the Queen.

• wedding services

Our dedicated service manager caters to your every matrimonial need. Our "Diamond in the Wilderness" offers full flexibility depending on your requirements with first class resources from catering and decorating to flowers and guestrooms.

The Pan Pacific Vancouver

VANCOUVER, BRITISH COLUMBIA, CANADA

Uniquely located on Vancouver's spectacular waterfront,

steps from entertainment, shopping and city sights, the Pan Pacific offers stunning panoramic views of rugged mountains, glimmering skyscrapers, and a harbor busy with cruise ships and sailboats, all delivered to your bedside from generous picture windows.

The Pan Pacific's unparalleled commitment to service has won it numerous top awards, including the prestigious AAA Five Diamond Award and the Mobil Four Star Award. The hotel has also attracted more royalty, visiting heads of state, and entertainment luminaries than any other hotel or resort property in Western Canada.

The award winning Pan Pacific is always finding luxurious new ways to make guests feel truly at home. Astounding vistas, plus an elegant sophistication and unparalleled Five-Diamond luxury and service, wrapped in friendly Canadian hospitality, awaits you. Begin a lifetime of memories at the Pan Pacific!

• ROMANTIC FEATURES •

Treat yourself to an unforgettable romantic getaway in one of world's most beautiful cities. Savor breakfast in bed as you watch the sun rise over the majestic North Shore Mountains, relax with a private spa treatment for two, enjoy a horse-drawn carriage ride around world famous Stanley Park or a stroll arm in arm along Vancouver's famous Seawall.

Whatever your pleasure, the Pan Pacific is the ultimate romantic destination. Once the sun sets, celebrate the end of another perfect day, and the start of a perfect evening, with an exquisite candlelight dinner in the award winning Five Sails restaurant overlooking the harbor.

• at a glance

Location: Vancouver, British Columbia, Canada
Mailing Address: 300 - 999 Canada Place Vancouver, BC. V6C 3B5 Canada
Reservations: 800-937-1515
Fax: 604-895-2469
Web Site: www.panpacific.com
Meeting Space: 20,000 square feet
Accommodations: 504 rooms and suites
Range of Rates: $290 - $365

about the area
Currency: CAD - Canadian Dollars
Weather: Temperate
Languages: English
Nearest Airport: Vancouver International

• nearby attractions

The Pan Pacific's downtown waterfront location puts you at the heart of Vancouver's fashionable shopping and entertainment district. Historic Gastown, the Vancouver Aquarium and Stanley Park are also a short walk away.

• onsite facilities

In addition to three great restaurants, the Pan Pacific features a heated outdoor pool, indoor and outdoor hot tubs and saunas, and a deluxe health club and spa with state-of-the-art equipment and a wide range of private spa treatments.

• wedding services

From formal dinners and rustic buffet luncheons, to receptions in our eight-storey atrium, our catering professionals will look after every detail for the perfect banquet, ceremony or reception indoors, outdoors, in your home or ours.

The Sutton Place Hotel

VANCOUVER, BRITISH COLUMBIA, CANADA

Welcome to The Sutton Place Hotel, Vancouver. With its

elegance and charm, Vancouver's Sutton Place Hotel brings a taste of Europe to one of North America's most beautiful cities.

The Sutton Place Hotel represents one of only two Five Diamond rated hotels in Canada. Luxury abounds from our 397 lavishly appointed guestrooms and suites, ranging in size from luxuriously appointed single accommodations to the

Presidential Suite. Each hosts a wide range of luxurious amenities. Dedicated professional staff provides the best accommodations in Vancouver with impeccable service and attention to detail. Entertain guests or share a quiet dinner in the elegant Fleuri Restaurant. Enjoy one of the city's best dining rooms for French continental cuisine. Restaurant Chef Michael Deutsch showcases his classical cooking as he presents house specials on an ever-changing menu. ❧

· ROMANTIC FEATURES ·

The Sutton Place Hotel is Vancouver's premier wedding hotel. From the moment you arrive, The Sutton Place in Vancouver will bring to mind all the warmth and charm one would expect to find only in the stately manors of long ago. Exquisite five diamond service amidst European elegance. Whatever you envision - cherished traditionalism, elegance and glamour, or exclusive intimacy - a Sutton Place wedding is uniquely yours. Our professional team offers worry-free wedding planning, exquisite cuisine, and excellence service.

Whether a bridal shower, rehearsal dinner, wedding ceremony and/or reception, we can design a truly personal experience that is a reflection of your unique style and taste. ❧

• at a glance

Location: Vancouver, British Columbia, Canada
Mailing Address: 845 Burrard Street Vancouver, BC, Canada V6Z 2K6
Reservations: 800-961-7555
Fax: 604-642-2928
Web Site: www.suttonplace.com
Size of Property: 21-story building
Meeting Space: 14,000 square feet
Accommodations: 397 rooms and suites
Range of Rates: $199 - $1,200

about the area

Currency: CAD - Canadian Dollars
Weather: Seasonal
Languages: English
Nearest Airport: Vancouver International Airport

• nearby attractions

Just steps away from Robson Street shopping, Vancouver Art Gallery, the Center for Performing Arts, downtown business district, theatres, Stanley Park, English Bay Beach, Pacific Centre Mall, and the Queen Elizabeth Theatre.

• onsite facilities

24-hour room service, Fleuri Restaurant - award-winning cuisine, Gerard Lounge - a celebrity favorite, La Boulangerie Bakery and Cafe, Le Spa Health and Beauty Fitness Centre, 16 sunlit function rooms, and multilingual concierge.

• wedding services

Our professional team offers worry-free wedding planning. We'll help you acquire photography, videography, and floral creation and decoration services. Exquisite cuisine and a beautiful wedding cake prepared to please you and your guests.

• **at a glance**
Location: Vancouver, British Columbia, Canada
Mailing Address: 845 Hornby Street Vancouver, BC V6Z 1V1 Canada
Reservations: 800-663-0666
Fax: 604-608-5348
Web Site: www.wedgewoodhotel.com
Meeting Space: 2,004 square feet
Accommodations: 83 rooms and suites
Range of Rates: $300 - $900

about the area
Currency: CAD- Canadian Dollars
Weather: Seasonal
Languages: Multilingual
Nearest Airport: YVR - Vancouver International

Wedgewood Hotel & Spa

VANCOUVER, BRITISH COLUMBIA, CANADA

The Wedgewood is a boutique luxury hotel nestled in

the heart of downtown that offers traditional European hospitality. With 83 elegant guestrooms and luxurious suites, the hotel caters to discriminating individual travelers and small upscale groups.

An abundance of flowers, fine antiques, original works of art and private balconies characterize guestrooms and the public areas of this exclusive Four-Diamond hotel while its award-winning restaurant, Bacchus, offers a truly unforgettable experience of modern French cuisine in a warm

and elegant setting with live entertainment nightly.

Our location is central to many fine restaurants, theatres and shopping in Vancouver's largest indoor mall as well as many designer-name brand shops.

The hotel was built in 1984 and has undergone its most recent renovations in 2003 including upgrades to the suites' bathrooms/decor and completion of a full-service luxurious Spa facility, carrying the renowned Epicuren cosmetic line. ❧

• ROMANTIC FEATURES •

Celebrate your special evening in one of our luxurious suites with a bottle of champagne upon arrival, breakfast in bed the following morning, and an authentic Wedgwood Jasper piece to treasure.

Relive your cherished memories and create new ones with a special evening in one of our elegant suites. A bottle of champagne will be awaiting your arrival, to be followed by a gourmet dinner for two in the romantic Bacchus Restaurant.

All guests will also receive a box of Belgian Truffles and a welcome note upon arrival. ❧

• **nearby attractions**

Central downtown location, within walking distance to Robson Street, Vancouver's entertainment, shopping, and dining district. Vancouver Art Gallery and Provincial Law Courts are across the street, with theatres and more close by.

• **onsite facilities**

Brand new luxurious Spa carrying the renowned Epicuren Discovery cosmetic line, Eucalyptus Steam Room, and Fitness Centre. Award-winning French restaurant Bacchus, with live entertainment nightly. State of the art business centre.

• **wedding services**

We specialize in intimate-sized weddings using our Eton/Cambridge Room for your ceremony and reception, and the Liaisons Room for your dinner and dance. The dining tables are decorated with a fresh floral centerpiece & votive candles.

U.S & CANADA

• **at a glance**

Location: Québec City, Québec Canada
Mailing Address: 1, rue des Carrières
Québec City (QC) G1R 4P5 Canada
Reservations: 800-441-1414
Fax: 418-692-1751
Web Site: www.fairmont.com
Size of Property: 18 acres
Meeting Space: 22,000 square feet
Accommodations: 618 rooms and suites
Range of Rates: $150 - $1,500

about the area

Currency: CAD - Canadian Dollars
Weather: Seasonal
Languages: French and English
Nearest Airport: Québec City
International Airport

• **nearby attractions**

Old Québec is on UNESCO's prestigious list of World Heritage Sites. Local attractions include: Petit-Champlain district with its European style boutiques, cafés and restaurants, Plains of Abraham, Île d'Orléans, Rue du Trésor and museums.

• **onsite facilities**

Health club which includes indoor swimming pool, fitness room and spa services, three restaurants including fine dining, room service, bar, business center, high speed internet, boutiques, on site hair salon and concierge services.

• **wedding services**

Banquet rooms available for wedding ceremony include a magnificent ballroom, dedicated wedding consultant, complimentary Deluxe accommodation for the bride and groom on their wedding night, and white-glove service for the reception and dinner.

Fairmont Le Château Frontenac

QUÉBEC CITY, QUÉBEC, CANADA

Our castle opens up its doors to celebrate your special day.

Since its birth in 1893, Fairmont Le Château Frontenac has played host to thousands of special occasions. Over the years, with complete dedication and expertise, our award winning Chefs and experienced Banquet team have mastered the art of taking care of you and your guests, making every reception a success that will be remembered for years to come.

Set in the heart of Old Québec—on Cap Diamond, above the St. Lawrence River, Fairmont Le Château Frontenac reigns as the symbol of the French-Canadian city loved by romantics worldwide. Views of Old Québec and the St. Lawrence River dominate every scene. A stay at the chateau permits you easy walking access to all of the wonderful sites and experiences that Old Québec has to offer.

In any one of our beautifully furnished 618 guestrooms and suites, you will feel an elegant touch of historic Europe. Our accommodations offer an unparalleled level of luxury and service.

• ROMANTIC FEATURES •

A synonym for romanticism - Fairmont Le Château Frontenac has been the scene of many love stories during its first century of existence. Couples come from everywhere to celebrate their union, reunion and honeymoon in a picture-perfect setting of classic romanticism. From a carriage ride under the starlit sky to a walk on the Dufferin Terrace or a romantic candlelit dinner in our fine dining room, romance is guaranteed to fill the air. You can trust us with your dreams.

Ice Hotel Québec-Canada © Xavier Dachez

Ice Hotel Québec - Canada

QUÉBEC, CANADA

This magnificent architectural marvel offers a distinctive

and incomparable experience to be enjoyed yearly from early January to April. Imagine sleeping in a work of art crafted each winter from the purest of nature's materials; ice and snow, and is destined to disappear every spring!

The unique North American Ice Hotel is made in

Ice Hotel Québec-Canada © Xavier Dachez

five weeks using 400 tons ice, and 12,000 tons of snow. Waiting for you are 18-foot high ceilings, original artwork and furniture carved from ice, many rooms and theme suites, exhibition rooms, a cinema, a magnificent chapel, the astonishing N'ice Club reception room and nightclub, functional fireplaces and hot tubs, and the famous Absolut Ice Bar. It is essential to savor a fine Absolut Vodka product served in our special ice glasses. Ice Hotel is a magical location to celebrate an engagement, a wedding, a honeymoon, a birthday, an anniversary, or to host a reception or special event.

· ROMANTIC FEATURES ·

Magical and romantic winter escapades are waiting for you, including champagne, wax-dipped roses, and candles. Spend a cozy night in the Ice Hotel, on deer pelts, tucked in warm sleeping bags, zipped together. Various activities are available including dog sledding, cross-country skiing, snowmobiling, and hot-air ballooning. In the evening, surrender to the calm tranquility of a hot tub under the stars. The perfect ending to a full day of outdoor recreation and the perfect beginning to the PURE SENSATION Winter Experience - a night at the Ice Hotel!

U.S & CANADA

• at a glance

Location: Québec, Canada
Mailing Address: 143, Route Duchesnay Pavilion L'Aigle Sainte-Catherine-De-La-Jacques-Cartier QC G0A 3M0
Reservations: 877-505-0423
Fax: 418-875-2833
Web Site: www.icehotel-canada.com
Size of Property: 30,000 square feet
Meeting Space: 10,000 square feet
Accommodations: 32 rooms and suites
Range of Rates: $150 - $300/person

about the area
Currency: CAD - Canadian Dollars
Weather: Wonderful Winter!
Languages: French, English
Nearest Airport: Jean-Lesage (YQB)

• nearby attractions

Historical and Dynamic Québec City: 25 min, Shopping Centers: 20 min, Museums & Galleries: 20 min, Ski and Winter Recreation Centers: 40 min, Casino: 90 min, The Cosmopolitan City of Montreal: 2 hrs

Ice Hotel Québec-Canada © Yves Tessier

• onsite facilities

32 Rooms and Theme Suites, Absolut Ice Bar, N'ice Club reception area and nightclub, Ice Chapel, 2 Exhibition Rooms, and Grand Hall. STATION TOURISTIQUE DUCHESNAY - 88 rooms and 14 cabins, Meeting Rooms

Ice Hotel Québec-Canada © Xavier Dachez

• wedding services

Civil wedding ceremonies with a celebrant can include champagne & ice goblets, musicians, photographer, video artist, floral arrangements, beauty salon services, limousine, fur cape and coat rental, special requests, and planning assistance

Loews Hotel Vogue

MONTREAL, QUÉBEC, CANADA

• at a glance

Location: Montreal, Quebec, Canada
Mailing Address: 1425 rue de la Montagne, Montreal (QC) H3G 1Z3
Reservations: 800-23-LOEWS
Fax: 514-849-8903
Web Site: www.loewshotels.com
Meeting Space: 6,500 square feet
Accommodations: 142 rooms and 16 suites
Range of Rates: Call for rates

about the area

Currency: CAD - Canadian Dollars
Weather: Temperate
Languages: French, English
Nearest Airport: Dorval International Airport

• nearby attractions

Visit historical landmarks and cultural neighborhoods. Local museums include Montréal Museum of Fine Arts; Sporting activities for winter and summer; nightlife, dining, and shopping.

Among the bustling business district where cafes, shops, and museums line the streets, is an enclave of luxuriousness yet to be duplicated. It's the Loews Hotel Vogue. A boutique hotel that reflects the rich, French heritage inherent to the city, and exemplifies the kind of personal service guests only dream of. Crowned by five stars by Canada Select, the Loews Vogue Hotel embodies the best of Montréal's past, present, and future. Work, sleep, and play in style when you stay in any one of our luxurious rooms. Silk upholstered furnishings and a marble bathroom are only the beginning of the indulgences we have in store for our guests. Neoclassical accents merge effortlessly with Late Empire furnishings. It's elegant. It's sleek. It's amour. Indisputably romantic, Loews Hotel Vogue is an ideal location for weddings and honeymoons. Always on the qui vive, our staff can help you execute the most lavish of events overseeing every detail. Creating a memory you'll enjoy for years to come. ⁊

• onsite facilities

24-hour concierge, full-service business center, limousine services, fitness center, and baby-sitting services. Banquet rooms including an outdoor terrace and beautiful ballroom accommodating up to 240 guests. Shops and exquisite dining.

• ROMANTIC FEATURES •

Imagine a destination that blends old-world charm with new-world style. Where every need is addressed with uncompromising personal service and every desire is fulfilled. Indisputably romantic, Loews Hotel Vogue is the perfect intimate and elegant location for weddings and honeymoons. Just beyond the lobby are the diverse sights, sounds and tastes of the best of Montreal. And inside is the personal service guests only dream of. Our luxurious accommodations will pamper you with amenities such as down duvets and pillows, a whirlpool bath, and a mini-bar stocked full of caviar. Loews Hotel Vogue. It's not only in the heart of the city. It's in the memory of anyone who's ever stayed here. ⁊

• wedding services

Loews can help make your memories cherished ones every step of the way. From choosing just the right engraver for your invitations to dressing the tables with the most beautiful flowers, Loews lets you focus on only one detail, your day.

• at a glance
Location: Quebec City, Quebec, Canada
Mailing Address: 1225 cours du General-De Montcalm, Quebec City (QC) G1R 4W6 Canada
Reservations: 800-23-LOEWS
Fax: 418-647-4710
Web Site: www.loewshotels.com
Meeting Space: 7,236 square feet
Accommodations: 404 rooms and suites
Range of Rates: Call for rates

about the area
Currency: CAD- Canadian Dollars
Weather: Temperate
Languages: French and English
Nearest Airport: Jean Lesage International Airport

• nearby attractions

Loews Le Concorde is only steps away from the winding cobblestone streets, monasteries, ancient universities, preserved battlefields, museums, and boutiques that characterize Old Québec.

Loews Le Concorde Hotel

QUÉBEC CITY, QUÉBEC, CANADA

A wonderland, be it winter, spring, summer or fall,

Quebec serves as the perfect backdrop for weddings. No hotel has a better view of that perfect backdrop than the Loews Le Concorde. Located on the highest point in Québec City at the entrance of the old walled city, Loews Le Concorde offers unobstructed, majestic views of the St. Lawrence River, Old Québec, and the Plains of Abraham. Its location on Grande Allee Street, the Champs-Elysées of Québec, is central to many sights, shops, and museums.

L'Astral, appropriately named, is the crowning star of our hotel. 540 feet in the air, this revolving restaurant serves up 13 miles of stunning 360-degree views. However, the fine regional cuisine is sure to compete for your attention.

Some of the largest guestrooms in town are also some of the most luxurious. Each room features amenities that duplicate the comforts of home. Our suites take it a step further, offering a cozy fireplace, sauna and whirlpool bath.

• onsite facilities

Business center with bilingual secretary, fitness Center with sauna and whirlpool, outdoor heated pool, boutiques, lounges, and intimate dining settings with spectacular views. Baby-sitting services and on-call doctor are also available.

• ROMANTIC FEATURES •

When you live in a city that celebrates everything from maple syrup to winter's denouement, you become quite adept at planning, organizing and hosting a myriad of events. This holds especially true for our hotel, where a dedicated staff and 28,000-square feet of space have one objective - to meet yours.

Our experienced, creative team makes every occasion special. Whether planning an intimate wedding or an elaborate celebration, allow us to handle all the arrangements, accommodations, and catering, along with all the other details that are customized, just for you. You just show up and shine! It will be an event with more joie de vivre than you ever thought possible.

• wedding services

Let our experienced, creative team of coordinators assist you with the special details of your event. From invitations and flowers, to catering and accommodations, let us show you how enjoyable an affair at Loews Le Concorde Hotel can be.

Princeville Resort

HANALEI, KAUAI, HAWAII, USA

HAWAII

• at a glance
Location: Hanalei, Kauai, Hawaii USA
Mailing Address: 5520 Kahaku Road
Princeville, HI 96722 USA
Reservations: 888-488-3535
Fax: 808-826-1166
Web Site: www.starwood.com/hawaii
Meeting Space: 13,000 square feet
(indoors)
Accommodations: 252 rooms and suites
Range of Rates: $450 - $1,900

about the area
Currency: U.S. Dollars
Weather: Tropical
Languages: English
Nearest Airport: Lihue Airport

• nearby attractions

Nearby attractions include Hanalei Valley Overlook, Limahuli Garden, and Kee Beach Park, with its view of the Na Pali Coast. Neighbors include the historic villages of Hanalei and Kilauea, with the Kilauea Point National Wildlife Refuge.

• onsite facilities

The Princeville Resort has over 13,000 square feet of wedding and banquet facilities, including the 6,600 square foot Grand Ballroom. The open-air Makana Terrace and Beach Gardens offer panoramic vista's for outdoor events.

• wedding services

The exquisite Princeville Resort, on Kauai's North Shore, offers discriminating honeymoon and wedding vacations. Visit us at www.starwood.com/hawaii and click on Romance for detailed wedding and honeymoon experiences.

Situated on a lush green bluff on Kauai's North Shore,

Princeville Resort offers 252 exquisitely appointed rooms and suites most with breathtaking views of Hanalei Bay and the azure Pacific. Here you can match wits with nature on two magnificent golf courses, the Prince or Makai, or pamper yourself in spa facilities that promise not just renewal of the body but rejuvenation of the soul. All rooms have air conditioning, color cable TV with in-room movies, in-room safe, telephone hook-up for laptop computers and complimentary coffee/tea. Guest rooms feature custom-designed furnishings, original artwork, and lavish bathrooms with oversized tubs. Princeville is a particularly wonderful place to golf, play tennis, hike, kayak and more — including spending a day luxuriating at the world-class Princeville Health Club & Spa. There is one fine dining restaurant, one full service restaurant, the elegant Living Room for cocktails and evening entertainment and 24-hour room service.

• ROMANTIC FEATURES •

Nothing else on earth is like Princeville. Sun-drenched days magically turn into soft, candlelit nights. The fragrance of exotic, tropical flowers is in the air. And so is romance. This is a place of such stunning beauty and romantic harmony, it quietly defines the meaning of forever. Whether beachside or on the Makana Terrace, you will find no more spectacular setting for your wedding vows than the Princeville Resort. For your honeymoon, a truly private and memorable dining experience for two can be had at a beautiful outdoor setting enhanced by soft candlelight and Hawaiian torchlight. Your private wait staff will greet you in the lobby and create a night that you won't soon forget.

• at a glance

Location: Poipu Beach, Kauai, Hawaii USA
Mailing Address: 2440 Hoonani Road
Poipu Beach, Koloa, HI
Reservations: 888-488-3535
Fax: 808-742-9777
Web Site: www.starwood.com/hawaii
Size of Property: 20 acres
Meeting Space: 9,900 square feet
Accommodations: 413 rooms and suites
Range of Rates: $325 - $2,600

about the area
Currency: U.S. Dollars
Weather: Tropical
Languages: English
Nearest Airport: Lihue Airport

• nearby attractions

Nearby attractions include Kiahuna Plantation Gardens, Waimea Canyon, Kokee Park, a 19th-century fort, and Hanapepe village, with its art galleries. From nearby Port Allen, boats depart to view the Na Pali Coast.

Sheraton Kauai Resort

KAUAI, HAWAII, USA

Sheraton Kauai Resort embraces sun-kissed Po'ipu beach where temperatures linger idly around 80 degrees. The resort's 20 acres span pristine beachfront - a playground for those who worship sun and waves - and tropical gardens filled with meandering waterways and romantic bridges that create a sense of serenity. 414 rooms and suites, many with connecting capabilities ideal for families and friends traveling together. All rooms feature private lanai, cable TV with in-room movies, video check-out and Sony Playstations. Two swimming pools, one oceanside, two children's pools and whirlpool fulfill your watersport desires. Our Galleria of Oceanfront Dining & Entertainment features superb American, Italian and Japanese Cuisine with entertainment ranging from traditional Hawaiian to classical piano, Jazz, Rock and Top 40 Hits. All around is the beauty and romance of spectacular oceanfront settings, dazzling sunrises, glorious sunsets, twinkling starlight and magnificent moonscapes.

• onsite facilities

The resort shuttle service can transport guests to golf, shopping, horseback riding and more. Other resort features include three restaurants and two bars, lit tennis courts, two swimming pools, and a fitness center.

• ROMANTIC FEATURES •

Sheraton Kauai has a variety of romantic wedding sites, from oceanfront beaches and lawns to lush tropical gardens with koi-filled lagoons. With four different wedding packages to choose from, as well as an ala carte wedding menu, couples can definitely create the wedding of their dreams. Receptions can range from just the bridal couple to 600 of your family and friends. A honeymoon on the Garden Island of Kauai has always been known for its romantic quality. Experience the spectacular scenic beauty, secluded beaches and majestic mountains and waterfalls. Romance is a part of the natural element of Kauai's charm.

• wedding services

Sunny Poipu Beach is home to the oceanfront Sheraton Kauai Resort, the perfect destination for your wedding or honeymoon vacation.

Visit us at www.starwood.com/hawaii and click on Romance for detailed wedding and honeymoon experiences.

The Lodge at Koele and Manele Bay

LANAI CITY, LANAI, HAWAII, USA

HAWAII

• at a glance

Location: Lanai City, Lanai, Hawaii USA
Mailing Address: P.O. Box 630310 Lanai City, HI 96763 USA
Reservations: 888-488-3535
Fax: 808-565-3686
Web Site: www.starwood.com/hawaii
Size of Property: .20+ acres
Meeting Space: 12,000 square
Accommodations: Lodge - 102 rooms; /Manele Bay - 249 rooms
Range of Rates: $400 - $2,200

about the area
Currency: USD - U.S. Dollars
Weather: Tropical
Languages: English
Nearest Airport: Lanai Airport

The Island of Lana'i is truly a Polynesian paradise, with spectacular year-round weather, a variety of restful diversions, and a land rich in history. Your pampering begins the moment you arrive, when you are greeted with a lei of freshly gathered flowers.

Overlooking America's most beautiful beach, the Manele Bay Hotel's 249 individually decorated rooms offer striking views of sculptured gardens and the opalescent sea. Here, you can pamper yourself with various spa treatments, indulge in a dazzling variety of dining experiences or accept the Challenge at Manele – 18 holes of unforgettable, championship golf. Upcountry at 1,600 feet above the sea in the cool highlands of Lanai, The Lodge at Koele sits amidst 20 acres of gardens. 102 guestrooms and suites marry the pastoral and the worldly with hand-carved four-poster beds and spacious balconies. The Lodge's award-winning golf course, the Koele, is consistently ranked among the world's finest.

• nearby attractions

From the refined to the hair-raising, you'll enjoy such diverse activities as four-wheel drive adventures, world-class golfing, clay target shooting, or even a game of croquet. Shopping and dining opportunities abound in Lana'i City.

• onsite facilities

The Lanai Conference Center offers over 12,000 square feet of indoor function space including the Kaunolu Room. Or choose the intimacy of the Trophy Room, Music Room, Formal Dining Room and Library or the Garden Terraces.

• ROMANTIC FEATURES •

It is perhaps the most anticipated event of one's life. And it must be everything you've dreamed of. Our dedicated staff of wedding professionals work tirelessly to ensure your ceremony is flawless. With unique wedding packages, you will surely be able to find something that can be customized to fit your wedding day desires. For the location of the event, your options are numerous — from dramatic cliffs above crashing seas, to lush tropical gardens — you will find a wide variety of dreamlike settings on the grounds of the Lodge at Koele or the Manele Bay Hotel. Our wedding specialists are at your beck and call to ensure that the most important day of your life comes off just perfect.

• wedding services

The Lodge at Koele and the Manele Bay Hotel are two of the finest Hawaii wedding or honeymoon vacation destinations. Visit us at www.starwood.com/hawaii and click on Romance for detailed wedding and honeymoon experiences.

Kapalua Bay Hotel

KAPALUA, MAUI, HAWAII, USA

HAWAII

• **at a glance**

Location: Kapalua, Maui, Hawaii USA
Mailing Address: One Bay Drive
Kapalua, Maui, Hi 96761-9099 USA
Reservations: 888-488-3535
Fax: 808-669-4694
Web Site: www.starwood.com/hawaii
Meeting Space: 6,500 square feet
(indoors)
Size of Property: 18 acres
Accommodations: 210 rooms, suites
and villas
Range of Rates: $390 - $935

about the area
Currency: U.S. Dollars
Weather: Tropical
Languages: English
Nearest Airport: Ahului Airport

• **nearby attractions**

Nearby attractions include the Haleakala National Park, the Kula Botanical Garden, the city of Lahaina and the Lahaina Whaling Museum, the Maui Tropical Plantation and others. Also, enjoy seeing Haleakala, the dormant volcano.

• **onsite facilities**

Onsite facilities include a beauty salon, specialty boutique shops, a fitness room equipped with machines and free weights, two swimming pools, daily laundry and dry cleaning services, as well as complimentary on call shuttles.

• **wedding services**

The luxurious Kapalua Bay Hotel offers oceanfront vistas for your wedding or honeymoon vacation. Visit us at www.starwood.com/hawaii and click on Romance for detailed wedding and honeymoon experiences.

Welcoming you to paradise, the Kapalua Bay Hotel sits at the heart of a magnificent resort. Stepping onto the lanai you are embraced by perfumed tradewinds and stunned by sweeping vistas of lush coastline and brilliant blue water. At once sensuous and stimulating, Kapaula Bay is the ideal place in which to nurture romance. In this idyllic spot, the mountains slope gently to the sea past orderly rows of pineapple and the emerald green of golf courses, to one of the world's finest beaches.

196 guest rooms and suites, 14 Villas and 6 luxury Coconut Grove Villas.

All rooms have air conditioning, private lanai, color cable TV with in-room movies ceiling fans, honor bar and in-room electronic safes, coffeemaker, daily newspaper and iron/board. Twice daily housekeeping service with evening turndown, 24-hour fitness center, two swimming pools and beach services, full service wedding coordinator, and three championship golf courses.

· ROMANTIC FEATURES ·

For a wedding location that you may not even have dreamed possible, The Point and Kapalua Bay defies description. Here, on a spectacular ocean-side expanse of emerald green velvet lawn, with the neighboring islands of Molokai and Lanai in the distance, and with thousands of tropical blooms as your witness, your vows are carried aloft by Pacific breezes. Each Kapalua Romance Package presents a unique moment in paradise, exceeding your expectations of romance and sophistication. And while our settings are second to none, you can expect the same from our dedicated staff. You will find pampering and unique luxuries that you have likely never experienced before.

Sheraton Maui

LAHAINA, MAUI, HAWAII, USA

HAWAII

• at a glance

Location: Lahaina, Maui, Hawaii USA
Mailing Address: 2605 Kaanapali Parkway Lahaina, HI 96761 USA
Reservations: 888-488-3535
Fax: 808-661-0458
Web Site: www.starwood.com/hawaii
Size of Property: 23 acres
Meeting Space: 11,000 square feet (Indoors)
Accommodations: 510 rooms and suites
Range of Rates: $350 - $970

about the area
Currency: U.S. Dollars
Weather: Tropical
Languages: English
Nearest Airport: Kahului Airport

Privately nestled against historic Black Rock, Sheraton Maui's

23 oceanfront acres flow gracefully from the crest of Pu'u Keka'a to the shores of Ka'anapali Beach. Home of the nightly Cliff Dive ceremony, this 510-room resort reflects a truly Hawaiian ambiance giving rise to 83% ocean view accommodations and lush tropical landscaping. All rooms feature private lanai, air conditioning, cable television, with On-command movies, voicemail, data port, in-room safe, coffee maker, hair dyer, ironing board, light waffle robes, and refrigerator. A 42-yard freshwater swimming lagoon with lava-rock waterways, and heated outdoor whirlpool offer a relaxing respite. Each guest is greeted with a fresh flower lei greetings upon arrival. There are two restaurants, a fitness center, three-night-lit tennis courts, 36-holes of championship golf, and international shops. And you can "Stay at One, Play at All, at Starwood Maui's sister hotels: the Westin Maui and Kapalua Bay Hotel. ✎

• ROMANTIC FEATURES •

White and gold beaches that go on for miles. Sunsets that last forever. An ocean with more shades of blue than the world has names for. With a setting this spectacular, romance comes with the territory. Allow us to be your guide. For a long-overdue romantic getaway, or for a once-in-a-lifetime event, The Sheraton Maui awaits you. Not only will you find our natural surroundings to be inspiring, but our unique spirit of service as well. Our Alii Presidential Suite, the ultimate honeymoon oasis, is truly fit for royalty with its private lawn and sweeping views of Kaanapali Beach, the West Maui Mountains, and neighboring islands of Molokai and Lanai. ✎

• nearby attractions

Historic Lahaina Town, Kaanapali Sugar Cane Train, Haleakala, Road to Hana, Maui Ocean Center, Snorkeling Black Rock, Whalers Village, Maui Arts and Cultural Center, Championship Golf, Molokini Island.

• onsite facilities

Over 11,000 square fee of wedding space including the grand Maui Ballroom with open-air courtyard. Ocean Lawn with stunning views of the Pacific and legendary Black Rock.

• wedding services

The Sheraton Maui's romantic oceanfront location offers the most memorable honeymoon and wedding experience. Visit us at www.starwood.com/hawaii and click on Romance for detailed wedding and honeymoon experiences.

• at a glance
Location: Kaanapali, Maui, Hawaii USA
Mailing Address: 2365Kaanapali Parkway Lahaina, HI 9676 USA
Reservations: 888-488-3535
Fax: 808-661-5764
Web Site: www.starwood.com/hawaii
Meeting Space: 45,000 square feet (indoor/outdoor)
Accommodations: 759 rooms and suites
Range of Rates: $350 - $3,000

about the area
Currency: U.S. Dollars
Weather: Tropical
Languages: English
Nearest Airport: Kahului

• nearby attractions

Nearby attractions include the Haleakala National Park, the Kula Botanical Garden, the city of Lahaina and the Lahaina Whaling Museum, the Maui Tropical Plantation and others. A trip on the Road to Hana is not to be missed!

Westin Maui

KAANAPALI, MAUI, HAWAII, USA

Set upon the finest stretch of Ka'anapali Beach, the Westin Maui lies between the shimmering Pacific Ocean and the verdant West Maui Mountains. The hotel is an aquatic playground offering snorkeling, scuba diving, five sparkling pools, plunging water slides and a swim-through grotto. 759 newly renovated rooms all with Westin's Heavenly Beds® and Heavenly Showers®. An 85,000 square-foot area featuring five heated swimming pools, two water slides, a swim-through grotto with twin waterfalls, and a hidden Jacuzzi. Steps away, the soft sands of Kaanapali Beach beckon - where you'll enjoy snorkeling, scuba diving, beach volleyball, windsurfing, and chartered catamaran adventures. Two championship golf courses and an 11-court tennis center are just a short walk away. You may also enjoy our full-service Health Club & Spa which provides complete massage and facial services, including rejuvenating full-body treatments. Westin Maui...where heaven and aloha meet! ॐ

• onsite facilities

Frolic in our 85,000 square foot aquatic playground or partake in one of many water sports available to you. Two championship golf courses as well as 11 tennis courts are just a short walk away. Spa and fitness facilities are also onsite.

• ROMANTIC FEATURES •

If you've always dreamed of a Hawaiian wedding, The Westin Maui has one of the most romantic settings in the islands: a white-column, open-air gazebo surrounded in lush tropical foliage, overlooking a shimmering blue ocean. To make your celebrated event as exciting and hassle-free as possible, we offer a variety of wedding and vow renewal packages, with a range of features and prices. After a blissful ceremony, continue the moment with a fabulous reception under the stars. Amidst cascading waterfalls and swaying palm trees, tailor your reception to be just as you dreamed. From simple appetizers to a lavish meal in a gorgeous outdoor setting, our wedding staff anticipates your every desire. ॐ

• wedding services

The art of creating the ultimate tropical wedding has been honed to perfection by The Westin Maui's knowledgeable Wedding department. Our staff can create a truly magical occasion whether you have a wedding party of two or two hundred.

Sheraton Molokai Lodge and Beach Village

MAUNALOA, MOLOKAI, HAWAII, USA

At the Sheraton Molokai Lodge and Beach Village, accommodations range from gracious rooms in a charming country lodge to fully furnished canvas bungalows situated along a white sand beach. Here, in the midst of 54,000 sprawling acres of Hawaiian wilderness, you will find unlimited opportunities for exploration and adventure as well as pure relaxation. Sheraton Molokai is Hawaii's only adventure resort offering luxuriously rustic accommodations and unlimited access to a host of extraordinary activities. Unmatched outdoor recreational activities include mountain biking, kayaking, horseback riding, archery and much more. The Lodge, located at an elevation of 1,200 feet, features 22 deluxe guest rooms, spa and fitness center, billiards room, bar and fine dining in the Maunaloa Dining Room. Kaupoa Beach Village delivers a relaxed beachfront experience with 40 two-bedroom canvas bungalows, each featuring solar-powered lights and ceiling fans, hot water showers and wooden footlockers. 🍃

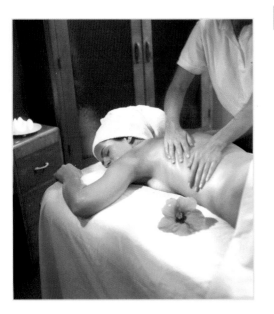

• ROMANTIC FEATURES •

It is every couple's dream: a wedding in paradise, on a secluded island at a romantic beachfront location surrounded by only the beauty of the Hawaiian landscape. Dreams come true at Sheraton Molokai Lodge with its Aloha Wedding package. Featuring a romantic private ceremony at the Sheraton Molokai Lodge or secluded Kaupoa Beach, the Aloha Wedding package offers couples the wedding of their dreams with none of the worries. For honeymooners, Kaupoa Beach Village is the Hawaii of honeymooner's dreams. Canvas bungalows dot green landscaped lawns...hammocks sway in the gentle trade winds...waves cascade onto the shore...and unobstructed sunsets paint the sky vivid shades of pink, orange and red. 🍃

HAWAII

• at a glance
Location: Maunaloa, Molokai, Hawaii USA
Mailing Address: 100 Maunaloa Highway Maunaloa, HI 96770 USA
Reservations: 888-488-3535
Fax: 808-552-2908
Web Site: www.starwood.com/hawaii
Size of Property: 54,000 acres
Meeting space: 540 square feet
Accommodations: 62 rooms and suites
Range of Rates: $285 - $459

about the area
Currency: U.S. Dollars
Weather: Tropical
Languages: English
Nearest Airport: Hoolehua Airport

• nearby attractions

Explore the beautiful terrain of Molokai via mountain biking, horseback riding, snorkeling, ocean kayaking, and Molokai Mule Rides. Enjoy visiting the Meyers Sugar Mill Museum, Halawa Valley Waterfall, and various coffee farms

• onsite facilities

A variety of intimate and private wedding settings for the active at heart. Choose from the charming ranch-style Lodge with panoramic views of rolling hills and the Pacific; or the natural beachfront Kaupoa Beach Village.

• wedding services

For the active at heart, the Sheraton Molokai Lodge & Beach Village is the perfect wedding or honeymoon destination. Visit us at www.starwood.com/hawaii and click on Romance for detailed wedding and honeymoon experiences.

The Royal Hawaiian

HONOLULU, OAHU, HAWAII, USA

W hen it opened in 1927, the "Pink Palace of the Pacific" made

Waikiki a world-class destination. Capturing the glamour of Old Waikiki, the bold pink facade, vaulted Spanish archways, gracious rooms and suites still kindle the hearts of travelers today. There are 528 rooms and suites, the richly appointed Tower Wing rooms are all ocean front with private lanais. All rooms have air conditioning, cable TV with in-room movies, refrigerator, TV internet and data ports on telephones and an in-room safe. Each guest is greeted with a fresh flower lei and freshly-baked Hawaiian banana bread. There is a fresh water swimming pool and

private beach area, two restaurants, the Mai-Tai Bar, and 24-hour in-room dining and full service Abahasa Spa.

The Royal Hawaiian offers you a virtually unlimited variety of things to do and see. In addition to sun-drenched outdoor activities, you'll also discover the finest in entertainment, cultural events and world class shopping, given our spectacular location.

· ROMANTIC FEATURES ·

For half a century, discriminating travelers have sought out the tropical serenity of The Royal Hawaiian, the most beloved landmark on Waikiki Beach. Today, our Celebration packages offer our treasured guests such luxuries as a bottle of special edition "Pink Champagne," an intimate dinner for two, and gifts that commemorate the classic traditions of The Royal Hawaiian.

Our 7,000-square foot Abhasa Waikiki Spa utilizes Hawaii's natural healing environment to promote the ultimate in beauty and rejuvenation at this world-class oasis known affectionately as the "Pink Palace." Individual, wedding and complete spa package rates are available.

HAWAII

• at a glance
Location: Honolulu, Oahu, Hawaii USA
Mailing Address: 2259 Kalakaua Avenue Honolulu, HI 96815 USA
Reservations: 888-488-3535
Fax: 808-931-7098
Web Site: www.starwood.com/hawaii
Size of Property: 1.2 acres
Meeting Space: 22,000 square feet (Indoors)
Accommodations: 528 rooms and suites
Range of Rates: $380 - $850

about the area
Currency: U.S. Dollars
Weather: Tropical
Languages: English
Nearest Airport: Honolulu International

• nearby attractions

The International Market Place, Waikiki Aquarium, Honolulu Zoo, Aloha Tower Marketplace, Pearl Harbor, Diamond Head, Iolani Palace, Pali Lookout, Polynesian Cultural Center, and Waimea Falls.

• onsite facilities

Onsite facilities include our famous Abhasa Waikiki Spa, beauty salon, boutique shops, and laundry/dry cleaning. Guests are also welcome to use the facilities at the Sheraton Waikiki (located adjacent to the property).

• wedding services

Since 1927, The Royal Hawaiian has fulfilled wedding and honeymoons dreams. Visit us at www.starwood.com/hawaii and click on Romance for detailed wedding and honeymoon experiences.

Sheraton Moana Surfrider

HONOLULU, OAHU, HAWAII, USA

For over a century, the Sheraton Moana Surfrider has been the

resort of choice for generations of families, romantic dreamers, and idealistic honeymooners seeking luxury and refinement in close proximity to Oahu's many wonders. Home to uncommonly gracious hospitality and a rich cultural heritage, including its famous "Hawaii Calls" radio broadcasts from the 1930's, the Sheraton Moana Surfrider is much more than a hotel - it is a Hawaiian legend that has created lifelong memories for a century of visitors from around the globe.

The grand columns of the porte cochere, the Palladian windows overlooking the ocean, the sweeping Banyan Veranda - all speak to the rich history of the Sheraton Moana Surfrider. Each guest is greeted with a fresh flower lei upon arrival. There is a fresh water swimming pool and private beach area, three restaurants, a beachfront bar with nightly entertainment, snack shop and 24-hour in-room dining. All guests have access to Sheraton Waikiki's Fitness Center.

· ROMANTIC FEATURES ·

Grand columns. Victorian elegance. Sweeping oceanfront vistas. When you first set eyes on the Sheraton Moana Surfrider, your heart will skip a beat. For the most historic hotel on Waikiki Beach is also surely the most romantic. For a storybook wedding, an unforgettable honeymoon, or simply a getaway to rekindle your love – The Sheraton Moana Surfrider is legendary.

We have several options available for your wedding ceremony, from the oceanfront Diamond Head Lawn, to the open-air Roof Garden. The Sheraton Moana Surfrider is also renowned for its wedding reception sites and menu options.

Create lasting memories by having your wedding and honeymoon here at the Sheraton Moana Surfrider.

HAWAII

• **at a glance**

Location: Honolulu, Oahu, Hawaii USA
Mailing Address: 2365 Kalakaua Avenue
Honolulu, HI 96815 USA
Reservations: 888-488-3535
Fax: 808-923-0308
Web Site: www.starwood.com/hawaii
Size of Property: .5 acres
Meeting Space: 15,000 square feet
Accommodations: 793 rooms and suites
Range of Rates: $270 - $1050

about the area
Currency: U.S. Dollars
Weather: Tropical
Languages: English
Nearest Airport: Honolulu
International

• **nearby attractions**

From visiting Diamond Head to the Waimea Falls, you'll also discover the finest in entertainment, cultural events, and world-class shopping. Should you need any assistance making reservations, our friendly staff is happy to help.

• **onsite facilities**

The Moana offers three restaurants and lounges along with a Snack Bar and Banyan Grill, 24-hour Room Service, and exceptional function space totaling over 12,000 square feet. An on-site salon and fitness center area are also available.

• **wedding services**

Since 1901, the Sheraton Moana Surfrider has welcomed wedding parties from around the world. Let us help you plan the wedding of your dreams. Visit us at www.starwood.com/hawaii and click on Romance for more information.

• at a glance

Location: Honolulu, Oahu, Hawaii USA
Mailing Address: 120 Kaiulani Avenue
Honolulu, HI 96815
Reservations: 888-488-3535
Fax: 808-931-4577
Web Site: www.starwood.com/hawaii
Size of Property: .5 acres
Meeting Space: 10,964 square feet
Accommodations: 1,152 rooms and
suites
Range of Rates: $165 - $595

about the area

Currency: U.S. Dollars
Weather: Tropical
Languages: English
Nearest Airport: Honolulu
International

• nearby attractions

From visiting Diamond Head to the Waimea Falls, you'll also discover the finest in entertainment, cultural events, and world-class shopping. Should you need any assistance making reservations our friendly staff is happy to help.

• onsite facilities

A fresh water swimming pool, two restaurants, a lounge, and nightly poolside entertainment as well as access to a fitness center are available to all guests. A travel and dining reservations desk is also available.

• wedding services

The Sheraton Princess Kaiulani is the ideal intimate location for your wedding or honeymoon vacation. Visit us at www.starwood.com/hawaii and click on Romance for detailed wedding and honeymoon experiences.

Sheraton Princess Kaiulani

HONOLULU, OAHU, HAWAII, USA

A crosswalk away from the crystal blue waters of world-famous Waikiki Beach, the hotel is situated at the former entrance to the royal estate of 'Ainahau, once home to Hawaii's most beloved Princess Victoria Kaiulani. The open-air lobby, decor and overall ambiance upholds the tradition of true Hawaiian hospitality.

We offer 1,152 rooms, many with private lanai, and all with air conditioning, color cable TV with in-room movies, refrigerator, in-room safe, and coffee-maker. There is one fresh water swimming pool, two restaurants, a lounge, food court and nightly poolside entertainment. All guests have access to Sheraton Waikiki's Fitness Center and Waikiki's most exciting dinner and cocktail show, "Creation – A Polynesian Journey;" a theatrical excursion through the South Pacific islands. The show takes the audience from the mythical creation of Polynesian man and woman to the tribal wars of Fiji, and from the romantic dances of Tahiti to the celebration of Hawaii's statehood.

• ROMANTIC FEATURES •

A garden oasis in the bustling core of Waikiki, The Princess Kaiulani is perfectly situated for a memorable wedding or scintillating honeymoon.

Whether you imagine moonlit walks along the sands of the world's most famous beach, or non-stop dancing in pulsating nightclubs, your dreams can become realities here.

The Sheraton Princess Kaiulani Hotel offers you a comprehensive wedding package, including our fine dining facilities and highly personalized service. For your reception, The Robert Louis Stevenson Room, on the penthouse level of the Princess Wing, is an ideal setting for up to 180 guests, offering a spectacular view of sunsets and the Pacific Ocean.

• nearby attractions

Sheraton Waikiki offers you a virtually unlimited variety of things to do and see. In additional to sun-drenched outdoor activities, you'll also discover the finest in entertainment, cultural events and world class shopping.

• onsite facilities

Guest amenities include access to our Fitness Center, Esprit, the only nightclub on Waikiki Beach, 2 cocktail lounges, and 20 gift and specialty shops. We also have two pools, three restaurants, water sports facilities and laundry services.

• wedding services

The Sheraton Waikiki is the ideal oceanfront location for your wedding or honeymoon.

Visit us at www.starwood.com/hawaii and click on "Romance" for detailed wedding and honeymoon experiences.

Sheraton Waikiki

HONOLULU, OAHU, HAWAII, USA

Rising on the graceful arch of the world's most famous beach, the Sheraton Waikiki Beach Resort reigns above Honolulu's glittering hub of excitement. With the brilliant Pacific and regal Diamond Head as a backdrop, our location is incomparable as a honeymoon location.

The Sheraton Waikiki commands breathtaking views of the azure Pacific, the Ko'olau mountains with their majestic silhouettes and Honolulu's whirling constellation of city lights.

Over two-thirds of the guest rooms and suites directly face the ocean. All rooms have air conditioning, mini-bar, color cable TV with in-room movies, Sony Play-station, TV internet and data ports on telephone. There are two fresh water swimming pools, three restaurants, two lounges, Waikiki's only beachfront nightclub, nightly poolside Hawaiian entertainment and 24-hour room service. The best luau in town can be found on our sister property, The Royal Hawaiian, every Monday night at 6:30pm.

• ROMANTIC FEATURES •

Five beautiful venues and four different wedding packages that range from an intimate reception for your closest friends and family, to hosting a glittering crowd of well wishers, the Sheraton Waikiki has a wedding package that will suit the most discriminating bride. A wedding on the Diamond Head Lawn at the Sheraton Waikiki can now be viewed by family and friends from around the world with Starwood Hotels in Hawaii's "Marriage Live" program. "Marriage Live" allows wedding couples to invite the world to their ceremony in real time, full-motion video and audio via a public or private portal over the Internet. Custom designed wedding receptions and honeymoon packages are also available.

Hotel Villa Vera
Spa and Racquet Club

ACAPULCO, GUERRERO, MÉXICO

Villa Vera hotel is located only 20 minutes away from the

Acapulco International airport, in the exclusive residential area of the Sport Club. Villa Vera Hotel offers a wide variety of comfortable rooms that are completely remodeled in our exclusive Mediterranean style decoration. These rooms are surrounded by breathtaking gardens and a unique atmosphere that is both private and tranquil, inviting relaxation. There are amazing views of the bay that will make your stay a total experience.

To stay at Villa Vera is a total experience. You will enjoy the magic of an incredible place that for ages has conquered the jet set as well as

famous people such as Elvis Presley, Elizabeth Taylor and other celebrity personalities.

The hotel's restaurant, Palma Real, has incomparable bay views and exquisite International and Mexican cuisine. Villa Vera also has the most complete and modern Spa, Gym with modern equipment, 2 tennis courts, 2 paddle courts, 2 meeting rooms, an on-site casino and award winning service.

· ROMANTIC FEATURES ·

A symbol of Acapulco's glory days when the jet set flew in from the French Rivera to the most fashionable resort of the moment to celebrate successes or triumphs, swim up to the very first pool bar in the world, Villa Vera has always belonged to the province of legends. Still nothing compares to the Romantic dining in the Restaurant Palma Real or to dining on the terrace of one of our villas with private pool. Here everyone finds the highest standards of hospitality, absolute privacy and all the diversions that continue seducing guests today, especially the honeymooners who find Villa Vera a pleasurable stay and absolute privacy, with everything they wish to have an unforgettable stay. Contact our wedding planner today for more information.

· at a glance
Location: Acapulco, Guerrero, México
Mailing Address: Lomas del Mar no. 35
Fracc. Club Deportivo Acapulco. Gro.
Mex. CP 39690 Mexico
Reservations: 888-554-2361
Fax: 52-55-5091-3293
Web Site: www.clubregina.com
Size of Property: 12,000 acres
Accommodations: 70 rooms
Range of Rates: $100 - $800

about the area
Currency: MXN - Mexican Pesos
Weather: Tropical
Language: Spanish
Nearest Airport: Acapulco
International Airport

· nearby attractions

Scuba diving, windsurfing, private yacht charter, city tours, coyuca lagoon tour, deep sea fishing, Palao tours, high cliff divers at night, jungle tour, morning and sunset cruises, bungie jumping, night clubs, discotheques.

· onsite facilities

Villa Vera is closely located to malls, amusement parks, golf courses, bowling, handball, basketball courts, and exclusive restaurants. Villa Vera has a Beach Club only 2 minutes away from the hotel.

· wedding services

Casa Lisa is an exclusive place to celebrate in "Villa Vera style" with an incomparable view of the bay and private swimming pool; professional decorating advice, set ups and arrangements, highly qualified chefs and much more are available.

MÉXICO

• at a glance

Location: Los Cabos, Baja California Sur, México
Mailing Address: 7.5 Carretera Transpeninsular, San Jose Del Cabo BCS, CP 23400 México
Reservations: 800-637-2226
Fax: 954-809-2347
Web Site: www.oneandonlypalmilla.com
Size of Property: 250 acres
Meeting Space: 5,000 square feet
Accommodations: 172 rooms and suites
Range of Rates: $325 - $1450

about the area

Currency: U.S. Dollars, MXN - Mexican Pesos
Weather: Temperate
Languages: English, Spanish
Nearest Airport: San Jose del Cabo

One&Only Palmilla Resort

LOS CABOS, BAJA CALIFORNIA SUR, MÉXICO

Resting on the tip of the Baja Peninsula where the azure ocean

greets the mountainous desert, where Pacific waters merge with the Sea of Cortez, is One&Only Palmilla. In January 2004, following an $80 million enhancement, One&Only Palmilla begins a new era as the quintessential embodiment of elegance.

In addition to world-class golf and exceptional accommodations, all with ocean views and your own personal butler offering a host of services, One&Only Palmilla will offer fine dining in two new restaurants, including "C", created by legendary Charlie Trotter.

The new One&Only Spa provides the perfect indoor/outdoor setting with private treatment villas for one or two people. The spa also features a full-service hair & nail spa, fitness center, outdoor hydrotherapy pool and a yoga garden.

• ROMANTIC FEATURES •

One&Only Palmilla provides an idyllic location for a wedding or honeymoon, including its own historic chapel which was built in 1956 along with the original hotel. Located on a hill in the center of the resort grounds, the chapel is in traditional Mexican style. The chapel can be used for private ceremonies, accommodating up to 50 guests. The new Spa will offer a special salon where wedding parties can prepare for the festivities, and a horse-drawn carriage will even be available to transport the bride and groom to the the chapel and reception. Beach weddings are also a popular favorite at this resort, given the spectacular coastline that One&Only Palmilla enjoys.

• nearby attractions

Just offshore, opportunities abound for sailing, kayaking, diving, and snorkeling. Los Cabos' natural reef rated among the finest in the world, offering underwater visibility of up to 120 feet. Deep-sea fishing is also a favorite sport.

• onsite facilities

Infinity-edged pools with swim up bar. Signature Jack Nicklaus golf course. 2 restaurants & 24-hour room service. One&Only Spa, fitness center & yoga garden. 2 tennis courts. Butler Service. Childrens pool.

• wedding services

Historic chapel available for private ceremonies for up to 50 guests. A 3,000 sq. ft. ballroom, and a broad range of choices for outdoor venues, including a central courtyard which takes full advantage of the resort's natural setting & beauty.

• **at a glance**

Location: Los Cabos, Baja California Sur, Mexico
Mailing Address: 5080 Bonita Road Suite E & F Bonita, CA 91902 Mexico
Reservations: 800-990-8250
Fax: 619-267-9009
Web Site: www.pueblobonito.com
Size of Property: 50 acres
Meeting Space: 1,645 square feet
Accommodations: 519 suites
Range of Rates: $195 - $1,800

about the area

Currency: U.S. Dollars, MXN - Mexican Pesos
Weather: Tropical
Languages: Spanish & English
Nearest Airport: San Jose del Cabo International

• **nearby attractions**

Lover's Beach at land's End, Santa Maria Bay, Chileno Bay, Coral Reef Diving at Cobo Pulmon, Whale Watching at Magdalena Bay, The Marina at Cabo San Lucas, Todos Santos, Glass factory at Cabo San Lucas, Exciting Nightlife.

Pueblo Bonito Sunset Beach

LOS CABOS, BAJA CALIFORNIA SUR, MÉXICO

The Pueblo Bonito Sunset Beach, our newest luxury resort in Los Cabos, is situated on the western side of the tip of Baja, overlooking the Pacific. Set away from the concentration of hotels along the Sea of Cortez, the resort's fifty-acre site and expansive, private beach provide guests with a uniquely tranquil and secluded setting.

The architecture features separate villas in a "Hacienda" style. And as with all Pueblo Bonito properties, lush and innovative landscaping blends with the unique terrain surrounding the Pueblo Bonito Sunset Beach resort.

Sunset Beach's initial phase includes 118 suites in total. Guests are offered a range of accommodations from Junior and Master Suites, to Presidential and Penthouse Suites. No matter which you choose, you can relax on your own private balcony at the end of the day enjoying a spectacular sunset. Come visit us, and lose yourself amongst the seclusion.

• **onsite facilities**

Expansive, free-form swimming pool with swim-up bar, children's pool, a Hydro-massage pool, large jacuzzi overlooking the ocean, two restaurants, fitness center, lighted tennis courts, in-room massage available, and 24-Medical clinic.

• ROMANTIC FEATURES •

Picture days of sun, sea, and pleasure on your own private beach. Tranquil evenings bathed in vivid sunsets. That's life at Sunset Beach, a fifty-acre resort overlooking the sparkling waters of the Pacific Ocean, where you can lose yourself among the pristine sands and lush gardens, and luxuriate in ocean view suites and splendid dining.

You'll be on the Western side of Baja, in a new and exclusive area, comfortably away from the hurly-burly of town and other hotels. Yet close to shopping and night life - all the enjoyment Cabo has to offer. Come and experience the very best of Mexico's warmth and charm in the comfort and luxury of your beautiful Pueblo Bonito Sunset Beach Hotel and Resort.

• **wedding services**

With an incomparable view of the Pacific, professional decorating advice, set ups, arrangements and much more, The Pueblo Bonito Sunset Beach is an exclusive place to celebrate in "Hacienda" style.

• at a glance
Location: Cancun, Riviera Maya, Quintana Roo México
Mailing Address: KM. 72 Carretera Cancún - Tulum, Riviera Maya, Q.Roo 77710 Mexico
Reservations: 011-52-984-875-1100
Fax: 011-52-984-875-1101
Web Site: www.palaceresorts.com
Size of Property: 85 acres
Accommodations: 1,266 rooms and suites
Rage of Rates: Contact Hotel for Rates

about the area
Currency: MXN - Mexican Pesos
Weather: Tropical
Languages: Spanish, English
Nearest Airport: Cancún Airport

• nearby attractions

Discover the unique archaeological site of Ek-Balam, known as the City of the "Black Jaguar," or take a first class boat ride to the private beach club of Isla Mujeres.

Aventura Spa Palace

CANCÚN, QUINTANA ROO, MÉXICO

Take your body, mind, and spirit on a journey that will

at once purify, restore, and revitalize the senses. Ideally positioned in the heart of the Riviera Maya, where the tropical sun meets the turquoise waters of the Caribbean Sea, the ultimate pampering experience of Aventura Spa Palace awaits you. This adults only resort is set within 85-acres of exuberant virgin jungle with wide and spacious lawns and gardens.

The focus of well-being extends to Aventura Spa Palace's six restaurants. Begin the day poolside with a delicious breakfast or take advantage of our room service menu and savor a romantic dinner for two in the privacy of your suite.

Aventura offers a wealth of fitness activities including spinning, step, yoga, meditation and exceptional therapeutic pools. Our cross-current marine pool refreshes with cascading waterfalls. Our lap pool energizes. Our sound pool soothes. And our outdoor pools encourage traditional lounging.

• ROMANTIC FEATURES •

Begin your lives in a breathtaking beachfront setting where every detail will be perfectly planned by our experienced wedding coordinators.

The Aventura Spa Palace offers a beautiful fairytale wedding, where the bride arrives on a horse-drawn carriage. The Palace brings seclusion and romance where the ceremony is held in a gazebo overlooking the ocean.

From the Aventura Spa Palace's central patio with its colonial fountain, through the romantic archways, down to the natural tile floor, to the carefully handcrafted furniture, it all combines to create a magical setting for your special wedding or honeymoon getaway.

• onsite facilities

Non-motorized water sports, dive tank, scuba lessons, therapeutic pools, fitness centers, outdoor free-weight gym, spinning room, aerobic room, yoga hut, and one pathway labyrinth. Spa facilities with resting lounge, Zen garden, & saunas.

• wedding services

A beautiful fairytale wedding, where every detail will be planned by our experienced wedding coordinators. Our three wedding packages, Free, Superior, and Deluxe, offer a variety of amenities and services to complement your special day.

Le Méridien Cancun

CANCÚN, QUINTANA ROO, MÉXICO

• at a glance
Location: Cancun, Quintana Roo, Mexico
Mailing Address: Retorno del Rey,
Cancun, Q. Roo 77500, Mexico
Reservations: 800-543-4300
Fax: 52-998-881-2201
Web Site: www.meridiencancun.com
Size of Property: 500 acres
Meeting Space: 9,378 square feet
Accommodations: 213 room and suites
Range of Rates: $200 - $1,500

about the area
Currency: U.S. Dollars
Weather: Tropical: Avg. 82 degrees
Languages: English, Spanish
Nearest Airport: Cancun
International

• nearby attractions

Located directly on the beach in the heart of the Hotel Zone. A wide choice of ground and sea excursions are available from the hotel: Water Parks, like Xcaret and Xel-Há; Archeological sites such as the Mayan Ruins, Chichen-Itzá and Tulúm.

• onsite facilities

Other on-site features include three upscale shops, a beautifully landscaped pool, beach front lounges and shelters, and two championship artificial grass tennis courts. Classes in basic Tae-Bo, Tai Chi, Yoga, stretching and water aerobics.

• wedding services

Wedding Package includes: Judge/Minister performing ceremony, Wedding license, All legal requirements made upon arrival, Wedding set up, Flower decoration, Wedding cake up to 10 people, One bottle of sparkling wine, Wedding Coordinator.

Merging the local flavour of Mexico with European flare,

Le Méridien Cancún Resort & Spa offers a high level of service and standards in all aspects of meals, accommodations and upscale boutiques. Stylish design creates an inviting atmosphere welcoming guests to a luxurious setting for those who seek excellence and demand quality.

Our 213 guestrooms and 26 suites have an ocean or lagoon view, with the majority of rooms having both views. The interior design elements are of a high quality and provide a residential atmosphere. Step through the vast elegant European style Spa and allow your body and mind to relax, revitalize, rejuvenate and rejoice in the finest European spa in Cancún - Spa del Mar. The spa has 14 treatment rooms offering a wide range of services, including three cascading pools, giving the sensation of swimming in the sea.

• ROMANTIC FEATURES •

Live the magic of this wonderful moment at this Mexican Caribbean Resort, honored with the Four Diamonds Award from the AAA. The delicate Mediterranean twist expressed in every single detail will make of your wedding date an unforgettable experience. Le Méridien Cancún has many beautiful and exclusive wedding locations overlooking the turquoise waters, perfect for a ceremony or smaller reception, or Martinière, the newest ballroom in Cancún, for up to 500 guests. At Le Méridien Cancun you can expect outstanding personalized service, luxury accommodations, and VIP treatment for you and your attendants, surrounded by elegance.

Moon Palace Golf Resort

CANCÚN, QUINTANA ROO, MÉXICO

Nestled between pristine white sand beach and acres of tropical, foliage the magnificent Moon Palace Golf Resort awaits you. This all-inclusive luxury resort offers an incredible 2,031 rooms in 3-story villas. Most with ocean views and all with a double Jacuzzi and private terraces.

Look no further than Moon Palace Golf Resort for fun and excitement. Our two outdoor pools are among the the largest lagoon-style pools in all of México. Each winds its way along the beach with Jacuzzis, swim-up bars, and children's areas.

In addition, our new Jack Nicklaus Signature course offers golfers championship greens on par with some of México's top courses. The resort features 10 exceptional restaurants so you can dine at a different spot every night of the week & sample some of México's best cuisine.

With the largest function space in Cancún and a grand ballroom that seats up to 3,000 guests, Moon Palace Golf Resort offers an inspired setting for your wedding or special event.

· ROMANTIC FEATURES ·

Imagine your wedding day amid palm trees and a warm ocean breeze where the bride arrives on a horse-drawn carriage. These are only some of the things that you can expect at Moon Palace Golf Resort.

With flexible indoor banquet facilities and expansive poolside terraces, we have the ideal location you desire. Themed events bring the flavor of Cancún to life and may be customized for your wedding event. Whether transforming our ballroom to a tropical paradise or setting up for a night under the stars, Moon Palace Resort's events and catering staff exceed your expectations and ensure guests an affair to remember.

Xpu-Ha Palace

RIVIERA MAYA, QUINTANA ROO, MÉXICO

• at a glance
Location: Riviera Maya, Quintana Roo México
Mailing Address: 6KM 265 Carretera Chetumal Puerto-Juarez Riviera Maya, México 77710
Reservations: 011-52-984-875-1010
Fax: 011-52-984-875-1012
Web Site: www.palaceresorts.com
Accommodations: 464 rooms and suites
Range of Rates: Contact hotel for rates

about the area
Currency: MXN - Mexican Pesos
Weather: Tropical
Languages: English, Spanish
Nearest Airport: Cancún Airport

Located in the Riviera Maya within wild tropical gardens

overlooking a white sandy beach is the magnificent Xpu-Ha Palace, the ultimate all-inclusive adventure for ecological and nature lovers.

Bungalow-style accommodations complement the resort's natural setting but don't be deceived. Under the thatched roofs you'll find plush beds, a double Jacuzzi and a large private terrace complete with hammock. Room service lets you enjoy a romantic meal on your terrace 24-hours a day.

With the Caribbean Sea in your backyard and an ecological park surrounding you, Xpu-Ha Palace offers more than just another day at the beach. Clear Caribbean waters guarantee excellent diving and snorkeling conditions and make for wonderful kayak excursions. Of course, those who prefer can also enjoy our private white sands and pools.

• ROMANTIC FEATURES •

The natural surroundings at Xpu-Ha Palace will delight you with a spectacular lagoon view for your ideal wedding location. Imagine your wedding day amid palm trees, a warm ocean breeze and the beauty of México. These are only some of the things that you can expect from Xpu-Ha Palace.

Our wedding packages have been designed to meet our clients' expectations and make this special day a memorable one. Our Free, Superior, and Deluxe packages offer a variety of amenities and services to complement your special day. Our free wedding package includes a wedding gazebo, documents and legal fees, white decorations, red carpet walkway, wedding coordinator, and much more.

• nearby attractions

Xpu-Ha Palace provides transportation to Playa Del Carmen, Moon Palace Golf Resort, Beach Palace and the Cancún shopping area. Take a first class boat ride to the quiet areas of Isla Mujeres or visit unique archaeological sites near by.

• onsite facilities

All-inclusive consist of non-motorized water sports, 24-hour room service, pools, private white sands, fitness center, scuba demonstration, kayaking & nightly dinner shows. Guests can also enjoy all of the amenities of the other Palace Resorts.

• wedding services

A wedding set in spectacular surroundings where every detail is planned by our experienced event coordinators. Our three wedding packages free, Superior, & Deluxe offer a variety of amenities and services to compliment your special day.

MÉXICO

• at a glance
Location: Colima, Mexico
Mailing Address: Mahakua Hacienda de San Antonio, Municipio de Comala, CP 28450, Colima, Mexico
Reservations: 800-477-9180
Fax: 65-6887-3338
Web Site: www.amanresorts.com
Accommodations: 25 suites
Range of Rates: $850 - $1,700+

about the area
Currency: MXN - Mexican Pesos
Weather: Temperate
Languages: Spanish, English
Nearest Airport: Colima

• nearby attractions

Guests can enjoy guided nature tours in the extensive resort grounds or explore the adjacent farm and dairy on horseback, foot or bicycle. There is also a 35 meter pool and tennis court, lounge room and well-stocked library.

• onsite facilities

The resort's own corral can host a charreada or Mexican rodeo - performances of extreme horsemanship and the volcanic stone amphitheater leads to a stage where performances of music, dance and drama are held.

• wedding services

Wedding venues include the amphitheater, by the pool overlooking the coffee plantation, avocado and pecan groves, or on the roof terrace looking out to one of Mexico's largest volcanoes. Fireworks and a mariachi or salsa band are available.

Mahakua - Hacienda de San Antonio

COLIMA, MÉXICO

Mahakua-Hacienda de San Antonio or "great community" is an elegantly restored, casa grande originally built by German planter Arnoldo Vogel and his Mexican wife in the 19th Century. Located at about 4,000 feet in the mountainous Western Mexican state of Colima, it spans over 470 acres within a 5,000 acre working ranch that includes an organic farm and coffee plantation. In the distance one can see a spectacular active volcano, Volcán del Fuego, Mexico's second largest. A large working aqueduct provides year-round water for the formal gardens inspired by Spain's famed Alhambra Palace where, along with fig and cypress trees are garden plants like the blue agave, from which tequila is made.

A range of experiences is available here, including riding through scenic countryside, cultural visits to traditional villages and local museums, bird-watching on nature walks through the Hacienda's grounds and classical gardens, or exploring further afield on horseback or by bicycle.

• ROMANTIC FEATURES •

All suites are located in a two-story wing which has its own private courtyard. A broad, winding volcanic-stone staircase connects the two floors and their 25 suites – some with balconies and views, others on the ground floor with direct access to the gardens. Each suite has its own name and theme. Some of the rooms are designed around the tapestries of the region or its charreada while others incorporate pre-Columbian legends and Spanish discoveries. The Dining Room is built on a vast scale with 15 foot high, barrel-vaulted brick ceilings and candlelit dinners can be enjoyed in various locations around the estate.

W Mexico City

MÉXICO CITY, MÉXICO

• at a glance
Location: Mexico City, Mexico
Mailing Address: Campos Eliseos 252:
Mexico City, 11560 Mexico
Reservations: 52-55-91381800
Fax: 52-55-91381899
Web Site: www.whotels.com
Meeting Space: 9 studios, totaling 6,860
square feet
Accommodations: 264 rooms and suites
Range of Rates: From $199

about the area
Currency: MXN - Mexican Peso
Weather: Semi-Dry, mild
Languages: Spanish, English
Nearest Airport: Mexico City Airport

• nearby attractions

The most sizzling sights and sensations of the world's largest city surround you – exclusive boutiques, art galleries, international luxury retailers and theatre.

Located in the trendy Polanco neighborhood, it's W's first hotel in Latin America and possibly the hottest experience yet.

By mingling modern design with a zealous commitment to comfort, W has created a sense of warmth and welcome that stays with you long past checkout time.

Meditate by one of the indoor koi ponds. Rekindle your spirits in the Red Lounge. Or stroll up to the guest room corridors, where dazzling images from around the world flicker continuously on a three-story projection wall. W Mexico City is the place to discover what you've been missing.

Sleek in design. Superior in service. From signature restaurants like Solea, serving contemporary coastal seafood with both Mexican and Asian flare, to The Coco Bar and Red Lounge with their seductive atmospheres, W Mexico City is a savvy blend of style and substance. Come discover the wonders within W Mexico City.

• onsite facilities

In-room massage, Solea restaurant, The Whisky Bar, Concierge Service, Whatever, Whenever Service, Sweat Fitness Center, Away Spa, Meeting & Event Facilities.

• ROMANTIC FEATURES •

W Mexico City is red hot with Romance. With pillow-top mattresses and feather beds, luxurious bath products and 24 hour concierge and room service you will want for nothing. Melt your cares away in the adobe sauna and relax in the Jacuzzi. For daytime delights, drift outside to the large terrace for an alfresco breakfast or lunch and let the outdoor rooftop bar with fire pit seduce you at night.

Come discover the passion burning within W Mexico City.

• wedding services

Let the elegant Great Room and restaurant-style food service from Solea turn your wedding red hot. W Mexico City will take personal care of your event to make sure it burns with the same passion that you do.

Westin Regina, Puerto Vallarta

PUERTO VALLARTA, JALISCO, MÉXICO

MÉXICO

• at a glance
Location: Puerto Vallarta, Jalisco Mexico
Mailing Address: Paseo de la Marina Sur #205 Puerto Vallarta, Mexico
Reservations: 800-228-3000
Fax: 52 322 226 1144
Web Site: www.westinpv.com
Size of Property: 21 acres
Meeting Space: 16,000 square feet
Accommodations: 280 rooms and suites
Range of Rates: $80 - $325

about the area
Currency: MXN - Mexican Pesos
Weather: Tropical
Languages: Spanish, Multilingual
Nearest Airport: Gustavo Diaz Ordaz International Airport

Hugged by the lush hills of the Sierra Madre and spectacular Banderas Bay, Puerto Vallarta charms visitors from the very first moment with its cobblestone streets and enchanting natural beauty...and at the heart of it all is the Westin Regina Resort, Puerto Vallarta ranked by Condé Nast Golden List as one of the best places to stay in the world.

This spectacular oceanfront resort, located in the exclusive Marina Vallarta, is nestled in an oasis of 600 palm trees and spectacular pools. Westin Regina combines the ambiance of colonial Mexico with the most sophisticated services and amenities, featuring all rooms and suites with private balcony, sweeping ocean views, and marvelous "Heavenly Bed."

Let the rest of the world slip away will you relax with a massage, body treatment, steam bath or sauna in the state-of-the-art fitness center and spa, play tennis in our lighted courts, parasail, play volleyball on the beach or a challenging round of golf, making each day memorable. ❧

• nearby attractions

There are many activities for guests to enjoy in Puerto Vallarta: Swimming with the dolphins, touring secluded beaches, horse back riding through tropical forests, sailing into the sunset, dining in Vallarta, and shopping in paradise.

• onsite facilities

New state-of-the art fitness center and full-service spa. Three lighted tennis courts. Parasail, play beach volleyball, or a challenging game of golf.

• ROMANTIC FEATURES •

Sense the fantastic atmosphere of this fascinating town and scenery where Richard Burton and Elizabeth Taylor fell in love...Puerto Vallarta. ... let be yourself enchanted by the Westin Regina Resort and delight in this perfect wedding and honeymoon site celebrating your life's most magical occasion at the Pacific Ocean shore, with a unique and beautiful sunset or a glowing moonlight in an absolute romantic atmosphere. Have your wedding become the most sublime and memorable moment of your life… forever!

To plan your wedding or make a honeymoon reservation, please contact us at info@westinvallarta.com. ❧

• wedding services

Westin Regina is an ideal spot for your wedding, with over 16000 sq ft of venue space to choose, whether small and intimate or a grand reception for 800 guests, qualified coordinators take every step to insure your event is a success.

Pueblo Bonito Emerald Bay

MAZATLAN, SINALOA, MÉXICO

• **at a glance**

Location: Mazatlan, Sinaloa, Mexico
Mailing Address: 5080 Bonita Road Suite E & F Bonita, CA 91902 Mexico
Reservations: 800-990-8250
Fax: 619-267-9009
Web Site: www.pueblobonito.com
Size of Property: 20 pristine acres
Meeting Space: 860 square feet
Accommodations: 258 Suites
Range of Rates: $135 - $700

about the area

Currency: U.S. Dollars, MXN - Mexican Pesos
Weather: Tropical
Languages: Spanish, English
Nearest Airport: Rafael Buelna

• **nearby attractions**

The Mueseo de Arqueologia, Casa de la Cultura, Museo Casa Machado, Teatro Angela Peralta, The Festival Sinaloa de las Artes, The Festival Cultural de Mazatlan, Plazuela Machado, and the Plazuela Republica.

• **onsite facilities**

Large swimming pool with swim-up bar, outdoor jacuzzi, gym, beauty salon with therapy rooms for massage and body treatment access to water sports and conveniences such as car rentals, travel arrangements and sight seeing tours.

• **wedding services**

Emerald Bay is the ideal location for your wedding. With many locations having an incomparable view of the Pacific, along with professional decorating, set-up and arrangements, Emerald Bay is an exclusive place to celebrate in style.

Discover the ultimate getaway - the gorgeous new

Pueblo Bonito Emerald Bay Resort in an exclusive new area of Mazatlan. This jewel among resorts, overlooking the Pacific Ocean and its own magnificent beach, is an ideal setting for relaxation, yet with easy access to Mazatlan's Golden Zone.

Emerald Bay's graceful architecture, gorgeous sorroundings and beautifully decorated ocean view suites provide every comfort and convenience. Relax on the beach or by the pool with swim-up bar. Have a massage, work out in the gym, or take advantage of the many nearby water sports. You'll discover fine dinning in the oceanview La Cordeliere Restaurant, and relaxed camaraderie in the extraordinary Kelly's Piano Bar with its Hemingway-esque atmosphere.

Emerald Bay is the perfect choice for vacation destination, away from it all but not too far away. Escape to a newfound paradise at the beautiful Pueblo Bonito Emerald Bay.

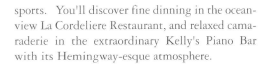

• ROMANTIC FEATURES •

Stroll for miles on a pristine beach. Lounge by a crystal clear pool and refresh yourself at the enticing swim-up bar. Experience the pleasure of a pampering massage or an invigorating workout at the health club. Sip a cool drink on an elegant veranda where the ambience echoes a gracious and glamorous past.

The setting is ideal for relaxation, yet with easy access to fishing, water sports, shopping and all that Mazatlan has to offer. The lovely ocean view suites, tropical gardens, fine dining and friendly service will have you dreaming of returning year after year.

Experience the very best in the comfort and casual luxury of your beautiful Pueblo Bonito.

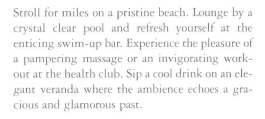

Pueblo Bonito Mazatlan

MAZATLAN, SINALOA, MÉXICO

• **at a glance**

Location: Mazatlan, Sinaloa Mexico
Mailing Address: 5080 Bonita Road,
Suites E & F, Bonita, CA 91902 USA
Reservations: 800-990-8250
Fax: 619-267-9009
Web Site: www.pueblobonito.com
Size of Property: 8 acres
Accommodations: 247 Suites
Range of Rates: $135 - $700

about the area

Currency: U.S. Dollars
MXN - Mexican Pesos
Weather: Tropical
Languages: Spanish, English
Nearest Airport: Rafael Buelna

• **nearby attractions**

Museo de Arqueologia, Casa de la Cultura, Museo Casa Machado, Plazuela Machado, Teatro Angela Peralta, The Festival Sinaloa de las Artes, The Festival Cultural de Mazatlan, Plazuela Republica, Cathedral de Mazatlan.

• **onsite facilities**

Two large free-form swimming pools featuring a convenient swim-up bar, fitness center, beauty salon, and three elegant restaurants.

P ueblo Bonito Mazatlan is located in this 400-year-old

city's scenic "Zona Dorado" (Golden Zone) on one of Mazatlan's finest beaches which stretches for miles, and offers panoramic views of the crystal blue Pacific Ocean. Pueblo Bonito Mazatlan, a premiere Mexico vacation destination, is beloved by those who know it. Guests return year after year for the charm of its relaxed ambience. Pueblo Bonito is Spanish for "Pretty Village." Right on the beach in a lush tropical setting, it is the ideal oasis for enjoyment of all that Mazatlan has to offer. Explore historic "Old Mazatlan." Shop for hand-made treasures. Walk or jog on one of the longest stretches of beach in Latin America. Golf, fish, engage in water sports. Laze by either of two large pools and enjoy the swim-up bar, waterfall, volleyball or outdoor jacuzzi. Dine grandly at the elegant Angelo's or casually at the oceanview Cilantro's. Watch the sunset-and fall in love with Pueblo Bonito, your own pretty village.

• ROMANTIC FEATURES •

Set in the Golden Zone beneath the majestic Sierra Madre, the Pueblo Bonito Mazatlan offers you the sights and sounds of this historic Mexican city. Each suite comes with an ocean view and amenities to meet your every expectation. Listen to the sound of waterfalls, relax in a tropical setting around two crystal clear pools, walk one of the longest stretches of beach in Latin America, sport fish, play golf, tennis, or any number of nearby water activities. At Pueblo Bonito Mazatlan, elegance, fine cuisine, and your choice to do it all or nothing at all awaits.

• **wedding services**

With an incomparable view of the Pacific from every location and a helpful staff, Pueblo Bonito Mazatlan is an ideal location to celebrate in style. To plan your wedding at Pueblo Bonito please call 800-990-8250.

Cliveden House

BERKSHIRE, UNITED KINGDOM

• at a glance
Location: Berkshire, United Kingdom
Mailing Address: Cliveden Taplow
Berkshire SL6 OJF United Kingdom
Reservations: +44-0-1628-668561
Fax: + 44-0-1628-661837
Web Site: www.clivedenhouse.co.uk
Size of Property: 376 acres
Meeting Space: 839 square feet
Accommodations: 39 rooms and suites
Range of Rates: $335 - $1,460

about the area
Currency: GBP - U.K. Pounds
Weather: Temperate
Languages: English
Nearest Airport: London Heathrow

• nearby attractions

Guests are free to explore the water garden and magnificent formal garden. Cliveden is also ideally located for visits to nearby Windsor and Eton and for experiencing the many and varied social events at both Henley and Ascot.

• onsite facilities

2 award-wining restaurants, 3 private dining rooms, Pavilion Spa with 7 treatment rooms, indoor and outdoor pools, Canadian hot tubs, sauna and steam rooms, indoor and outdoor tennis courts, 3 vintage launches, 376 acres of grounds.

• wedding services

There are 5 licensed areas within Cliveden for civil services. Personal wedding coordinator organizes everything including cake, flowers, entertainment, transport and even fireworks. For weddings over 60 guests, exclusive use is possible.

Cliveden is Britain's only five star hotel that is also a stately home. Set in spectacular surroundings on the banks of the River Thames and within 35 minutes drive of central London.

The unique combination of the House, the setting, hospitality, service and fine dining makes Cliveden an unforgettable experience. Indulgence is found in either of the award winning restaurants, relaxation is assured in the tranquil setting of the Pavilion Spa, and contentment confirmed with a leisurely cruise down the River Thames aboard one of the Cliveden vintage launches.

• ROMANTIC FEATURES •

As Britain's highest rated five star hotel, Cliveden is the ultimate wedding venue. With its fairy tale architecture, rich interiors and breathtaking views, there can be few better places for a wedding or marriage blessing. Add to that our reputation for offering excellent service, hospitality and food, and you could not hold your ceremony or reception in a more superior location.

Among the ingredients we add to your wedding day are accommodations in a suite on the eve of your wedding; the French Dining Room for your Wedding Breakfast; the Mountbatten/Lady Astor Suite for the Wedding Ceremony; fresh flowers; a harpist to play during the proceedings and a suite for your wedding night.

Lé Meridien Piccadilly

CENTRAL LONDON, UNITED KINGDOM

EUROPE

• **at a glance**

Location: Central London, United Kingdom
Mailing Address: 21 Piccadilly, London W1J 0BH UK
Reservations: 44-0-870-400-8400
Fax: 44-0-20-7437-3574
Web Site: www.lemeridien.com
Size of Property: 15 acres
Meeting Space: 9 function rooms, max 240 guests
Accommodations: 26 rooms and suites
Range of Rates: $330 - $4,300 (VAT included)

about the area
Currency: GBP - U.K. Pounds
Weather: European
Languages: English
Nearest Airport: London Heathrow

The perfect celebration location for those looking to indulge in

five-star luxury, haute cuisine, fine wines, first class leisure facilities and unsurpassed levels of service. Spaced over 9 floors, the hotel's 266 classically decorated and well appointed bedrooms and sumptuous suites reflect the hotel's theatrical Edwardian origins, whilst offering every luxury that you would expect from a five-star establishment.

Hotel guests can also relax in marbled splendor at the hotel's very own Champneys Health Club & Spa, offering an unrivaled range of health and beauty treatments, spas, saunas, Turkish baths, a spacious swimming pool, gym cardiovascular room, and even its own squash courts.

Le Méridien Piccadilly has a tasteful collection of restaurants and banqueting rooms to suit every requirement.

The world renowned Terrace Restaurant & Bar and the Oak Room are both unique places to host weddings, receptions, dinner dances, or any grand occasion!

• ROMANTIC FEATURES •

EXQUISITE WEDDING PACKAGE: Our $120 package price includes 2 glasses of Sparkling Wine or Pimms, a mouth-watering 3 course dinner with coffee and petit fours, a bottle of selected house wine, Menu printing VAT @ 17.5 % and Room Hire.

Special occasions deserve some extra special touches, and we are delighted to offer a complimentary room night for the Bride & Groom which includes full use of the spectacular Champneys Health Club & Spa!

You may upgrade your wedding package with a Champagne reception, pre-dinner canapés, dinner menu upgrades, Flower arrangements, digestives, calligraphy, place-cards, coordinated table cloths & chair covers, and more. Pure elegance and luxury!

• **nearby attractions**

Le Méridien Piccadilly is located in the heart of London's West End. You'd be hard-pressed to find a more convenient location in London – everything you could possibly fancy is at the doorstep!

• **onsite facilities**

Our guests have complimentary use of the facilities in the exclusive Champneys Health Club & Spa. The Glass-Roof Terrace Restaurant & Bar is one of London's trendiest restaurants. Come and enjoy the perfect culinary experience.

• **wedding services**

Our banqueting facilities include the famous Oak Room & Lounge with its magnificent and original oak-wood paneling and spectacular Venetian Chandeliers. The Oak Room is the picture perfect ballroom for a breathtaking Wedding.

Swissôtel The Howard, London

LONDON, UNITED KINGDOM

• at a glance

Location: London, England - United Kingdom
Mailing Address: Temple Place, London, WC2R London
Reservations: 800-63-SWISS
Fax: 44-20-7379-4547
Web Site: www.swissotel.com
Meeting Space: 2 facilities for 2 - 150 people
Accommodations: 189 rooms and suites
Range of Rates: $470 - $1,350

about the area

Currency: GBP- U.K. Pounds
Weather: Temperate
Languages: Multilingual
Nearest Airport: London City Airport

• nearby attractions

Just a short walk from Covent Garden with its theatres, restaurants, nightlife and shopping and world famous landmarks such as St Paul's Cathedral.

• onsite facilities

Its contemporary minimalist culinary presentations are created from the finest produce from the regions seas, lakes and lands. Jaan's cuisine is inspired by modern french cooking.

• wedding services

Our banquet team will tailor your wedding or event to reflect your personal style. From a simple dinner to a reception for 150 we will ensure that every stage of your event from the enquiry through to the departure of the guests is perfect.

Truly a Five-Star Experience. The newly designed

Swissôtel the Howard London has recently completed a full refurbishment offering a contemporary yet elegant hotel. Sandblasted glass windows in the entrance lobby, marble columns, and ornate cornicing , which with a personalized service, provides the perfect setting for distinguished

tastes. Our staff of dedicated professionals cater to your needs and ensure a memorable stay.

Just a short walk from Covent Garden with its theatres, restaurants, nightlife and shopping and world famous landmarks such as St. Paul's Cathedral, Swissôtel The Howard enjoys one of the best locations in town. Set in a quiet oasis just off the Strand overlooking both the River Thames and its own courtyard garden, guestrooms enjoy either river or garden views. Escape and enjoy the tranquility and pampered comfort of your room with all the facilities you would expect from a five star hotel.

• ROMANTIC FEATURES

Many of our executive rooms and suites have balconies which have beautiful panoramic views across the River Thames, where you can enjoy a glass of champagne or admire the lights of London.

Our candlelit restaurant, Jaan, is the perfect place to enjoy a special dinner. With views overlooking our courtyard garden and its soothing waterfall, the atmosphere at Jaan is a rare find in London.

Grand Hotel du Cap-Ferrat

ST. JEAN CAP FERRAT, FRANCE

• at a glance

Location: St. Jean Cap Ferrat, France
Mailing Address: Grand Hotel du Cap Ferrat, 71 Bldv, General de Gaulle St Jean Cap Ferrat, 06230 France
Reservations: 33-4-93-76-50-50
Fax: 33-4-93-76-50-76
Web Site: www.grand-hotel-cap-ferrat.com
Size of Property: 17 acres
Meeting Space: 500 square feet
Accommodations: 53 rooms and suites
Range of Rates: 355-2,550 EUR

about the area
Currency: Euros
Weather: Mediterranean, Mild
Languages: French
Nearest Airport: Nice International

• nearby attractions

St Jean Cap Ferrat: Ephrussi de Rothschild Villa Monaco: casino, restaurants, night life San Remo, Italy: shopping and boutiques. Eze: medieval town overlooking the sea. St Paul de Vence: medieval village, large artist community and museum.

• onsite facilities

53 rooms and suites; Restaurant Le Cap; Le Club Dauphin with swimming pool and restaurant; Somerset Maughan Bar

• wedding services

Full catering and banquet facilities for weddings up to 150 persons either by the swimming pool or in our gardens.

The Grand-Hotel du Cap-Ferrat represents the very essence of luxury. Come to the Grand-Hotel nestled peacefully on the tip of the Cap-Ferrat peninsula, to dream and admire beauty, where a perfect holiday will be assured. Set by the shade of pine trees dominating the sea, in a private park at the very end of the coast and brimming with a myriad of glorious flowers, the hotel is a true paradise, built in 1908 during the "Belle Epoque." Time has not tarnished its beauty, and the hotel has kept its refined atmosphere, yet no modern conveniences have been spared. The hotel has kept its old-world feel, a hint of the "Roaring Twenties" with the refined atmosphere of a place worthy of the greatest.

• ROMANTIC FEATURES •

44 rooms and 9 suites: cozy and exclusive atmosphere, inviting furniture, sumptuous carpets and bathrooms with rare marble.

Restaurant Le Cap: culinary creations that are both inventive and original offered in peaceful luxury overlooking the pine trees and the sea.

Club Dauphin: Olympic sized salt water heated swimming pool with a pool side restaurant serving delicate perfumes and Mediterranean flavors that blend harmoniously with the scents of the sea.

Somerset Maughan Bar: somewhere between a lounge bar and a cigar cellar boasting an atmosphere both rich and comfortable.

Gardens: 17 acres of exquisite, enchanting and breathtaking, luxuriant, rich and exotic vegetation and flowers.

• at a glance
Location: Paris, France
Mailing Address: Hôtel de Crillon 10, Place de la Concorde 75008 Paris, France
Reservations: + 33-1-44-71-15-01
Fax: + 33-1-44-71-15-03
Web Site: www.crillon.com
Accommodations: 147 rooms and suites
Range of Rates: $570 - $5,000

about the area
Currency: Euro
Weather: Temperate
Languages: All current languages
Nearest Airport: Orly, Roissy CDG

Hotel de Crillon

PARIS, FRANCE

Legendary and enchanting, the Hotel de Crillon, whose design was commissioned by Louis XV, shares its incomparable history with the glorious Place de la Concorde. Offering a unique proximity to fashionable "Rue du Faubourg St Honoré", the charming Palace is within walking distance to the Champs Elysées, the Louvre Museum, the Madeleine area and the Opéra.

Celebrated for its outstanding service, the hotel has recently completed a $30 million renovation, which included redesign of all bedrooms, bathrooms and luxurious suites, now equipped with remote-controlled air-conditioning, high speed internet access, modem connections, satellite television, and direct-dial telephones with voice mail.

L'Ecole des Fleurs, the renowned flower arranging school, offers 90-minute to all-day classes on most weekdays. There are also special programs for pets, children and women. Banquet rooms have a unique history and most overlook the Place de la Concorde and have private terraces.

• ROMANTIC FEATURES •

Most enchanting and romantic Palace of Paris. A real home feeling, a very special place for unforgettable events. Les Ambassadeurs, the Hotel Gastronomic restaurant, is ideal for a proposal or a special evening, overlooking the Place de la Concorde, beautifully appointed with marble walls and Baccarat eighteenth century unique chandeliers. The Hotel de Crillon has the best suite offer within Paris. Every suite has a separate living room and a separate bedroom, all renovated in 2003, giving a unique private apartment feeling. Definitely the most famous and romantic Hotel in Paris, and the most dedicated staff.

• nearby attractions

Ideally located on the place de la Concorde, around the Champs Elysées Avenue and the most fashionable shopping street Rue du Faubourg St Honoré. 10 minutes walking from the Louvre Museum, the Galeries Lafayette, and the Opéra.

• onsite facilities

State-of-the-art, 24-Hour fitness center, beauty spa offering à la carte treatments, massage, hairdressing and make-up appointments.

• wedding services

"Noces de Crillon" Honeymoon package including a fantastic VIP set-up in the suite, champagne welcome, breakfast, Crillon bathrobes, airport limousine transfers (complimentary late check out upon request), and a wonderful dedicated staff.

Hotel de Vendome

PARIS, FRANCE

Guests at Hotel de Vendome may be inclined to call it home during their stay as it is a place where luxury and refinement has lived for centuries. Located in Place Vendome, this extraordinary hotel embraces its architectural roots suggestive of the Louis IV period, while firmly founded at the site of its namesake, the Vendome family's ancient mansion.

Such a lengthy tradition of sophistication and elegance is evident in all that makes Hotel de Vendome an illuminating testimony to the "City of Light's" penchant for style and finesse, from distinctive dining and discerning shopping to luxurious surroundings and the ultimate in service. The management and staff invite visitors to explore Hotel de Vendome's many marvels that will richly reward guests with its palatial panache and welcoming warmth. And, when visitors are ready, they can explore the various cultural and historical sites of Paris just outside Hotel de Vendome's doors. ♈

· ROMANTIC FEATURES ·

Each of the Hotel's 29 rooms (19 rooms and 10 suites) are uniquely decorated in styles ranging from traditional to contemporary, adroitly combining a distinct sense of time-honored European luxury with modern conveniences for guests traveling for business or pleasure.

Throughout the Hotel de Vendome guests move from room to room with magnificent marble or plush carpet under their feet, while hands discern elegant yet understated wood paneling, detailed moldings or textured wallpaper, the beauty of which is illuminated by crystal chandeliers or decorative light fixtures. Of course lavish furniture, artwork and decorations give each room its own unique identity and individual sense of grandeur. ♈

EUROPE

· at a glance

Location: Paris, France
Mailing Address: 1 Place Vendome
75001 Paris France
Reservations: 33-1-55-04-55-00
Fax: 33-1-49-27-97-89
Web Site: www.hoteldevendome.com
Accommodations: 29 rooms and suites
Range of Rates: $370 - $2,410 EUR

about the area

Currency: Euro
Weather: Continental
Languages: French, English, German, Arabic
Nearest Airport: ORY, CDG

· nearby attractions

The 5 star deluxe Hotel de Vendome is centrally situated in the very heart of Paris, close to the Louvre museum, fashion shops & famous jewelers, the opera, and shopping streets.

· onsite facilities

The Hotel de Vendome is the smallest Palace in Paris. The 29 rooms & suites are all different in colors & furniture. The style is Baroque, Classic, Art deco. Piano bar & restaurant on the 1st level with great cocktails and french cuisine.

· wedding services

For weddings we have our famous honeymoon package with accommodation in a junior or a deluxe suite, breakfast in room, bottle of champagne in room with flowers.

Hotel Lancaster

PARIS, FRANCE

• at a glance

Location: Paris, France
Mailing Address: 7, rue de Berri,
Champs Elysées 75008 Paris France
Reservations: 33-1-40-76-40-76
Fax: 33-1-40-76-40-00
Web Site: www.hotel-lancaster.fr
Size of Property: 8 floors
Meeting Space: 323 in square feet
Accommodations: 60 rooms and suites
Range of Rates: $490-$1,973

about the area

Currency: Euro
Weather: Temperate
Languages: French, English, Italian
Nearest Airport: Orly, Roissy, CDG

• nearby attractions

Situated very close to the Champs Elysées, a few steps away from Paris' Haute-couture boutiques and fashion shops. Historic buildings: Arc de Triomphe, Place de la Concorde, Invalide.

The Lancaster, an elegant 19th century townhouse, in the heart of Paris just off the Champs-Elysées, epitomizes tradition, art de vivre and elegance, with an intimate and discreet decor where antiques and works of art are enhanced by contemporary touches.

The 60 individually appointed rooms and suites each with lots of charm, evoke a residential feel, and draw their freshness from the scented zen-like courtyard garden, where meals can be enjoyed in the summer months. A palace for the discerning traveller, a hotel for those who appreciate quality over ostentation and elegance over fashion.

The Emile Wolf suite is dedicated to the Swiss hotelier who created the Lancaster and amassed the exceptional collection of antiques in the hotel today.

This magnificent suite of autumnal coloring has pale gold silk covered walls and curtains, hand-painted renaissance toile in guise of wardrobe doors, and is exquisitely furnished with a grand piano played by illustrious stars of cinema.

• onsite facilities

The Lancaster offers CD/DVD players, Wifi wireless Internet connection, a fitness centre with sauna, a zen-like courtyard garden, an exclusive dog-bed, a private car park.

• ROMANTIC FEATURES •

Honeymooners can appreciate the rooms with balconies offering a view of Paris' most romantic places such as "Le Sacré Coeur" in Montmartre or The Eiffel Tower. The hotel Lancaster hosts an exceptional collection of French antiques and original works of art.

A suite is dedicated to the actress Marlène Dietrich who lived in this room in the 1930's for over 3 years. This particularly romantic suite is decorated in her favorite colors of lilac and is full of unusual and tasteful "objets d'art."

• wedding services

The Lancaster can organize flowers, photographers, reservations in refined Parisian restaurants, hair dresser, limousine service, facial treatments, massages, manicure, make-up.

• at a glance

Location: Paris, France
Mailing Address: 14 rue de la Tremoille, 75008 Paris France
Reservations: 33-1-56-52-14-00
Fax: 33-1-40-70-01-08
Web Site: www.hotel-tremoille.com
Meeting Space: 700 square feet
Accommodations: 93 rooms and suites
Range of Rates: $480 - $1,140

about the area

Currency: Euros
Weather: Temperate
Languages: English, French
Nearest Airport: Roissy-Charles de Gaulle

• nearby attractions

Within walking distance: Eiffel Tower, Louvre Museum, Champs Elysees, Bateaux Mouche, Arc de Triomphe, famous restaurants (Alain Ducasse...)

La Tremoille

PARIS, FRANCE

The Hotel de la Tremoille is ideally located in the city's most prestigious area, the "Golden triangle", between the avenue Champs-Elysees, avenue George V and avenue Montaigne.

The property has been fully renovated in 2002 after a 15-month complete closure for an extensive renovation program. Since its re-opening, it has already been dubbed "the only left bank hotel on the right bank" because of its very particular and trendy atmosphere.

The rooms have been decorated with a constant care for comfort and are all equipped with the most recent technologies   (CD and DVD players in all rooms, complimentary high-speed internet access...).

Additional services include the trendy restaurant & bar Senso (Sir Terence Conran's latest addition to the parisian scene), a very intimate fitness centre, 24 hour room service..etc

Quite simply, La Tremoille offers warm service as well as peace and privacy in what is possibly the best location in the heart of romantic Paris.

• onsite facilities

Free access to fitness center (cardio-training room, two treatment rooms, jet shower room, sauna) Restaurant & bar Senso decorated by the famous designer Sir Terence Conran.

• ROMANTIC FEATURES •

With its unique location, La Tremoille offers many possibilities for a romantic breakaway.

You are only one hundred meters from the Bateaux-Mouche and the most romantic cruise and candlelight dinner possible on the river Seine.

Most of the trendiest parisian restaurants are within walking distance as well as the most famous luxury shops (Christian Dior, Cartier, Louis Vuitton...).

• wedding services

We offer upgrade upon availability to honeymoon couples. A bottle of champagne is graciously offered upon arrival. Special Honeymoon packages upon request at the reservation department.

• at a glance

Location: Courchevel 1850
Mailing Address: Rue de Bellecôte, 73120 Courchevel 1850, France
Reservations: 65-6887-3337
Fax: 65-6887-3338
Web Site: www.amanresorts.com
Size of Property: 31 suites and rooms
Accomodations: $625 - $2,400+

about the area

Currency: Euros
Weather: Continental
Languages: French, English
Nearest Airport: Geneva / Lyon St Exupéry

• nearby attractions

Les Trois Vallées is the world's largest ski area with more than 600km of groomed trails and 200 lifts. Just 200 metres away is the cosmopolitan village centre with its ski lifts and school, tourist office, upmarket shops and restaurants.

• onsite facilities

Heated boot racks and bell-boys who lay out your skis on the snow ready to go are part of the service. Also on offer is a fumoir, turkish hammam, two jacuzzis, indoor pool, gym, library, sundeck, salon as well as a restaurant and bar.

• wedding services

What better way to start a honeymoon than with fresh tracks through the powder snow followed by a steam in the turkish hammam, a swim, a candlelit gourmet dinner and then a cigar and dijestif in the salon?

Le Mélézin

COURCHEVEL 1850, FRANCE

Le Mélézin is ideally placed with its ski-in ski-out facilities

onto the Bellecôte slope of Courchevel 1850, to take advantage of the superb skiing available in Les Trois Vallées, the world's largest ski area. Skiing and winter activities such as snowshoeing, snowmobiling, ice skating and ice climbing are a highlight, and Le Mélézin can arrange for a personal ski instructor or mountain guide.

The resort, an Alpine retreat, has a classic ambience with oak beams up to 200 years old gracing both the classically patterned parquet flooring and lobby panelling. Après-ski activities include relaxing in the salon with its cozy open fireplace,

enjoying a cigar in the intimate fumoir, enjoying the Turkish hammam, jacuzzi or swimming pool and gym, or simply sitting on the outdoor sundeck and terrace where lunch is served. A selection of books, magazines and CDs are also available in the library which is decorated with antique carpentry tools. This winter season runs from 19th December 2003 to 12th April 2004.

• ROMANTIC FEATURES •

The views from Le Mélézin are to forests of pine and the ski slopes beyond. Head above the village, however, and the vistas open all the way from the French to the Swiss Alps. Even Mont Blanc is visible.

Several rooms offer balconies with views of the pistes and surrounding peaks. All have a large, separate dressing area, CD player and television with DVD. The bathrooms are finished in rose-tinted granite and offer twin washbasins, a deep bathtub and a separate shower. Most have views of the pistes.

The dining room offers gourmet French cuisine adapted to the lighter demands of the modern diner. Guests sit in an elegant manor-house setting, amidst old oak beams, engravings and frescoes.

• **at a glance**
Location: Bremen, Germany
Mailing Address: Im Burgerpark 28209
Bremen, Germany
Reservations: 49-421-3408-0
Fax: 49-421-3408-602
Web Site: www.park-hotel-bremen.de
Meeting Space: 7 meeting rooms from
130 square feet to 4,520 square feet
Accommodations: 138 rooms, 12 suites
Range of Rates: 180 - 850 Euros

about the area
Currency: Euro
Weather: Temperate
Languages: German, English, French
Nearest Airport: Bremen Airport

Park Hotel Bremen

BREMEN, GERMANY

The Park Hotel Bremen looks like part of a grand estate,

uniquely located in the 202 hectare Bürger Park, with a fountain, beautiful gardens and a lake.

The hotel offers luxury and comfort in a 1200-year old city that has been a trading centre since medieval times. There are 150 rooms, decorated with prestige furnishings in extravagant Italian, Moorish, Pompeiian and Japanese themes. Many have a calming view of the park or lake. There is room service from 6am till midnight, satellite television, CD sound system, fax and a modem for internet use. There is also a computer with Internet access.

Experience classic french cuisine at the elegant Park Restaurant, with over 450 wines from all over the world. Try also the homemade pastries at the "Café am Hollersee" in the hotel. Activities available nearby include swimming, riding, tennis, jogging, biking, and boat trips on the River Weser. The Park Restaurant is the place to indulge in gourmet international cuisine.

• ROMANTIC FEATURES •

The stunning Roman-style Douglas beauty spa and the "Spa'rks" fitness centre are spread over 1200 square meters on four floors. This unique spa features a heated, 13x5 metre outdoor pool and a grotto--heated Roman bath, sauna, aroma steam cabinet and a jacuzzi. The gold and blue tiled steam room with tropical rain showers is pure Arabian Nights. There are also thalasso baths, massages and Douglas beauty spa facials, pedicures, manicures and body treatments.

The fully equipped gymnasium teaches yoga, T'ai Chi and aerobics. The Spa'rks menu has mouth-watering fresh juices, power shakes and light meals.

• **nearby attractions**

The charming Schnoor quarter in Bremen's historic centre has 15th and 16th century gabled brick houses, with artisans, gold-smiths, galleries, cafés, restaurants, theatres, a toy museum, Christmas shop and the inspiring St. Petri Cathedral.

• **onsite facilities**

Seven elegant salons of various sizes for banquets, meetings, and private functions for up to 800 people. Two new conference suites each for up to six people, one kilometer from the center of the city. Underground garage and valet parking.

• **wedding services**

The Park Hotel Bremen enjoys a well-deserved reputation for distinguished hospitality in a country house atmosphere. With its unique location on the edge of Burgerpark, the hotel is the ideal location for wedding celebrations.

• at a glance
Location: Hamburg, Germany
Mailing Address:
Neuer Jungfernstieg 9-14
20354 Hamburg Germany
Reservations: +49-40-3494-3151
Fax: +49-40-3494-2606
Web Site: www.raffles-hvj.de
Meeting Space: 247 - 3,444 square feet
Accommodations: 156 rooms and suites
Range of Rates: $260 - $2,175

about the area
Currency: Euro
Weather: Temperate
Languages: German, English, French
Nearest Airport: Hamburg
Fuhlsbuettel

• nearby attractions

St. Michaelis church, "Hamburger Michel":
3 km; Harbour of Hamburg and
Speicherstadt: 3 km; Fish Market: 3 km;
St. Katharine church: 5 km; Deichstraße
and Cremon: 2 km; Blankenese; the historical suburb of Hamburg: 15 km.

• onsite facilities

Shopping facilities: The Jungfernstieg,
Hanseviertel, Mönckebergstraße,
Hamburger Hof and Gänsemarkt are all
within walking distance.

• wedding services

Our limousine service, cosmetic and massage treatments from our Amrita Spa as
well as the wedding coiffure by our in-
house hairdresser complete the arrangements and leave you with more time to
enjoy your once-in-a-lifetime event.

Raffles Hotel Vier Jahreszeiten

HAMBURG, GERMANY

This is the grand hotel of Hamburg, with a deserved

reputation as one of the best hotels in the world. Situated at the banks of the city's Inner Alster Lake, its incomparable location is in the heart of the city's financial and shopping district. The classic lines of its exterior are complemented by its warm and attractive interior spaces. It is not by chance that this hotel has long been regarded by Hamburg's elite as their own special meeting place. The 156 guestrooms have their own indi-vidual touch. Their design speaks for themselves with its tasteful elegance and timeless luxury. The ambience is rounded off by exquisite antiques and the breathtaking view on the Inner Alster Lake. For relaxation, wellness and fitness, the luxurious Amrita Spa offers a wide range of treatments and facilities.

Additional services: 4 restaurants • 2 bars • 5 meeting rooms • Valet parking • 24-hour room service • Concierge desk • Hairdresser • Wireless LAN in all guestrooms and public areas.

• ROMANTIC FEATURES •

"When it comes to comfort, design and the most obliging service, nothing can surpass Hamburg's Raffles Hotel Vier Jahreszeiten. On the banks of Inner Alster Lake, the hotel has been welcoming guests since 1897. The grand old German oak and marble lobby and the oak paneled lounge create an atmosphere much like of a palatial estate, while the restful living room provides a quiet retreat in the heart of the city. Consistently rated as one of the finest hotels in the world, the Raffles Hotel Vier Jahreszeiten has hosted royals and dignitaries for a century. Here in addition to impeccable service and luxurious accommoda-tion you'll find some of the best restaurants in Hamburg.

The Regent Schlosshotel Berlin

BERLIN, GERMANY

Y ou are our guest and we provide a world in which everything
is as you wish it to be. Featuring state of the art conveniences necessary for our guests' comfort, our 54 rooms, including 12 suites, combine modern sensibilities with an elegantly historic ambience for the most discerning guest.

Experience the magical atmosphere in our bar "Le Tire Bouchon"with its open fireplace, enjoy the gourmet cuisine in the restaurant "Vivaldi" and breakfast in our wintergarden "Le Jardin" with view over the Schlossgarten. Our private rooms are the ideal setting for celebrations, cocktail parties and dinners for up to 200 guests.

Relaxation is what matters most at The Regent Schlosshotel Berlin. The roman-style pool with three saunas and fitness area is ideal for unwinding. The comprehensive service amenities also include a beauty-studio with a variety of different massages.

Indulge your senses and experience Regent's world-renown personalized service. ❧

· ROMANTIC FEATURES ·

To be happy. To marry. A fairy-tale wedding in a castle. A day full of emotions and feelings. Romance in incomparable surroundings. And behind the scenes, we provide all the care and attention that is second nature to us.

A private wedding, a grand wedding, a golden wedding or a honeymoon to Berlin. Our wedding planner includes every detail. We plan, we advise, we prepare, and we are the magic elves, ensuring that your celebration at the Regent Schlosshotel Berlin is an unforgettable occasion. ❧

• at a glance
Location: Berlin, Germany
Mailing Address: The Regent Schlosshotel Berlin Brahmsstrasse 10 14193 Berlin Germany
Reservations: +49-30-895-84-464
Fax: +49-30-895-84-800
Web Site: www.schlosshotelberlin.com
Meeting Space: 36,694 square feet
Accommodations: 42 rooms, 12 suites
Range of Rates: $275 - $431

about the area
Currency: Euro
Weather: Temperate
Languages: German
Nearest Airport: Int. Airport Tegel

• nearby attractions

Situated in the exclusive residential area of Grunewald, the Schlosshotel offers an oasis of tranquility within easy reach of the city's main attractions close to the Kurfürstendamm and not far from the new city center Potsdamer Platz.

• onsite facilities

The Regent Schlosshotel Berlin was built as a private mansion and preserves the dignified charm of a European Grand Hotel. Here you will find a hotel that combines gracious accommodations, gourmet cuisine and exceptional recreation.

• wedding services

Your personal wedding concierge includes every detail which needs to be taken care of before and on the day itself. Stylish invitations, a wedding carriage drawn by horses, magnificent flower decorations, festive music, and a sumptuous menu.

• at a glance

Location: Nikiti, Halkidiki, Greece
Mailing Address: 63088 Nikiti Halkidiki Greece
Reservations: 0030-23750-22310
Fax: 0030-23750-22591
Web Site: www.dbr.gr
Size of Property: 7.4 acres
Meeting Space: 1 meeting room for up to 30 people
Accommodations: 60 suites and villas
Range of Rates: $350 - $7,000

about the area
Currency: Euro
Weather: Mediterranean
Languages: Greek
Nearest Airport: Thessaloniki (SKG)

Danai Beach Resort & Villas

NIKITI, HALKIDIKI, GREECE

A luxurious hideaway perched on the bluffs of the Aegean Peninsula; the Danai Beach Resort & Villas was created to offer secluded luxury and attentive service in a setting where deep waters meet azure skies and white sandy beaches.

The nine elegant buildings of suites and villas feature cool and spacious accommodations with a variety of amenities for the comfort and convenience of the guests. Here they will find themselves hidden among lush gardens, where lovely squirrels and singing birds complete the most charming ambience. Barbeque sea food and great steaks are served in the "Seahorse Grill" restaurant, whereas gourmet cuisine is to be enjoyed in the open air, sea view restaurant, "The Squirrel". Mediterranean plates are served at the "Andromeda".

The hotel is a leisurely 50 minute drive from the International Airport "Macedonia" of Thessaloniki SKG and is situated between two traditional villages.

• ROMANTIC FEATURES •

The Danai Beach Resort & Villas is a very romantic destination for many honeymoon couples or couples who want to get married at the hotel's beautiful church.

The Danai Beach Resort & Villas offers all the amenities for an unforgettable stay. Thirteen of the Suites and all the Villas have a private swimming pool on the terrace. Room service is available 24 hours a day. For more romance we suggest private dining on the beach, in the room or even in our wine cellar under the candlelight.

Another suggestion is a private boat cruise along the coast of Mount Athos with lunch on board, combined with a stop for swimming in a secluded beach at the west side of Sithonia.

• nearby attractions

The whole peninsula of Sithonia, where the hotel is situated, has small villages & beautiful beaches, while Athos, the unique Monk Republic, is in the third peninsula. Thessaloniki, the second largest city of Greece, only an hour away.

• onsite facilities

Three restaurants with gourmet, Mediterranean & Greek cuisine. A variety of treatments in our 'St. Barth' Wellness & Spa. Tennis, fitness room, water sports and also golf course nearby. Wine & olive oil tasting, theme nights and excursions.

• wedding services

We have 3 and 7-night honeymoon packages, which include accommodations in one of our suites, transfers to/from the airport, champagne breakfast in bed, dinner for two in gourmet restaurant, private boat cruise, massage, olive oil tasting.

• at a glance
Location: Elounda, Crete, Greece
Mailing Address: 72 053 Elounda, Crete, Greece
Reservations: 30-28410-63813
Fax: 30-28410-41783
Web Site: www.eloundabay.gr
Size of Property: 20 acres
Meeting Space: 5,000 square feet
Accommodations: 273 rooms, bungalows and villas
Range of Rates: $110 - $4,230

about the area
Currency: Euro
Weather: Mediterranean
Languages: Greek and English
Nearest Airport: Heraklion Crete

• nearby attractions

Nearby to Aghios Nikolaos, the Fishing village Elounda, Minoan Palaces of Knossos, Malia and Phaestos, and Lasithi plateau.

Elounda Bay Palace

ELOUNDA, CRETE, GREECE

Member of The Leading Hotels of the World & 5-Star

Diamond Award recipient Elounda Bay Palace is a picturesque resort of Cretan architecture set amidst lush green gardens and a sparkling coastline. Natural beauty combined with all the advantages of modern living make Elounda Bay ideal for those seeking a relaxing honeymoon.

Dressed in unpretentious elegance, each room and bungalow creates a unique atmosphere of warmth and comfort with magnificent views of the bay. For our guests who choose for one of our

Mediterranean Villas with private pool, or the unique Palace Suite with private pool and gym, we extend the privilege of butler service. Your personal assistant is always at hand so you receive the undivided attention you deserve, from unpacking your wardrobe and planning your meals, to maintaining your pool and garden.

Each of our restaurants and bars boasts its own unique style and atmosphere. Our expert chefs provide a wide variety of Greek and International Cuisine.

• onsite facilities

The Oloundian, an open-air amphitheater seating up to 600. Watersports Center; scuba diving, sailing, waterskiing, windsurfing, and parasailing. Tennis courts, white sand beaches, fitness center, 2 pools, and a European-style beauty salon.

• ROMANTIC FEATURES •

In a tranquil setting overlooking the breathtaking Mirabello Bay, a feeling of divine lingers on. The gods of Greek mythology continue to have a way of smiling upon the Elounda Bay Palace. The lush gardens, secluded white sandy beaches, and superb restaurants create the consummate Greek Island experience and the ideal atmosphere to enjoy a romantic honeymoon getaway or the perfect setting for an unforgettable wedding ceremony and celebration. A romantic dinner just for the two of you, prepared in the privacy of your suite is only one of the many special services offered at the Elounda Bay Palace that will make your stay a memory that will live with you forever.

• wedding services

The hotel offers various wedding packages according to the guest's personal taste and style. The lush green gardens, private white sandy beaches, and on-site venues offer many choices for ideal ceremony and reception locations.

Elounda Beach Hotel & Villa

ELOUNDA, CRETE, GREECE

• at a glance

Location: Elounda, Crete, Greece
Mailing Address: 72053 Elounda Crete, Greece
Reservations: 30-28410-63721
Fax: 30-28410-41373
Web Site: www.eloundabeach.gr
Size of Property: 40 acres
Meeting Space: 5,000 square feet
Accommodations: 258 rooms and suites
Range of Rates: $450 - $580

about the area

Currency: Euro
Weather: Mediterranean
Languages: English, Greek
Nearest Airport: Heraklion Crete

• nearby attractions

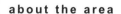

The Elounda Beach Hotel is nearby to Aghios Nikolaos; the fishing village Elounda; the Minoan Palaces of Knossos, Malia and Phaestos; and the Lasithi plateau.

The Elounda Beach Hotel, a member of "The Leading Hotels of the World", is undoubtedly Greece's most exclusive and internationally acclaimed deluxe 5 star resort hotel. Set on 40 acres of colorful gardens, the resort combines natural beauty with all the advantages of modern living.

The Elounda Beach Hotel overlooks the breathtaking Mirabello Bay and the island of Sponalonga with its Venetian fortress. All accommodations are decorated with regional flair and fitted with hand-made furnishings, marble bathrooms, and all of the modern amenities.

The resort upholds the Greek tradition for fine dining, evidenced by a Five Star Diamond Award from the American Academy of Hospitality for its outstanding cuisine.

Surrounded by colorful fragrant gardens, the hotel consists of two buildings and a bungalow complex, almost all enjoying exceptional views out to sea or built directly on the waterfront, with some accommodation categories offering the luxury of a private swimming pool.

· ROMANTIC FEATURES ·

Here in a tranquil setting overlooking Mirabello Bay, a feeling of divinity lingers on. The gods of the Greek mythology continue to have a way of smiling upon the Elounda Beach Hotel.

Services for guests range from personal trainers to private chefs and sommeliers. Guests residing in the Royal and Imperial suites even have a luxury car at their disposal, indoor and outdoor heated swimming pools, and private pianists on call to perform on custom grand pianos.

The gardens, onsite facilities, and restaurants create the consummate Greek island experience and the ideal atmosphere to enjoy a unique wedding or relaxing honeymoon where romance flourishes under the Mediterranean sky.

• onsite facilities

Outdoor seawater swimming pool, five tennis courts, Aphrodite Health Center with beauty salon, fitness center & turkish baths, white sand beaches, and Watersports Center hosts scuba diving, waterskiing, windsurfing,and more.

• wedding services

The hotel offers various wedding packages at different prices according to the guests requirements. The basic package includes the ceremony, gift to the mayor, bride's flower bouquet, make-up and hairdressing.

Hotel Gritti Palace

VENICE, ITALY

• at a glance

Location: Venice, Italy
Mailing Address: Campo S. Maria Giglio, 2467 30124 Venice, Italy
Reservations: 888-625-5144
Fax: 39-041-520-0942
Web Site: www.starwood.com/italy
Size of Property: One block
Meeting Space: 1,940 square feet
Accommodations: 82 rooms and 9 suites
Range of Rates: $920 - $4,750

about the area

Currency: Euro
Weather: Temperate
Languages: Italian, English
Nearest Airport: Marco Polo International

• nearby attractions

Saint Mark's Square: 300m; Grand Canal: 1m; Doges Palace: 450m; Correr museum: 350m; Guggenheim Museum: 200m; La Fenice Theater: 100m; Murano Island: 5 km; Lido Beach: 2 km; Casino of venice: 1 km

• onsite facilities

Private round-trip boat service is available to Venice Lido, where our sister hotels, The Westin Excelsior and Hotel Des Bains, await. Discover and enjoy private beach facilities, swimming pools, tennis and golf.

• wedding services

The Hotel Gritti Palace is an ideal venue for weddings and unique meetings of up to 90 participants. Our banqueting facilities can host everything from theme parties to gala dinners to working luncheons.

Situated on the Grand Canal, with an incomparable view of the

water, the Hotel Gritti Palace was built in 1525 as the residence of the Doge of Venice, Andrea Gritti. Our ideally located hotel continues to attract elite guests, with luxuriously appointed rooms, attentive service, and the savory cuisine of the Restaurant Club del Doge. Ernest Hemingway once appreciated the hotel "as the best hotel in a city of great hotels."

The Hotel Gritti Palace is a splendid little Palazzo that preserves within its walls stories of illustrious visitors such as the British Royal family, the Duke of Windsor, Princes of Monaco, and Hollywood stars.

• ROMANTIC FEATURES •

Each guest room gracefully reflects the warmth and rich cultural heritage of Venice. Superb accommodations await guests of the Hotel Gritti Palace - where special courtesies are provided in an elegant, refined setting.

All guest rooms are conveniently furnished with air conditioning, a direct-dial phone, television and minibar. Precious decorations and beautiful antique furnishings enhance the atmosphere and luxurious comfort of the 91 guest rooms and suites. Your wish is our command. Discover all that we have to offer.

Hotel Danieli

VENICE, ITALY

• **at a glance**
Location: Venice, Italy
Mailing Address: Castello,
4196 30122 Venice Italy
Reservations: 888-625-5144
Fax: 39-041-520-0208
Web Site: www.starwood.com/italy
Size of Property: One block
Meeting Space: 2,971 square feet
Accommodations: 222 deluxe rooms
and 11 suites
Range of Rates: $800 - $5,200

about the area
Currency: Euro
Weather: Mild
Languages: Italian, English
Nearest Airport: Marco Polo
International

• **nearby attractions**

Saint Mark's Square: 50m; Grand Canal: 150m; Doges Palace: 50m; Correr Museum: 200m; Guggenheim Museum: 800m; La Fenice Theater: 500m; Murano Island: 5km; Lido Beach: 2km; Casino of Venice: 2km

The Hotel Danieli is a masterfully restored palace synonymous with the splendor and romance of Venice. We are just steps away from the Piazza San Marco and its Basilica as well as legendary sites such as the Doge's Palace and the Bridge of Sighs. Our main building is the original 14th century palace of Doge Dandolo's family, a Venetian gothic landmark lavishly appointed with pink marble, stained glass, ceilings decorated with golden leaves, Murano glass chandeliers, and antiques. These glorious interiors are rivaled only by the captivating panoramic views from our rooftop restaurant, La Terrazza Danieli.

Named in Condé Nast Traveler's 2002 Gold List and 2001 Readers' Choice Awards List, the Hotel Danieli has been the luxury hotel preferred by discerning visitors to Venice for generations.

Designed in the late 14th century to meet the demands of Europe's traveling nobility, the Hotel Danieli continues to set the standard for hospitality at its best.

· ROMANTIC FEATURES ·

From the luxurious linens to the antique furnishings, the decor of Hotel Danieli makes every guest feels like they are royalty. A magnificent atrium, a golden staircase, a palace in Venetian Gothic style, the spell of magical, enchanting Venice. Extraordinary atmosphere, extraordinary comfort. Romantic witness to events and passions, an architectural treasure that for generations has hosted the most discerning travelers. Like a painting of Canaletto, like a Vivaldi concerto, a symbol of the city built on water.

• **onsite facilities**

Take advantage of our private boat service to and from Venice Lido - where private beach facilities, swimming pools, tennis and golf await at our sister hotels, The Westin Excelsior and Hotel Des Bains.

• **wedding services**

The Hotel Danieli is an ideal venue for unique receptions and weddings for up to 120 participants. Banqueting facilities can host theme parties, gala dinners, and stunning weddings.

Hotel Des Bains

VENICE, ITALY

• at a glance

Location: Venice, Italy
Mailing Address: Lungomare Marconi 17
30126 Venice Lido Italy
Reservations: 888-625-5144
Fax: 39-041-526-0113
Web Site: www.starwood.com/italy
Size of Property: One block
Meeting Space: 5,366 square feet
Accommodations: 172 rooms and 19 suites
Range of Rates: $460 - $2,300

about the area
Currency: Euro
Weather: Temperate
Languages: Italian, English
Nearest Airport: Marco Polo International

• nearby attractions

Saint Mark's Square: 1 km; GrandCanal: 1 km; Doges Palace: 1 km; Correr Museum; 1 km; Guggenheim Museum: 2 km; La Fenice Theatre: 2 km; Murano Island: 6 km; Downtown Venice: 1 km; Casino of Venice: 3 km;

Come and discover the Hotel Des Bains, a charming resort situated on Venice Lido. Surrounded by a lovely, large private park and opposite the legendary beach, we're just a 15-minute boat ride from St. Mark's Square. Built in pure Palladian style with Art Nouveau decorations, the Hotel Des Bains has welcomed international guests since 1900 and has been the preferred holiday destination of many.

A grand hotel of the Belle Epoque minutes away from St. Marks Square via private shuttle service. A charming resort immersed in a splendid park and facing a private beach, offering an outdoor pool, tennis courts and water sports.

The Hotel Des Bains is the perfect honeymoon location featuring 2 restaurants, piano bar, poolside buffet and bar, beach bar with snack service, private beach, outdoor pool, 2 outdoor tennis courts, golf course, horseback riding, water sports, gymnasium, massages, sauna and more.

• ROMANTIC FEATURES •

A 15-minute private boat ride will take you across the Venice lagoon between the Venetian minor islands - from The Westin Excelsior's private pier to Venice historical center.

The Hotel Des Bains is also the perfect venue for an exceptional and unforgettable wedding conference. We're able to accommodate weddings for up to 350 people. Experience mouth watering Mediterranean cuisine and elegant dining in the Liberty Restaurant. Or nibble on authentic Italian pizza in the casual Pagoda Restaurant while enjoying the view from the terrace right on the beach. At sunset the terrace of the Piano Bar Colony is the best place to grab a cocktail and traditional Venetian appetizer.

• onsite facilities

A grand hotel of the Belle Epoque just minutes away from St. Mark's Square via private shuttle service. A charming resort surrounded by a splendid park and facing a private beach, offering an outdoor pool, tennis courts and water sports.

• wedding services

To celebrate the most important day of your life in a unique and unforgettable way: the Hotel Des Bains offers you its more refined services and banquet facilities up to 360 participants.

• at a glance
Location: Sardinia, Italy
Mailing Address: Località Chia - 09010
Domus de Maria (CA) Sardinia - Italy
Reservations: 0039-070-923-93-431
Fax: 0039-070-923-01-44
Web Site: www.lemeridien-
chialaguna.com
Size of Property: 9.8 acres
Accommodations: 376 rooms and suites
Range of Rates: $170- $580 per person

about the area
Currency: Euro
Weather: Sub-tropical
Languages: Italian, English, French
Nearest Airport: Cagliari - Elmas

Le Méridien Chia Laguna

SARDINIA, ITALY

L e Méridien Chia Laguna, a four-star resort is set in the most stunning scenery in Sardinia, Italy. Its style and design express a fusion between antique and modern where current architectural innovation is combined with the design and style of the ancient traditions of South Sardinia.

The resort is in a splendid location with numerous local attractions and an enchanting landscape that includes the beautiful Tower of Chia, a cultural and artistic monument built around the year 1200. A serene and relaxing atmosphere is combined with a rustic elegance.

A private beach, 700 meters from the resort, provides ample opportunity for water sports and a complimentary mini-train service provides easy accessibility to the beach from outside the main reception.

• nearby attractions

Set by Bay of Chia which has some of the most amazing beaches in Sardinia. Just 55 minutes from Cagliari, Sardinia's main Airport. The resort is surrounded by the typical Mediterranean vegetation. It lies in a valley surrounded by mountains.

• onsite facilities

Serene and relaxing atmosphere with 2 different types of accommodation. Private beach only 500m away and a complimentary disney-like train service to/from the beach. A spa is available for those who want to regenerate.

• ROMANTIC FEATURES •

Le Méridien Chia Laguna has two different types of accommodation, cottages and hotel rooms, which offer ideal surroundings for a romantic honeymoon.

Cottage rooms are spread throughout the Mediterranean landscape and are decorated with traditional Sardinian design. Some of them have a patio with a garden while others have a balcony. Sea view rooms are available with a lovely view of the Mediterranean.

Rejuvenate and enjoy the many activities available at the property including tennis, beach volleyball, canoeing, water sports and mini-golf; or simply relax in the sun on the white sandy beaches of the Bay of Chia.

• wedding services

Deluxe Rooms, Junior Suites and Suites facing one of the most stunning sceneries on the Chia Lagoon and Spanish Tower. Serene and relaxing atmosphere for young couples makes this location ideal for honeymooners.

• at a glance

Location: Venice, Italy
Mailing Address: San Marco
2159 30124, Venice Italy
Reservations: 888-625-5144
Fax: 39-041-523-1533
Web Site: www.starwood.com/italy
Size of Property: One block
Meeting Space: 1,713 square feet
Accommodations: 167 rooms, 8 suites
Range of Rates: $730 - $2,850

about the area

Currency: Euro
Weather: Temperate
Languages: Italian, English
Nearest Airport: Marco Polo
International

• nearby attractions

Saint Mark's Square: 100m; Grand Canal: 1m; Doges Palace: 200m; Correr Museum: 100m; Guggenheim Museum: 200m; La Fenice Theatre: 200m; Murano Island: 5km; Casino of Venice: 1km

Westin Europa

VENICE, ITALY

An architectural landmark on the Grand Canal, just steps from the Piazza San Marco, The Westin Europa and Regina, Venice offers an ideal combination of traditional elegance and modern technology. New rooms in the magnificently restored, centuries-old hotel feature the same Grand Canal views that inspired Monet, who painted the city while visiting.

Chefs are ready to prepare savory regional dishes in the show kitchen at La Cusina. The salon atmosphere of Bar Tiepolo is ideal for tea or cocktails.

During the summer season, the famous private beaches of the Lido - along with tennis, golf and boating at the hotel's sister properties - are just a complimentary boat ride away. Visit and see for yourself why our lovely hotel was recently listed in the Condé Nast Traveler's 2002 Gold List.

Historic accommodations, appointed in traditional Venetian style, extend throughout the hotel's five buildings, which date from the 17th to the 19th centuries.

• ROMANTIC FEATURES •

Private beach facilities, swimming pools, tennis and golf are just a private, round-trip boat ride away at Venice Lido at our sister hotels. The Westin Europa and Regina, Venice welcomes guests to two charming venues overlooking the Grand Canal.

The Westin Europa and Regina, Venice welcomes guests to two charming venues, overlooking the Grand Canal. The elegant gourmet restaurant La Cusina features savory regional dishes, prepared by artistic chefs.

• onsite facilities

Restaurant, piano bar on outdoor terrace during the summer, private launches to airport and Venice Lido, where private beach facilities, swimming pools, tennis and golf await at our sister hotels, The Westin Excelsior and Hotel Des Bains.

• wedding services

The Westin Europa & Regina is the ideal venue for weddings and receptions for up to 110 participants. Banqueting facilities can host theme parties, gala dinners and wedding receptions.

• at a glance

Location: Venice, Italy
Mailing Address: Lungomare Marconi; 41
30126 Venice Lido
Reservations: 888-625-5144
Fax: 39-041-526-7276
Web Site: www.starwood.com/italy
Size of Property: One block
Meeting Space: 15,327 square feet
Accommodations: 178 rooms, 19 suites
Range of Rates: $750 - $3,980

about the area
Currency: Euro
Weather: Temperate
Languages: Italian, English
Nearest Airport: Marco Polo
International

• nearby attractions

Saint Mark's Square: 1 km; Grand Canal: 1 km; Doges Palace: 1 km; Correr Museum: 1 km; Guggenheim Museum: 2 km; La Fenice Theatre: 2 km; Murano Island: 6 km; Venice Downtown: 1 km; Casino of venice: 3 km.

• onsite facilities

The Moorish charm of guest rooms and suites is complemented by the finest in modern comfort. Three restaurants, three bars, each different, each inviting. In addition to a private beach, swimming pool, 6 tennis courts and water sports, guests may enjoy horseback riding and golf at the exclusive Golf Club Venezia.

• wedding services

The Westin Excelsior is an ideal venue for receptions and banquets for up to 440 participants. Magnificent rooms and a patio overlooking the sea: splendid settings for an unforgettable wedding.

The Westin Excelsior, Venice Lido

VENICE, ITALY

The charms of Venice Lido, from the casino to its exclusive private beaches, are legendary. Look forward to a rejuvenating vacation when The Westin Excelsior, Venice Lido opens its doors for another season of bustling activity and blissful relaxation.

Overlooking the beach and just a short boat ride from Piazza San Marco (St. Mark's Square), the hotel spotlights Venetian cuisine at its three restaurants. Ivory stucco and crystal chandeliers create an atmosphere of refinement throughout.

Lounge by the pool, improve your tennis game on the clay courts, and enjoy water sports, from parasailing to water-skiing.

The guest rooms at The Westin Excelsior, Venice Lido have been sumptuously decorated in Iberian-Mauresque style. All accommodations feature magnificent views of the sea, lagoon, or the city, and offer welcome comforts and thoughtful amenities including in-room refreshment centers.

• ROMANTIC FEATURES •

The Tropicana Restaurant offers a relaxed, elegant ambience for all-day dining during low season. During the summer, La Terrazza Restaurant provides a magnificent seaside setting perfect for candlelight dinners complemented by live music. Check out the open-air setting of Restaurant Taverna for breakfast and lunch daily.

Water Taxis are available from the waterfront immediately outside the railway station. Guests may preferably arrange a private transfer with the chief purser on board or contact the hotel to arrange a transfer. For further details, please contact the concierge desk at the hotel.

Gran Hotel Bahia del Duque

CANARY ISLANDS, SPAIN

The Gran Hotel Bahía del Duque Resort is located on the shoreline of the fashionable Costa Adeje in southern Tenerife. Washed by a 900 meter long sandy beach, the outline of La Gomera Island can be made out in the distance.

The hotel is a perfect setting for a family holiday. You can relax on the beach or be as active as you choose, with an array of fine sports facilities, both land and water based. The latter comprise 8 swimming pools, including 2 children's pools, 1 salt water pool and 2 heated pools, a beach club, watersports including waterskiing and parascending, 3 floodlit tennis courts, 2 squash courts, fitness center, jogging circuits, 5 nearby golf courses, games room, beauty salon, boutiques, gift and tobacco shops.

• ROMANTIC FEATURES •

The hotel retains a peaceful and private atmosphere as the rooms are spread across twenty houses, all reflecting traditional Canarian architecture, with Victorian and Venetian turn-of-the-century influences and set amongst luxuriant gardens sloping down to the beach. The philosophy of the hotel can be clearly perceived as soon as you see the building from a distance. "Live the difference" is what is offered to all who stay here, from the first moment guests arrive until they leave. Just outside the entrance area is the beginning of a lake that is formed by several swimming pools that are connected by waterfalls. Amongst the gardens is an impressive selection of 11 fine restaurants, 10 bars and cafés to choose from. Cuisines range from Spanish, French, and Italian to typical Canarian, Latin American and Gourmet.

EUROPE

• at a glance

Location: Canary Islands, Spain
Mailing Address: 38660 Costa Adeje - Tenerife Sur Canary Islands, Spain
Reservations: 34-922-74-69-00
Fax: 34-922-74-69-16
Web Site: www.bahia-duque.com
Meeting Space: 53,819 square feet
Accommodations: 482 rooms and suites
Range of Rates: $340 - $6,540

about the area

Currency: Euro
Weather: Mild
Languages: Spanish, English
Nearest Airport: Tenerife South Airport

• nearby attractions

The Gran Hotel Bahía del Duque Resort has 56,000sq meters of exuberant tropical and sub-tropical vegetation, which has created a particular microclimate, with all kinds of trees, cacti and different European plants.

• onsite facilities

The rooms have been decorated in a style that is equally baroque and simple with moroccan influences, with the light and freshness provided by their ochre and sienna-colored tones.

• wedding services

From the moment of your first contact with the Gran Hotel Bahía del Duque Resort you will be attended to by highly qualified personnel who speak several languages so that you may use your native language at all times.

Hotel Ritz, Barcelona

BARCELONA, SPAIN

EUROPE

• at a glance

Location: Barcelona, Spain
Mailing Address: Gran Via de les Corts
Catalanes, 668 08010 Spain
Reservations: +34-93-510-11-61
Fax: +34-93-412-75-79
Web Site: www.ritzbcn.com
Meeting Space: 4,338 square feet
Accommodations: 125 deluxe rooms
and suites
Range of Rates: $355 - $2430

about the area

Currency: U.S. Dollars
Weather: Temperate
Languages: Spanish and Catalan
Nearest Airport: El Prat International

A major landmark of Barcelona, the Ritz is an elegant and emblematic hotel, built in 1919 and recently renovated. It has preserved its period charm and distinction of its setting, though provides amply to the needs of the modern executive.

Situated on a pleasant tree-lined boulevard in the heart of the city, guest rooms are bright, spacious and comfortable, while suites feature strong period tones.

Diana restaurant offers quality Mediterranean and international cuisine in an airy dining room with smooth and professional service. Decorated elegantly in shades of blue and presided over by a beautiful and unique period fireplace, Diana restaurant is an ideal setting in which to enjoy the most select, top-level, creative cuisine.

The hotel is situated in Barcelona city center, close to the Gothic Quarter, the Paseo de Gracia, the Ramblas, and surrounded by many of Gaudi's and other world-renowned modernist architect's buildings. Also located close to the sea front. ✿

• ROMANTIC FEATURES •

When you visit the Ritz Hotel, your honeymoon dreams become memories that last a lifetime.

Elegant, sophisticated and romantic, the Hall makes you feel like an international celebrity. The Concierge will be more than happy to arrange just about anything.

You will feel far away from the crowds but will really be in the heart of the downtown excitement.

The Ritz is located in the trendiest area for restaurants and boutiques. ✿

• nearby attractions

In Barcelona, you can enjoy the unique constructions of the modernist architect Gaudi, its excellent shopping, its delicious gastronomy and never-ending list of leisure and cultural activities. Fun is guaranteed day and night.

• onsite facilities

The Ritz has 125 spacious, totally renovated rooms with minibar, double windows, safe, phone, satellite TV, air conditioning and walk in closet. 24 hours room and laundry service. Health club, Beauty Parlour, Hairdressing and Business corner.

• wedding services

The hotel offers 10 meeting rooms up to 300 people, ideal for wedding celebrations. Audiovisual equipment available at the hotel. The Ritz offers its more romantic rooms for wedding couples with special services & upgrades upon availability.

• at a glance

Location: Barcelona, Spain
Mailing Address: Ramblas 111, Barcelona, 08002, Spain
Reservations: 800-543-4300
Fax: 34-93-301-7775
Web Site: www.lemeridien.com
Meeting Space: up to 250 people
Accommodations: 212 rooms and suites
Range of Rates: 175 - 1,800 Euros

about the area

Currency: Euro
Weather: Temperate
Languages: Spanish, English
Nearest Airport: El Prat International

• nearby attractions

Close to the Gothic quarter, Palau de la Musica, the Picasso Museum, and the harbor. Montjuic Park, with the Olympic Stadium, Greek Theatre and Miró Museum, are easily accessible. Restaurants, bars and museums are also nearby.

Le Méridien Barcelona

BARCELONA, SPAIN

Superior bedrooms, superb service, and breathtaking suites

with unique views of the Barrio Gótico - Your Barcelona experience starts at Lé Meridien. Located in the very center of town on the world-famous Las Ramblas, minutes away from everything that makes Barcelona one of Europe's most exciting cities.

Le Méridien Barcelona is often referred to as 'the star's hotel, as many world-famous personalities have crossed the threshold, including Pavarotti, Zubin Mehta, the Rolling Stones, Madonna, and many more. The top floors feature beautiful suites in three main color schemes. Orange, green (reflecting the Mediterranean sun and sea), and classic creme.

The warm and cozy decoration of Le Patio restaurant offers a perfect combination of the Mediterranean-style cuisine and the peaceful, traditional atmosphere of a Catalan patio. There is no better place to spend the evening in Barcelona than Le Piano Bar where guests can enjoy one of our special cocktails while listening to live music.

• onsite facilities

We offer 24 hour front desk and concierge, a 24 hour currency exchange, bellman and porter, business and internet center, and a doctor on call.

• ROMANTIC FEATURES •

Enjoy champagne on arrival, celebrate over a three course dinner, and relax with breakfast in bed. Le Méridien Barcelona's Mediterranean Suites offers a spacious sitting area and private dressing room. All have spectacular terraces offering views over Barcelona's city center. These suites are ideal for enjoying breakfast in the Mediterranean sun and romantic dinners under the stars.

The Mediterranean Suites are a honeymooners' preferred choice. They can be used for small, private cocktail parties, including before and after wedding celebrations.

• wedding services

Eight versatile function rooms are located on the 1st floor overlooking Las Ramblas. Perfect for your wedding reception. From simple and elegant to a grand event, we can cater 10 to 350 guests, cocktail style, and up to 250 for banquets.

• at a glance
Location: St. Moritz, Switzerland
Mailing Address: Via Serlas 27 CH -
7500 St Moritz, Switzerland
Reservations: 41-81-8371100
Fax: 41-81-8372999
Web Site: www.badruttspalace.com
Size of Property: 6 acres
Meeting Space: 694 - 4,185 square feet
Accommodations: 180 rooms and suites
Range of Rates: $200 - $5,000

about the area
Currency: CHF - Swiss Francs
Weather: Temperate
Languages: German, Italian, English
Nearest Airport: Zurich and Milan

• nearby attractions

Winter: skiing, bob sleighing, sledding, curling. Events like Polo World Cup, White Turf on the frozen lake. Summer: St Moritz offers many outdoor activities, including golfing, hiking, biking, and water sports. Visit Zurich, Milan and Lake Como for a day trip.

Badrutt's Palace Hotel

ST. MORITZ, SWITZERLAND

Badrutt's Palace Hotel, situated amidst breathtakingly beautiful

and unspoiled scenery, has long been hailed as a landmark in the center of St. Moritz and is the ultimate expression of the Swiss Alps region. A favorite of celebrities and royalty alike since its opening in 1896, The Palace Hotel offers 180 guest rooms and suites with stunning views of the Swiss Alps.

Badrutt's Palace is a celebration of style, sports, cuisine and fashion, with discreet service and traditional elegance evoking an atmosphere of pampered luxury for all. An ideal destination in both winter and summer, the hotel is located in one of the most challenging ski areas in the world and offers a wide range of summer alpine activities. Guests find the ultimate in relaxation at the spa, exciting nightlife at the Kings Club, and world-renowned cuisine in the hotel's restaurants and nearby Chesa Veglia. ॐ

• onsite facilities

7 Restaurants and Bars, Kid's Club Palazzino, Health Club, Daniela Steiner Beauty Spa, Ski Rental & Ski School, Tennis courts (Summer),Gift Shop, Luxury boutiques, 24 hour Concierge & Room Service, Ice Rink (Winter),

• ROMANTIC FEATURES •

Badrutt's Palace Hotel is situated like a fairy-tale castle in the centre of St. Moritz overlooking the lake of St. Moritz and the Swiss Alps. A large variety of Junior Suites and Suites with private balconies, Awarded Beauty Spa for couple treatments, large variety of Restaurants for Candle Light Dinners and wedding functions, Famous Night Club "King's Club", romantic horse drawn carriage trips, many sport activities available in Winter & Summer (i.e. skiing, paragliding, hiking, biking, horseback riding, sailing and 4 golf courses in close proximity), romantic picnics in the countryside. Furthermore St. Moritz offers the ultimate shopping experience. ॐ

• wedding services

Special Honeymoon treatments, Rolls Royce transfer within St. Moritz, florist on property, Private Salons for Cocktails and dinner events, Personal Suite Butler, Chesa Veglia - Swiss Chalet for diner events, awarded Executive & Pastry Chefs.

• at a glance

Location: Zurich, Switzerland
Mailing Address: Talstrasse 1 8022 Zurich Switzerland
Reservations: +41-1-220-50-20
Fax: +41-1-220-50-44
Web Site: www.bauraulac.ch
Meeting Space: Up to 200 guests
Accommodations: 125 rooms and suites
Range of Rates: $365 - $1700

about the area
Currency: CHF - Swiss Francs
Weather: Temperate
Languages: German
Nearest Airport: Zurich Airport

• nearby attractions

The opera, the art museum, the concert hall, the bahnhofstrasse (the world's most beautiful shopping mile), the lake of Zurich.

• onsite facilities

Picnic on the shore of Lake Zurich. Visit the elegant Le Restaurant Français for classic French fare, Le Pavillon for romantic garden dining. Also available: La Terrasse, Rive Gauche & Bar, Health Club overlooking the lake and Alps, Beauty Salon, Night Club.

• wedding services

Honeymoon Special quoted for two people in a Double room with upgrade to a Suite. The package includes fruits, flowers and sweets, bottle of Champagne, cocktail on the terrace at the romantic Schanzengraben river and buffet breakfast.

Baur au Lac

ZURICH, SWITZERLAND

Baur au Lac is Zurich's prestigious landmark of unequalled hospitality, elegance and impeccable service, with more than 158 years of hosting royalty, celebrities and international travelers. In its own private park on the lake shore with a unique location at the upper end of fashionable Bahnhofstrasse, Zurich's famous shopping and business districts, the Hotel is only a stone's throw away from all major cultural and tourist attractions. The hotel offers the ultimate in luxury, comfort and modern amenities, evoking the intimate atmosphere of a private home.

Baur au Lac is Internationally renowned for superior cuisine and outstanding wines. Enjoy elegant Le Restaurant Français for classic French fare, Le Pavillon for romantic garden dining in a unique setting, La Terrasse for outdoor snacks and Rive Gauche, downtown's latest "in" restaurant for informal dining and the American Bar for cocktails and after-dinner drinks.

The hotel also boasts excellent meeting/banquet rooms, business center, disco club, fitness room, garage.

• ROMANTIC FEATURES •

Le Pavillon for romantic garden dining in a unique setting. Park on the shore of lake Zurich. Honeymoon suite 529.

In its own private park on the lake shore, with a unique location at the upper end of fashionable Bahnhofstrasse, Zurich's famous shopping and business districts, the hotel is only a stone's throw from all major cultural and tourist attractions. After major renovations, the hotel offers the ultimate in luxury, comfort, and modern amenities, evoking the intimate atmosphere of a private home.

• at a glance
Location: CH - Lausanne, Switzerland
Mailing Address: Place du Port 17-19
CH - 1006 Lausanne, Switzerland
Reservations: +41-21-613-33-33
Fax: +41-21-613-33-34
Web Site: www.brp.ch
Size of Property: 10 acres
Meeting Space: 12 rooms /19,000 square feet
Accommodations: 140 rooms, 29 suites
Range of Rates: From $360 + up

about the area
Currency: CHF-Swiss Francs
Weather: Temperate, Mild
Languages: French
Nearest Airport: Geneva International Airport

• nearby attractions

Olympic Museum, Lausanne Cathedral and Old Town, Cruise on Lake Geneva, Chillon Castle, Diablerets Glacier 3000, Gruyères (a typical Swiss medieval village), and Evian, a French spa resort.

Beau-Rivage Palace

LAUSANNE, SWITZERLAND

A few steps from the Olympic Museum, the Beau-Rivage Palace is set in a magnificent 10-acre private park, right on Lake Geneva, overlooking the Alps. Next to the harbour, yet only ten minutes away from Lausanne's shopping district, the hotel provides guests seeking a retreat from everyday life with the opportunity to enjoy many cultural and sporting activities, while offering impeccable service and exquisite cuisine.

Richly appointed with fine fabrics, tapestries and period furniture, the rooms offer the utmost in elegance and comfort. Seven suites were created to be different and unique in style, each one to suit the most demanding of guests.

For excellent French cuisine in a truly regal setting, reserve a table at La Rotonde. The "Café Beau-Rivage," modelled after a Parisian brasserie, is perfect for those seeking a more informal meal. The Bar Anglais is where business meets pleasure and Le BaR, at lake-level, is a lively place to see and be seen.

• onsite facilities

Fine-dining restaurant, French brasserie, 2 bars with live music, in and outdoor swimming-pool, 2 tennis courts, fitness center, massage and beauty treatments, sauna, solarium, steambath.

• ROMANTIC FEATURES •

Honeymoon Package:
- Two nights in a Deluxe room with lake view.
- Welcome glass of Champagne upon arrival
- Fruits, flowers and chocolates in the room
- Champagne in the room
- Full Buffet breakfast in "Salon Grammont"
- Candlelight dinner in our French fine-dining restaurant "La Rotonde"
- Relaxing body massage or facial treatment in our fitness centre
- Limousine transfer in Rolls Royce from Geneva International Airport
- Free use of the swimming-pool, fitness centre and tennis courts

• wedding services

Our team can organize your wedding from A to Z. Beautiful banquetting space, including amazing Belle Epoque ballroom, catering, decorations, flower arrangements, music and entertainment, limousine service (Rolls Royce), honeymoon suite.

Le Montreux Palace

MONTREUX, SWITZERLAND

EUROPE

• at a glance

Location: 1820 Montreux, Switzerland
Mailing Address: Grand-Rue 100 CH -
1820 Montreux Switzerland
Reservations: 412-1-962-1100
Fax: 412-1-962-1717
Web Site: www.montreux-palace.com
Meeting Space: 12 conference rooms
Accommodations: 235 rooms and suites
Range of Rates: $277 - $725

about the area

Currency: CHF - Swiss Francs
Weather: Temperate
Languages: French
Nearest Airport: Geneva
International Airport

• nearby attractions

Golf; Summer and winter sport activities including water-skiing, windsurfing, skiing, hang-gliding, rafting, mountain biking, horse-back riding, hiking, boating, tennis, hot-air ballooning and many others.

L e Montreux Palace, "The Pearl of the Swiss Riviera," situated on the fabled shores of lake Geneva, overlooking the lake and the Alps, is a jewel of the Belle Epoque architecture.

Built in 1906, the hotel offers a traditional and elegant atmosphere where each guest can experience personalized service and attention to detail in the true Swiss tradition.

The 235 rooms and suites, all recently renovated, combine elegance and refined decoration, so that each guest can have an exquisite experience.

Dining at Le Montreux Palace is a delightful experience offering a wide array of tastes to suit every palate.

Discover the notion of well-being at the Amrita Wellness Centre, an exclusive top-of-the-line complex with a surface of 20,828 square feet as well as underground parking. Besides its indoor/outdoor swimming pool, a fitness centre, saunas, hammams, Jacuzzis and steam baths, the Amrita Wellness Centre will provide a vast choice of therapies, treatments and massages. ✎

• onsite facilities

Amrita Wellness Centre includes; swimming pool, fitness equipment, saunas, hammams, jacuzzis, and steam baths. Underground parking, hairdresser, discotheque, and newsstand.

· ROMANTIC FEATURES ·

A dream-like natural setting and a romantic decor, combined with luxury, elegance and comfort, set the mood for that special occasion. A champagne cocktail in the Golden Rose bar, with the sunset over the lake and Alps as a back drop, followed by a candlelight dinner in the intimacy of your suite, adds serenity and revitalization of your body and mind with the spirit of Amrita Wellness. Our simultaneous soothing massages and treatments in your private room for two will enhance your beauty and harmony on this journey of a life time... so many small details to ensure that your stay at Le Montreux Palace is unforgettable. ✎

• wedding services

Honeymoon package includes, room hire with floral decoration, 1 hour cocktail service, 4-course menu (as per our proposal), wedding cake with champagne, luxurious honeymoon suite and a spa treatment for the couple at the Amrita Wellness Centre.

Swissôtel Geneva Métropole

GENEVA, SWITZERLAND

• at a glance

Location: Geneva, Switzerland
Mailing Address: 34 Quai Général Guisan, 1204 Geneva, Switzerland
Reservations: 41-22-318-3350
Fax: 41-22-318-3300
Web Site: www.swissotel.com
Meeting Space: 48,000 square feet
Accommodations: 127 room and suites
Range of Rates: $250 - $12,300

about the area

Currency: CHF- Swiss Francs
Weather: Temperate
Languages: English, French, German, Italian
Nearest Airport: Geneva-Cointrin

• nearby attractions

Located in the heart of the business and shopping district, Swissôtel Metropole is a brief walk to the cities most noted attractions. Central station provides guests with excellent connections to national and international destinations.

• onsite facilities

Swissôtel Métropole offers guests 7 banquet and meeting rooms, a rooftop terrace, a restaurant with international, seasonal cuisine, a stylish piano bar, "Swissôffice" business center, and brand new Amrita Fitness Center equipped with the best fitness machines.

• wedding services

Our team of event coordinators can arrange all of the details for your special day. Simple and elegant or an elaborate celebration, our coordinators will create an atmosphere of refinement that reflects your personal style and dreams.

Located in the heart of the city's business and shopping

district with splendid views of Lake Geneva, the Five-Star De Luxe Swissôtel Metropole Geneva is the perfect venue for your wedding and honeymoon. Recently renovated with 16 new suites, Swissôtel Metropole offers its guests an extensive range of services to render their stay most enjoyable and memorable. The absolute highlight is the Presidential Suite, which offers the highest level of elegant living-comfort. With a direct view over the lake, the Presidential Suite presents an inviting living room and dining room. The impressive master bedroom offers a private luxurious bathroom, equipped with a sauna, Turkish bath and Jacuzzi. Large Plasma-TV screens and decor of wonderful oriental upholstery throughout make for a stay in the highest level of style.

Swissôtel Métropole offers a restaurant with international cuisine, a stylish piano bar, and 2 panoramic terraces on the top floor with a view over the lake and its Jet d'eau. ❧

• ROMANTIC FEATURES •

Imagine your wedding cocktail on the panoramic terrace with magnificent views over the lake. Surprise your guests with the refinement of a five-star cuisine and the elegance of the decor.

You can rely on the Swissôtel Métropole to help you organize the most beautiful day of your life on the shores of Lake Geneva. The hotel, ideally located in the city center, will charm you with its Belle époque style and its 127 rooms and suites offer yourself and guests the best comforts. ❧

Four Seasons Hotel Sydney

SYDNEY, AUSTRALIA

AUSTRALIA

• **at a glance**

Location: Sydney, Australia
Mailing Address: 199 George Street
Sydney, NSW 2000 Australia
Reservations: 61-2-9238-0000
Fax: 61-2-2-9251-2851
Web Site: www.fourseasons.com/sydney
Size of Property: 1 city block
Meeting Space: 14,176 square feet
Accommodations: 531 rooms and suites
Range of Rates: $320 - $3,150

about the area
Currency: AUD - Australian Dollars
Weather: Temperate
Languages: English
Nearest Airport: Kingsford-Smith
International

Voted Best Hotel in the Pacific Rim by the Condé Nast Traveler 2003 Readers' Choice awards, Four Seasons Hotel Sydney offers the most outstanding hotel location in the city at the juncture of the business and leisure districts.

Ideally located in the historic Rock's area, overlooking the Opera House and the Sydney Harbour Bridge, the hotel's 531 luxurious guest rooms and suites provide breathtaking harbour and city views. At the same time, it is literally a few steps away from the Central Business District.

Four Seasons Hotel Sydney is the place for business, leisure and important celebrations in Sydney – as much a part of the city's life and landscape as the Opera House itself.

For wedding receptions large and small, Four Seasons boasts 1,317 sq metres of function space, including Sydney's finest ballroom, a magnificent pillarless Grand Ballroom with elegant dinner seating for maximum of 540 guests.

• ROMANTIC FEATURES •

Couples enjoy The Spa's exclusive couples' treatment room, including a hydrotherapy bath, steam room and shower; poolside massage and drinks in The Cabana; romantic award-winning dining in Kable's with Contemporary Italian cuisine by Executive Chef Marc Miron; and comfortable, well-appointed rooms including the trademark Four Seasons bed with 220-count Egyptian cotton linens – slumber comfortably in elegance.

Enjoy easy access to all areas of the city from this central location and the dedicated attention of the concierge who can organize a picnic basket for two, tours to wine country and anything your romantic heart desires.

• **nearby attractions**

Four Seasons Hotel Sydney offers the most outstanding hotel location in the city at the juncture of the business and leisure districts. Ideally located in the historic Rocks District, meters from the Opera House and Circular Quay.

• **onsite facilities**

Features harbourfront and city views, gourmet dining at Kable's restaurant and bar, a luxurious spa with Australian aromatherapy treatments, 24/7 state-of-the-art Fitness center, full-service business center and exclusive Executive Club.

• **wedding services**

With breathtaking views of Sydney's signature landmarks, the Opera House and Harbour Bridge, weddings take on a remarkable magic. Celebrate in the most elegant surroundings, with exquisite cuisine and unparalleled service.

• at a glance

Location: Melbourne, Australia
Mailing Address: 495 Collins Street
Melbourne, 3000 Australia
Reservations: 61-3-9620-9111
Fax: 31-3-9614-1219
Web Site: www.lemeridien.com
Meeting Space: 5,600 square feet
Accommodations: 244 rooms and suites
Range of Rates: From $181

about the area

Currency: AUD - Australian Dollars
Weather: Temperate
Languages: English
Nearest Airport: Melbourne
International Airport

• nearby attractions

Located at the blue-chip address of Collins Street; close to the Stock Exchange, Colonial Stadium, Melbourne Exhibition, and Convention Centre and the Casino.

Le Méridien at Rialto

MELBOURNE, AUSTRALIA

B uilt at the end of the 19th century, Le Méridien at

Rialto is one of Australia's finest examples of 'fin de siècle' architecture. Located in the heart of Melbourne, it is only a short stroll from Melbourne Exhibition and Convention Center, Colonial Stadium, theaters and well-known shopping areas. The European style of each bed-

room makes for elegant and intimate accommodations.

The hotel has 244 rooms, all of which have individualized European-style interior furnishings, creating elegant, intimate and comfortable zones. Room types consist of Standard, Deluxe, Premier and suites - offering all guests something suitable for their needs. Le Méridien at Rialto has 44 suites. Each suite is different and highlights the architectural features of the room. One of our most popular suites is the Courtyard Suite with a romantic turret bedroom and elegant furnishings. French style flows through the Standard rooms. Each Standard room has a warmth and unique quality which only time can produce.

• onsite facilities

The hotel incorporates all the amenities that you would expect in a Le Méridien, including bellman and porter, beauty salon, currency exchange, doctors on call, elevator, valet parking and much more.

• ROMANTIC FEATURES •

Premiere Suite utilizes the recently refurbished Premier room type. It has been designed with the needs of the most discerning executive traveller in mind.

Premier rooms are equipped with four phone lines, cordless phone, fax, stereo, video machine, oversized bathrooms.

• wedding services

We have a dedicated Wedding coordinator who will personalize your Special Day, to ensure it is everything you dreamed it would be.

Park Hyatt Melbourne

MELBOURNE, VICTORIA, AUSTRALIA

AUSTRALIA

• at a glance
Location: Melbourne, Victoria, Australia
Mailing Address: 1 Parliament Square
Melbourne VIC Australia 3002
Reservations: 61-3-9224-1234
Fax: 61-3-9224-1200
Web Site: www.melbourne.park.hyatt.com
Meeting Space: 10 - 500 people
Accommodations: 240 rooms
Range of Rates: $220 - $520

about the area
Currency: AUD - Australian Dollars
Weather: Four seasons in one day!
Languages: English
Nearest Airport: Tullamarine International

• nearby attractions

Melbourne is a multi-cultural city with a vibrant artistic life and is regarded as one of the culinary, sporting and shopping capitals of Australia, with a wide selection of museums, art galleries, theatres and festivals.

• onsite facilities

Dine in the award winning Radii restaurant, or relax in the sumptuous Park Club Health & Day spa with a la prairie or Aveda body treatment. Park Hyatt Melbourne, your private haven!

• wedding services

Catering executives can assist with all your needs: Location, Reverend/Judge Service, Music, Food and Beverage, Cake, Decor, Flowers.

Conveniently situated in one of Melbourne's most historic areas, at the top of Collins Street and opposite St. Patrick's Cathedral, Park Hyatt Melbourne overlooks a district of Victorian architecture and is bordered by Melbourne's delightful Fitzroy Gardens. Just 13 miles from Melbourne Airport and convenient to the city's attractions, this boutique-style Hyatt hotel provides a warm ambience and an exceptional level of personalized service to its guests.

Capturing the very essence of Melbourne today, the hotel's facilities are sophisticated and contemporary, offering spacious and beautifully presented accommodations in a wide choice of rooms and suites.

In keeping with the cultural vibrancy of Melbourne, and with the attention to detail usually reserved for a private collection, specially commissioned contemporary works of art from local and international artists are displayed throughout the hotel.

· ROMANTIC FEATURES ·

Melbourne, the gateway to Victoria, is an eclectic city of casual elegance, characterized by an interesting blend of modern and Victorian architecture, attractive parks and lush ornamental gardens. Set on the banks of the Yarra River, the city's unique geographical position means that it is possible, within a day, to visit the coast, ski in the Victoria Alps and visit one of the many Yarra Valley and Mornington Peninsula vineyards that produce world-class red and white wines. Melbourne is a multi-cultural city with a vibrant artistic life and is regarded as one of the culinary, sporting and shopping capitals of Australia, with a wide selection of museums, art galleries, theatres and festivals

• at a glance
Location: Sydney, Australia
Mailing Address: The Wharf at Woolloomooloo, 2011
Reservations: 61-2-9331-9000
Fax: 61-2-9331-9031
Web Site: www.whotels.com
Meeting Space: 1,076 square feet
Accommodations: 104 rooms and lofts
Range of Rates: From $210

about the area
Currency: AUD - Australian Dollars
Weather: Four Distinct Seasons
Languages: English
Nearest Airport: Sydney International Airport

W Sydney

SYDNEY, AUSTRALIA

Amidst the heart of Sydney's luxury marina stands the boutique hotel, W Sydney. It's warm. It's on the water. It's located on the Wharf at Woolloomooloo. It exclaims, "Welcome to Sydney!" W Sydney always provides the utmost dedication to service and excellence. Whatever you want, Whenever you want it.

The W Sydney retains the authenticity and charm of the historic wharf building but offers the latest in modern luxury. The Water bar, named "Bar of the Year" by the Sydney Morning Herald, is where one can lounge on the vast ottomans, enjoy a cocktail, and soak in the rhythm of Australia.

Guests really experience the lap of luxury. Every amenity has been carefully designed to stimulate the guest and create a world of relaxation. Revel in the indoor heated pool or rejuvenate yourself in the spa. This alluring hotel is a Conde Nast Traveler 2001 "Hot List" award winner.

• nearby attractions

Visitors will feel immediately at ease knowing that all major attractions like Bondi Beach, Star City Casino and The Sydney Opera House are a short drive away. Wherever you want to go, Whatever you want to do. Go Wild.

• onsite facilities

24 hour in room massage, 24 hour in room dining, charming restaurants, Concierge service, Indoor pool, W café, Water Bar, The W Living Room, Wired Services, Meeting and Event Facilities.

• ROMANTIC FEATURES •

The ultra lofts are the ultimate in luxury suites filled with romance. The split level, apartment sized unit is 98 square meters. Relax in the comfort of your own lounge or dining and entertainment area in the downstairs of your suite. Drift away on chocolate brown suedette furnishing while taking in the panoramic views of the city skyline and marina. Head upstairs to wrap yourself in a Terry pique spa robe and bathe with the luxurious bath products. Schedule an in room. Then snuggle in the ultimate bed with fluffy goose down duvets and pillows and soft 250 thread count linens. Let the W Sydney relax and romance you.

• wedding services

Let the W Sydney take care of all your wedding needs. Experts are on hand for Whatever you want, Whenever you want.

• at a glance

Location: Matangi Island, Fiji

Mailing Address: P.O. Box 83 Waiyevo Taveuni , Fiji

Reservations: 1-888-628-2644

Fax: 679-8-880-274

Web Site: www.matangiisland.com

Size of Property: 240 acres

Meeting Space: 10,000 square feet

Accommodations: 11 bungalows & 3 tree houses

Range of Rates: $450 - $780

about the area

Currency: FJD - Fiji Dollars

Weather: Tropical

Languages: English

Nearest Airport: Taveuni Island

• nearby attractions

Bouma waterfalls and walking trails on the island of Taveuni. Villages on the island of Qamea. Scuba diving and snorkeling on nearby reefs. Matangi's gorgeous Horseshoe Bay - perfect for private picnics.

Matangi Island Resort

M A T A N G I   I S L A N D ,   F I J I

Matangi Island Resort Fiji is a truly unique small island in the South Pacific Islands. Set on a 240-acre private Fiji island, our enviable setting offers gorgeous beaches, tropical rain forest and some of the world's best scuba diving sites. This small luxury Fiji resort offers just eleven individual beachfront and ocean view bungalows, all handcrafted from local materials, plus three Tree House Bures overlooking the beach and ocean.

The resort is undoubtedly one of the finest romantic beach resorts in Fiji, specializing in intimate honeymoons, weddings and anniversaries and offering fine dining and spa services.

Offshore scuba diving and light tackle sport fishing are both exceptional. And our surrounding islands are truly beautiful with stunning bays, breath-taking waterfalls, remote villages and secluded hiking trails. Above all else, Matangi Island offers an exceptional service in a friendly down-to-earth atmosphere – it is the ultimate destination to relax, meet like-minded visitors and to escape the commercial world of tourism. ॐ

• ROMANTIC FEATURES •

Matangi's intimate setting and relaxed atmosphere make it the perfect location for a memorable Fiji wedding. Our staff make sure your wedding is a hassle free occasion - all you need to do is obtain your marriage license, choose when and where you would like your wedding to take place, who you would like as your witnesses, and we do the rest. Professional photography is available.

Matangi's intimate setting on its own private island makes it the perfect location to celebrate your honeymoon. One of the most popular spots for honeymooning couples is the secluded Horseshoe Bay with its enclosed beach setting. And if Horseshoe Bay has already been booked, we have plenty of other secluded beaches where the only footprints are your own. ॐ

• onsite facilities

Bar and dining room on our over-the-water deck. Activities Center offering snorkeling, sailing, kayaking, windsurfing, hiking and fishing. Full Service PADI and SSI Dive Centre. Massage, Spa, and Boutique.

• wedding services

Island Wedding Package - Registration, Minister, wedding coordinator, decorated site, witnesses, floral leis, floral headpiece, bouquet, choir, rum punch, appetizers, cake, private dinner, bottle of champagne.

• at a glance

Location: Motu Toopua, Bora Bora, Tahiti
Mailing Address: B.P. 175, Vaitape Bora
Bora French Polynesia
Reservations: 011-689-604002
Fax: 011-689-604003
Web Site: www.boraboralagoonresort.ori-
ent-express.com
Size of Property: 13 acres
Meeting Space: Approx. 1,000 square
feet
Accommodations: 80 rooms and suites
Range of Rates: $450 - $1800

about the area

Currency: XPF - French Pacific Franc,
Euros
Weather: Tropical
Languages: French, English, Tahitian
Nearest Airport: Bora Bora

• nearby attractions

Bora Bora Lagoon Resort is surrounded by
the most beautiful lagoon in the world. Most
activities take place in, on and under the
lagoon - snorkeling, scuba diving, shark
feeding. The main village of Vaitape is just
5 minutes away.

• onsite facilities

Resort features two restaurants; two bars;
swimming pool; fitness center; two tennis
courts; Game room; wide selection of water
sports; beaches and snorkeling and, new
for 2004, a beachfront, tree-house style
Spa.

• wedding services

Whether renewing vows or celebrating a
new beginning, two Tahitian style blessing
ceremonies are available. One takes place
at the hotel, the other on a private motu.
Both include the blessing, flowers, entertainment and a romantic dinner.

Bora Bora Lagoon Resort

MOTU TOOPUA, BORA BORA, FRENCH POLYNESIA

From its ideal location on its own lush motu (islet) in the center of Bora Bora's spectacular lagoon, Orient Express Hotels' award winning Bora Bora Lagoon Resort features 80 luxurious bungalows in over-water, beach and garden settings and serves as Tahiti's most authentic luxury resort. Each air-conditioned bungalow offers a private terrace, television with DVD, telephone, mini-bar, coffee/tea maker and personal safe; overwater bunga-lows feature glass-topped coffee tables for unique views of Bora Bora's abundant marine life. Guests dine on the finest cuisine in the islands in two superb restaurants. Activities offered daily include swimming pool, tennis courts, state of the art fitness center, a full array of water activi-ties, and boat shuttle service to Vaitape, just five minutes across the lagoon. Bora Bora Lagoon Resort embodies the ideal South Seas hideaway - the seclusion of a private island setting, yet within easy reach of the main attractions of Bora Bora island. ᐧᐧ

• ROMANTIC FEATURES •

Voted #1 Honeymoon Suite/Overwater Bungalows and #1 Most Secluded Resort three years in a row by the readers of Modern Bride Magazine, the Bora Bora Lagoon Resort is the ideal South Seas Island honeymoon resort. The resort's white sand beaches, swaying palms, lush gardens, beautiful scented flowers, crystal blue waters teaming with bright, colorful fish, magi-cal sunsets and romantic, starry nights create the perfect setting for a celebration of love. At Bora Bora we offer a range of romantic packages and an exclusive Tahitian wedding ceremony, which takes place on the main beach and is carried out in traditional Tahitian style. ᐧᐧ

Hotel Bora Bora

BORA BORA, FRENCH POLYNESIA

• at a glance
Location: Bora Bora, French Polynesia
Mailing Address: Point Raititi, BP1, Nunue, Bora Bora, French Polynesia
Reservations: 65-6887-3337
Fax: 65-6887-3338
Web Site: www.amanresorts.com
Accommodations: 54 bungalows and fares
Range of Rates: $700 - $975+

about the area
Currency: XPF - French Pacific Franc
Weather: Tropical
Languages: French, English, Tahitian
Nearest Airport: Papeete

• nearby attractions

What makes Hotel Bora Bora so unique is its location. The lagoon's coral gardens and tropical fish combine to create a spectacular setting offering a range of watersports from snorkeling and diving to sailing, fishing and cruising.

• onsite facilities

Island and sea excursions can be arranged at the Raititi Lounge, there are two tennis courts, lit for night play, and the resort also offers basketball and volleyball. Beauty treatments are available in the privacy of guest suites.

• wedding services

Traditional Polynesian ceremonies take advantage of the dramatic setting and are held at the lagoon's edge at sunset, officiated by a native Polynesian. Crowns of gardenia and tapa cloth certificates add an authentic touch.

Hotel Bora Bora is located on the island of Bora Bora, just 10 km long and four km wide and one of the many islands of French Polynesia in the South Pacific. Hotel Bora Bora sits nestled beneath the green volcanic peaks of Mount Otemanu (Mountain of the Bird). Not only does it have as a backdrop the lush vegetation and volcanic peaks of Bora Bora island but it also faces one of the world's most spectacular lagoons.

The resort has three white sand beaches and is fringed by a barrier reef offering a variety of colorful marine life for snorkelers and divers.

These underwater treats are available to non-divers who can experience an aqua safari. Sailing and deep sea fishing are popular and typical catches range from tuna and wahoo to marlin and mahimahi. A number of secluded beaches on deserted motu (islets) nearby make good picnic destinations on a cruise boat. There are a number of treks across the island and guests can explore on either horseback, jeep or foot.

• ROMANTIC FEATURES •

Hotel Bora Bora's 54 Polynesian-style bungalows and farés (the Tahitian term for home) enjoy a variety of settings, from garden view and beachfront to overwater locations. Rooms take on the eclectic taste of an old trader's house with rattan and bamboo, Tasmanian oak floors, red-cedar walls, ceilings of pandanus lashed to beams of Douglas fir, cast-iron tubs and overhead fans. Interiors also include a collection of Polynesian craft, from canoe paddles to fish-hooks, and facilities include CD players and personal safes.

The breezy Matira Terrace Restaurant overlooks the lagoon with tables built from monkey-pod trees and a roof of pandanus thatching. Local musicians play here nightly.

InterContinental Beachcomber Resort Bora Bora

BORA BORA, FRENCH POLYNESIA

• at a glance

Location: Bora Bora, Tahiti
Mailing Address: BP 156 Vaitape Bora Bora, 98730 French Polynesia
Reservations: 1-888-303-1758
Fax: 689-604-999
Web Site: http://borabora.french-polyne-sia.intercontinental.com
Size of Property: 5 acres
Accommodations: 50 overwater and 14 beach bungalows
Range of Rates: $655 - $945

about the area

Currency: XPF - French Pacific Franc
Weather: Tropical
Languages: French, English
Nearest Airport: Bora Bora

• nearby attractions

Activities are plentiful! Outrigger canoeing, windsurfing, engine-powered Hobie cat, jet skiing, 4x4 safaris, horseback rides on the beach, and deep-sea fishing. Snorkel and scuba dive with tropical fish in our crystal clear blue waters.

• onsite facilities

Experience our magnificent fresh water sandy bottom pool with its waterfall and luxurious vegetation. Twenty-four hour room service as well as a business center are also available. Various Polynesian cultural activities are also available.

• wedding services

Many couples dream about celebrating their wedding in the Polynesian tradition. For years, brides and grooms from Japan, the US and Europe have entrusted us with the preparation and celebration of their weddings at our Polynesian resorts.

I nter-Continental Beachcomber Bora Bora Resort is situated on the island's famous Matira Point. It is surrounded by white sand and azure water. Forty-one over-water bungalows have glass topped coffee tables in room (for lagoon viewing!), and 10 air-conditioned beach bungalows are nestled on the most beautiful beach in Bora Bora. Guests may partake in shark and ray feeding excursions, private motu (islet) picnics and a variety of other activities. Bora Bora Intercontinental is the most exclusive and intimate resort for the perfect romantic vacation. Bora Bora is the Pearl of the Pacific, where time stands still. The lagoon, with its infinite shades of blue, is known for being one of the most breathtaking in the world. To top it off, themed evenings with beach barbeques, Polynesian activities (buffet with Tahitian dancing and music, mamas making crafts, and local artisans), and Soirée Merveilleuse (buffet with a fabulous dance and music show).

• ROMANTIC FEATURES •

Honeymooning guests receive special gifts upon arrival. If you would like a more romantic touch, we have lots of suggestions from which you may choose. You may have exotic flowers spread on your bed and in the room, crowns of fresh tropical flowers with exhilarating scents, a private mini Polynesian dance-show, or an hour of live traditional music only for you. Enjoy cocktails served on the veranda of your private bungalow under a tropical moon or sail off for a romantic picnic on one of the surrounding islets where you can spend the afternoon sun bathing and swimming, finished with a truly unforgettable romantic dinner by the light of the moon.

• **at a glance**

Location: Bora Bora, French Polynesia
Mailing Address: BP 190 Vaitape Bora
Bora Polynésie Française
Reservations: 00-689-47-07-29
Fax: 00-689-47-07-28
Web Site: www.lemeridien.com
Size of Property: 5 acres
Accommodations: 100 bungalows
Range of Rates: Beach Bungalows $650

about the area

Currency: XPF- French Pacific Franc
Weather: Tropical
Languages: French, Tahitian
Nearest Airport: Bora Bora Airport

Le Méridien Bora Bora

BORA BORA, FRENCH POLYNESIA

Le Méridien Bora Bora is located in the Southern tip of

a motu, facing the island of Bora Bora, with an open view on the famous Mountain Otemanu.

The hotel is only 20 minutes from the airport by private boat, and 5 minutes from the main island, and just some knocks of palms from the "Lagoonarium."

Stay in one of our 65 overwater bungalows, 16 premium bungalows, or one of our 18 beach bungalows with private beach.

The bungalows provide an exceptionally warm welcome with their burnished hardwoods, louvred windows, thatched ceilings and earth-toned

fabrics. Each bungalow includes a main room and a terrace, and a wide glass window integrated into the floor allows guests to admire the submarine life in the lagoon.

All rooms and bungalows include air-conditioning, a dressing-room, tea and coffee facilities, mini-bar, cable television, safe, direct telephone, and a separate shower and bath. The two restaurants in the hotel offer a variety of local and european specialities.

• ROMANTIC FEATURES •

With an enchanting setting and beautiful sunsets, Le Méridien offers you a traditional Polynesian wedding ceremony with costumes, Polynesian dances, and a priest sermon.

In their bungalow, the bride and groom are dressed by the "Mamas." The groom travels to the ceremony location on board a Polynesian pirogue. A Tahitian dancer and a second pirogue accompany the groom as he crosses the lagoon. The bride and bridesmaids travel to the ceremony site sitting in a "Pomare" chair carried by a Maohi warrior, in accordance with the tradition. At the end of the ceremony, the bride and groom board a boat where they will enjoy the sunset on the mountain...

• **nearby attractions**

Le Méridien Bora Bora is located on a 10 km long "motu" islet within the most beautiful lagoon in the world. Water sports and idle pleasure will be the key words of your stay! You will enjoy our private lagoon and the turtle's care centre.

• **onsite facilities**

Le Méridien offers 15 beach bungalows and 85 overwater bungalows with a windowed surface in the floor to observe the underwater world. The hotel's restaurants combine the delights of authentic local dishes and international cuisine. You will enjoy the spa with a wide selection of massages and treatments.

• **wedding services**

Le Méridien Bora Bora provides tailor-made wedding ceremonies with flowers, dinner, dancing, and more! You can also experience a Polynesian wedding and enjoy the church located on the motu (note: the Polynesian wedding has no legal value)

• at a glance

Location: Moorea, French Polynesia
Mailing Address: PO Box 1019 Moorea, French Polynesia Papetoai
Reservations: 1-888-303-1758
Fax: 689-55-1955
Web Site: www.moorea.intercontinental.com
Size of Property: 12 acres
Meeting Space: 2,500 square feet
Accommodations: 143 rooms and bungalows
Range of Rates: $310 - $630

about the area

Currency: XPF - French Pacific Franc
Weather: Temperate
Languages: English, French
Nearest Airport: Moorea

• nearby attractions

Moorea's coral reefs and rich marine life make scuba an ideal activity. When on land visit rain forests, cascading water falls and tropical fruits. Finally, stop by Tiki village, which is a recreation of an old Polynesian tribal village.

• onsite facilities

Food and beverages may be served to your room or bungalow upon request 24 hours a day, while bar is located between the lobby and the pool. It provides a relaxing atmosphere and breathtaking colors at sunset.

• wedding services

Many couples dream about celebrating their wedding in the Polynesian tradition. For years, brides and grooms from Japan, the US and Europe have entrusted us with the preparation and celebration of their weddings at our Polynesian resorts.

InterContinental Beachcomber Resort Moorea

MOOREA, FRENCH POLYNESIA

Moorea, with its picturesque silhouette, is one of the windward islands of the Society Archipelago situated in the middle of the tropical South Pacific. It faces the generous contours of Tahiti - the main island of French Polynesia. A deep channel 11 miles (17 km) wide separates these two volcanic islands, each of which is surrounded by a blue lagoon.

Moorea's natural beauty appeals to many thousands of visitors and adventurers every year, and the Moorea Beachcomber Inter Continental Resort is one of their favorite hotels. On a unique site nestled between the mountains and the blue lagoon, the hotel consists of 143 rooms and bun-

galows all offering the highest standard of comfort.

Facing the lagoon and the blue Pacific, a private beach outlines the resort with fine white sand. One of the main attractions of the Moorea Beachcomber is its Dolphin lagoon where these friendly mammals play and swim along with the guests, offering a unique experience. ❦

• ROMANTIC FEATURES •

Honeymooning guests receive special gifts upon their arrival. If you would like a more romantic touch, we have lots of suggestions from which you may choose. You may have exotic flowers spread on your bed and in the room, crowns of fresh tropical flowers with exhilarating scents, a private mini Polynesian dance-show, or an hour of live traditional music only for you.

Enjoy cocktails served on the veranda of your private bungalow under a tropical moon or sail off for a romantic picnic on one of the surrounding islets where you can spend the afternoon sun bathing and swimming, finished with a truly unforgettable romantic dinner by the light of the moon. ❦

InterContinental Beachcomber Resort Tahiti

TAHITI, FRENCH POLYNESIA

The Tahiti Beachcomber Inter-Continental is the first international hotel of Tahiti, the main island of French Polynesia, situated between California and Australia in the South Pacific.

Recently renovated and decorated in traditional Polynesian style, the resort has a total of 271 rooms and bungalows settled in the heart of a magnificent tropical garden and two spectacular infinity pools.

Located on the sunny West coast of Tahiti, the resort's 30 acres of beautiful land, facing Moorea island and the reef, have their own private sand beach and lagoon. Polynesian dance shows and live music perform every night in the restaurant

opening out on water's edge.

The resort is directly accessible from the airport where international flights bring visitors from around the world. Papeete, capital of French Polynesia, with its typical shops and marketing streets, is only ten minutes from the resort by bus or taxi.

· ROMANTIC FEATURES ·

Honeymooning guests receive special gifts upon their arrival.

If you would like a more romantic touch, we have lots of suggestions from which to choose. You may have exotic flowers spread on your bed and in the room, crowns of fresh tropical flowers with exhilarating scents, a private mini Polynesian dance-show, or an hour of live traditional music only for you.

Enjoy cocktails served on the veranda of your private bungalow under a tropical moon, or sail off for a romantic picnic on one of the surrounding islets where you can spend the afternoon sun bathing and swimming, finished with a truly unforgettable romantic dinner by the light of the moon.

· at a glance
Location: Tahiti
Mailing Address: InterContinental Hotels TAHITI BEACHCOMBER I-C RESORT BP 6014 Papeete PAPEETE, 98702 FRENCH POLYNESIA
Reservations: 011-1-689-86-5110
Fax: 011-1-689-86-5130
Web Site: www.tahiti.interconti.com
Size of Property: 30 acres
Meeting Space: Yes
Accommodations: 271 rooms

about the area
Currency: CFP-Central Pacific Franc
Weather: Tropical
Languages: French, English
Nearest Airport: Papeete (PPT)

· nearby attractions

Visit The Market Place, Paofai Church, Matavai, Pointe Venus Papenoo Beach, The Tree Waterfalls of Tefa Aurumai, Gauguin Museum, Botanic Garden, Matatoa Garden, Marae Arahurahu, Museum of Tahiti and her Islands, Le Lagoonarium

· onsite facilities

The Tahiti Beachcomber Inter-Continental has specialized in organizing banquets, cocktails, weddings, meetings and conferences in its fully equipped banquet rooms, or in its lush tropical gardens.

· wedding services

Many couples dream about celebrating their wedding in the Polynesian tradition. For years, brides and grooms from Japan, the US and Europe have entrusted us with the preparation and celebration of their weddings at our Polynesian resorts.

Le Méridien Tahiti

TAHITI, FRENCH POLYNESIA

• at a glance
Location: Tahiti, French Polynesia
Mailing Address: BP 380595 Tamanu - Punaauia Tahiti Polynésie Française
Reservations: 00-689-47-07-29
Fax: 00-689-47-07-28
Web Site: www.lemeridien.com
Meeting Space: 300 - 500 square feet
Accommodations: 150 rooms and suites
Range of Rates: Lagoon View Rooms from $391

about the area
Currency: XPF - French Pacific Franc
Weather: Tropical
Languages: French, Tahitian
Nearest Airport: Faa'a International Airport

• nearby attractions

Le Méridien Tahiti is located on a natural white sand beach facing the island of Moorea. Le Méridien's beach is considered by connoisseurs to be one of the most beautiful in Tahiti.

L e Méridien Tahiti is located along the beach in the

picturesque Punaauia region on the main island. It is only 15 km from Papeete, 9 km from Faa's International Airport and 20 minutes from the Atimaono International Golf Course, the botanical gardens, and the Gauguin Museum. It is only a few minutes walking distance from the Museum of Tahiti and its islands.

Le Méridien's beach is considered by connoisseurs as one of the most beautiful sites of Tahiti, facing the island of Moorea in a majestic environment of mountains, and just a few kilometers from the capital Papeete.

You will enjoy 130 spacious rooms of 47 m2- 5 Junior Suites - 2 Senior Suites - 1 Presidential Suite - 12 Deluxe air-conditioned bungalows on pilotis.

Le Méridien Tahiti offers a surprising culinary variety mix of local and European cuisines.

Le Méridien Tahiti offers a wide range of activities including a swimming pool with white sand bottom (the largest in the South Pacific), and many water sport activities. ॐ

• onsite facilities

The hotel features 138 rooms and suites overlooking the lagoon, and 12 Polynesian-style overwater bungalows. The property proposes two restaurants with a surprising culinary mix of local and European cuisines.

• wedding services

Le Méridien provides tailor-made wedding services: flowers, photographers, gala dinners. You can also discover the traditional Polynesian wedding with costumes, Polynesian dances and a priest's sermon.

· ROMANTIC FEATURES ·

Enjoy amazing sunsets over the lagoon and Moorea Island.

Our gourmet restaurant "Le Carré" will welcome you for a romantic dinner beside the lagoon in a trendy atmosphere. ॐ

• at a glance

Location: Kedewatan, Ubud, Bali, Indonesia
Mailing Address: Amankila, Kedewatan, Ubud, Bali,Indonesia
Reservations: 65-6887-3337
Fax: 65-6887-3338
Web Site: www.amanresorts.com
Accommodations: 30 suites
Range of Rates: $650 - $1,300+

about the area

Currency: IDR - Indonesian Rupiah
Weather: Tropical
Languages: Bahasa, English
Nearest Airport: Denpasar, Bali

Amandari

BALI, INDONESIA

• nearby attractions

Amandari is located in the central hill district and artistic centre of Ubud, famed for its traditional crafts. Besakih, Bali's mother temple, is also nearby, and trekking and hiking through the terraced paddy fields are a highlight.

Perched on an escarpment high above the Ayung River gorge,

Amandari means "peaceful spirits." It is located just outside the art community of Ubud, in Central Bali, and was designed as a traditional Balinese village. River-stone walkways with shrines and high paras-stone walls link the 30 thatched roof suites, each of which has its own walled garden. The open-air lobby was designed after a wantilan, or village meeting place, and the pathway that runs through Amandari and down the valley to the river below is sacred land. Every

six months for hundreds of years, Balinese have taken the path down to a pool of holy water. Just above this spring-fed pool sit three modest shrines and an ancient tiger carved into rock.

Amandari's trained guides can offer guests a variety of hiking experiences in the hills and terraced rice fields that surround the resort. White water river rafting along the Ayung River below and mountain biking are alternative ways to enjoy this lush countryside close-up.

• onsite facilities

The health and fitness centre includes a gym with views of the surrounding lotus pond, sauna and steam rooms and a spa where beauty treatments can be enjoyed in massage bales. A tennis court is floodlit for night play.

• ROMANTIC FEATURES •

Balinese-style stone gateways front Amandari's walled, thatched-roof suites, each with a private garden courtyard. Suites either feature a large combined bedroom and living room, or a bedroom with queen-sized bed on a mezzanine level. The bathroom, fitted out in Javanese marble, includes twin vanities and dressing areas with separate shower and toilet rooms and an outdoor sunken marble bath.

The alfresco Restaurant is crafted largely of teak wood and overlooks Amandari's 32 meter green-tiled horizon pool which lies close to the lip of the gorge. Each evening, a traditional Balinese gamelan orchestra performs in the music pavilion just beyond the pool.

• wedding services

For an intimate ceremony, the Ayung River Gorge bale is an ideal venue, with its views that stretch over the verdant terraces and river below, decorated in local flowers and lit with flaming bamboo torches.

• at a glance

Location: Central Java, Indonesia
Mailing Address: Amanjiwo,
Borobudur, Central Java, Indonesia
Reservations: 65-6887-3337
Fax: 65-6887-3338
Web Site: www.amanresorts.com
Accommodations: 36 suites, some with
pools
Range of Rates: $650 - $2,600 +

about the area

Currency: IDR-Indonesian Rupiah
Weather: Tropical
Languages: Bahasa, English
Nearest Airport: Jakarta, Indonesia

• nearby attractions

Amanjiwo is located in one of the most scenic parts of Java and provides the opportunity for immersion in Javanese culture, offering trips to ceremonies, nearby temples and antique shops as well as private visits to Borobudur.

• onsite facilities

Amanjiwo offers two tennis courts with a thatched roof pavilion for shady breaks and a 40 meter amphitheatre-style swimming pool. Beauty treatments, including traditional Javanese creme baths, are also available.

• wedding services

The Dalem Jiwo suite is ideal for a wedding ceremony, with its own private entrance surrounded by rice fields and classical rotunda leading down to a private pool finished in green Javanese stone.

Amanjiwo

CENTRAL JAVA, INDONESIA

Amanjiwo, or "peaceful soul," takes its inspiration from the surrounding culture of Central Java. The resort is located within a natural amphitheatre with the limestone Menoreh Hills rising directly behind, the Kedu Plain and Tidar, the mystic hill known as the geographic centre of the island, in front and no less than four volcanoes gracing the horizon. It looks out onto rice fields and beyond, and to Borobudur, the largest Buddhist sanctuary in the world which is mirrored in its design and central dome.

Some of Asia's most ancient and important religious monuments and temples are nearby; and Amanjiwo, as a result, offers a certain spiritual quality. Regular exhibitions are held in the art gallery where Amanjiwo's informal artist-in-residence keeps a studio, and a meditation garden can be found in a quiet corner of the resort below the Menoreh Hills. Personalized tours can also be arranged from the resort to discover Central Java, its art and culture and its centuries of temple architecture.

• ROMANTIC FEATURES •

Amanjiwo is constructed from paras yogya – the local limestone. 36 suites radiate outward from the main building in two deep crescents and are rimmed by high walls set off by spider lilies and morning glory. Each features terrazzo flooring, high ceilings, domed roofs and sliding glass doors that open onto a garden terrace with a view of Borobudur. All suites include a thatched-roof gubug (pavilion) with a daybed for outdoor lounging and dining. Interiors include a central, four-pillar bed on a raised terrazzo platform, sungkai wood screens, coconut wood and rattan furniture, old batik pillows in classic Yogyakarta style, traditional glass paintings and a sunken outdoor bathtub.

• **at a glance**

Location: Manggis, Bali, Indonesia
Mailing Address: Amankila, Manggis, Bali, Indonesia
Reservations: 65-6887-3337
Fax: 65-6887-3338
Web Site: www.amanresorts.com
Accommodations: 34 suites, some with private pool
Range of Rates: $650 - $2,600+

about the area
Currency: IDR - Indonesian Rupiah
Weather: Tropical
Languages: Bahasa, English
Nearest Airport: Denpasar, Bali

• **nearby attractions**

Amankila is located in Bali's most traditional regency. A hypnotic mix of religion, royal culture and architectural splendour lie within easy reach of the resort with two of the island's most important temples and royal palaces nearby.

• **onsite facilities**

Snorkelling, windsurfing, sailing and kayaking are some of the seasonal watersports on offer at the Beach Club. Spa treatments can also be enjoyed here at two teakwood massage tables hidden away beneath the coconut palms.

• **wedding services**

All weddings at Amankila are unique. Flower arrangements, traditional Balinese dances and musicians can all be arranged. Ideal settings for a wedding include the grassy seaside coconut grove or alongside the three-tiered horizon pool.

Amankila

BALI, INDONESIA

Amankila, which means "peaceful hill," is set on a cliffside overlooking the Lombok Strait in East Bali. Beyond the open-air lobby, the signature three-tiered horizon pool cascades down the hill towards the sea. All suites are connected to the reception and restaurant area by stepped walkways and are elevated to take advantage of the spectacular views. Below the resort is a private stretch of sand and beach club with eight private bales set back in the tropical foliage. A range of seasonal watersports are available including windsurfing, kayaking or sailing on the outrigger. Adjacent is the emerald green tiled 41 metre pool which stretches out alongside the coconut grove.

Balinese cooking classes, market tours, temple visits and guided jeep rides or treks through the surrounding hillsides and paddy fields of "Old Bali" are a highlight at Amankila. Two private bales located in the hills offer a panoramic picnic spot with spectacular views of rice fields, banana trees and Amuk Bay. ❧

• ROMANTIC FEATURES •

The 34 free-standing suites, with their alang alang roof thatching, are fashioned as beach houses with a twist. They reflect the lines and flow of their East Bali surroundings, in particular the royal water palace just outside Amlapura, the district's capital.

Each suite features a large bedroom with wide window views, a canopied, king-size bed and a writing desk. The bathroom is divided, with a window-side divan, a soaking tub and separate shower and toilet rooms which give way to coconut-shell dressing areas and double terrazzo vanities. The suite's outdoor terrace is furnished with a daybed, coconut-shell table and rattan chairs suitable for alfresco private dining. ❧

• at a glance

Location: Bali, Indonesia
Mailing Address: Amanusa, Nusa Dua, Bali, Indonesia
Reservations: 65-6887-3337
Fax: 65-6887-3338
Web Site: www.amanresorts.com
Accommodations: 35 suites, some with pools
Range of Rates: $650 - $1,300+

about the area

Currency: IDR-Indonesian Rupiah
Weather: Tropical
Languages: Bahasa, English
Nearest Airport: Denpasar, Bali

• nearby attractions

Guests can spend the day in one of the ten thatched roof bales at the Beach Club, enjoy the range of seasonal watersports on offer, or play golf on one of Indonesia's finest courses.

Amanusa

BALI, INDONESIA

Amanusa means "peaceful isle". From its hillside position it overlooks the Bali Golf and Country Club, the Indian Ocean and sacred Mount Agung on the far horizon. The colonnaded open-air lobby, lined with baskets of white tuberoses, leads to a teak sculpture illustrating scenes from the epic poem, the Ramayana. 35 thatched-roof suites are set behind foliage and mossy paras stone walls and are linked by stone walkways. The terrace bar and Indonesian restaurant offer sweeping views of the surroundings whilst the Restaurant offers gourmet Mediterranean food in an elegant high-celinged room which looks out onto the pool. Here there is an alfresco dining area surrounded by flowering frangipani trees.

Watersports, including surfing off Amanusa's private beach with the Amanusa surf instructor, and golfing on the adjacent course are a highlight, and for those who want to venture further afield, the cosmopolitan shopping areas and restaurants of Sanur and Kuta are nearby.

• onsite facilities

Amanusa facilities include a beach club, 24 meter swimming pool, two tennis courts and beauty treatments. Golf is also available on the neighbouring course, and shopping and nightlife are only a fifteen minute drive away.

• ROMANTIC FEATURES •

All suites have a queen size, canopied four-poster bed with a bay window sofa, a sunken indoor bath overlooking a japanese-style water garden, and an outdoor shower lined with tropical plants. A garden courtyard with table and chairs offers a private outdoor dining area; there is also a terrace with a spacious canopied day bed for lounging.

Amanusa's resident masseuses mix traditional Balinese massage with Swedish massage and acupressure. These are available in the suites, on your private terrace, poolside or on one of the Beach Club bales. A private barbeque dinner for two on the beach with toes in the sand, beneath the light of the moon, is a romantic way to start a honeymoon.

• wedding services

Amanusa's courtyard, which overlooks the pool, surrounded by towering stone walls and framed by flowering bougainvillea, provides a stunning wedding setting, as does the private golden sand beach with its ten thatched-roof bales.

Amanwana

MOYO ISLAND, INDONESIA

• at a glance

Location: Moyo Island, Indonesia
Mailing Address: Amanwana, Moyo Island, West Sumbawa Regency, Indonesia
Reservations: 65-6887-3337
Fax: 65-6887-3338
Web Site: www.amanresorts.com
Accommodations: 20 luxury tents
Range of Rates: $650 - $750+

about the area

Currency: IDR - Indonesian Rupiah
Weather: Tropical
Languages: Bahasa, English
Nearest Airport: Denpasar, Bali

• nearby attractions

The nature reserve of Moyo Island is a haven for nature lovers, and a number of walks begin directly from the camp. Watersports such as sport fishing are available on the resort's fleet of boats, and a number of deserted beaches are nearby.

• onsite facilities

Spa treatments are available in the alfresco Jungle Cove Massage area beneath the tamarind trees overlooking Amanwana Bay. Afterwards, the adjacent Music Pavilion offers a quiet place to relax and contemplate the peaceful surroundings.

• wedding services

An intimate Indonesian blessing can be held in one of Moyo's secluded inland jungle clearings. A short trek leads to a picture-postcard waterfall where green waters mirror the dense foliage of the jungle canopy above.

A manwana, or "peaceful forest," is an adventure camp of 20 luxury tents set on the nature reserve of Moyo Island. A wide variety of animal and bird life inhabit the vegetation which ranges from savannah to tropical jungle. Macaque monkeys and the occasional deer wander through the camp whilst the turquoise waters in front of the tents teem with tropical fish.

Diving and snorkelling are a highlight here with turtles and sharks sometimes spotted. Sailing, cruising and sport fishing on one of Amanwana's fleet of boats in the crystal clear waters of the Flores Sea are also popular.

The Dining Room and Bar are located in an open-air pavilion facing the sea which has a Sumbawan epil wood floor and soaring bamboo roof with pillars of solid coconut. The fresh menu changes daily and features both western and Indonesian specialities. Other facilities include a wooden boardwalk with loungers that face out to the sea, and a fresh water dipping pool that is set against a wall of coral rock.

· ROMANTIC FEATURES ·

Each 58-square-meter luxury tent is partially enclosed by a solid wall with a soft waterproof external roof and a separate canvas interior. A coral-stone deck surrounds each tent and there is hardwood flooring throughout. Inside, the air-conditioned tents feature banks of windows offering views of either the ocean or the jungle. Tents feature Indonesian island artwork, a sitting area with comfy lounging divans, king-size bed draped in netting, a writing desk and a large bathroom with twin vanities. Sand paths link the tents to one another and lead to the beach, boardwalk and jetty where guests can enjoy private starlit dinners or barbecues.

Le Méridien Nirwana Golf and Spa Resort

BALI, INDONESIA

• **at a glance**

Location: Bali, Indonesia
Mailing Address: PO Box 158, Tabanan 82171. Bali, Indonesia
Reservations: 62-361-815-900
Fax: 62-361-815-901
Web Site: www.lemeridien-bali.com
Size of Property: 250 acres
Accommodations: 278 rooms, suites, and villas
Range of Rates: $100 - $900

about the area

Currency: IDR - Indonesian Rupiah
Weather: Tropical
Languages: English, Bahasa
Nearest Airport: Denpasar

• **nearby attractions**

Overlooking Tanah Lot Temple, a 45 minute drive to the artist colonies of Ubud, Mas & Celuk. Kuta, Legian & Seminyak for shopping and fabulous restaurants are 30 minutes away. On a clear day the top of the Agung Volcano can be seen.

• **onsite facilities**

Our leisure facilities include 4 interconnecting swimming pools, a 54-meter water slide, a man-made white sand beach, floodlit tennis courts, air-conditioned squash courts, and a fully equipped spa and fitness center.

• **wedding services**

Partnering with professional local wedding consultants, every detail large or small can be arranged in advance from Bali. Choose from religious civil, or Balinese Hindu blessings ceremonies to mark the nuptials.

Set serenely amidst landscaped gardens and gently sloping rice terraces, Le Méridien Nirwana Golf & Spa Resort fronts the dramatic coastline of south-west Bali, in the Tabanan regency.

The 278-room hotel is part of the prestigious 100-hectare Nirwana Bali integrated resort offering an unparalleled array of luxurious resort facilities, including an 18-hole par 72 Greg Norman designed signature golf course and a spa.

Overlooking the Indian Ocean, spectacular vistas of the coast are possible from most parts of the hotel, and memorable sunset views of Tanah Lot temple are highlights of any stay at Le Méridien Nirwana.

Large standard guestrooms at Le Méridien Nirwana are a generous 44 square meters, including a balcony.

Twelve traditionally-styled one and two-bedroom villas offer guests a totally Balinese experience within their spacious confines. Each luxury villa features full facilities, including private plunge pool with adjoining terrace and courtyard, and both indoor and outdoor pavilions.

• ROMANTIC FEATURES •

Dreamtime weddings are a specialty at Le Méridien Nirwana, with a stunning setting of rose garlands, a chapel of daisies, a sunset over the Indian Ocean or the backdrop of Tanah Lot Temple. The Nirwana cliff lawn is perfect for outdoor catered weddings with traditional Balinese or western decor. The Grand Ballroom with its elegant furnishings is suitable for up to 300 guests. We are proud to have played host to many weddings from simple yet traditional settings for two to elaborate floral chapels for 200.

Honeymoon under a Bali moon, where a world of pampering and graceful elegance awaits you. "Surprise & Delight" honeymoon amenities ensure that your stay is enjoyable and memorable.

Hilton Maldives Resort & Spa

THE MALDIVES

• **at a glance**
Location: The Maldives
Mailing Address: PO Box 2034, South Ari Atoll, Republic of the Maldives
Reservations: 960-450-629
Fax: 960-450-691
Web Site: www.hilton.com/worldwideresorts
Size of Property: Two islands
Accommodations: 150 bungalows
Range of Rates: $250 - $5,000

about the area
Currency: U.S. Dollars
Weather: Tropical
Languages: English, German, Japanese
Nearest Airport: Male

• **nearby attractions**

The Maldives is a stunning archipelago of over 1000 islands, set in the jewel-blue waters of the Indian Ocean. Nearby attractions include coral reefs and fishing. The capital city of Male, 100km away by local dhoni boat, is of interest.

• **onsite facilities**

The resort offers some of the most luxurious Water Villas in the Indian Ocean, first class dining in 5 outlets, the only in-house sommelier in the Maldives, its own reef, water sports, dive centre, tennis court & a stunning over-water spa.

• **wedding services**

As one of the most idyllic settings in the world, couples can chose from 3 ceremonies, each including a wedding cake, Champagne, bouquet, photography, complimentary 'pre-wedding' Spa treatments, sunset cruise on a yacht, and dinner.

Reached by seaplane, the Hilton Maldives Resort & Spa on Rangali Island has become one of the Maldives' premier resorts and lies in one of the most beautiful areas in the world. Complemented by two uninhabited islands and a deep blue lagoon surrounded by a dramatic reef, the resort fulfills the ideal dream of a tropical paradise.

Rangali Island is home to 40 Water Villas and eight Deluxe Water Villas, all built over the crystal-clear Indian Ocean. Completely self-contained and air-conditioned, their wooden interiors evoke the best of the tropics. Surrounded by a natural lagoon, all Water Villas boast ocean view baths and sun terraces with lagoon access. Two secluded Sunset Water Villas are also available. These unrivaled, private villas boast an array of luxurious amenities including personal butler service, a jet boat shuttle and a divine circular bed which rotates 180 degrees to follow the sunset.

The hotel is proud of its fresh and innovative cuisine, available to guests in each of its restaurants. An eclectic mix of East meets West and a cross-section of ingredients and flavors combine to produce a totally new eating experience. First-class dining includes the sand-floored, buffet style Atoll Restaurant; the beautifully located Sunset Grill standing 50 meters out to sea; a la carte dining at the Vilu Restaurant; and Japanese style Teppan Yaki at the Koko Grill. The two underground wine cellars are home to over 10,000 bottles of wines selected by the resort's Wine Master. Its dedication to providing exquisite cuisine and delectable wines, topped with warm and friendly service, has put the hotel on the map as being one of the most unique fine dining experiences in Asia Pacific.

Five-star treatment continues at the overwater Spa, designed to let the mind and body unwind in harmony with the beauty of the natural environment. The ultimate relaxation therapies have been effortlessly combined to provide all guests with a chance to experience the best massage and 'wellness' treatments in the world. An extensive selection of treatments is offered by a team of professional therapists who pamper to guests wishing not only to have a relaxing vacation but also a revitalizing or healthy break in paradise. A full glass floor gives guests stunning views of the beautiful marine life whilst being pampered by expert therapists. Reached by a 40m bridge, the four treatment rooms are all well planned with cool, nautical interiors. Three have spectacular glass floors providing unbeatable views of the colorful marine life below whilst guests enjoy the wonderful selection of treatments. Guests can also relax in the open air Jacuzzi in the tranquil relaxation area looking out onto the Indian Ocean. Couples wishing to have the most romantic 'honeymooners' experience ever can enjoy joint massages and treatments in a double treatment room. The Spa treatments range from traditional Thai and Swedish massages, E'Spa facials, holistic and phytomer skin care programs, cleansing and detoxifying treatments and soothing body masks of seaweed and mineral extracts. All therapy sessions can be reserved ahead of time and individual Spa programs can be tailored to suit each guest.

Leisure facilities are equally outstanding with an on-site dive centre, fishing, watersports, tennis and numerous excursions available each day. A stunning coral reef is within paddling distance of the hotel's sandy white beaches.

For the more energetic guest, there is a host of recreational activities available. Excursions to neighboring islands, snorkeling safaris, windsurfing, big-game fishing, jet skiing, catamaran sailing and cruising aboard the resort's luxury yacht 'Goma' are always popular. Fitness fanatics also enjoy the gymnasium, the tennis court and beach volleyball. The Maldives is a popular destination for SCUBA divers and the resort's dive centre, managed by Sub Aqua, offers PADI courses and guided dives for certified divers daily so that guests can explore the wonderful underwater world nearby. ꕥ

• ROMANTIC FEATURES •

The Hilton Maldives Resort & Spa is extremely popular with couples wishing to have the ultimate romantic wedding ceremony. Couples can choose from three 'Renewal of Love' packages, each containing all the symbolic activities that nuptial ceremonies do, but taking place in paradise! All three ceremonies include a beautiful wedding cake, Champagne, bouquet, photography and complimentary 'pre-wedding' Spa treatments for him and her. Following the ceremony, the newly-weds sail into the sunset aboard the resort's yacht before returning for a gourmet, Champagne wedding dinner at the Sunset Grill Restaurant set 50m out to sea over a coral reef. The evening ends in a specially decorated wedding bed in their villa . . . ꕥ

• over-water spa

Indulge yourself with the best treatments in the world set in stunning rooms with underwater views. Choose from relaxing massages or pampering E'Spa treatments.

• wedding services

50 of the world's finest water villas await you, each offering stunning views of the ocean, Bose surround sound system, spacious bathrooms, and personal butler.

Raffles The Plaza

SINGAPORE

SOUTH PACIFIC & ASIA

• at a glance

Location: Singapore
Mailing Address: Raffles The Plaza, 2 Stamford Road, Singapore 178882
Reservations: 65-6837-3883
Fax: 65-6336-6210
Web Site: www.raffles-theplazahotel.com
Meeting Space: 70,000 square feet
Accommodations: 769 rooms and suites
Range of Rates: $390 - $3500

about the area

Currency: SGD - Singapore Dollars
Weather: Tropical
Languages: Chinese, Malay, Tamil, English
Nearest Airport: Changi International Airport

• nearby attractions

Singapore Art Museum at Bras Basah Road. CHIJMES offers dining, shopping, leisure and entertainment experience. Esplanade Theatres On The Bay, a total lifestyle experience, performing arts, shopping, dining and other cultural entertainment.

• onsite facilities

12 Restaurants and 5 Bars, Raffles Inc Premier Exec Club facilities, 24-hour-in-room dining services, 6 tennis courts, Amrita Spa Raffles City is Asia's largest spa, 2 outdoor swimming pools.

• wedding services

Our personal wedding concierge is dedicated to providing all the support and assistance needed on the couple's big day. A bridal suite for the wedding night is available.

Ideally located at the heart of Singapore's business, cultural, shopping and entertainment districts, Raffles The Plaza provides easy access to most parts of Singapore.

Following a recent $45 million renovation of guestrooms, this modern contemporary hotel is now a proud winner of the Gold Key Awards for excellence in hospitality designs.

Raffles The Plaza offers a choice of 12 restaurants and 5 bars, including Italian, Japanese and Szechuan cuisines as well as Singapore's latest dining and entertainment concepts in the Equinox Complex. In addition, guests have access to the 50,000 sq. ft. Amrita Spa, Asia's most extensive spa and fitness facility, offering the best in spa and skincare treatments as well as two outdoor pools, six tennis courts, meeting facilities in the 70,000 sq ft Raffles City Convention Centre and the adjacent Raffles City Shopping Centre.

• ROMANTIC FEATURES •

Ever dream of having a romantic and memorable wedding with exclusive personalized service from our Wedding Concierge?

Raffles Romance implies service beyond the ordinary. And the theme line 'Weddings to Remember' reflects exactly what the bride and groom desire where Raffles Romance's services are designed to turn wedding receptions into a worry-free and truly unforgettable celebration to seal your love. The team shares a wealth of experience, having planned and attended to more than 2,000 weddings at Raffles The Plaza. Every couple celebrating their wedding here will have the luxury of enjoying this exclusive butler service providing you with a one-stop service point in style.

Swissôtel The Stamford

SINGAPORE

• at a glance

Location: Singapore
Mailing Address: 2 Stamford Road, Singapore 178882
Reservations: 65-6339-6633
Fax: 65-6336-5117
Web Site: www.swissotel-thestamford.com
Meeting Space: 70,000 square feet
Accommodations: 1,262 guestrooms and suites
Range of Rates: $360 - $3300

about the area

Currency: SGD - Singapore Dollars
Weather: Tropical
Languages: English, Chinese, Malay, Tam
Nearest Airport: Changi International Airport

• nearby attractions

Clarke Quay situated along Singapore River, a festival village combining entertainment, food and shopping. *Peranakan Place situated along Orchard Road. Colorful and unique culture is vibrantly depicted in the beautiful buildings.

Southeast Asia's tallest hotel located in the heart of Singapore, The Stamford boasts a prime location that is within walking distance from Suntec Singapore & the central business district. The Mass Rapid Transit Station at City Hall, one of the two major interchanges, is located beneath the hotel complex, allowing easy access to Singapore Expo· & the rest of the island. The meeting facilities are unparalleled, from the technologically advanced Executive Conference Centre to the award-winning Raffles City Convention Centre servicing team, with its "under one roof" meeting concept. Providing an all encompassing convenience for all meetings, exhibitions & incentive groups. Other services include concierge assistance at the touch of a button to the relaxation facilities at Amrita Spa. For dining and entertainment, you can choose to dine at any of the 17 restaurants and bars which include Equinox Complex. ৯

• onsite facilities

Business Center with Secretariat Services, Amrita Spa Raffles City is Asia largest spa, 2 outdoor swimming pools, 12 restaurants & bars, 24-hour-in-room dining services.

· ROMANTIC FEATURES ·

The Wedding Concierge, newest addition to the Romance Team, is dedicated to providing all the support & assistance needed & unstinting attention to every nuance of a wedding celebration. Every couple will have the luxury of enjoying this exclusive butler service that is distinctively and genuinely warm, attentive, gracious, professional & confident. On top of that, every couple will also receive a "Feed at Raffles" membership card & a supplementary card which allows them to enjoy great discounts & promotions when dining at the wide range of restaurants & bars at Raffles The Plaza, Raffles Hotel, Swissôtel The Stamford, Equinox Complex & Swissôtel Merchant Court. ৯

• wedding services

From florists to bridal services, photographers to limousines, musicians to wedding gifts and accessories, Our wedding consultants will be able to introduce you to the services that best suit your style.

• at a glance

Location: Singapore
Mailing Address: 100 Orchard Road
Singapore 238840
Reservations: 65-6739-8337
Fax: 65-6235-0743
Web Site: www.lemeridien.com
Meeting Space: 20,500 square feet
Accommodations: 407 rooms and suites
Range of Rates: SGD $618 - $988 nett

about the area

Currency: SGD - Singapore Dollars
Weather: Tropical
Languages: English, Mandarin, Malay
Nearest Airport: Changi International Airport

Le Méridien Singapore

SINGAPORE

Located along the legendary Orchard Road, in the hub of the shopping, entertainment and business districts, Le Méridien Singapore offers all the conveniences of an international hotel complemented by traditional Asian hospitality.

The only hotel to boast a prestigious neighbor, The Presidential Palace, Le Méridien is also in close proximity to famous tourist spots and three museums.

The hotel has 407 guestrooms and suites, two restaurants and two lounges. Café Georges, the premier dining room, serves a lunch and dinner buffet on weekdays and Singapore High Tea on weekends and public holidays.

Thirteen function rooms offer space for conferences, meetings, workshops, dinner and dances, product launches and gala dinners. Complete with audio-visual and meeting equipment, there is also a banquet and conference coordinator in attendance.

Sandwiched between two subway train stations, the hotel's strategic location makes accessibility to all parts of the island easier.

• ROMANTIC FEATURES •

Wedding couples have five good reasons to choose Le Méridien Singapore to hold their banquet.

- Location - Situated along Orchard Road, the hotel is strategically located in the heart of the bustling city.
- Convenience - A short 5-minute walk, either way from Somerset or Dhoby Ghaut subway stations.
- The Margaux Ballroom, decorated in opulent black and gold, makes for a sleek and stylish venue for a wedding.
- Cantonese style cuisine - Pick and choose to make up your own 8-course or 9-course Chinese menu.
- Personalized attention - An experienced Catering Sales team is backed up by an attentive banquet operations staff.

• nearby attractions

Close proximity to Chinatown, Little India, Singapore Botanic Gardens. Ten minutes away from three museums: National Heritage, Asian Civilizations and Singapore Art. The Jurong Bird Park, Reptile Park and Night Safari are recommended.

• onsite facilities

Four outlets comprising two restaurants and two bars. On level four are the Fitness Center and an outdoor swimming pool, nestled amidst palms and blue skies. The Business center is on lobby level, next to the reception area.

• wedding services

Fitted with chandeliers, the pillarless Margaux Ballroom can accommodate up to 53 tables of ten persons each for a wedding banquet dressed according to a theme - Garden or Candlelight.

• at a glance
Location: Pamalican, Philippines
Mailing Address: c/o A. Soriano Air
Corporation, A. Soriano Hangar, Andrews
Avenue, Domestic Airport, Pasay City
1300, Philippines
Reservations: 65-8887-3337
Fax: 65-6887-3338
Web Site: www.amanresorts.com
Accommodations: 40 casitas
Range of Rates: $625 - $2,950+

about the area
Currency: PHP - Philippines Peso
Weather: Tropical
Languages: English, Tagalog
Nearest Airport: Manila

• nearby attractions

The abundant and beautiful reef waters
that surround Pamalican and its neighboring islands are ideal for snorkeling, diving
and cruising. Trips can also be made to
Manomoc island with its traditional village
and spectacular sand bar.

• onsite facilities

A garden walkway leads down from the 30
meter pool to the sand beach and open-air
Beach Club with its mattresses and pillows
spread out facing the sea and lounge
chairs lining the beach.

• wedding services

A wedding ceremony can be celebrated on
the champagne-soft powder beach set up
with a coconut palm arch and aisle adorned
with seasonal tropical flowers. Local
Filipino musicians serenade the couple
with traditional guitar and harp music.

Amanpulo

PAMALICAN, PHILIPPINES

Amanpulo means "peaceful island" and is set on the secluded,

private island of Pamalican. Pamalican is part of
the Quiniluban group, which makes up the
northern half of the Cuyo Islands and is one of
nearly 1,800 islands in Palawan, the largest
province in the Philippines. A low-lying coral
island, Pamalican is rimmed by seven square
kilometers of pristine reef making it a romantic
getaway with abundant sun, sand and surf.

While some guests might prefer to laze and bask
in sunshine and tranquillity, the rich marine
waters and surrounding reef provide a host of
options from diving, windsurfing, snorkeling
and fishing to cruising to nearby islands. There
are also a number of bush paths and two modest
hills to explore on foot or by bicycle. All rooms
have their own golf cart for exploring the island
and two synthetic-grass, floodlit tennis courts
are located adjacent to the Clubhouse, with rest
pavilions for refreshments. Balls, rackets and
playing partners are available.

• ROMANTIC FEATURES •

40 casitas (65-square-meter cottages in hillside
and beachfront settings) are modeled after the
Philippine bahay kubo (native dwelling). Inside,
decorative details pay homage to neighboring
islands: pebble-washed walls, coconut-shell
tables, rustic Palawan rice and knife baskets, a
king-size bed with a rattan headboard and slid-
ing-glass doors that reveal outdoor decks with
his-and-her divans.

Nearly half the space in a casita is given over to
a Cebu-marble bathroom, with twin vanities,
separate changing areas, a shower and an elegant
bathtub. Romantic starlit barbecue dinners on
the beach are a highlight.

• at a glance

Location: Phuket, Thailand
Mailing Address: Pansea Beach, Phuket 83000, Thailand
Reservations: 65-6887-3337
Fax: 65-6887-3338
Web Site: www.amanresorts.com
Accommodations: 40 pavilions
Range of Rates: $650 - $7,300+

about the area

Currency: THB - Thailand Baht
Weather: Tropical
Languages: Thai, English
Nearest Airport: Phuket

Amanpuri

PHUKET, THAILAND

Amanpuri, or "place of peace," was the very first Amanresort

and reflects the style and elegance of Thai culture. Thai-style pavilions and villa homes are interspersed amidst a coconut plantation on a headland overlooking the Andaman Sea. Elevated walkways connect the pavilions with the resort facilities and steps lead down from the 27 metre freshwater infinity pool to the private sand beach. Here, a variety of seasonal watersports are on offer such as sailing, snorkelling, diving, fishing or cruising on one of Amanpuri's extensive range of vessels.

Other facilities include a gym which is located by the beach with floor to ceiling window views of the sea and Amanresorts' first Aman Spa which opened alongside Amanpuri in December 2001. Aman Spa is a holistic sanctuary which nurtures both body and mind. Six spacious treatment rooms are scattered amidst the trees where health and beauty treatments may be enjoyed together with guided meditation and yoga classes. ❧

• nearby attractions

Amanpuri offers six floodlit tennis courts; equipment and professional coaching are available. Five international-standard golf courses are located within 30-40 minutes of Amanpuri, and complimentary golf clubs can be provided

• onsite facilities

Amanpuri's Amancruises fleet numbers more than 20 luxury cruisers and sailing craft for half, full day and overnight trips to explore the many beautiful islands and coves around Phuket. Starlit dinner cruises are also available.

• ROMANTIC FEATURES •

Blessed with a seaside setting of rare beauty, Amanpuri offers a tranquil retreat in elegant Thai surroundings. The resort's Thai-style pavilions are 115 square meters each, including their own private outdoor terrace. All pavilions feature an outdoor sala suitable for private dining, a king-size bed, separate bath and shower and CD player.

The Restaurant specializes in Italian cuisine and overlooks the sea, whereas the open-air Terrace by the pool serves Thai specialities. In the evening, chairs are set out along the terrace between the pool and the steps leading to the beach for the spectacular view of the sun setting on the Andaman Sea. ❧

• wedding services

A traditional Thai Buddhist ceremony can be performed in one of the villa homes decorated with flower petals, fragrant jasmine, orchids and a floral archway. It is performed by up to five monks who garland and bless the bride and groom.

• at a glance •
Resort Guide

Features and Amenities

	Anse Chastanet Resort	Atlantis, Paradise Island	Beaches Turks and Caicos Resort	British Colonial Hilton	Cap Juluca	The Caves	Cobblers Cove	CuisinArt Resort & Spa, Anguilla	The Fairmont Glitter Bay	The Fairmont Royal Pavilion	Frenchman's Reef & Morning Star	Half Moon, Montego Bay	Horned Dorset Primavera	Le Méridien L'Habitation	One&Only Ocean Club	Raffles Resort	Renaissance Jamaica Grande Resort	Royal Plantation Spa & Golf Resort	San Souci Resort and Spa	Sandals Antigua Resort & Spa	Sandals Dunn's River	Sandals Grande St. Lucian	Sandals Negril Beach Resort & Spa	Sandals Regency St. Lucia
Hotel Amenities																								
Airport Transfers	•	•	•		•		•				•	•			•	•		•	•	•	•	•	•	•
All Inclusives			•			•						•						•	•	•	•	•	•	•
Bar(s)	•	•	•	•	•	•	•	•	•	•	•	•	•	•	•	•	•	•	•	•	•	•	•	•
Beach/Ocean Front Rooms	•	•	•	•	•		•	•	•	•	•	•	•	•	•	•	•	•	•	•	•	•	•	•
Concierge		•		•	•		•	•	•	•	•	•	•	•	•	•	•	•	•	•	•	•	•	•
Conference Room(s)		•	•	•	•		•	•	•	•	•	•		•	•	•	•	•	•	•	•	•	•	•
Dry Cleaning		•	•	•	•		•	•	•	•	•	•	•	•	•	•	•	•	•	•	•	•	•	•
Fine Dining	•	•		•	•			•	•	•	•	•	•	•	•	•	•	•	•	•	•	•	•	•
Fitness Equipment		•	•	•	•		•	•	•	•	•	•		•	•	•	•	•	•	•	•	•	•	•
Honeymoon Packages	•	•	•	•	•		•	•	•	•	•	•	•	•	•	•	•	•	•	•	•	•	•	•
Honeymoon Suites	•	•	•	•	•	•	•	•	•	•	•	•	•	•	•	•	•	•	•	•	•	•	•	•
Laundry Service	•	•	•	•	•		•	•	•	•	•	•	•	•	•	•	•	•	•	•	•	•	•	•
Rental Cars	•				•	•	•	•					•							•	•	•	•	•
Restaurant(s)	•	•	•	•	•	•	•	•	•	•	•	•	•	•	•	•	•	•	•	•	•	•	•	•
Room Service		•	•	•	•	•	•	•	•	•	•	•	•	•	•	•	•	•	•	•	•	•	•	•
Shops/Boutiques	•	•	•	•	•		•	•	•	•	•	•		•	•	•	•	•	•	•	•	•	•	•
Spa Services	•	•	•	•	•		•	•	•	•	•	•	•	•	•	•	•	•	•	•	•	•	•	•
Special Offers		•	•	•			•	•	•	•	•	•	•	•	•	•	•	•	•	•	•	•	•	•
Room Information																								
Air Conditioning		•	•	•	•		•	•	•	•	•	•	•	•	•	•	•	•	•	•	•	•	•	•
Balcony or Terrace	•	•	•		•		•	•	•	•	•	•	•	•	•	•	•	•	•	•	•	•	•	•
Ceiling Fan	•				•	•	•	•	•	•	•	•	•	•	•		•		•	•		•	•	•
Coffee/Tea Facilities	•		•	•		•	•	•	•	•	•	•	•	•	•	•	•	•	•	•	•	•	•	•
Data Port			•	•	•			•	•	•	•	•		•	•	•	•	•	•	•	•	•	•	•
Hair Dryer	•	•	•	•	•		•	•	•	•	•	•	•	•	•	•	•	•	•	•	•	•	•	•
Iron/Ironing Board	•	•	•	•	•		•	•	•	•	•	•	•	•	•	•	•	•	•	•	•	•	•	•
Jacuzzi		•	•		•		•											•	•	•			•	•
Kitchen(ette)					•	•	•				•				•									
Minibar or Refrigerators	•	•	•		•		•	•			•	•	•	•	•	•	•	•	•	•	•	•	•	•
Private Pool			•		•			•				•	•	•	•	•		•		•				•
Safe	•							•	•	•	•	•	•	•	•	•	•	•	•	•	•	•	•	•
Telephone		•	•	•	•		•	•	•	•	•	•	•	•	•	•	•	•	•	•	•	•	•	•
Television/Cable		•	•	•	•	•	•	•	•	•	•	•	•	•	•	•	•	•	•	•	•	•	•	•
Whirlpool Bath		•	•															•	•	•		•	•	•
Recreation																								
Beach(es)	•	•	•	•	•		•	•	•	•	•	•	•	•	•	•	•	•	•	•	•	•	•	•
Game Room		•	•					•				•					•	•	•	•	•	•	•	•
Golf		•	•					•	•	•	•	•		•	•	•	•	•	•	•	•	•	•	•
Horseback Riding		•					•	•				•					•		•					•
Jacuzzi or Sauna		•	•		•	•	•	•			•	•		•	•		•	•	•	•	•	•	•	•
Nightclub/Discotheque	•	•	•	•								•					•		•					•
Swimming Pool(s)	•	•	•	•	•	•	•	•	•	•	•	•	•	•	•	•	•	•	•	•	•	•	•	•
Tennis		•	•		•			•	•	•	•	•		•	•	•	•	•	•	•	•	•	•	•
Volleyball		•	•	•	•			•			•	•		•	•		•	•	•	•	•	•	•	•
Water Sports	•	•	•	•	•		•	•	•	•	•	•	•	•	•	•	•	•	•	•	•	•	•	•

Resort Guide

Features and Amenities

	Caribbean				United States																			
	Sandals Royal Bahamian	Sheraton Grand Resort Paradise Island	The Westin Rio Mar Beach Resort	Westin St. John	Algonquin Hotel	Amangani	Arizona Biltmore Resort & Spa	The Drake Hotel	Estancia La Jolla Hotel & Spa	The Gant	The Greystone Inn	The Grove Park Inn Resort & Spa	Hard Rock Hotel at Universal Orlando	Hilton Tucson El Conquistador	Hotel Plaza Athenee	The Inn at Fisher Island	Inn at Lost Creek	The Inverness Hotel	Le Parker Méridien New York	Le Merigot	Litchfield Plantation	Little Palm Island Resort & Spa	The Little Nell	Manchester Grand Hyatt San Diego
Hotel Amenities																								
Airport Transfers	•		•	•		•				•		•	•	•		•		•				•	•	
All Inclusives	•	•							•		•													
Bar(s)	•	•	•	•	•	•	•	•	•	•		•	•	•	•	•	•	•	•	•	•	•	•	•
Beach/Ocean Front Rooms	•	•	•	•												•					•			
Concierge	•	•	•	•	•	•	•	•	•		•	•	•	•	•	•	•	•	•	•	•	•	•	•
Conference Room(s)	•	•	•	•			•	•	•	•	•	•	•	•	•	•	•	•	•	•	•		•	•
Dry Cleaning	•	•	•	•			•	•	•	•	•	•	•	•	•	•	•	•	•	•			•	•
Fine Dining	•	•	•	•	•	•	•	•	•		•	•	•	•	•	•	•	•	•	•	•	•	•	•
Fitness Equipment	•	•	•	•	•	•	•	•	•	•	•	•	•	•	•	•	•	•	•	•		•	•	•
Honeymoon Packages	•			•			•		•		•	•	•	•	•	•	•	•	•	•	•	•	•	
Honeymoon Suites	•	•	•	•		•		•	•	•	•	•	•		•	•	•	•	•	•	•	•	•	
Laundry Service	•	•	•	•			•	•	•	•	•		•	•	•	•		•	•				•	•
Rental Cars		•	•	•				•							•	•		•	•					
Restaurant(s)	•	•	•	•	•	•	•	•	•		•	•	•	•	•	•	•	•	•	•	•	•	•	•
Room Service	•	•	•	•		•	•	•	•		•	•	•	•	•	•	•	•	•	•		•	•	•
Shops/Boutiques		•	•	•		•	•			•		•	•	•		•						•	•	•
Spa Services	•		•	•		•	•		•		•	•	•	•	•	•	•	•	•	•	•	•	•	•
Special Offers	•	•	•	•			•	•	•		•		•	•	•				•				•	•
Room Information																								
Air Conditioning	•	•	•	•	•	•	•	•	•		•	•	•	•	•	•	•	•	•	•		•		•
Balcony or Terrace	•	•	•	•		•	•		•	•			•	•	•	•	•	•			•	•	•	
Ceiling Fan			•					•	•												•	•	•	
Coffee/Tea Facilities	•	•	•	•			•	•		•		•		•			•	•	•	•		•	•	•
Data Port		•	•	•	•		•	•		•		•	•	•	•	•	•	•	•	•			•	•
Hair Dryer		•	•	•		•	•	•	•			•	•	•	•	•	•	•	•	•		•	•	•
Iron/Ironing Board	•	•	•	•		•	•	•	•			•	•	•	•	•	•	•	•	•	_•_		•	•
Jacuzzi	•			•							•	•	•		•		•				•	•	•	•
Kitchen(ette)						•				•						•	•						•	
Minibar or Refrigerators	•	•	•	•	•	•	•	•	•		•	•	•	•	•	•	•	•	•	•		•	•	•
Private Pool		•		•									•							•				
Safe	•	•	•	•		•	•	•	•	•		•	•	•	•		•	•	•	•			•	•
Telephone	•	•	•	•	•	•	•	•	•		•	•	•	•	•	•	•	•	•	•		•	•	•
Television/Cable	•	•	•	•	•		•	•	•		•	•	•	•	•	•			•	•	•		•	•
Whirlpool Bath	•															•				•	•		•	•
Recreation																								
Beach(es)	•	•	•	•				•	•							•					•	•		•
Game Room	•		•						•			•												
Golf			•				•					•	•	•	•	•	•	•					•	
Horseback Riding	•					•					•	•											•	
Jacuzzi or Sauna	•	•	•				•		•			•	•	•	•	•	•	•		•		•	•	•
Nightclub/Discotheque	•							•					•											
Swimming Pool(s)	•	•	•	•		•	•	•	•		•	•	•	•	•	•	•	•	•	•		•	•	•
Tennis	•	•	•			•	•		•		•	•		•		•	•	•			•	•	•	•
Volleyball	•	•	•					•					•								•	•	•	•
Water Sports	•	•	•					•	•							•						•	•	•

	United States																			Canada								Hawaii		
	Montage Resort & Spa	Mountain Lodge Telluride	Pinehurst	Portofino Bay Hotel, A Loews Hotel	Raffles L'Ermitage Beverly Hills	Rancho Valencia	The Regent Beverly Wilshire	San Francisco Clift	South Seas Resort	The Stanhope Park Hyatt New York	The Sutton Place Hotel - Chicago	Universal's Royal Pacific Resort	W Chicago Lakeshore	W New York - The Court	The Westin Chicago River North	Westin Grand Bohemian	The Westin St. Francis	Wild Dunes Resort	Woodlands Resort & Inn	Chateau Lake Louise	Fairmont Le Château Frontenac	Ice Hotel Quebec - Canada	Loews Hotel Vogue	Loews Le Concorde Hotel	The Pan Pacific Vancouver	The Sutton Place Hotel	Wedgewood Hotel & Spa	Kapalua Bay Hotel & Ocean Villas	The Lodge at Koele and Manele Bay	Princeville Resort
	•			•	•			•	•			•				•		•							•				•	•
								•										•				•								•
	•		•	•	•		•	•	•		•	•	•	•	•	•	•	•	•		•		•	•	•	•	•			•
	•			•		•	•	•		•		•		•	•		•		•		•	•	•				•	•	•	•
	•	•		•	•	•	•	•			•	•		•		•	•	•	•				•	•	•	•	•	•	•	•
	•	•		•	•	•		•			•			•		•	•		•			•	•	•	•	•	•	•	•	•
	•	•	•	•	•	•		•			•			•								•				•	•	•	•	•
	•			•	•			•																						
	•			•				•	•			•		•	•	•		•				•				•	•	•	•	•
			•		•		•	•				•		•				•								•	•	•	•	•
			•					•						•				•								•		•	•	•
	•				•			•			•		•	•	•		•					•	•	•	•	•	•	•	•	•
	•	•	•	•	•			•					•			•	•	•				•	•	•	•	•	•	•	•	•
	•	•	•	•	•			•						•								•				•	•	•	•	•
	•	•	•	•	•	•		•			•			•								•	•	•		•	•	•	•	•
	•		•	•	•			•						•								•				•		•	•	•
	•		•	•	•		•	•			•	•	•	•	•	•	•	•	•	•	•		•	•	•	•	•	•	•	•
		•		•	•	•		•	•					•					•				•				•	•	•	•
				•				•																		•				
	•	•	•	•	•	•		•			•		•	•	•	•	•	•	•		•		•	•	•	•	•	•	•	•
	•	•	•	•	•	•	•	•	•	•	•	•	•	•	•	•	•	•	•	•	•	•	•	•	•	•	•	•	•	•
	•	•	•	•	•	•		•	•		•	•	•	•	•	•	•		•		•		•	•	•	•	•	•	•	•
		•			•			•	•																•		•		•	•
		•			•		•	•							•						•									
	•			•	•			•	•					•		•			•		•		•	•	•	•	•	•	•	•
		•		•		•		•						•				•			•				•		•	•	•	•
			•	•	•	•	•	•						•							•		•	•	•	•	•	•	•	•
	•	•		•	•	•		•						•							•				•	•	•	•	•	•
		•	•		•									•														•	•	•
	•		•		•			•				•																•	•	•
	•			•				•				•													•				•	•
								•																					•	•
	•	•	•	•	•	•		•						•							•	•	•				•	•	•	•
	•	•		•		•		•						•								•				•	•	•	•	•
	•	•						•						•														•	•	•
	•							•				•																•	•	•

Resort Guide

Features and Amenities

	Hawaii								México												Europe			
Hotel Amenities	The Royal Hawaiian	Sheraton Kauai Resort	Sheraton Maui	Sheraton Moana Surfrider	Sheraton Molokai Lodge	Sheraton Princess Kaiulani	Sheraton Waikiki	Westin Maui	Aventura Spa Palace	Hotel Villa Vera Spa and Racquet Club	Le Méridien Cancun	Mahakua Hacienda de San Antonio	Moon Palace Golf Resort	One & Only Palmilla Resort	Pueblo Bonito Emerald Bay	Pueblo Bonito Mazatlan	Pueblo Bonito Sunset Beach	Xpu-Ha Palace	W Mexico City	Westin Regina Resort, Puerto Vallarta	Badrutt's Palace Hotel	Baur au Lac	Beau-Rivage Palace	Cliveden House
Airport Transfers											•		•		•	•	•	•	•		•	•	•	•
All Inclusives	•									•			•							•				
Bar(s)	•	•	•	•	•	•	•	•	•	•	•		•	•	•	•	•		•	•	•	•	•	•
Beach/Ocean Front Rooms	•	•	•	•	•	•	•	•			•		•	•	•	•	•	•		•	•	•	•	
Concierge	•	•	•	•		•	•	•	•	•	•	•	•	•	•	•	•	•	•	•	•	•	•	•
Conference Room(s)	•	•	•	•		•	•	•	•	•	•	•	•	•	•	•	•	•	•	•	•	•	•	•
Dry Cleaning	•	•	•	•	•	•			•		•	•	•	•	•	•	•		•	•	•	•	•	•
Fine Dining	•	•	•		•			•	•	•	•	•	•	•	•	•	•	•	•	•	•	•	•	•
Fitness Equipment	•	•	•	•		•	•	•	•	•	•	•	•	•	•	•	•		•	•	•	•	•	•
Honeymoon Packages	•	•	•	•				•					•	•	•					•	•	•	•	•
Honeymoon Suites	•	•	•	•		•	•	•					•	•	•					•	•	•	•	•
Laundry Service	•	•	•	•	•	•	•	•	•		•	•	•	•	•	•	•	•	•		•	•	•	•
Rental Cars	•	•	•	•	•	•	•	•	•		•	•	•	•	•	•	•	•	•	•	•	•	•	•
Restaurant(s)	•	•	•	•	•	•	•	•	•	•	•	•	•	•	•	•	•	•	•	•	•	•	•	•
Room Service	•	•	•	•	•	•	•	•	•	•	•	•	•	•	•	•	•	•	•	•	•	•	•	•
Shops/Boutiques	•	•	•	•	•	•	•	•	•	•	•		•	•	•	•	•	•	•	•	•	•	•	•
Spa Services	•	•	•	•	•	•	•	•	•	•	•	•	•	•	•	•	•	•	•	•	•	•	•	•
Special Offers	•	•	•	•	•	•	•	•	•		•		•											

Room Information																								
Air Conditioning	•	•	•	•	•	•	•	•	•	•	•	•	•	•	•	•	•	•	•	•	•	•	•	•
Balcony or Terrace	•	•	•	•		•	•	•	•	•	•	•	•	•	•	•	•	•	•	•		•	•	•
Ceiling Fan			•						•		•		•					•						
Coffee/Tea Facilities	•		•	•	•	•	•	•				•		•	•	•	•		•	•	•	•	•	•
Data Port	•	•	•	•	•	•	•	•	•		•	•	•	•	•	•			•	•	•	•	•	•
Hair Dryer	•	•	•	•	•	•	•	•	•	•	•	•	•	•	•	•	•	•	•	•	•	•		•
Iron/Ironing Board	•	•	•	•	•	•	•	•	•			•	•	•	•	•	•	•	•	•	•	•		•
Jacuzzi	•	•	•						•	•	•		•					•						
Kitchen(ette)									•					•	•	•								
Minibar or Refrigerators	•	•	•	•		•	•	•	•	•	•	•	•	•	•				•	•	•	•	•	•
Private Pool	•	•	•	•	•	•	•	•	•					•										
Safe	•	•	•	•		•	•	•	•	•	•		•	•	•	•			•	•	•	•	•	•
Telephone	•	•	•	•		•	•	•	•	•	•	•	•	•	•	•	•		•	•	•	•	•	•
Television/Cable	•	•	•	•		•	•	•	•	•	•	•	•	•	•	•	•		•	•	•	•	•	•
Whirlpool Bath											•	•		•									•	

Recreation																								
Beach(es)	•	•			•	•	•	•			•		•	•	•	•	•	•		•	•	•	•	
Game Room									•	•			•						•					•
Golf	•	•	•			•	•	•				•	•	•					•					•
Horseback Riding			•		•							•			•	•	•	•						•
Jacuzzi or Sauna		•	•					•	•		•		•						•	•		•	•	•
Nightclub/Discotheque	•		•	•	•	•	•														•	•	•	
Swimming Pool(s)	•	•	•		•	•	•	•	•	•	•	•	•	•	•	•	•	•	•	•	•	•	•	•
Tennis		•	•						•	•		•	•	•	•	•	•	•		•	•	•	•	•
Volleyball					•				•				•		•	•	•	•						
Water Sports	•	•	•	•	•	•	•	•	•		•		•	•	•	•	•	•		•			•	

	Europe																								Australia				South Pac.		
	Danai Beach Resort & Villas	Elounda Bay Palace	Elounda Beach Hotel & Villa	Gran Hotel Bahia del Duque	Grand Hotel du Cap-Ferrat	Hotel Danieli	Hotel de Crillon	Hotel de Vendome	Hotel Des Bains	Hotel Gritti Palace	Hotel Ritz Barcelona	La Tremoille	Le Mélézin	Le Méridien Barcelona	Le Méridien Chia Laguna	Le Méridien Piccadilly	Le Montreux Palace	Park Hotel Bremen	Raffles Hotel Vier Jahreszeiten	The Regent Schlosshotel Berlin	Swissotel Metropole Geneve	Swissotel The Howard, London	Westin Europa	The Westin Excelsior, Venice	Four Seasons Hotel Sydney	Le Méridien at Rialto	Park Hyatt Melbourne	W Sydney	Amandari	Amanjiwo	Amankila

at a glance

Resort Guide

Features and Amenities

	South Pacific														
	Amanpulo	Amanpuri	Amanusa	Amanwana	Bora Bora Beachcomber	Bora Bora Lagoon Resort	Hillton Maldives Resort & Spa	Hotel Bora Bora	Le Méridien Bora Bora	Le Méridien Nirwana	Le Méridien Singapore	Le Méridien Tahiti	Matangi Island	Moorea Beachcomber	Swissotel The Stamford
Hotel Amenities															
Airport Transfers	•	•	•	•	•	•	•	•	•		•	•	•	•	•
All Inclusives															•
Bar(s)	•	•	•	•	•	•	•	•	•	•	•	•	•	•	•
Beach/Ocean Front Rooms	•	•	•	•	•	•	•	•	•			•	•		
Concierge	•	•	•	•					•	•	•			•	•
Conference Room(s)	•	•	•			•		•		•	•	•		•	•
Dry Cleaning	•	•	•					•	•		•			•	•
Fine Dining	•	•	•	•		•	•	•	•			•		•	•
Fitness Equipment		•				•	•	•			•	•		•	•
Honeymoon Packages					•	•	•					•	•	•	
Honeymoon Suites					•						•	•	•	•	
Laundry Service	•	•	•	•		•	•					•	•	•	•
Rental Cars						•				•	•		•		
Restaurant(s)	•	•	•	•	•	•	•	•	•		•	•	•	•	•
Room Service	•	•	•	•	•	•	•		•	•	•	•		•	•
Shops/Boutiques	•	•	•	•	•	•	•	•		•	•	•	•	•	•
Spa Services	•	•	•	•		•	•		•				•	•	•
Special Offers	•		•	•		•	•				•			•	•
Room Information															
Air Conditioning	•	•	•	•	•	•	•	•	•	•	•	•		•	•
Balcony or Terrace	•	•	•	•	•	•	•	•	•	•	•	•	•	•	•
Ceiling Fan	•	•	•	•	•	•	•	•	•			•	•	•	
Coffee/Tea Facilities					•	•	•			•	•	•	•		•
Data Port	•	•	•				•	•		•	•	•			•
Hair Dryer	•	•	•	•			•				•	•		•	•
Iron/Ironing Board	•	•			•	•	•		•		•			•	•
Jacuzzi							•								•
Kitchen(ette)															•
Minibar or Refrigerators	•	•	•	•	•	•	•	•	•	•	•	•	•	•	•
Private Pool		•	•					•							
Safe	•	•	•	•	•	•	•		•	•	•	•		•	•
Telephone	•	•	•	•	•	•	•		•	•	•	•		•	•
Television/Cable	•			•	•		•	•		•	•	•		•	•
Whirlpool Bath														•	
Recreation															
Beach(es)	•	•	•	•	•	•							•	•	
Game Room						•	•	•	•					•	
Golf		•	•							•					
Horseback Riding					•	•		•						•	
Jacuzzi or Sauna							•			•				•	
Nightclub/Discotheque															
Swimming Pool(s)	•	•	•				•			•	•	•		•	•
Tennis	•	•	•			•	•	•				•		•	
Volleyball					•	•	•	•	•						
Water Sports	•	•	•	•	•	•	•	•	•			•	•	•	